TOWAR
PNEUMATOLOGICAL
THEOLOGY

Pentecostal and Ecumenical Perspectives on Ecclesiology, Soteriology, and Theology of Mission

Veli-Matti Kärkkäinen

Edited by
Amos Yong

University Press of America,® Inc.
Lanham · New York · Oxford

4720 Boston Way
Lanham, Maryland 20706

PO Box 317
Oxford
OX2 9RU, UK

Printed in the United States of America
British Library Cataloging in Publication Information Available

ISBN 978-0-7618-2389-6

™ The paper used in this publication meets the minimum requirements of American National Standard for Information Sciences—Permanence of Paper for Printed Library Materials, ANSI Z39.48—1984

We dedicate this volume to two ecumenical heroes,
the long-standing co-chairs of the Catholic-Pentecostal dialogue,
an exercise on the frontiers of ecumenism
and pneumatological theology,

Kilian McDonnell, O.S.B.
Institute for Ecumenical and Cultural Research

and

Cecil Mel Robeck, Jr.
Fuller Theological Seminary

Table of Contents

Preface

In my recent textbook, *Pneumatology: The Holy Spirit in Ecumenical, International, and Contextual Perspective,*[1] I argued that any talk about the Spirit must be both contextual and ecumenical. In other words, the Spirit of God is no general spirit hovering above the world, nor does any one Christian tradition or church have a monopoly on the Spirit. The Spirit of God takes root and is being manifested in particular contexts, among specific people, and saves and heals real people and communities. The Spirit champions and fosters variety and richness. Yet as the bond of love between the Father and Son and, consequently, between God's people and God and the world, the Spirit is also the principle of unity-in-diversity.

In a sense, the present collection of essays is a case study and elaboration of this foundational affirmation. It is both a proposal for the possibility of a genuinely pneumatological theology—a theology informed by and founded on the Spirit of the Triune God—and an inquiry into some specific challenges in the life and mission of the Christian church.

In 1996, the Catholic Theological Society in the United States held its annual meeting under a groundbreaking title, "Toward a Spirit Theology." Since then many other meetings on the relationship between the Spirit and theology have been held, but that one title still catches much of what I believe is crucial to the future of Christian theology. Pneumatological theology is not, as is often assumed, a theology centered on the Spirit as such, nor is it a collection of scattered references to the Third Person of the Trinity. In the Bible and in Christian tradition, the Spirit's role in the Divine Trinity is to turn our eyes to the Son and in doing so return us to the Father. The Spirit is the contact point, so to speak, not the focus. But neither is the Spirit to be the "Third Unknown," a more or less useless appendix to Christian systematic theology. It is not only a theology of the "third article" (in reference to the last section of the creed) but rather a theology of all three articles of the Christian faith. A truly spirited theology is fully trinitarian, a theology in which all the persons of the Trinity are honored in their own specific, yet unified personhoods and ministries. This collection of essays provides some tentative perspectives on some hermeneutical, soteriological, ecclesiological, and missiological issues from that perspective.

I develop my reflections on a pneumatological theology in critical dialogue with Pentecostal and Catholic traditions, two traditions that are seemingly at the opposite end of the ecumenical spectrum. I believe the time has come for Pentecostals to engage in mutual learning and exchange with other traditions, not only in sharing their charismatic, dynamic spirituality but also their emerging theology. Theology is nothing other than reflection on Christian life and experience. In that sense, all churches and denominations do theology. I speak not only to Pentecostals and Catholics but also to Orthodox, Lutheran, and other Protestant theologies in their specific contexts. I also continue learning from all of them and being enriched by their insights. Doing so I am also reflecting my own ecumenical and cross-cultural journey: theologically, I was trained by Lutheran, Eastern Orthodox, and Roman Catholic mentors on both sides of the Atlantic, and I have lived and taught in Europe, Asia, and the United States of America.

I continue to be fascinated by systematic theology in all its variety and richness. Theology should never be done in a vacuum, but be informed not only by biblical and historical studies but also by the full spectrum of contemporary "mainline," contextual, global, and cross-cultural voices, including challenges from other religions. Therefore, fittingly I believe, this collection of essays ends with a reflection on the theology of religions (which deals with the question of the relation of Christianity to other religions) from a pneumatological perspective.

Recently, as I received feedback from my peers concerning my application for a sabbatical, I was both commended and warned: commended for my continuous writing activities on various topics, the present compilation of essays being an example, and warned about interest in too many areas, implying a lack of focus. Grateful for mentoring from my more seasoned colleagues, with a smile—yet, I hope, seriously—I promised that the time will come when I tighten the reins of my theological horse. The present essays, however, originated during my formative theological years when no or only a few ecumenical, topical, or cultural boundaries were honored, and so they offer a theological smorgasbord with a focus on a pneumatological theology for the Christian *oikoumene*.

I am grateful to Amos Yong, my younger colleague and friend, for this careful editing and creative restructuring of these materials as well as making my "Finnish English" readable.

On the eve of Pentecost 2002
and the everlasting Feast of the Spirit
Temple City, California,
Veli-Matti Kärkkäinen

Acknowledgements

We are grateful to the managing and permissions editors of the following journals and books for non-exclusive rights to reproduce these essays, albeit in revised format from their original publication:

Chapter 1: "Pentecostal Hermeneutics in the Making: On the Way from Fundamentalism to Postmodernism," *Journal of the European Pentecostal Theological Association* 18 (1998): 76–115.

Chapter 2: "Authority, Revelation, and Interpretation in the Roman Catholic-Pentecostal Dialogue," *PNEUMA: The Journal of the Society for Pentecostal Studies* 21, 2 (1999): 89–114.

Chapter 3: "'Anonymous Ecumenists?': Pentecostals and the Struggle for Christian Unity," *Journal of Ecumenical Studies* 37, 1 (Winter 2000): 13–27.

Chapter 4: "On Free Churches' Identity in Ecumenical Context: Pentecostalism as a Case Study," *MID-STREAM: The Ecumenical Movement Today* (forthcoming).

Chapter 5: "The Ecumenical Potential of Pneumatology," *Gregorianum* 80, 1 (1999): 121–45.

Chapter 6: "Spirit, Church, and Christ: An Ecumenical Inquiry into a Pneum-tological Ecclesiology," *One in Christ* 36, 4 (2000): 338–53.

Chapter 7: "'Trinity as Communion in the Spirit': *Koinonia*, Trinity, and *Filioque* in the Roman Catholic-Pentecostal Dialogue," *PNEUMA: The Journal of the Society for Pentecostal Studies* 22, 2 (2000): 209–30.

Chapter 8: "Church as Charismatic Fellowship: Ecclesiological Reflections from the Pentecostal-Roman Catholic Dialogue," *Journal of Pentecostal Theology* 18 (2001): 101–22.

Chapter 9: "The Calling of the Whole People of God into Ministry: The Spirit, Church and Laity," *Studia Theologia: Scandinavian Journal of Theology* 54, 2 (2000): 144–62, reproduced by permission of Taylor & Francis AS [www.tandf.no/studtheol].

Chapter 10: "Spirit and Supper: On the Pneumatological Understanding of the Lord's Supper," previously unpublished.

Chapter 11: "The Doctrine of Theosis and Its Ecumenical Potential," *Sobornost/Eastern Churches Journal* 23, 2 (2001).

Chapter 12: "Theology of the Cross: A Stumbling Block to Pentecostal-Charismatic Spirituality," in *The Spirit and Spirituality: Essays in Honor of Russell P. Spittler*, edited by Wonsuk Ma and Robert Menzies (forthcoming). Our special thanks to the editors in this case for allowing publication of this piece in this collection first.

Chapter 13: "Are Pentecostals Oblivious to Social Justice? Theological and Ecumenical Perspectives," *Missiology: An International Review* 29, 4 (Oct. 2001): 417–31.

Chapter 14: "The Problem of Proselytism in the Relations between Older and Younger Churches: A Theological Inquiry," *Ecumenical Review* 52, 3 (July 2000): 379–90.

Chapter 15: "Culture, Contextualization, and Conversion: Missiological Reflections from the Catholic-Pentecostal Dialogue (1990–1997)," *Asian Journal of Mission* 2, 2 (2000): 149–77.

Chapter 16: "'Truth on Fire': Pentecostal Theology of Mission and the Challenges of a New Millennium," *Asian Journal of Pentecostal Studies* 3, 1 (2000): 33–60, and "Spirit, Eschaton and Mission: A Contribution to Pneumatological Missiology/Missiological Pneumatology," an unpublished paper read at the European Pentecostal Charismatic Research Association's Annual meeting at the Missionsakademi, University of Hamburg, Germany, August 1999.

Chapter 17: "Toward a Pneumatological Theology of Religion: Pentecostal-Charismatic Contributions," *International Review of Mission* 91, 361 (2002): 187–98.

Introduction: Pentecostalism and a Theology of the Third Article

Over the past few years I have taught at Pentecostal institutions (at Bethany College in Santa Cruz, California, and North Central University in Minneapolis, Minnesota) an upper division undergraduate course on the Holy Spirit which has included, as part of the traditional theological loci, ecclesiology and soteriology, among other topics. Throughout this period of time, I have been looking for a text that deals with at least some of these pneumatological topics from an explicitly Pentecostal theological perspective in order to suggest to my students the possibility of thinking theologically as Pentecostals, and to model for them what it means to do so while retaining the authenticity of their Pentecostal identities. The collection of essays in this book meets exactly this pedagogical need. More than that, it does so by confronting head on the questions concerning Pentecostal identity, both ecclesially and theologically, without avoiding the complexity of the ecumenical issues and implications that are involved. Specifically, this book is one of the first which goes beyond simply a Pentecostal theology of baptism in the Holy Spirit and of the charismata toward a Pentecostal ecclesiology, soteriology, and theology of mission (the subtitle), and that from an explicitly pneumatological starting point (the main title). Let me briefly elaborate on this.

It is fair to say that Pentecostal theology as a systematic enterprise is finally coming of age. In the past, Pentecostals have relied upon and borrowed from their Fundamentalist and—since their alliance with the National Association of Evangelicals in the 1940s—Evangelical brothers (few sisters have been involved in the theological task in these traditions). Over the course of the twentieth century, Pentecostal theology came to be seen as Evangelical theology plus an additional chapter or two on Spirit-baptism and the charismatic gifts.[1] More recently, however, questions have been raised about the validity of such an enterprise from both ecclesiological and theological perspectives. The former queries about the *sus generis* nature of Pentecostalism as a movement while the latter wonders whether the distinctiveness of Pentecostal spirituality does not occasion or even demand its own theological account. This is not to say, of course, that there are no connections, even intimate ones, between Pentecostals and Evangelicals. Yet it certainly is the case that Pentecostals have not developed in detail either an ecclesiological or theological self-understanding, at least not to date.

The formation of the Society for Pentecostal Studies (SPS) in 1970 and the European Pentecostal Theological Association (EPTA) in 1979 marked important steps forward for the maturing Pentecostal movement. Although the earliest members of (especially) the SPS were primarily historians interested in documenting the roots and origins of the twentieth century Pentecostal revival, the emergence of these academic societies created space for biblical and theological reflection from explicitly Pentecostal perspectives. In the SPS, for example, tracks in biblical studies, in religion and culture, in theology, and, most recently, in philosophy were gradually added to the program structure of the annual meetings. Correlatively, members of both societies have gained academic expertise in these areas, some of which have appeared over the years in the biannual *Pneuma: The Journal of the Society of Pentecostal Studies* and the annual *EPTA Bulletin: Journal of the European Pentecostal Theological Association*. Over the last three decades, then, the emergence of a distinctive Pentecostal theological self-understanding has been facilitated by these societies and their respective organs of publication.

These developments have accelerated especially during the 1990s. In 1992, the faculty of the Church of God Theological Seminary (Cleveland, Tennessee) joined with Sheffield Academic Press (as of 2002 an imprint of Continuum) to publish the biannual *Journal of Pentecostal Theology* and the occasional *JPT* Supplemental Series. Over twenty theological monographs have since appeared in the series, besides the over 100 articles in the journal. In addition, the 1990s has seen the flowering of the Pentecostal academy worldwide: the European Pentecostal Charismatic Research Association; the Pentecostal and Charismatic Research Fellowship of England; the Commission Evangelical Pentecostal Latinoamerica; the Society for Pentecostal Theology in South Africa (and its journal

Pneumatikos); the Asia Pacific Theological Association (which, in collaboration with the Asia Pacific Theological Seminary, produces the *Asian Journal of Pentecostal Studies*); the Asian Pentecostal Society; the Indian Conference of Pentecostal Theologians: the Korean Pentecostal Society (with its journal *Spirit and Church*); the Asian Charismatic Theological Association; the Association of Pentecostal and Charismatic Bible Colleges of Australasia (PCBC, with its *PCBC Journal*, and its sister publication, the *Australasian Pentecostal Studies*); and the Fellowship for Pentecostal Studies in Aotearoa, New Zealand (with its journal *Renewal Theology*), just to name the most prominent.

Veli-Matti Kärkkäinen is one of the few Pentecostal theologians who has not only engaged this worldwide conversation but is capable of representing it. Fluent in a number of languages (including one Asian) and educated at Fuller Theological Seminary and the University of Helsinki (both of the schools in which he currently teaches in systematic theology and ecumenism respectively), he has already established himself as a voice to be reckoned with in the theological academy. His over 100 published articles in various kinds of confessional, ecumenical, theological and missiological journals have addressed readers in the West and the Asian world. More importantly, he has published seven major monographs over the last five years. The first two, his doctoral dissertation and *Habilitationsschrift* on the Roman Catholic-Pentecostal dialogue, established Kärkkäinen's credentials as a Pentecostal and ecumenical thinker.[2] More recently, his five introductory volumes on pneumatology, ecclesiology, soteriology, christology, and theology of religions will continue to add to Kärkkäinen's reputation as an ecumenical theologian.[3]

These five recent monographs, however, do not highlight the confessional Pentecostal location that informs Kärkkäinen's theology. Further, as introductory texts, they only anticipate the kind of constructive theological program that Kärkkäinen the Pentecostal and ecumenist has been developing. The collection of essays in *Toward a Pneumatological Theology* therefore provides more explicit glimpses of this aspect of Kärkkäinen's constructive work which has been done over the past five plus years, and brings them together in ways which complement the other book-length publications. They will therefore appeal to Pentecostal and non-Pentecostal theologians alike not only for their potential use in the classroom, but also for what they represent as the convergence of Pentecostal and ecumenical theology. Seeking to explore the question of what it means to do theology from a distinctively Pentecostal perspective, this volume addresses issues in ecclesiology, soteriology, and theology of mission which take up the theological question of what it means to be Pentecostal in the twenty-first century. As such, Kärkkäinen's theological project involves helping Pentecostals give a theological account of their confessional identity to the other Christian churches specifically, and, as the last essay in this volume suggests, perhaps also to the wider *oecumene.*

But what exactly lies at the core of the Pentecostal ecclesiological and theological identity? Perhaps, Kärkkäinen suggests, Pentecostal spirituality—symbolized most vividly by the distinctive Pentecostal testimony of encounter with the Spirit of God. This leads to the explicitly pneumatological orientation that underlies this volume specifically and that is seen to hold forth potential for Christian theology in the twenty-first century more generally.

It should be remembered that what Kärkkäinen calls the "pneumatological renaissance"—the resurgence of theological thinking about the Holy Spirit, long recognized as the shy, silent, or even forgotten member of the Trinity[4]—has been underway at least since the middle of the twentieth century. Well into his *Church Dogmatics*, Karl Barth himself suggested in an address given in 1957 that perhaps the way forward for Christian theology was to be reconceptualized within a pneumatological framework. He said,

> There is certainly a place for legitimate Christian thinking starting from below and moving up, from man who is taken hold of by God to God who takes hold of man...one might well understand it as a theology of the third article....Starting from below, as it were, with Christian man, it could and should have struggled its way upward to an authentic explication of the Christian faith.[5]

Tillich attempted such a reconfiguration, at least in outline, between the second and third volume of his *Systematic Theology*.[6] In neither Barth's nor Tillich's cases, of course, did either man work through the implications of what it means to rethink Christian theology from a pneumatological starting point.

Against this background, it is understandable that during the past generation, the number of studies on pneumatology has exploded.[7] Yet, it is not only the case that Christian theology is taking pneumatology seriously as a topic for theological reflection. In addition to this, a variety of theological topics have been re-examined from distinctively pneumatological perspectives.[8] This pneumatological reframing of older theological subjects has shed new light on the issues for our time. The promise of pneumatological thinking—what Kärkkäinen calls the "pneumatological potential" of theological efforts to think creatively and constructively—across the theological disciplines should therefore not be underestimated. This is especially the case given the increasingly ecumenical direction of theology.

The ecumenical character of theology was given further impetus by the Charismatic renewal movement of the 1950s and 1960s. Even during the 1950s, the ecumenical potential of a pneumatological theology was recognized.[9] In the meanwhile, the Charismatic Catholic theologian Donald L. Gelpi, S.J., was one of the first to attempt this task in a comprehensive manner.[10] Others who have contributed to this conversation include the Charismatic Baptist Clark H. Pinnock and the Pentecostal (Assemblies of God) born and raised now United Methodist D. Lyle Dabney. The former has produced a systematic theology written from the perspective of pneumatology, including chapters on the Trinity, christology, creation, ecclesiology, soteriology, eschatology, and revelation.[11] The latter has laid the groundwork for a multi-volume systematic theology beginning with the Spirit. Dabney's theological project will be to argue for a distinctively pneumatological theology that gives a theological account of what it means to be a Christian in the twenty-first century. His anticipated theology of the Third Article will not only complement and supplement the medieval and Scholastic patrological theology and the Reformation christological theology, but also seek to revision the theological loci and content from a pneumatological starting point.[12] My own work seeks to build on the labor of these others toward what Kärkkäinen calls a "consensual hermeneutic and theological method," one that precisely by beginning with the Spirit, overcomes false dichotomies and formerly intractable dualisms toward an ecumenical approach to theological thinking.[13]

Toward a Pneumatological Theology by Kärkkäinen participates in and contributes to this ongoing theological discussion in the academy regarding the possibility of a truly pneumatological theology. Such a theology of the Third Article is still truly in its infancy. Yet what it aspires to is not just one alongside the many other proliferations of theology produced by the Reformation. Rather, Kärkkäinen points the way forward toward a truly ecumenical theology, yet one which does not compromise the distinctively particular features of all viable Christian theologies which arise out of confessional and liturgy—yes, even Pentecostal theologies are embedded in liturgical—practices and contexts. The value of Kärkkäinen's project, of which this volume gives a sampling, is that it traverses grounds heretofore considered to be in opposition—Pentecostal and ecumenical; Free Churches and historical churches; charismatic experiences and liturgical experiences; praxis and reflection; oral and narrative patterns of theologizing and discursive modes of theological reflection; East and West; and so on. This is a testimony to Kärkkäinen's capacity to cross over, return, and therefore bridge multiple worlds. Here is truly a theology that emerges from living on the boundaries and walking along the margins, especially since, in our time, the center which once held no longer holds. And why not, if Christian theology today seeks to follow after the Spirit who blows where she wills (cf. John 3:8)?

Many college and seminary programs in biblical and theological studies still divide their theological curriculum into the traditional three courses sequence of patrology (God the Father), christology (God the Son) and pneumatology (God the Spirit). This book appeals to educators looking for Pentecostal and ecumenical perspectives on the last named topic, even while it retains its own intrinsic theological appeal for students and scholars working in these areas. It is divided into four sections. Part One focuses on Pentecostal hermeneutics, but sets that discussion within the larger framework of Pentecostal identity. The rationale, of course, is that the hermeneutical question (chapters one and two) cannot be isolated from the identity question (chapters three and four), since decisions made in either area, whether consciously or not, inform the other. Here, then, the relationship between Pentecostalism and the Ecumenical movement generally and the Roman Catholic Church in particular is initially posed, and the question is raised about whether or not there may be pneumatological resources which could adjudicate some of the issues that arise in considering these relationships (chapter five).

Part Two takes up the ecclesiological question in earnest by beginning with the application of the pneumatological resources suggested in chapter five to the doctrine of the Church. Chapters six and seven consider the ecclesiological implications of considering the Trinity as communion in the Spirit, while chapter eight is an extension of that idea toward a theology of ministry. The final chapter of this part explores a pneumatological theology of the sacraments by looking at the relationship between the Spirit of God and the Lord's Supper. In one sense, the essays in this section constitute the heart of Kärkkäinen's theological program. The proposals contained here regarding the doctrine of the Church are seen to have ramifications not only for the more abstract Christian doctrines like Trinity and filioque, but also for the existentially felt doctrine of salvation and the practically urgent theology of mission (the next two sections). They also bring to light aspects of the Pentecostal dialogue with the Roman Catholic Church (since 1972) which capture the history and emerging trajectories of thinking in both camps—not only for ecclesiology but also, as the remainder of this volume bears out, for the theological task as a whole—as they enter into the third millennium.

For these reasons, soteriology is taken up after and not before ecclesiology in this book. Yet here as well, the question concerns that of reconceptualizing soteriology in pneumatological perspective. Chapter eleven sketches the outlines of a response to this question by considering, in dialogue with Eastern Orthodoxy and recent Luther research, the ways in which the New Testament motifs of being transformed into the image of God and being made partakers of the divine nature are central to the experiencing and understanding of Christian salvation. Chapter thirteen explores how a pneumatological spirituality can inform Christian life in the face of tragedy and the ambiguities of history. While written originally for the journal *Missiology*, the argument in chapter fourteen on social justice is as much theological and soteriological as it is missiological. Its inclusion in the section on soteriology is meant to highlight the need for Christians in general and Pentecostals in particular to reconceive the doctrine of salvation in social rather than only individualistic terms.

The last section of essays focuses on a pneumatological theology of mission that is nevertheless informed by Pentecostal and ecumenical perspectives. Chapter fourteen on proselytism as an ecclesiological issue enables us to see further how theology and praxis are interconnected, and how a robust pneumatological approach may be suggestive regarding one way forward. The next two chapters explore traditional missiological questions within pneumatological, eschatological, and social frameworks. The last chapter takes up the urgent question of the non-Christian faiths—perhaps one of two such issues which require intense Christian theological reflection in the twenty-first century (the other being the relationship between religion and science)—and proposes a pneumatological program of inquiry.

Most of the seventeen essays in this volume have been published elsewhere. Each essay has been revised, some substantially so, especially with an eye toward a North American readership (even if Kärkkäinen's international relevance should attract attention from around the world).

Because these essays originated as journal articles with no intention then of being collected into a book, overlaps in content are inevitable. In this volume, then, I have tried to eliminate redundancy as much as possible while staying true to the spirit of the original publications. Chapter titles and many section titles have been modified from their original versions. In some cases, the number of footnotes has been reduced by up to 75%—either by elimination, absorption into the text, or consolidation into one at the end of a paragraph—in order to minimize intrusions in the flow of the argument. Those interested in the detailed documentation provided by Kärkkäinen, especially the numerous foreign language sources he has worked with, can look up the original publications as noted in the preceding "Acknowledgements." Consistency of documentation has been applied throughout. Gender inclusive language has been used except when quoting from original sources.

I am grateful to Veli-Matti Kärkkäinen for trusting me with his previously published work, and for his expedient responses to my seemingly endless stream of questions along the way. Chelsea DeArmond typeset the manuscript and prepared the camera-ready copy for publication, and she and Nicole Benson proofread the manuscript; to them we owe a great debt of gratitude. Thanks are also due to Deans Debra Harless and Rich Sherry of Bethel College and Professor Glen Menzies of the Pastoral Ministries Department at North Central University for finding funds for this project from these respective institutions to see this book through to publication.

Amos Yong
Crystal, Minnesota
May 2002

Abbreviations

DPCM	*Dictionary of Pentecostal and Charismatic Movements.* Edited by Stanley M. Burgess and Gary B. McGee. Grand Rapids: Zondervan, 1988.
ER	*The Ecumenical Review*
FR I	Final Report of the International Roman Catholic/Pentecostal Dialogue (1972–1976). *PNEUMA: The Journal of the Society for Pentecostal Studies* 12, 2 (1990): 77–84. Also in the *Information Service* 32 (1976): 32–7.
FR II	Final Report of the International Roman Catholic/Pentecostal Dialogue (1977–1982). *PNEUMA: The Journal of the Society for Pentecostal Studies* 12, 2 (1990): 85–96. Also in the *Information Service* 55 (1984): 72–80.
FR III	Final Report of the International Roman Catholic/Pentecostal Dialogue (1985–1989). *PNEUMA: The Journal of the Society for Pentecostal Studies* 12, 2 (1990): 97–116. Also in the *Information Service* 75 (1990): 179–91.
FR IV	The Report from the Fourth Phase of the International Dialogue (1990–1997) between the Roman Catholic Church and Some Classical Pentecostal Churches and Leaders. *PNEUMA: The Journal of the Society for Pentecostal Studies* 21, 1 (1999): 11–51.
IBMR	*International Bulletin of Missionary Research*
IRM	*International Review of Mission*
JES	*Journal of Ecumenical Studies*
JPT	*Journal of Pentecostal Theology*
JPTSup	Journal of Pentecostal Theology Supplemental Series
PG	*Patrologia Graeca*
PNEUMA	*PNEUMA: The Journal of the Society for Pentecostal Studies*
PCTSA	*Proceedings of the Catholic Theological Society of America*
SIHC	Studies in the Intercultural History of Christianity
WCC	World Council of Churches

Vatican II documents:

AA	*Apostolican Actuositatem*
DV	*Dei Verbum*
LG	*Lumen Gentium*
UR	*Unitatis Redintegratio*

Part One

Hermeneutics and Identity: Pentecostal and Ecumenical

Chapter One

Hermeneutics: From Fundamentalism to Postmodernism

Hermeneutics has been a "hot topic for Pentecostals" in recent years.[1] Walter Hollenweger's dedication of his groundbreaking work *The Pentecostals* with these words is illustrative: "To my friends and teachers in the Pentecostal movement who taught me to love the Bible and to my teachers and friends in the Presbyterian church who taught me to understand it."[2] Hollenweger's chiding remark, while valid when the book was written, is no longer true. In an article on Pentecostal hermeneutics in 1992, Hollenweger himself says that today "one finds scores of first-class Pentecostal scholars" and that these scholars "deserve to be taken seriously." He concludes this article by saying: "Pentecostalism has come of age. It is now possible to be filled with the Spirit, to enjoy the specific Pentecostal charismata and Pentecostal spirituality, to believe in Pentecostal mission, and at the same time to use one's critical faculties to develop them and to use them—as any other charisma for the Kingdom of God."[3]

A recent issue of *Concilium*, the bastion of ecumenical scholarship, was devoted to the theme of "Pentecostal Movements as an Ecumenical Challenge." Editors Jürgen Moltmann and Karl-Josef Kuschel state that "today a generation of Pentecostals has grown up which need not be afraid of comparisons with the theology of the traditional churches in academic discussion or in exegetical and systematic development of faith."[4] So it means that nowadays Pentecostals are no longer noted "for their bad hermeneutics" as Pentecostal exegete Gordon Fee ironically contended some time ago.[5]

The growing recognition of Pentecostal work in the area of hermeneutics does not, however, mean that the issue of interpretation of Scripture is settled for Pentecostals. Quite the contrary; living as we are in the days of a major paradigm shift that affects the whole of our culture, Pentecostals are left with enormous challenges in terms of approaching and appropriating Scripture for the third millennium. Biblical interpretation in the pews—if not in the pulpits also—seems to go on like nothing has happened. One does not need to be a prophet to foresee that sooner or later confusing questions will have to be addressed. Older denominations started this struggle much earlier than Pentecostals. Bible colleges and seminaries will be the first ones to tackle these issues. Increasing ecumenical contacts will also push Pentecostals to clarify their own position.

The purpose of this chapter is to offer a descriptive survey of the short history of Pentecostal interpretation. I am not going to suggest my own views about the issues under consideration but will outline a schema of development based on the Pentecostal literature. Although a comprehensive analysis of the history and development of Pentecostal hermeneutics remains to be completed, a broad outline could be presented in these four movements: (1) the oral, pre-reflexive stage of early Pentecostal bible reading; (2) the trend toward Fundamentalist-Dispensational interpretation in alliance with Evangelicalism; (3) the quest for a distinctive pneumatic exegesis; and (4) emerging postmodern developments.

Oral, Charismatic Spirituality in Early Pentecostal Bible Reading

Charismatic, eschatologically flavored spirituality lies at the heart of the Pentecostal phenomenon, and thus of its Bible reading. The starting point is the essence of Pentecostalism with "its persistent emphasis upon the supernatural within the community,"[6] and the supernaturalistic horizon of Pentecostalism "marked by living in and from the eschatological presence of God."[7] This ethos was succinctly captured in the beginning of the International Roman Catholic-Pentecostal Dialogue, which began in 1972, as it defined the "essence of Pentecostalism": "It is the personal and direct awareness and experiencing of the indwelling of the Holy Spirit by which the risen and glorified Christ is revealed and the believer is empowered to witness and worship with the abundance of life as described in Acts and the Epistles."[8] Pentecostalism's manifestations of charismatic gifts "offered invincible certitude that the supernatural claims of the gospel were really true."[9] It is this supernatural, charismatic ethos, coupled with an intense eschatological expectation, which naturally informs Pentecostal hermeneutics. The powerful outpouring of the Spirit at Azusa Street, and soon all over the world, was seen as a decisive step to final consummation, when the Kingdom will be ushered in.

Preaching and Bible teaching shaped the character of the early Pentecostal movement. Preaching was essential to the spread of the Pentecostal movement and its incipient, practically oriented theologizing. Testimonies were one of the basic tools to "spread the fire." It was primarily through personal testimonies that "the Pentecostal community participated in the hermeneutical process."[10] For this reason, access to God was not controlled by a few professionals, nor was preaching relegated only to trained clergy. After all, the Spirit had accredited ordinary people to preach "the everlasting Gospel." A short note in the October 1906 *Apostolic Faith* magazine, the first Pentecostal paper, gives a clear picture of the prevailing attitude:

> God does not need a great theological preacher that can give nothing but theological chips and shaving to people. He can pick up a worm and trash a mountain....[H]e is using even the children to preach His gospel. A young sister, fourteen years old was saved, sanctified and baptized with the Holy Ghost and went out, taking a band of workers with her and led a revival in which one hundred and ninety souls were saved.[11]

Preaching was included in the overall trajectory of worship services, but it was not necessarily the climax of the service. The congregation participated in the sermon in terms of responding, but the sermon also allowed for participation of the congregation more fully in the altar call. The sermon was an occasion for the listener to immediately experience the biblical message rather than being characterized by a hermeneutics that spent its time exegeting a text in historical-critical manner. The preacher focused on the immediate meaning of a text.

The early Pentecostals' use of the Bible, still the dominant pattern in churches, can be summarized as follows. First, Scripture is the inspired Word of God, authoritative and wholly reliable; this has often led to the downplaying of the role of human authors. Second, Pentecostals have not recognized a historical distance between themselves and the text: there has thus been an emphasis upon the immediate meaning and context. Third, the early Pentecostals' "operative principle of interpretation was the conviction that exegesis is best when it is as rigidly literal as credibility can stand."[12] Little or no significance was placed upon the historical context, and the Bible was understood at face value. Fourth, the Pentecostals' interpretation was theologically colored by the christological "full gospel" pre-understanding, where Jesus stood at the center of charismatic life. Last, the prime interpreter and preacher was the local pastor, most of whom were uneducated, ordinary folk. Church of God theologian, Steve J. Land, illustrates the early ethos of Pentecostalism and Pentecostals' understanding of Scripture:

> The faith, worldview, experience and practice of Pentecostals was thoroughly eschatological. They lived both in tension of the already but not yet consummated Kingdom....Time and space were fused and transcended in the Spirit, and at the heart of testimony, expectation and worship was Jesus, the Savior, Sanctifier, Healer, Baptizer with the Spirit, and Coming King.[13]

Experience came first; theology followed: "In the beginning there was an experience and a testimony, then came an explanation in the form of a theological construct."[14]

The major mode of Pentecostal theology has thus been from the beginning orality, a mode that still dominates in the Two-Thirds World. Although western theological scholarship has tended to downplay the oral way of doing theology as something "primitive," there are certain strengths to it. Because "our knowledge of God is relational, and not merely informational, theology can be better expressed orally, because that is the primary mode of relational communication among ordinary people in the community of faith"; because this process is oral and experiential, it includes the uneducated and uninitiated. "[I]t puts the 'modern' person at a distinct disadvantage!"[15]

Catholic Walter J. Ong has done groundbreaking research into the nature and significance of orality in relation to literacy in general and Christian writings in particular.[16] He traces the "stages of the Word" from oral (oral-aural) to script to electronic. He shows convincingly how vast a difference there is between oral culture and our western technological mindset and how difficult it is to get into the sphere of a genuine oral communication.

A Move toward Fundamentalism and Alliance with Evangelicalism

When Pentecostalism was birthed it existed on the fringes of the society and ecclesial spectrum. Pentecostals were both rejected and eschewed by those who had power. In order to improve their status, Pentecostals sought for more respected colleagues in society. Fundamentalism and Evangelicalism were natural friends although the courtship was not self-evident. All Fundamentalists and most Evangelicals looked with suspicion at Pentecostals but they were wise enough not to turn Pentecostals down. Soon it became clear that the courtship was beneficial to both. To Fundamentalists and Evangelicals it gave more influence because of rapidly growing numbers of Pentecostals, and for Pentecostals it meant entrance to a more respected company.

Pentecostals, primarily from white denominations such as the Assemblies of God and the Foursquare, readily accepted the fundamentalist-dispensational hermeneutic where literalism and inerrancy are emphasized.[17] Fundamentalism, of course, emerged out of a critique of modernism with its championing of historical-critical study of the Bible. Fundamentalists and Pentecostals sought to fight against modernism and the historical-critical study of the Bible within the confines of the very same epistemological outlook. Because of its Fundamentalist heritage, Pentecostalism is marked by a strong anti-intellectualism that persists even to the present day.

Pentecostalism's fundamentalistic traits became apparent in the Roman Catholic-Pentecostal dialogue. Scripture and its interpretation was one of the first topics to be taken up. Pentecostals insisted on inerrancy and the plenary inspiration of Scripture, while opposing the use and principles of critical methods (see *FR* II.23).

Several theologians have shown convincingly that both modernism and its critique in the form of Fundamentalism share a key epistemological presupposition. Modernism finds its epistemological roots in the Enlightenment ideal of "objectivity"; this objectivist/positivist presupposition is then brought into the service of a historicist view of meaning. We might have expected conservative Fundamentalists in general, and Pentecostals in particular, to "counter that there is a supernatural reality which transcends objectivistic categories; however, in that they too were children of the Enlightenment and shared its positivistic epistemology," that was not the case.[18]

Along with the association with Fundamentalism there arose the "evangelicalization of Pentecostalism." Evangelicalism emerged within the conservative bloc of Christianity as an attempt to preserve classical Christian doctrines on the one hand, and to be more open to the challenges of the modern world on the other. Pentecostal participation in the National Association of Evangelicals in the 1940s was motivated by the desire to receive acceptance from the larger Evangelical movement. At the same time it meant adjusting Pentecostalism in tune with Evangelical concerns, one of the most important of which was biblical inerrancy.

Pentecostals within the academy have tended to align themselves with Evangelicals in their move toward adopting the methods of historical criticism while maintaining a commitment to the reliability of the biblical narrative. As a result, Pentecostal biblical scholars have increasingly emphasized the historical contexts of biblical narratives and reduced their focus on the intent of the inspired authors. These and other developments have, of course, meant either denying or downplaying the earlier emphasis on the immediacy of the text, its multiple meanings and relevance "here and now." This has led to a growing divergence in the practice of biblical interpretation between Pentecostals in the parish and in the academy.

Now, before proceeding in our survey, we have to ask of ourselves: what are we to think of the developments of the Pentecostal interpretation paradigm along these lines? Several Pentecostal theologians have recently contended that the fundamentalist-type understanding of inerrancy is not necessarily part of the original Pentecostal heritage, and more importantly, does not relate directly to the question of authority of Scripture among Pentecostals.[19] Those Pentecostals who have questioned the legitimacy of Evangelization of Pentecostalism do not generally oppose the idea of trustworthiness of Scripture nor do they suggest succumbing to an irresponsible use of critical methods. What they are concerned about is the narrowing down of Pentecostal hermeneutics to the point where its distinctives might be lost altogether.

In fact, Pentecostals have never grounded their understanding of the authority of Scripture on a bedrock of doctrine—doctrine of inerrancy or any other doctrine—but, rather, on "their experiences of encountering a living God, directly and personally."[20] Some of them even claim that it is possible to question and even cast serious doubts on traditional understandings of and proofs for infallibility and inerrancy among Pentecostals without seriously challenging their understanding of the Bible as the authoritative word of God. This, of course, does not mean that doctrines are unimportant *per se* for Pentecostals, but that the basis for the doctrinal process is the experience of the community of faith. Neither does it mean that Scripture would not be the ultimate norm of faith and practice, but it means that this "belief is not a matter of dogma but arises from repeated observations of the way in which God utilizes Scripture interactively."[21]

If doctrine (of inerrancy, etc.) is not the basis for the authority, what is? Some Pentecostal theologians argue Scripture to be "Spirit-Word," a dynamic interaction of written text and the Holy Spirit. Steven J. Land, for example, write that,

> The Spirit that inspired and preserved the Scriptures illuminates, teaches, guides, convicts and transforms through the Word today. The Word is alive, quick and powerful, because of the Holy Spirit's ministry. The relation of the Spirit to Scripture is based on that of Spirit to Christ. Even as the Spirit formed Christ in Mary, so the Spirit uses Scripture to form Christ in believers and *vice versa*.

In so doing, Land boldly places the authority of the Spirit ahead of the authority of Scripture.[22]

This makes it understandable why Pentecostals of this generation have not felt it necessary to draw a sharp distinction between the "inspiration" of the original text by the Spirit and the "illumination" of the read text by the same Spirit, although for many Fundamentalists and conservative Protestants this would be a test of orthodoxy. "When one encounters the Holy Spirit in the same apostolic experience, with the same charismatic phenomenology accompanying it, one is then in a better position to come to terms with the apostolic witness in a truly existential manner."[23] Given this ambivalent attitude toward the dominating views of either "liberalism" or Evangelicalism-Fundamentalism, it is no wonder that some Pentecostals have entertained the idea of a distinctive *Pentecostal hermeneutics*. Is it possible? And if so, what are the parameters?

Toward a Distinctive Pentecostal "Pneumatic" Hermeneutics

Once again we see that ecumenical contacts have pushed Pentecostals to think through theological issues from the vantage point of their charismatic experience. Howard M. Ervin, a Baptist theologian who has been actively involved with Pentecostal issues and has been in the Pentecostal team in the earlier phases of the Catholic-Pentecostal dialogue, has been the first to suggest a distinctively Pentecostal interpretation scenario. I am here making use of his dialogue-paper from the Second Quinquennium (1978–1982), since position papers are supposed to be more than just personal opinions. Its title is revealing: "Hermeneutics: A Pentecostal Option."[24] It suggests that there is something like a distinctive Pentecostal view of the Scripture and interpretation. He calls it "pneumatic exegesis."

According to Ervin, "[e]pistemology is a question fundamental to any discussion of hermeneutics." He criticizes the overall tendency of western culture to accept as axiomatic two ways of knowing, namely, reason and sensory experience. As a consequence, a theology that limits itself to these two ways, "finds itself faced with an unresolved dichotomy between faith and reason." This leads either to "traditional hermeneutics" with its strong commitment to a critical-historical exegesis or to a "dogmatic intransigence," or even to a "non-rational mysticism." What is needed, according to Ervin,

> is an epistemology firmly rooted in the biblical faith with a phenomenology that meets the criteria of empirically verifiable sensory experience (healing, miracles, etc.) and does not violate the coherence of rational categories. A pneumatic epistemology meets these criteria, and provides (a) a resolution of the dichotomy between faith and reason that existentialism consciously seeks to bridge; (b) the antidote to a destructive rationalism that often accompanies a critical-historical exegesis; (c) and a rational accountability for the mysticism fostered by a piety grounded in *sola fide*.[25]

Why is there a need for a "pneumatic epistemology" as a basis for a "pneumatic" Pentecostal hermeneutics? For Ervin, "[i]t is the transcendent word. It is the word beyond all human words"; actually "[i]t is a word for which *there are no categories endemic to human understanding*. It is a word for which, in fact, there is no hermeneutic unless and until the divine *hermeneutes* (the Holy Spirit) mediates an understanding."[26]

The biblical precondition for understanding the Word of God is "man's ontological re-creation by the Holy Spirit (the new birth) that makes humans partakers of the divine nature." This re-creation, however, does not erase the boundary between the Creator and the creature, even if "the conditions for hearing and understanding the Word are now present for we become by grace what He is by nature." This distance—"bridged" but not "erased"—renders the word ambiguous until the Holy Spirit interprets it. Thus hearing and understanding the word is a "theological *theos logos* communication in its deepest ontological context." Hearing the word in this sense is not simply grasping the kerygma cognitively. "It is being apprehended by Jesus Christ, not simply in the letter-word but the divine-human word. *Herein lies the ground for a pneumatic hermeneutic*."[27]

Pneumatic hermeneutics, according to Ervin, gives a legitimate place for "an intuitive, non-verbal communication between God and man namely, miracles. The reality of a direct encounter between God and man is precisely what the biblical record of dreams, visions, theophanies, miracles, etc., is saying to us."[28] It would be a fatal misinterpretation of biblical revelation to overlook the importance of the direct encounter with miracles and visions. The repudiation of a concept of a direct miraculous encounter with God leads to a one-sided view of revelation merely as cognitive data, whereas experiential dimension is neglected. For Ervin, the Pauline concept of "demonstration of the Spirit and of power" (1 Cor. 2:4) is by definition miraculous. Furthermore, reminiscences of the words and the deeds of Jesus constitute historical data and indispensable to faith. The contribution to hermeneutics of the present Charismatic and Pentecostal renewal of the Church is "its insistence upon the experiential immediacy of the Holy Spirit."[29]

Ervin's synthesis of a pneumatic epistemology, and thus a pneumatic hermeneutics, is revealing:

> A pneumatic epistemology posits an awareness that the Scriptures are the product of an experience with the Holy Spirit which the biblical writers describe in phenomenological language. From the standpoint of a pneumatic epistemology, the interpretation of this phenomenological language is much more than an exercise in semantics or descriptive linguistics. When one encounters the Holy Spirit in the same apostolic experience, with the same charismatic phenomenology accompanying it, one is in a better position to come to terms with the apostolic witness in a truly existential manner. One then stands in "pneumatic" continuity with the faith community that birthed the Scriptures.[30]

This pneumatic continuity creates a deepening respect for the witness of the Scriptures to themselves, thus making the Bible "alive" in a new, fresh way.

By championing "pneumatic epistemology," and as a consequence, "pneumatic hermeneutics," Ervin is sensitive to the dangers of subjectivism that he believes are inherent in the New Hermeneutics (and one could add, in the post-modern hermeneutics of our day).[31] While sympathetic to the intentions of the New Hermeneutics to be sensitive to the "numinous" quality of the written text—over against the basic ethos of traditional hermeneutics—he warns that "the hermeneutical enterprise by its subjectivity in its efforts to reconstruct the numinous intentionality of the text" may lead to "demythologizing of Scripture because of its dis-ease with the biblical world view," thus "rob[bing] exegesis of its critical-contextual historicity and facticity. Hermeneutics is then an exercise in *private reconstruction of the intentionality of the text.*"[32] Ervin forcefully argues for the legitimacy and importance of a sound "grammatico-historical, critical-contextual exegesis."[33] In this Ervin strikes a note different from most of the Pentecostal theologians of the day when the text was written. For him "there can be no hermeneutical integrity apart from a critical, contextual exegesis." But exegesis as a human enterprise is not enough: "It is only as human rationality *joined* in ontological union with the 'mind of Christ' (1 Cor. 2:16) is *quickened* by the Holy Spirit that the divine mystery is understood by man."[34]

Ervin's proposal for pneumatic hermeneutics has interesting ecumenical implications: "...the Scriptures are now read within the pneumatic continuity of the faith community and that community is much larger than the post-Reformation communities of the West. There is a growing sense of accountability to and for the cumulative consensus of the Church to the deposit of the faith once for all delivered." As a consequence, hermeneutics needs to relate its insights to the historical succession of church tradition, over against a sectarian understanding of interpretation. It even affects the way the Pentecostals see the role of tradition. Ervin states, "Thus it seems at least to this writer, that the hermeneutical enterprise must entertain seriously the insight of the Eastern church that, 'tradition is the life of the Spirit in the Church.'"[35]

Ervin's theory of pneumatic epistemology and pneumatic hermeneutics has been taken up and expanded by French L. Arrington. Pentecostal hermeneutics arises out of the Pentecostal theology of the Spirit.[36] Pentecostals have understood that the Scriptures can be interpreted properly only through the agency of the Holy Spirit (cf. John 14:26, 16:13). Convinced of the importance of the Holy Spirit to the interpretative process, they bear a distinctive witness to an experience and life in the Spirit, out of which Pentecostal hermeneutics and theology have emerged. According to Arrington, the Pentecostal method of interpretation stands on three pillars: 1) pneumatic, 2) experiential and 3) historical narrative. Like Ervin, Arrington sees no obstacle for Pentecostals to use critical tools of historical-contextual exegesis while at the same time appreciating the spiritual nature of the text and its interpretation. In other words, Pentecostals must give proper recognition to both the divine and human elements in Scripture.

Ervin's and Arrington's suggestion of a pneumatic exegesis, while entertaining legitimate Pentecostal intentions to have pneumatology inform interpretation, has met with critique from Catholics and Pentecostals. According to Catholic Paul D. Lee, much depends on the exact meaning of the endeavor: "Does it mean the search for a deeper spiritual meaning of the biblical text through the eyes of faith? Does it foster a union of our modern historical sense with the 'sense of history,' viz., the historicity of the mystery (a personal entry of God into human history)? Does it imply the pilgrim Church's expectation for the fulfillment of God's word?" If the answer is "yes," then Lee is ready to embrace it, because in that case Pentecostal hermeneutics would mean establishing comprehensive spiritual exegesis. But when it comes to the necessity of a distinctive Pentecostal hermeneutic itself, Lee in unsure. His problem is with the seemingly dualistic (he calls it also "gnostic") impression from the pneumatic epistemology: "If Scripture is written in human language and is capable of communicating God's word, his [Ervin's] insistence on the total incapacity of the human hermeneutic of language to understand Scripture seems unreasonable."[37]

In Arrington's development of a pneumatic exegesis, the dualism is not so apparent. Arrington starts with God's willingness to reveal himself, first through the Incarnation and the gift of the Holy Spirit, and then through the Bible. This makes the inspiration of the Scripture a "mystery of the divine-human encounter" (Lee's paraphrase of Arrington). This creates a "spiritual kinship" between the ancient writer and the modern reader: "It is the experience of the Holy Spirit that reenacts the apostolic experience of the Spirit. The Spirit serves as the 'common context,' the bridge between the writer and the reader." Lee appreciates Arrington's emphasis on "a mutual conditioning between interpretation and experience" and his insistence on the parameters within the "pneumatic continuity of the faith community" as a warrant against undue subjectivism. He also gives credit to Arrington's salient effort to go beyond the verbal dictation theory. Even with these modifications, Lee advises Pentecostals, instead of "insisting on a questionable Pentecostal hermeneutics," to consider more seriously human existence as a Spirit-event created by God's word in his image and likeness, where spiritual conversion would be not a mystical, dramatic event, but a gradual conformity and transformation of the human subject into the image of God through the Spirit. This, Lee contends, would lead to a legitimate and sound spiritual exegesis, without a distinctive Pentecostal-Charismatic hermeneutic as such. Living in the Spirit is a "constant struggle yet a graced dialectic," he argues.[38]

Several Pentecostal scholars have addressed the Ervin-Arrington proposal with a view to modify it. For Timothy Cargal, Ervin's attempts at articulating a Pentecostal epistemology were naïve because Ervin sought, on the one hand, to re-adopt the first-century worldview with all its corollaries in opposition to our modern positivist-mechanistic outlook, and, on the other hand, to satisfy the requirements of a rationalist-modernist philosophical paradigm. The problem is that it evidences the general fundamentalist appropriation of modernist philosophy which, however, is the main target of Fundamentalistic critique, and furthermore, that the postmodern paradigm shift is already moving beyond such a positivistic worldview. In addition, Cargal, like Lee, is not happy with Ervin's insistence on the "transcendent word," "the word beyond all human words," because this leads to a sort of "docetic" view of the Bible. According to Cargal, however, this is not a Pentecostal view of inspiration, because no hermeneutic—not even one guided by Pentecostal pneumatic illumination—would then make Scripture comprehensible.[39]

Now, the correction to Ervin is that Pentecostal doctrines of inspiration are not docetic. Pentecostals emphasize that the special characteristic of Scripture is that it is the "Word of God" expressed in human words. Scripture then is in one sense comprehensible apart from pneumatic illumination, thus making critical-historical exegesis necessary. "Pneumatic illumination" becomes a factor in understanding the "Word of God" quality of scripture, that is the "'deeper significance to the biblical text that can only be perceived through the eyes of faith' and with the aid of the Holy Spirit."[40] This is what Lee also called for, naming it comprehensive spiritual exegesis. Cargal shows that this understanding of interpretation accords well with the original Pentecostal ethos, and perhaps ironically, with the mindset of postmodern hermeneutics, in its insistence on the immediacy of the text and multiple dimensions of meaning.

We may conclude from this section that Ervin's attempt to construct a distinctive Pentecostal hermeneutics is commendable in principle, if not totally satisfactory in its present form, because it is an effort to let pneumatology inform scriptural interpretation. A truly Pentecostal theology and hermeneutics cannot help but investigate the pneumatological (spiritual) resources for interpretation. With the major revisions posed by Catholic and Pentecostals colleagues, Ervin's pneumatic exegesis raises the same legitimate concerns as the spiritual exegesis, well attested both in church history and among some representative theologians of our day: this is to seek the "Word of God," "the deeper meaning," "the spiritual meaning" of the biblical text, in addition to the meaning derived from critical-historical study. When biblical studies comprise both sound critical-historical study and the search for spiritual meaning, in the context of the Spirit-informed Church-koinonia, with the openness to the transcendent meaning of the Word, basic elements of consensual reading are there. It is not the purpose of this chapter to investigate whether a distinctive Pentecostal-Charismatic hermeneutics is needed. This question must be left open. Suffice to say that the Pentecostal-Charismatic community has contributed in a significant way to the emergence of a pneumatic/spiritual dimension of biblical interpretation.

The Promise and the Problematic of an Emerging Postmodern Paradigm

It is one of the dictums of our day that a fundamental paradigm shift is emerging in the western societies as we approach the end of this millennium. Broadly speaking it is often called postmodernism. Postmodernism emerged out of the critique of the hegemony of the modern western worldview, which was associated with a positivistic philosophy and a mechanistic outlook. Postmodernism does not mean so much a critique of reason and rationality *per se*. Rather, it rejects the *hegemony* of rationalism as the *only* way of interpreting our world, especially human life. It is in this sense that advocates of postmodernism speak of a post-critical—but not anti-critical nor pre-critical—stance.

Pentecostal theologian, Jackie David Johns, in a programmatic article, "Pentecostalism and the Postmodern Worldview," has noted that, according to some observers of Pentecostalism, certain characteristics of the movement "make it the probable dominant expression of Christianity in the postmodern age," and that inside the movement, scholars have focused on the connection between postmodernism and Pentecostal hermeneutics.[41] The main characteristics of a Pentecostal worldview are outlined by Johns as follows. First, the Pentecostal worldview is God-centered: "All things relate to God and God relates to all things." Second, because Pentecostalism is God-centered, it is holistic. Consequently, Pentecostals are inclined to think systematically, as is evidenced especially in their eschatology. Third, characteristic of a Pentecostal worldview is its "transrationalism": "Pentecostals do not limit truth to the realm of reason. For them the spectrum of knowledge includes cognition, affection and behavior, each of which is fused to the other two." Fourth, there has been an emphasis on the apocalyptic, since Pentecostalism emerged in the nineteenth-century holiness movement embedded with premillennial eschatological vision. Fifth, Pentecostals are more inclined toward action than toward reflection. Lastly, Pentecostals have a strong sense of needing to be separated from the world.[42]

Out of this distinctive worldview emerges elements of a Pentecostal paradigm which would also inform hermeneutics. A God-centered, holistic worldview focused on encountering God is supported by an "epistemology which is based upon personal revelation and response."[43] Johns notes, furthermore, that rationalism and empiricism and any combination of the two are rejected as adequate sources of knowledge. Rather, a *yada*-kind of knowledge, based on Hebrew tradition, is seen as that which negates neither reason nor sensory experiences, but rather, accepts them as designed to facilitate knowledge of and relationship to God, albeit now distorted by sin. Following therefore in the tradition of Wesleyanism, the center of authentic Christianity is the transformation of the heart. Of course, Pentecostals are concerned with truth, but not just propositional truth: "[i]n their paradigm orthodoxy, orthopraxy and orthopathy form the purpose, function and structure/essence of truth."[44] Several Pentecostal scholars have criticized the one-sided western way of knowing as something objective and divorced from experience, emotions, and supernatural. What is needed is what Peter Stuhlmacher has called an "openness to transcendence" as a deliberately adopted methodological presupposition, which conforms much more to the "object" (i.e., the text) of our hermeneutical investigation.[45]

Postmodern developments of Pentecostal hermeneutics arose out of the conviction that, as Cargal says, "the traditional features of Pentecostal appropriation of the Bible such as multiplicity of meanings and the dialogical role of experience in the interpretational task have affinities with and could benefit from the insights of a variety of postmodern approaches to texts."[46] Cargal notes that this is actually the only way to do relevant interpretation today. A younger generation of Pentecostal scholars has thus interacted actively in recent decades with such writers as Wilhelm Dilthey, Martin Heidegger, Hans-Georg Gadamer, Paul Ricoeur, and Jürgen Habermas among others. While critical of many of their presuppositions, Pentecostal scholars have eagerly engaged with the proposals of these writers.

In line with latest developments of postmodern hermeneutics, Pentecostal scholars have broadened the area of hermeneutics. The first shift involves the move from regional hermeneutics to general hermeneutics. It was, of course, Schleiermacher who first extended the domain of hermeneutics from the principles of interpretation for a particular field of texts (e.g., biblical texts) to a general theory of the operation of understanding involved in the interpretation of all texts. The second shift "results from the understanding that the human sciences involve a domain distinct from the natural sciences and as such require a different approach in their study."[47] The issue at stake here grows from the question of what it means to study history in a scientific mode, in accordance with what Kant had done in clarifying the method of the natural sciences in his *Critique of Pure Reason*. The third shift concerns the notion of "text" itself. For the postmodern paradigm the text is, besides what the original author meant, also what the text "claims about the world and the appropriation of the message of the text by the interpreter in the direction of the text itself."[48] Whereas traditional hermeneutics utilized "principles of interpretation" to achieve "explanation," the postmodern appreciates as well the "understanding" process.

Pentecostal scholars' use of the famous French philosopher Paul Ricoeur may be due to the fact that Ricoeur mediates between the hermeneutic which attempts objectively to reconstruct the meaning of a text in its original context and the hermeneutic which attempts existentially to appropriate a text.[49] In this sense Ricoeur offers a hermeneutical theory "vastly superior to a narrowly conceived 'evangelical hermeneutics,'" while at the same time his approach is relatively conservative.[50] Surprisingly, Pentecostal scholars have followed Ricoeur's lead in understanding the real nature of "myth." As is well known, Ricoeur rejects Bultmann's definition of myth contending that myth is more than an explanation of the world and history. Myth is not a "false explanation by means of images and fables"; rather, myth is "a traditional narration which relates to events that happened at the beginning of time and which has the purpose of providing grounds for the ritual actions of men of today and, in a general manner, establishing all the forms of action and thought by which man understands himself in his world."[51] This definition of myth as a collection of symbols in narrative form is not far from the (pre-critical) Pentecostal interpretation where "biblical narratives have a symbolic nature as well as a historical nature" especially in preaching and testimonies.[52] Pentecostals' insistence on the importance of narrative texts of the Bible, which originates from reading especially the book of Acts as *the narrative*, echoes the views of postmodernism. With the ascendance of systemic thinking and the decline of historicism, postmodernism has rehabilitated the role of narratives, and even created a so-called "narrative theology" of its own. Narrative has always been an indispensable part of Pentecostalism. It is no longer necessary, nor right, to hold a sharp distinction between biblical narrative and theological instruction.[53]

Ricoeur's proposal is suggestive for Pentecostals who hold both a historical and a symbolic nature of Scripture. In the process of interpreting symbols, Ricoeur suggests the use of a dialectical movement between *Verstehen* (understanding) and *Erklären* (explanation), and does not regard them as opposite to each other like Romanticist hermeneutics falsely thought.[54] The dialectic between understanding and explanation, where the interpreter moves from understanding to explanation and then from explanation to comprehension, is appreciated by Pentecostal interpreters. In other words, one moves from the "first naiveté" ("guesses at the meaning") to a "second naiveté" (a post-critical stage). Explanation or critical consciousness validates the interpretation and thus mediates between the initial stage of understanding and a second informed level of understanding (i.e., second naiveté). Ricoeur describes the movement from the first to the second naiveté in terms of a hermeneutical circle or arc. Pentecostals have recognized the role of the "experience" of the interpreter within the hermeneutical circle. As Arrington puts it, not only must "the interpretations drawn from Scripture impact Pentecostal experience," but such "personal and corporate experience informs the Pentecostal hermeneutical process."[55] The importance of personal experience as a legitimate part of the interpretation process is linked with multiple meanings of the biblical text and with Bible reading and testimonies:

> The place of the Pentecostal experience of the Spirit in the hermeneutical enterprise is first of all in the ontological locus of the interpreter in "the world" according to Gadamer's analysis. It is with a Pentecostal experience as a part of the interpreter's horizon that one approaches a text's horizon....Thus is a legitimate part of understanding to bring one's experience to the interpretive event. It is also legitimate to probe the horizon of the text for an understanding of the commonality as well as the divergence of the experience of God which is involved in the horizon of the text and the horizon of the interpreter.[56]

A Pentecostal/charismatic experience is not something to be resisted in the interpretation process, and it is not necessarily opposed to being critical, in a positive sense of the word, as a part of scientific investigation.[57]

In addition, however, the move beyond the positivist-mechanistic outlook of western scholarship has helped Pentecostals to appreciate the role of the affections in Bible reading and interpretation, which has been an indispensable part of Pentecostal ethos since the beginning of the movement. Pentecostals have never approached the Bible solely from the perspective of an objective "outsider." Robert O. Baker, taking the lead of Land and other Pentecostal scholars' insistence on holistic reading, has proposed "a model of reading for the formation of Christian affections." Applying this model to read the *paraclete*-passages in John 14–16, Baker argues that this is a contribution to a wider ecumenical guild of interpreters. As a corrective to an affectionless, "objective" western understanding of knowledge, Pentecostal scholars have proposed the Hebrew notion of *yada* which sees knowing in active relationship, as opposed to a Greek philosophical understanding of reality which sees the "knower" as subject and the thing known as object in dualistic opposition.[58]

In fact, the latest developments in postmodern hermeneutics have informed Pentecostal interpretation and helped it to mature. Pentecostal hermeneutics, so it seems, has been given a chance to move beyond the impasse of the fundamentalist-modernist controversy and to look for a more distinctive Pentecostal, yet at the same time more ecumenical, appropriation of hermeneutical principles. This has made it possible, first, for Pentecostal theologians to get out of the self-made ghetto and to participate in discussions with Catholics and other theologians. Second, as a consequence, it has been possible for Pentecostal exegetes to make use of critical methods of modern biblical scholarship, while at the same time being critical of some of their misguided implications. Third, the role of experiences and emotions has been emphasized much more than before. This has always been part of Pentecostal Bible reading and proclamation.

The fact that Pentecostal hermeneutics has been informed in some measure by the latest postmodern developments does not, of course, mean that there are not limitations to postmodernism. In fact, some Pentecostal scholars have raised serious questions about adopting a postmodern mindset uncritically. Robert Menzies's critique has been the most harsh, with his advice to "jump off the postmodern bandwagon" and instead to align with Evangelicals. Even those who have seriously inspected the possible commonalities have expressed reservations and warnings.[59] Much work is still to be done and many philosophical and theoretical questions to be inspected.

Pentecostal Hermeneutics On the Way

This chapter has traced the development of Pentecostal Bible reading and interpretation in four movements: from an initial charismatically flavored literalism to Fundamentalism to an attempt to construct a distinctively "pneumatic exegesis" to, finally, considerations in relation to an emerging postmodern outlook. Our survey shows that a Pentecostal interpretation is in the making. As being on the way, we have noted a bewildering array of road signs both on the "right" and on the "left." Pentecostal hermeneutics has, of course, many affinities with a conservative ethos with its high view of revelation and commitment to the reliability of Scripture. At the same time, it differs significantly from a Fundamentalist-conservative agenda in that it—at least, it should be—is open to the charismatic power of the Spirit to make the text alive "here and now." Theologically, this openness to the Spirit should shape Pentecostal views of revelation and tradition. Although Pentecostals insist upon the once-and-for-all-nature of revelation in Christ, their view seems to see revelation also as a continuing dynamic process. The written text is the ultimate norm but it is not only an ancient document.

Although the alignment with Evangelicals and Fundamentalists has been beneficial to Pentecostals, one hopes that it will not force Pentecostals to overlook their charismatic distinctives. It is also good to remember that no other movement has ever been so hostile to Pentecostal distinctives (charismata, Pentecostal interpretation of Spirit-baptism, etc.) than reactionary Fundamentalism. Whatever good may be gleaned from that association, its dark side must not be ignored.

Attempts to construe a distinctive Pentecostal hermeneutics have not been successful thus far, although they reflect legitimate concerns to let the openness to the Spirit inform the model of Bible reading. In fact, I am not sure if a distinctively Pentecostal hermeneutics is needed. Dangers are twofold. On the one hand, the attempts often border on Pentecostal ideology. On the other hand, they add to the endless fragmentation of Protestantism and the larger *oikoumene*. Instead, let Pentecostals seek a legitimate Pentecostal contribution to a conciliar Bible reading that would strengthen ecumenical commitment to Scripture and help open up its meaning in a postmodern world.

The courtship of some Pentecostal exegetes and theologians with an emerging postmodern mindset is—to say the least—an ambiguous enterprise. That it cannot—and should not—be avoided is obvious if Pentecostals have anything to say to people preparing to cross over into the third millennium. There is always a danger for sectarian groups to lose their voice in their (often exclusivist) attempt to protect their own territory. Honest dialogue with intellectual developments of any age has characterized dynamic, living traditions. So, from that perspective, one hopes that many more conversations will occur between Pentecostals and postmodernists.

Let us, however, be cautious. It seems to me that the alleged similarities between Pentecostalism and postmodernism are not that obvious when the issues are pressed. True, there are many potential convergences—plurality of meaning in any text, the plural meanings of the biblical text, the role of affections in reading, etc.—but the convergences might exist only on the "surface level." Between postmodernism(s) and Pentecostalism there is such a wide gap in terms of presuppositions that one is wise not to exaggerate apparent similarities. For example, there is no "big story" for postmodernists, but there is one for Pentecostals; there is not absolute truth of any kind for postmodernists, but there is *the* truth for Pentecostals. It is these kind of foundational philosophical presuppositions that should be considered carefully before the wedlock is celebrated.

To be on the way is better than to settle down, even if wandering is sometimes troublesome and confusing. Much philosophical, historical, theological, and exegetical work waits the new generation of Pentecostals who want to preserve their identity and at the same time relate to other Christians and to the world around them.

Chapter Two

Authority, Revelation and Interpretation

Roman Catholics and Pentecostals have in been in dialogue since 1972. Discussion about Scripture and related topics such as tradition, inspiration, authority, and interpretation, continued to surface throughout the various phases of the dialogue. It was on the agenda of each of the first three quinquennia.

The dialogue has been both enriched and confused by the fact that both Roman Catholic and Pentecostal hermeneutics are still in the making. Roman Catholics, for example, experienced a dramatic shift during Vatican II as "*Dei Verbum* laid the foundations for a profoundly reconceived theology of revelation."[1] This major shift in the Catholic theology of revelation saw the replacement of the dominantly propositional or doctrinal view of revelation for a more personalist, trinitarian, experience-oriented, and *koinonia*-related view. The older propositional model—which, perhaps, can also be called a "revelational positivism"[2]—presented divine revelation as the communication of fundamental truths about God, with the consequence that assent to these truths was equivalent to assent to Catholic faith. This view was presupposed in the draft document on divine revelation at Vatican II, but was firmly rejected and replaced. A more personalist and trinitarian approach is clearly evident in the first chapter of the constitution:

> By this revelation, then, the invisible God..., from the fullness of divine love, addresses men and women as friends..., and moves among them, in order to

> invite and receive them into his own company. This economy of revelation is realized by deeds and words, which are intrinsically bound together. As a result, the works performed by God in the history of salvation show forth and bear out the doctrine and realities signified by the words; the words, for their part, proclaim the works, and bring to light the mystery they contain. The most intimate truth which this revelation gives us about God and the salvation of humanity shines forth in Christ, who is himself the mediator and the sum total of revelation. (*DV* 2)

One emphasis warmly welcomed by Pentecostals in the dialogue is *Dei Verbum*'s insistence on the priority of the Word of God in spirituality and theology. This means that the Church transcends itself in an attitude of openness and receptivity to a word it receives as servant rather than as master. It also puts the teaching authority into its right place. The authority of the Church teaching office depends on the authority of God, and consequently is exercised within and not above the Church.

An ecumenically important corollary is that the whole people of God, not just the hierarchy/magisterium, is addressed by the word of God, incarnate in Jesus Christ and dwelling in the Church by the power of the Holy Spirit. This is clearly brought home in Vatican II's pneumatological emphasis on divine revelation, which complements the christological orientation. This pneumatological perspective negates any attempt to conceive of God's word as the unique possession of any one group within the Church. God's word continues to abide in the whole Church through the Holy Spirit.

Of course, the major shift we have been describing does not mean that Catholics do not any more think of revelation in propositional, factual terms; this would make dialogue with Pentecostals, who have inherited some fundamentalist views, extremely difficult. What it means is that revelation is not understood *primarily* and *merely* as propositional. Here Catholic theology must steer a middle course between completely rejecting any cognitive content to divine revelation and seeing it merely as a factual "deposit of faith."

This dilemma is not unlike Pentecostals' attempt to balance their older, fundamentalistically-oriented view with a pneumatic, postmodern notion. The Pentecostal view of revelation and the interpretation paradigm are, of course, not as evident as the Catholic. Since I have in the previous chapter delineated the major stages of development in Pentecostal hermeneutics, my purpose here is to inquire into four definitive issues about revelation and interpretation which seem to have been crucial in the Roman Catholic-Pentecostal dialogue during the first three quinquennia (1972–1989) in order to continue thinking about what a constructive Pentecostal hermeneutic might look like. These issues are: (1) the nature of infallibility and inerrancy of the inspired Scriptures; (2) the relationship between critical study of the Bible and Spirit-inspired interpretation; (3) the criteria for interpretation: "sensus-fidei" (collegial) or "clarity of Scripture" (individual); and (4) the role of (post-biblical) tradition. Before I go into each of these questions, I will briefly summarize the common agreement between Catholics and Pentecostals.

Common Ground between Catholics and Pentecostals

First, Roman Catholics and Pentecostals agree on Jesus Christ as the final revelation, the consummation of God's speaking to us: "Together we believe that our Lord Jesus Christ revealed God in a perfect way through his whole ministry: through his words and deeds, his signs and wonders, but especially through his death and glorious resurrection from the dead, and finally by sending the Spirit of truth (cf. John 15:26; 16:7, 12)" (*FR* III.15; cf. *FR* III.14). Second, Roman Catholics and Pentecostals agree on the basic affirmation of biblical inspiration by the Holy Spirit: "We believe together that the books of the Old and New Testaments have been written, in their entirety, under the inspiration of the Holy Spirit. Scripture is the Word of God written in human words in history" (*FR* III.18). Third, there is common agreement upon the infallibility of Scripture as a logical result of its inspiration by the Spirit: "The Scripture teaches faithfully and without error that truth which God wanted to put into the sacred writings for our salvation (cf. 2 Tim 3:16)" (*FR* III.18).[3]

Fourth, there is consensus between Catholics and Pentecostals about the necessity of the Holy Spirit in understanding and appropriating the Word of God: "Both Pentecostals and Roman Catholics agree that Scripture, inspired by the Spirit, can be properly interpreted only with help of the Holy Spirit. 'So also no one comprehends the thoughts of God except the Spirit of God' because spiritual things 'are spiritually discerned' (1 Cor. 2:11, 14)" (*FR* III.24). The Catholic team argued that the "same Spirit who inspired the Scripture also opens the sense of the Scripture to the People of God, so that it nourishes their faith" (*FR* III.21, 24, and 26), and, the Pentecostal team affirmed that "the interpretation of Scripture can only be discerned through the Holy Spirit" (*FR* II.20 and 27). The obvious reason for the emphasis on the role of the Spirit in interpretation is that both Catholics and Pentecostals think revelation is *both* past *and* present. Catholic expert on the theology of revelation Gerald O'Collins affirms that this is the view of Vatican II. In order to preserve orthodoxy, he qualifies the statement by adding, "[p]resent revelation actualizes the living event of the divine self-revelation without adding to its content."[4] That is why several Catholic theologians who have assessed the contributions of Vatican II have called for "a more spiritual exegesis."[5]

Fifthly, Catholics and Pentecostals reached a significant ecumenical milestone when they achieved consensus concerning the integral relationship between Spirit, Word and *koinonia*/communion. Catholic ecumenist Paul D. Lee writes: "The Spirit, as the principle of interiority, provides inspiration for the prophets, scriptural writers, Jesus and the apostles, as well as for the text and the interpreter of the Bible. The Spirit, as the principle of unity, brings the Bible into a coherent whole. The Spirit, as the principle of communion, bridges the interpreters and the authors so as to bring forth a communion."[6] The very fact that the title for the Third Quinquennium was "*Koinonia*" is a powerful reminder of the close link between the Spirit's work as a principle of unity, and the role of church community. It was the "[c]hurch [that] recognized the New Testament writings as the Word of God addressed to humanity" (*FR* III.22), and in this sense the very same Spirit, working in the living church-communion, "is the ultimate redactor of the canonical Scripture."[7] Catholic co-chair Kilian McDonnell has noted in his most recent writings the integral relationship between *koinonia*, Spirit, and the formation of canon. Even the process of determining the canon of the Scripture was a process of the self-identification of the *koinonia*: "The *koinonia*, the power of the Spirit, recognizes its deepest self in identifying the canon."[8]

Such are, then, the convergences between Roman Catholics and Pentecostals in the understanding of revelation, inspiration, and interpretation. While we need to acknowledge the ecumenical significance of this common foundation, there is no denying some major differences, to which I turn next.

The Inerrancy, Infallibility and Authority of Scripture

Above we noted that both Pentecostals and Catholics agree on their basic affirmation of the infallibility of Scripture. The problem arises when we press the language used in the *Final Reports*. For Catholics, the infallibility of Scripture refers to the salvific intent of Scripture, not necessarily freedom from accidental errors.

The Pentecostal view is unclear. During the Second Quinquennium Pentecostals insisted on a "plenary inspiration" (*FR* II.23), while during the Third Quinquennium the adjective is dropped (*FR* III.17, 24). The confusion in the Pentecostal camp is enhanced by the reference to Black Pentecostals to whom the question of scriptural infallibility is not defined along the lines of strict "plenary" inspiration. It is evident that for non-white Pentecostals, a label like "neo-evangelical" would fit better than the inerrantist label.[9] Now, seeing inspiration as "plenary inspiration" carries with it overtones of the fundamentalist doctrine of Scriptural inerrancy. Pentecostals have been unsure about whether to side with Fundamentalist view or not.

The *Final Reports* prompt Paul D. Lee to observe: "Whether or not Pentecostals intended this deletion is not clear."[10] If the dropping is accidental, it shows that inerrancy is not of major importance to Pentecostals. If, on the other hand, the dropping is intentional, it shows that Pentecostal exegesis is moving beyond a literal-fundamentalist notion of inerrancy. In any case, the Pentecostal side of the dialogue chose to reject completely critical studies of the Bible (this was during the late 1970s). This extreme attitude toward modern biblical scholarship is a strong indication of the fundamentalist attitude.

Interestingly, the Pentecostal dialogue-paper by Howard M. Ervin does not even address this issue(!), a strong indication that the issue itself is of not of primary interest to this last generation of Pentecostals involved in the dialogue. In order to get a proper perspective on the issue of inerrancy/infallibility we need to recall aspects of the Pentecostal movement from fundamentalism to postmodernism discussed in the previous chapter. First, the fundamentalist-type understanding of inerrancy is not necessarily part of the original Pentecostal heritage.[11] This is especially the case if, as already intimated, the early Pentecostal affective and non-rationalistic epistemology stands out in stark contrast to the objectivist and positivist epistemology shared by modernism and Fundamentalism alike. Second, while the "evangelicalization of Pentecostalism" during and since the 1940s meant adjusting Pentecostalism, for instance in their "Declarations of Faith," in tune with Evangelical concerns, one of the most important of which was biblical inerrancy,[12] more recent Pentecostal scholars have drawn on postmodern theories of narrative in order to maintain and invigorate their own Pentecostal commitments to the reliability of the biblical (meta-) narrative. Third, there is an emerging realization that Pentecostals have never grounded their understanding of the authority of Scripture on a bedrock of doctrine—the doctrine of inerrancy or any other doctrine—but, rather, on their experiences of encountering in a direct and personal way the living God. In this case, it is the living Spirit of God who secures the authority of the living Word of God for the believer.

If all this is the case, then the Catholic emphasis on the salvific intent of infallibility is by no means an obstacle to Pentecostals. This issue also relates to the question of the legitimacy of critical study of Scripture. While it is certainly the case that the *FR* of the Second Quinquennium reflects the fundamentalist-literal type of understanding of inerrancy in all factual matters, yet the Pentecostal stance about the nature and definition of infallibility/inerrancy is not absolutely clear in the *FR* of the Third Quinquennium. But insofar as recent Pentecostal scholarship has opted to start with the original charismatic spirituality of the movement and has called for a distinctive Pentecostal notion of authority—and thus inspiration, where the role of the Spirit is appreciated as the ultimate criterion—instead of relying upon the fundamentalist and/or Evangelical notions of authority, to that extent, Pentecostals are moving beyond the impasse of the Fundamentalist understanding toward a more conciliar view.

Critical Bible Study and Spirit-informed Interpretation

For Pentecostals, according to the second *FR*, there is no way to do any kind of critical study of the Bible: "Pentecostals reject the philosophical and theological principles of form and redaction criticism as militating against the plenary inspiration. They insist on the necessity of the light given by the Holy Spirit if the reader is to respond with faith and understanding to the Word of God" (*FR* II.23). While this attitude is certainly changing among Pentecostal academics, it still holds true for many Pentecostal clergy, and certainly most laity. The reason why Pentecostals do not accept the standard critical methods of modern scholarship stems from their inherited understanding of inspiration in a literal-fundamentalist way. Critical studies on the one hand, and the attitude of faith from the Bible student's part to the light given by the Holy Spirit on the other hand, are seen as opposites by Pentecostals. In other words, it is not possible to be at the same time a critical student of the Bible and a believer surrendering to the illumination of the Spirit. One underlying factor among Pentecostals is the fear of rationalism, i.e., human reason taking the place of the Spirit: "In the determination of the limits and validation of religious knowledge, it was agreed that faith and reason cannot be polarized. However, Pentecostals place a greater emphasis *upon pneumatic inspiration and supernatural manifestations, than on reason,* for determining the limits and validity of religious knowledge" (*FR* II.28, emphasis mine). But it should also be suggested that Pentecostals are reacting to the theological principles behind these higher-critical methods of study rather than to the methods itself. In the final analysis, the Pentecostal attitude toward the study of the Bible remains unclear in *FR* II; the closest we get to a sort of definition is this: "The Pentecostal form of exegesis, while having its roots in evangelicalism, is not specifically defined. It is admittedly in a formative stage. Current exegesis would tend to be a pneumatic literal interpretation" (*FR* II.25).[13]

Ironically enough, Catholics oppose the "secular" presuppositions of modern critical scholarship, but they do not see any objection to using these very same methods: "Roman Catholics believe that the light of the Holy Spirit given in and through the Church is the ultimate principle of interpretation of Scripture. They reject any exegetical method that would deny this. However, they believe that critical methods are compatible with a Spirit-inspired exegesis and consider them necessary for a proper understanding of the text" (*FR* II.24). Catholics did not see any contradiction between a careful use of critical studies and openness to the guidance of the Holy Spirit. Catholics would, one suspects, understand well the hesitance of Pentecostals toward a more critical attitude since it was not so long ago when Catholic theology itself was wrestling with the same issue. It was not until after Vatican II that the official permission came from the highest church authority for Catholic scholars to pursue critical studies.

The reservation on the part of Pentecostals, however, reflects their being children of their time. In light of the Pentecostal dialogue-paper and the practice of modern Pentecostal scholarship, there has arisen a much more positive attitude toward generally accepted methods of biblical scholarship. Ervin's attitude, expressed in his dialogue-paper where he calls for Pentecostal pneumatic exegesis, is clearly much more positive toward historical-critical methods than the *FR*. As we saw earlier, he even thinks it is necessary, as does Arrington in his *DPCM* article on hermeneutics.[14] Several Pentecostal scholars have distinguished themselves in using the latest critical methods, even those explicitly condemned in the

FR, i.e., form-criticism and redaction-criticism. James B. Shelton, using redaction criticism, emphasizes the distinct contributions and viewpoints of each New Testament writer, and Donald A. John's study on the distinctives of New Testament writers' theologies utilizes form and genre criticism as well as redaction criticism.[15] From these examples Catholic Paul D. Lee observes that "[t]he growing emergence of a more sophisticated Pentecostal scholarship seems to discard the naive plenary verbal inspiration theory."[16]

The conclusion is that although *FR* II clearly rejected Pentecostals' use of critical methods because of the underlying philosophical principles, both dialogue-papers, *DPCM* and recent Pentecostal scholarship leave no doubt about the use of sound critical methods, in accordance with the emphasis on the Holy Spirit, in the Pentecostal interpretative process. *FR* II, thus, reflects either older Fundamentalist-oriented skepticism against all kinds of modern biblical scholarship or the general attitude among ordinary church members and a majority of Pentecostal preachers in the parishes.

Sensus Fidei and *Claritas Scripturae*

Both sides recognize that Scripture is of necessity linked to interpretation, and there is thus an urgent need for interpretation (cf. *FR* II.52). At the outset it was affirmed that there is, however, "a significant divergence as to the nature of interpretation which is necessary to understand Scripture accurately" (*FR* III.25). The basic question here is: "Who has the right to correctly interpret Scripture, especially when Scripture seems to contradict itself?"[17] The major divergence is clearly spelled out:

> Disagreement centers around what or who is an authoritative interpreter. To the Pentecostal it is the right interpretation under the illumination of the Holy Spirit leading to consensus. To the Roman Catholic, it is the church interpreting Scripture as understood by the people of God and discerned by the teaching office of the church. Both Pentecostals and Roman Catholics see interpretative authority as an expression of the activity of the Spirit in the Church. (*FR* II.52)

The only criterion for Pentecostals is the "Holy Spirit's guidance" when there are conflicting interpretations of Scripture. This understanding, of course, carries with it subjectivism, a problem not properly dealt with by Pentecostals (cf. *FR* II.27). Pentecostals believe that God has given special gifts for teaching the believing community, but they emphasize more than Catholics the role of every believer in the interpretation process. For Pentecostals Scripture is "clear" when interpreted and discerned in the power of the Spirit (see *FR* III.26).[18]

Pentecostal understanding of the interpretation process, according to the *Final Reports*, can be summarized in three statements. First, they rely upon supernatural charismatic gifts provided sovereignly by God. Second, they insist upon the "clarity of Scripture" principle inherited from Protestant Reformation. Third, Pentecostals do not accept any kind of authority, church or collegiality, beyond every believer's private judgment, although the help of the discerning Christian community is acknowledged. This right of individual judgment pertains to both faith and practice.

In his response to *FR* III, Hollenweger rightly wonders how the seemingly dramatic differences in matters of both faith and practice among Pentecostal churches are to be understood.[19] For him the Pentecostal handling of Scripture is by no means clear. The question is: who is the discerning Christian community and what are the instruments by which it expresses its judgment? The Pentecostals have not yet provided a credible solution to this major problem of interpretation.

As is well known, the Catholic Church opts for collegial interpretation with the help of the Spirit and of the believing community on the one hand (*FR* III.25), and the warrants of the living tradition on the other hand (*FR* II.101). Among Catholics this discerning sense of the believing community has come to be known as *sensus fidei*. "The whole body of the faithful who have an anointing that comes from the Holy One cannot err in matters of belief (cf. 1 John 2:20, 27)" (*FR* III.25, quoting *LG* 12).[20] Catholics untiringly stress the indispensable link between believing community, living tradition and guidance from the Holy Spirit who is both the inspirer and illuminator of divine truths: "The proper interpretation of Scripture must be made in the communion of the believers, within the living Tradition which is guided by the Holy Spirit. This same Spirit who inspired the Scripture also opens the sense of the Scripture to the People of God, so that it nourishes their faith" (*FR* III.21; cf. *FR* II.51).

Although Pentecostals give credit to the interpretation process in the Catholic Church, they firmly object to *sensus fidei* as a guarantee of not erring in faith or practice (see *FR* III.26). Ironically, both sides refer to a kind of supernatural endowment of Spirit in leading to the fullness of the truth in interpretation. For Pentecostals it is the supernatural charismatic gift of teaching and discernment, for Catholics, the supernatural *sensus fidei*. What, then, are the essential differences and similarities in all of this? The dialogue itself does not make this clear, and needs further analysis.

So far we have operated at the level of *Final Reports*. To further our discussion, it will be useful to have a look at a second Pentecostal dialogue-paper by Howard M. Ervin, where his argument is much more in tune with the Catholic understanding of interpretation than the *Final Reports* show. Ervin sees the Reformers' *sola scriptura* principle as problematic in some ways, because it raises the private, individual judgment too high, thus creating more fragmentation of the Church. Referring to the *sola scriptura*, he writes: "But as so frequently happens, its strength is also its weakness. For the right of private judgment coupled with the ultimate and absolute authority of the Scripture has accelerated the fragmentation of the Church to an alarming degree. In the final analysis, however, it is not Scripture that possesses final authority, but the private interpretations of the individual that are authoritative."[21] The problem in overemphasizing *sola scriptura* is the failure to recognize that Scripture, too, has its own history. As a way out of this one-sided Protestant Reformation heritage, Ervin suggests a more communal mode of interpretation, based on an important New Testament example in Acts 15 where the integral relationship between the Spirit, community and interpretation is manifested. In the first Christian council in Jerusalem, the criterion for interpretation was that "it seemed good to the Holy Spirit and to us" (Acts 15: 28) and "to the apostles and the elders with the whole church" (Acts 15: 22). In other words, there was "collegial consultation among responsible leaders ratified by the consensus of the whole community...(as) twin principles for discerning the direction of the Spirit's inspiration."[22]

Interestingly, the most recent Catholic theology of the Magisterium has come to emphasize more and more the role of the whole community both in receiving God's word, and in determining what is the truth. The notion of *sensus fidei* thus becomes more communal and the emphasis on *infallibility* denotes primarily the validity of the communal judgment of the whole body of believers rather than the primary role of the teaching magisterium/hierarchy. Although this emphasis can be clearly seen in Vatican II (e.g., in *Lumen Gentium* and *Dei Verbum*), its implications have not been that clear from the beginning. It is especially the pneumatological (*LG* 4 and 12) and prophetic (*LG* 12 and 35) emphases, coupled with the communal that would be warmly welcomed by Pentecostals (see *LG* 4, 12 and 35). The new emphasis on the role of the people of God in receiving the word of God emerged out of the ecclesiology of communion going back to patristic theologies where it is very evident.[23]

Catholic Jeremy Miller has characterized the movement of discernment through the Spirit of God in the community in three distinct moments: (1) the *articulation* of the faith in liturgy, devotions, and the like; (2) the *pedagogy*, in which the ecclesiastical magisterium discerns that which is articulated in the faith of the faithful; (3) and the *reception*, in which the faithful either do or do not recognize the faith authoritatively proclaimed as their own.[24] This model is not far from the Pentecostal scenario as explained above, although the terminology, of course, differs. "Each believer, by virtue of baptism," states Catholic Gaillardetz (and Pentecostals would qualify, "by virtue of baptism in the Spirit"), "has a supernatural instinct or sense of the faith that allows each to recognize divine revelation and to respond to it in faith. The infallibility of the whole people of God, however does not refer to the individual exercise of this *sensus fidei* but to the corporate belief of the whole people of God."[25] *Sensus fidei*, then, becomes what it actually denoted in the patristic theologies: *sensus fidelium*, or even more clearly, *consensus fidelium*. This notion overcomes the artificial separation between church *in credendo* (passively receiving the deposit of faith from the teaching office) and church *in docendo* (in worship), while leaving intact the legitimate distinction of different functions.

The dialogue could not resolve the issue under consideration. There are clear differences among Catholics and Pentecostals in the interpretation process. While Catholics stress strongly the collegial, community-related interpretation, Pentecostals emphasize private, individual judgment and the clarity of Scripture, which makes collegial interpretation and church tradition unnecessary. However, a Pentecostal dialogue-paper calls for revision of the Protestant *sola scriptura* principle associated with private interpretation toward a more dialectical, collegial interpretation. This is in accordance with the recent development of Pentecostal hermeneutics that seeks to re-establish the role of community/collegiality of the Spirit-filled church in the interpretation process. Here scholars are probing to the early roots of the movement. These developments seem to be extremely fruitful in terms of ecumenical developments, especially in relationship to Roman Catholic and Eastern Orthodox Churches.

Tradition as the bearer of the Spirit?

"The relationship between Scripture and Tradition is the most acute point of disagreement in the discussion of the Word of God in the Pentecostal/Catholic dialogue."[26] The issue surfaced in every quinquennium. Although there are major differences between Catholics and Pentecostals in their understanding and appropriation of tradition, the basic consensus was reached already during the First Quinquennium as to the inevitability of tradition and the need for caution: "A discernment must be made on these developments (i.e. traditions) by the Churches" (*FR* I.30). The basic Catholic view is clearly stated:

> Roman Catholics in the dialogue explain tradition in a two-fold sense, each sense related to the other. Tradition, here spelled with a capital T, stands for everything that is being and has been handed down, the once for all revelation made by God in Jesus Christ, the Word of God proclaimed in written and oral form, and the whole of the Spirit-filled community's response to the truth of the Gospel. As such, Tradition contains both an active element of handing down by the church, and a passive one of the material handed down. Within Tradition in this sense, the Word of God as Scripture has a kind of primacy. In this understanding Tradition is a continuous process. (*FR* II.55)

The Catholic position has several fundamental characteristics. An important conceptual distinction is made between Tradition (capital) which designates the whole of the Church's response throughout history to revelation, and tradition(s) (lower case) which designates material not found in Scripture, of which those relative to faith are normative and those related to Church practice and discipline are not (cf. also *FR* II.56).[27] The three-fold sense of the Word of God is explicated as the core of the Tradition: as incarnate, as written and as oral. Furthermore, the indispensable role of the Spirit is emphasized both in the response of the Spirit-filled community to the Tradition and in the actual handing down of the tradition. The work of the Holy Spirit in the process makes the Tradition living, thus "a continuous process."[28] Finally, and this is important for Pentecostals as well, the Scripture, the written word of God, is given primacy in the Tradition (see *FR* II.26 and 30).

Catholics emphasize that the handing down of the Scripture through the centuries is a result of living tradition, guided by the Holy Spirit (*FR* II.19; cf. *LG* 8). Vatican II, while insisting on the permanence of the covenant established in Christ, recognized that God is not silent in our time. While Jesus Christ was God's definitive self-expression, nevertheless that Word is received by humanity in history and is kept alive in the living memory of the Church. "As a dynamic, living Word, it speaks anew to each generation of believers."[29] This is the understanding of tradition in its most dynamic sense, as God's Word actualized in the life of the Church (see *DV* 8). Tradition, as "a living Gospel," rather than standing over against the written Word of God, is seen as an avenue for the Spirit to guide the believers toward fuller understanding and to guard them in the truth of God (*FR* II.26). "To deny present revelation is to doubt the active power here and now of the Holy Spirit as guiding the Tradition and mediating the presence of the risen Christ."[30] While Protestants and Pentecostals tend to interpret this as a second source of revelation, Catholics think in terms of single source of Revelation flowing in two streams (*FR* II.19 and 20). This is the official stand of *Dei Verbum* (*FR* II.30, citing *DV* 10).[31]

Pentecostals agree with the traditional Protestant Reformation denial of the legitimacy of post-biblical tradition as normative. Scripture must always stand as the criterion for tradition and its legitimacy (see *FR* II.20 and 57, and III.23). Consequently, Pentecostals do not believe it is right to go beyond the written Word of God in establishing doctrines. Two concrete examples in the *Final Reports* show this difference of opinion. First is the church's attitude toward those who have not heard the Gospel (*FR* II.14); second is the role of Mary (*FR* II.59). Without going into the intricacies of these two disputed questions, suffice it to say that Pentecostal doctrine itself offers at least one major article of faith in the same category as these two Catholic issues, namely the doctrine of speaking in tongues as "the initial (physical) evidence" (of reception of the baptism with the Holy Spirit). Regardless of one's view of that particular doctrine, it makes the point that I want to highlight here: if Catholic doctrines are not "purely" based on the Scripture, neither are Pentecostal doctrines. And how could they be!

Ecumenically, a much more fruitful approach for Pentecostals, instead of insisting on the impasse created by what they think is the Reformation denial of tradition (although, mainline Reformation theology has already moved much closer to the Catholic position), would be to uncover the pneumatological resources for the proper understanding of tradition. And Catholic theology should do much more homework in the fashioning of that—what seems to me, the *major*—problem, namely, criteria for distinguishing between what is good in the development of tradition and what is not. I do not see anything in Pentecostal theology which would necessarily oppose the (Catholic and Orthodox) idea of tradition as the dynamic bearer of the Spirit, but I am concerned if criteria for discerning the result of tradition are not spelled out.

That the understanding of tradition as a dynamic, Spirited living Gospel is not foreign to Pentecostalism is seen in Ervin's dialogue-paper.

In tune with Catholic understanding, Ervin appreciates a living ecclesial tradition against the numerous sectarian interpretations of Scripture. While arguing on the primacy of written tradition over the oral, Ervin emphasizes that "tradition is the life of the Spirit in the Church illuminating and communicating truth anew." Interestingly enough, he connects this with his earlier emphasis on the need for "the apostolic witness of Scripture in terms of apostolic experience" which has been one of the hallmarks of Classical Pentecostalism.[32]

One way to help both Catholics and Pentecostals think through the issues of tradition is to draw attention to the notion of *anamnesis*, one of the most recent developments in the postconciliar theology of revelation. Memory, dynamically understood, can illuminate the category of tradition both in its active sense as a process of handing on the apostolic faith and in its objective sense as the actual content of that faith. Memory here is not, of course, meant in its everyday meaning in which it refers to a mere recalling things from the past, but in its ancient biblical and liturgical usage in which the transformative power of past events is brought to bear on present realities, as in the Eucharist. Tradition can be viewed as the "memory" (*anamnesis*) of God's word residing in the corporate consciousness of the Church. Memory in the biblical sense of the term is not simply storage of the sediment of the past. It is also the "humus from which life never stops borrowing." Tradition as understood this way, rather than undermining the role of the written Word, enhances it: "As the memory of the Church, Tradition represents the permanence of a Word which is always alive, always enriched, and yet radically always the same, where the Church never ceases to nourish its faith."[33]

Here we come to the problem that was addressed tentatively above, namely, that of distinguishing between right and wrong developments. The written Word becomes *the* criterion to distinguish between what is right and what is wrong in the development of tradition. Not every move in the tradition can be welcomed. More than occasionally the Church has gone astray in its understanding.[34] The critical role of the Scripture should have been stressed more.

In sum we may state that in terms of understanding the nature and role of tradition, there is a real, thus far unresolved difference, between Catholics and Pentecostals. Pentecostals align with the "standard" Reformation stance (which, though, as we mentioned already, has been superseded in the mainline ecumenical theology). At the same time, there are hopeful signs toward a more consensual understanding, if not unanimity, when the pneumatological resources for the understanding of tradition and its formation are uncovered. Interestingly enough, this means going back to the roots of Pentecostal theology, with its insistence on the continuing revelation of the Spirit and the (more) communal mode of interpretation. The developments of the post-conciliar Catholic Church in moving toward a more dynamic, Spirit-informed notion of tradition as a part of rethinking of Catholic ecclesiology (e.g., the Church as a sacrament, filled with the Spirit, equipping each member for spiritual ministry) seem to make it easier for Pentecostals to approach Catholics in this matter.

Transitions

This chapter has analyzed Catholic and Pentecostal views of Scripture, authority, and interpretation. There is a significant agreement on the finality of Jesus Christ as the ultimate norm of revelation as well as the inspiration and interpretation of the written Word in the Spirit of God. There is also a helpful reference to *koinonia*.

Four topics were highlighted since they have been issues of contention. Two of them appear to have much potential for convergence if not for consensus, namely, the nature of infallibility and the legitimacy of critical studies. In fact, in reference to the latter, it seems that the new generation of Pentecostal exegetes is taking for granted a responsible use of standard critical tools while at the same time expressing reservations about the underlying philosophical presuppositions, as Catholics are doing also. The dramatic shift in biblical methodology, as a result of the emerging postmodern mindset, has appeared to contribute to this change of attitude among Pentecostals.

When it comes to the definition of infallibility, ambiguity exists in the Pentecostal camp. Several theologians, so it seems, might be quite willing to champion a sort of infallibility where the emphasis is on the salvific function of Scripture (cf. Catholics) rather than on the fundamentalistic notion, but the general ethos among lay people and preachers alike adds polarity rather than leads to a consensus. It is to be seen which direction the pendulum is going to take in the near future. These two notions are not, of course, contradictory, but there is a clear tension when the issue is pushed.

Two other issues, discussed in this chapter, appear to be much more complicated. Pentecostals strongly prefer individual right to interpretation since they believe that Scripture is clear and is not in need of hierarchical/collegial interpretation. Catholics stress the primacy of collegial/magisterial right to interpretation. These traditional dividing lines, however, seem to begin to eradicate as, on the one hand, Pentecostals are re-appropriating a more communal interpretation paradigm (cf. Acts 15), and, on the other hand, Catholics have had to take another look at what the notion *sensus fidei* really means. Is it not, first and foremost, an affirmation of the work of the Spirit in all the faithful rather than just in the hierarchy? The new emerging *koinonia*-ecclesiology, with rehabilitation of the Spirit in the church, clearly points to this direction.

The question of tradition has been, and continues to be, the hardest issue. Without watering down the remaining differences, some hopeful signs are in the horizon. Some Pentecostals are willing to have another look at what role the Spirit plays in the growth and reappropriation of the biblical tradition. Here they are gleaning from insights of Eastern Orthodox and some Catholic traditions.[35] Catholics, at the same time, are looking for parameters to assess whether growth of the tradition in the church is right or not. Here the role of the written Word, after Vatican II, has been much more clearly affirmed than before. Catholics also show signs that they are willing to learn from Christian *oikoumene* since the more recent view of revelation regards even the Catholic "deposit of faith" as eschatological rather than complete. The significant reformulation of the Catholic theology of revelation with its personalist, pneumatological, and *koinonia*-oriented emphases carries with it enormous ecumenical potential.

It has been said that "A closed Bible unites us; an open Bible divides us!"[36] Unfortunately, Scripture has been an occasion of divisions and conflicts, especially when it has been opened in the ecumenical table. Catholics and Pentecostals have dared to open the Bible and have taken honest looks at some fundamental issues. Clearly, the engagement has been fruitful to both parties. Let us hope that as the dialogue continues, there will come another occasion to retrieve some of these issues.

Chapter Three

Pentecostals as "Anonymous Ecumenists"?

The leading Pentecostal ecumenist, Cecil M. Robeck, Jr., has recently said: "We Pentecostals are ecumenical, we just don't know it!"[1] Karl Rahner spoke of "anonymous Christians." In a similar vein, we could say that Pentecostals are "anonymous ecumenists."

We have a paradox: "Pentecostalism" and "ecumenism" do not seem to match. You are either/or, not both. If you are Pentecostal, you are narrow-minded and exclusivistic. On the contrary, ecumenical Christians—so the general thinking goes—are tolerant and open to others. What Pentecostals think of as legitimate "soul-winning," other Christians often regard as blunt proselytism. To be honest, most Pentecostals do not regard themselves as ecumenical. If they have any thoughts about Christian unity, it usually means relating to those who are of the same mind. Pentecostals prefer to speak about "spiritual ecumenism."

The Spirit of God has not, however, been satisfied with this kind of exclusivism. Just as in the times of the Judges, the Spirit comes suddenly like a rushing wind upon a Pentecostal and urges that person to relate to others. The rest of the Pentecostals often look incomprehensibly at these Gideons or Samsons.

One wonders if a chapter on Pentecostals and ecumenism will be rather short, since there is not much to tell about. Or is there? Actually, the most noted observer of the Pentecostal phenomenon, Walter J. Hollenweger, has recently outlined four phases of ecumenical development among Pentecostals. The first phase was the beginning of

Pentecostalism as an ecumenical movement. During the second phase, Pentecostals started forming local congregations and aligning themselves with Fundamentalists and Evangelicals. Phase three saw a blurring of the ecumenical vision as national and international denominations were organized. Finally, during phase four, some Pentecostals have begun to return to their ecumenical roots by engaging in formal ecumenical dialogue.[2] According to Hollenweger, in general a phase takes a generation. He argues that the older classical Pentecostal denominations are now somewhere between phases three and four, while the charismatic renewal in the mainline churches must be placed between phases one and two.[3]

Although Hollenweger's outline is helpful in many ways, for our purposes here I have chosen a different schema. It seems to me that the emergence and development of a Pentecostal ecumenical perspective could be summarized in five major stages: (1) the initial ecumenical emphasis of the new movement; (2) the development of an exclusive attitude toward other churches, because of their hostility toward Pentecostals; (3) a redefinition of unity as "spiritual unity"; (4) the emergence of cautious openness toward the ecumenical movement; and (5) the establishment of relationships with the Roman Catholic Church, and later, with other churches, in terms of Christian unity and exchange.

The purpose of this chapter is to offer a descriptive survey of the short history of the emergence of the Pentecostal ecumenical vision based on this outline, and to present some challenges not just to Pentecostals, but also to a wider *oikoumene* since the way of ecumenism is by definition a two-way street. If Pentecostals have not been very active—and most of them still entertain doubts—in ecumenical work, there must be some reason, since Pentecostalism could have provided potential for an unprecedented effort to unite Christians. That was at least the dream of the pioneers. In order to re-appropriate that dream let us return to the origins of modern Pentecostalism.

The Original Vision of Christian Unity

Although the story of the birth of Pentecostalism at Azusa Street (Los Angeles, California) at the turn of the twentieth century is well known, there is not yet a consensus among researchers of Pentecostalism as to the exact origins of the movement.[4] Four main proposals have been set forth. The first is proposed by those who desire to connect the origins of the modern Pentecostal movement with the work of Charles F. Parham and his students at Topeka, Kansas. The second is argued by non-white historians and theologians of the movement who often emphasize the primary role of the Black Holiness preacher William Joseph Seymour and the Apostolic Faith Mission that arose in Los Angeles in April 1906. The third is suggested by others who see themselves as constituting the earliest Pentecostal denominations, thereby claiming to be the original Pentecostals, because some of their leaders or members spoke in tongues prior to either Parham or Seymour. Finally, there are those who view the origins of Pentecostalism as a sovereign work of God which can be traced to no single leader or group, but rather to a spontaneous and simultaneous outpouring of the Holy Spirit.[5]

Whatever one's view of the origins, one thing seems undisputed: "the Pentecostal Movement started as an ecumenical revival movement within the traditional churches."[6] Robeck, referring to the ethos of the earliest Pentecostal leaders, follows the conclusions of Hollenweger by arguing that, "the Pentecostal Movement was going to be the answer to Jesus' prayer in John 17:21 regarding Christian Unity."[7]

This ecumenical theme has thus been part of the Pentecostal movement since its inception. The mission statement of the Azusa Street Mission—the first Pentecostal church—proclaimed that "THE APOSTOLIC FAITH MOVEMENT stands for...Christian Unity everywhere."[8] Charles F. Parham, the Bible teacher in the Topeka Bible College where the first outpouring of the Spirit of the emerging Pentecostal movement was experienced, regarded himself as an "Apostle of Unity."[9] W. F. Carothers, one of the pioneers, wrote in the first year of the Azusa Revival: "...the restoration of Pentecost means ultimately the restoration of Christian unity and the two messages have come to us together in this [Apostolic Faith] Movement."[10]

The motto of Dutch Pentecostal pioneer Gerrit Roelof Polman (1868–1932) was: "The purpose of the Pentecostal revival is not to build up a church, but to build up all churches."[11] Cornelius van der Laan calls Polman "a failed ecumenist," "a sectarian against his will." Van der Laan summarizes his analysis of this profound Pentecostal leader:

> Polman's ecumenical heart collided with his fundamentalistic Evangelical head. His Spirit baptism had generated a loving attitude toward all fellow Christians, but he was unable to fully assimilate this ecumenical experience into his thinking....Surely this was not his fault alone. He received no help from his Evangelical colleagues nor from the academic theologians.[12]

Other Pentecostal pioneers and leaders could be singled out, e.g., Thomas Ball Barratt from Norway who brought the Pentecostal message to several Scandinavian countries. In an inclusive vision, he dreamed of the "very Revival Christ had in His mind when He prayed that *all His disciples might be* one."[13]

Rejection by Other Churches Led to Exclusivism

But it was with great disappointment that these new Pentecostals came to realize that most of organized Christendom did not want them and would not accept them. All kinds of complaints and accusations were leveled against them. Partially because of some extremes in their worship, and partially because of the rigidity of some of the older denominations, the Pentecostals found themselves at odds with established denominations. The more Pentecostals came to be marginalized by the establishment, the more there arose among Pentecostals prejudices toward other Christians, especially the Roman Catholic Church. Finally this led to exclusivism.

Pentecostalism has provoked controversy at almost every stage of its development. This has been true not merely because of its tradition-breaking form of worship and practice, but also, significantly, because it has challenged the so-called cessationist principle, which holds that miracles or extraordinary charismata were terminated at or near the end of the apostolic age. The older scholars of church history and historical theology had asserted and explained the disappearance of the "religion of the Spirit and of power" in the earliest church. Against this view, "the salient characteristic of Pentecostalism is its belief in the present-day manifestation of spiritual gifts, such as miraculous healing, prophecy and, most distinctively, glossolalia. Pentecostals affirm that these spiritual gifts (charismata) are granted by the Holy Spirit and are normative in contemporary church life and ministry."[14] Many observers of the movement hold that this challenge, in spirituality and enthusiasm—in the "revalorization of the Charismata"—rather than in theological analysis, entails the most important contribution of Pentecostalism and later Charismatic movements.[15] Unfortunately, most churches, especially before the birth of the Charismatic movement in the mainline denominations, did not heed the Pentecostal message, nor were they willing to learn from these "enthusiasts."

What could a movement do in a situation like this other than what similar movements had done before: to start over again? Pentecostals started to build churches and form Pentecostal constituencies that soon meant departure from the early vision of unity. Instead of unity, the main purpose came to be survival and competition with others. In a few decades, Pentecostals consolidated their status as a religious constituency. Alignment with Fundamentalists, who, ironically, were one of their most bitter enemies theologically but were willing to allow a kind of "contract-marriage," led to an even more exclusivist attitude. The enemies of Fundamentalists, and later on of Evangelicals, became enemies of Pentecostals, too.

A Vision of "Spiritual Unity"

Now the crucial question is, to quote Robeck again: "But if this is true, if Pentecostals are truly ecumenical, why do we not recognize that fact?" Or to put it another way: if the Pentecostal movement started with a clear ecumenical vision, why is it that today most Pentecostals are suspicious of, even when not hostile to, the idea of ecumenism, especially "formal ecumenism"—e.g., membership in the WCC or even the prospects of discussions with the Roman Catholic Church? Robeck gives the obvious answer to his own question: "The answer, of course, lies in the definition given to the term and to the history of how this definition gained supremacy."[16]

Harvard professor Harvey Cox rightly acknowledges this perspective. While giving credit to the fact that early Pentecostals were, indeed, ecumenical, he remarks that "ecumenism" was defined strictly by these Pentecostals:

> The early Pentecostals were obviously not ecumenists, at least not in today's sense. If God was now forming a new church to replace the old, corrupt ones, then why waste time worrying about ecclesiastic unity? Most people who became Pentecostals joined the new movement from other denominations, so were not eager to cooperate with them. They had left them for what they considered to be good reasons, and now they had also been rejected by them. Such churches, some of them believed, were led by wolves in sheep's clothing, craven hirelings who were misleading the flock. "Be not unequally yoked together with unbelievers," Paul had plainly said. They took him at his word, and they urged the members of other churches who dropped in on their revivals to do the same. Many did.[17]

Consequently, Pentecostals have insisted on "invisible"—one could say "spiritual"—ecumenism rather than on visible unity, for they believe that unity is something already there for Spirit-filled Christians. Unity for them is not something we do but something that comes from the Spirit. One of the most influential leaders of Pentecostalism, Donald Gee of England, wrote: "We do not come together to 'make' unity for it already exists by the grace of God. It only needs to be cherished."[18]

When the modern ecumenical movement took form in the WCC, Pentecostals rejected it quickly, because it looked to many of them too much like a human attempt to do the work of God. "It made visible what was rightfully invisible, and it empowered a structure (the WCC) or a series of structures (the constituent denominations), with power that Pentecostals believed was best left to the Holy Spirit."[19] Furthermore, issues that have led Pentecostals to reject the modern ecumenical movement go beyond the matter of visibility. Visibility itself was important because of the Pentecostal fear, grounded in an interpretation of prophecy, that a worldwide church will ultimately become a tool of the antichrist. But added to this are fears of the undervaluing of evangelism in favor of social service and theological liberalism. These are the reasons why some Pentecostal denominations disapprove of ministers who are too closely related to WCC or other agencies of the formal ecumenical movement.[20]

There is, however, an inconsistency to be found in the Pentecostal "criteria" for ecumenism. On the one hand, as Pentecostal spokesman Donald Gee expressed many decades ago, the only test of Christian unity is the "mutual acceptance of the Lordship of Jesus Christ"; on the other hand, Pentecostals reject outright both the WCC, which understands itself to be "a fellowship of churches which confess the Lord Jesus Christ as God and Savior according to the Scriptures," and the National Council of Churches of Christ in the United States, with a preamble to its constitution that declares it to be a "community of Christian communions which, in response to the gospel as revealed in the Scriptures, confess Jesus Christ, the incarnate Word of God, as Savior and Lord."[21] Robeck puts the situation in proper perspective:

> To note all of this, however, is not to say that Pentecostals have rejected ecumenism, only that they have rejected one particular form or instrument of ecumenism. If ecumenism is viewed as something "spiritual," something created by the Holy Spirit, a genuine unity or *koinonia* in the Spirit, a fellowship of all those who are "blood bought Christians," then Pentecostals have embraced rather than rejected ecumenism.[22]

Pentecostals have indeed been involved with ecumenism when they have found it in accord with their own viewpoint. In 1947 the First

Pentecostal World Conference convened in Zurich, Switzerland, giving rise to the Pentecostal World Fellowship whose long-time chairman was the celebrated Pentecostal ecumenist David J. du Plessis. It was meant to build unity among Pentecostal churches worldwide. The same can be said of the Pentecostal Fellowship of North America (PFNA), founded in 1948 "to demonstrate to the world the essential unity of Spirit-baptized believers, fulfilling the prayer of the Lord Jesus 'that they all may be one.'"[23] Pentecostals have also been active in the World Evangelical Fellowship and the Lausanne Committee for World Evangelization, transconfessional organizations with formulated doctrinal bases. From all this Robeck draws the conclusion:

> Each of these examples, then, supports the basic assertion that Pentecostals view themselves as ecumenical, but they do not understand that this is so. They tend to overlook the reality that these organizations, like the National Council of Churches or the World Council of Churches, are humanly formed. They emphasize the fact that they are merely participating in the summons of the Holy Spirit to enter into an answer to Jesus' urgent prayer for unity among his disciples. While the WCC is described as "making" unity happen, Pentecostals deny that their groups do this. They are simply recognizing that their unity already exists.[24]

The Emergence of an Ecumenical Perspective

Two developments opened the eyes of (at least some) Pentecostals to the challenge of ecumenical activities. First, there was the untiring work of the late David du Plessis in establishing contacts with both Roman Catholic and Protestant churches.[25] Born in South Africa in 1905, du Plessis was ordained as Pentecostal minister of Apostolic Faith Missions of South Africa in 1928. He served as General Secretary of the Mission until elected General Secretary of the World Pentecostal Conference in 1948. A personal word of prophecy to du Plessis by an illiterate Pentecostal evangelist, Smith Wigglesworth, played a crucial role in driving Mr. Pentecost toward ecumenical contacts with Rome. Before receiving the prophecy, du Plessis—according to his own testimony—shared the same kind of prejudices so prevalent among Pentecostal ministers: "I couldn't see anything else but old-line Pentecostalism. I was in a sort of Pentecostal hothouse, having no part or dealings with anything or anyone outside.…I have never loved Catholics. I have felt never any consideration for them. I have been brought up to despise them, reject them."[26]

Very soon his attitude began to change. A few years after the word of prophecy from Wigglesworth, du Plessis lay for a few months in a hospital because of a car accident. There he reflected on the possibility of reaching out to older churches:

> In 1951 the Lord spoke to me and clearly told me to go and witness to the leaders of the World Council of Churches. In my prayers I said: "Lord, I have preached so much against them. What do I say to them now? They will not listen to me. Their churches have put our people out of their fellowship. That is why we have now a separate Pentecostal Movement. The churches were not willing to listen to the testimony of those who speak with tongues." But the Lord kept telling me to go and witness to them.[27]

Already in 1951, du Plessis had visited the WCC office in New York. The next year he was seen at the International Missionary Council session in Willingen, Germany. In 1954 he was invited by W. A. Visser't Hooft, General Secretary of the WCC, to participate in the Evanston Assembly. Thereafter he visited a number of ecumenical offices as well as theological schools in the United States, both Protestant and Catholic, lecturing on Pentecostalism and the Pentecostal movement. In 1964 du Plessis was invited by Cardinal Bea as the only Pentecostal observer to the third session of Vatican Council II.

The second development which introduced Pentecostals to the challenge of ecumenical activities is the emergence of the Charismatic movement in older churches. Although at first highly suspect among classical Pentecostals, this movement came to be seen in due course as divine confirmation of the sovereignty of the Spirit. The charismatic renewal movement in the Roman Catholic Church, for example, was central to the development of relationships between Rome and some Pentecostals. While I will return to this matter shortly, it is important to note that charismatic renewal provided additional impetus for Pentecostal participation in formal ecumenism.

Examples of this emerging ecumenical openness can be seen in the two Brazilian and Chilean Pentecostal churches which first joined the WCC in the 1960s.[28] The presence of Pentecostals at the World Council Assembly in Canberra 1991 took on a particular importance. The theme "Come Holy Spirit - Renew the Whole Creation," and the establishment of a special group on "Pentecostal and Charismatic Movements" in Section III of the Assembly, "Spirit of Unity—Reconcile Your People," made this an especially important moment for the witness of the Pentecostal churches.[29]

In the Faith and Order movement, within both the WCC and the National Council of Churches (USA), there has been considerable effective Pentecostal witness, especially in Santiago de Compostela in 1993. Pentecostal theologian Simon Chan of Singapore made a major presentation on the Trinity, and several Pentecostal leaders took part in the work of various groups.[30] Jeffrey Gros notes that in the discussions of the differences between East and West over the trinitarian faith and processions, "the Pentecostal voice played a unique and important role"; he concludes: "Indeed, after the Santiago meeting, it will be difficult for Pentecostals in the future to disown the World Council and the Faith and Order movement and their theology, without disowning the contribution of their own churches and movement."[31]

Against this background it is no wonder that a growing number of both Pentecostals and non-Pentecostals urge Pentecostals not to be afraid to take part in formal ecumenical work. It has been argued that besides being able to contribute uniquely to other churches, Pentecostals will reap good fruit themselves as well. This will not mean denying the Pentecostal distinctives but affirming them. Kilian McDonnell, the co-founder and Catholic co-chair of the Roman Catholic-Pentecostal dialogue, has urged Pentecostals and Catholics to unite in common witness because there is enough "theological basis" for this. [32]

Roman Catholic-Pentecostal Dialogue: An Exercise on the Frontiers of Ecumenism

One of the best kept secrets of recent ecumenical developments is the International Roman Catholic-Pentecostal dialogue which started in 1972. The dialogue is an honest confrontation of the currently two largest Christian groups, both of whom are outside of the WCC. The mutual talks between these two "giants" carries much potential and, hopefully, points to the future of ecumenism where the "Free Churches" are drawn to dialogue as equal partners.

There was roughly a sixty-year period between the formation of the first Pentecostal bodies and the beginning of official dialogue between Roman Catholics and Pentecostals. It is obvious that something significant had to take place after the beginnings of the Pentecostal movement and within the Roman Catholic Church before there could even be a suggestion of some kind of discussion together. Dialogue had its beginning when Pentecostals Rev. David du Plessis and Rev. Ray

Bringham contacted Catholic Kilian McDonnell, O.S.B. Ecumenically it is of the highest importance that the initiative came from the Pentecostal side. Catholic Paul D. Lee, who wrote his doctoral dissertation on the dialogue, has neatly summarized the major phases of the Roman Catholic-Pentecostal dialogue in these terms: (1) The Stage of Mutual Introduction (the First Quinquennium, 1972–1976); (2) The Phase of Contra-Positions (the Second Quinquennium, 1977–1982); (3) The Search for Common Identity (the Third Quinquennium, 1985–1989); and (4) The Potential of Mutual Cooperation in the Christ-given Mission (the Fourth Quinquennium, 1990–1996).[33]

The first dialogue sessions (1972–1977) were a time for establishing mutual trust and understanding. Discussions were mainly on the phenomenon of Pentecostalism, an area unfamiliar to most of the Catholic team members. At this first stage of mutual encounter and introduction, efforts were made to see the correlation between the two traditions. The Catholics emphasized the sacramental and personal element of the faith experience in the Church, while the Pentecostals stressed the communitarian character of renewal experience and worship.

The second phase (1978–1982) covered such topics as speaking in tongues, faith and experience, hermeneutics, healing, tradition, the church as communion, Mary, and ministry. The result of the discussion was the appreciation of Pentecostal openness to, and receptiveness of, spiritual manifestations, especially speaking in tongues and healing, in the Catholic charismatic renewal. The Church as a lived experience of community was emphasized throughout the discussion. There was a surprising degree of agreement on healing, including healing as a sign of God's kingdom, healing as a means of wholeness, Jesus Christ as the healer and anointer, and the Eucharist as a source of healing. Disagreements touched on issues like the relationship between Scripture and tradition, the guidance of the Spirit and the authority of authentic interpretation, the question of Mary, and the priesthood of all believers.

The overall theme for the Third Quinquennium (1985–1989) was "Communion of Saints." Topics for dialogue were: "Communion of Saints" (1985), "The Holy Spirit and the New Testament Vision of Koinonia" (1986), "Koinonia, Church and Sacrament" (1987), and "Koinonia and Baptism" (1988). This third phase was more concentrated than the previous two. Despite the initial intention of the Pentecostal participants not to deal with unity or ecclesiological questions, the topics that were discussed such as ministry, tradition, and others gradually led to the question of ecclesiology.

The Fourth Quinquennium ended in the summer 1997. Its overall topic was "Evangelization, Proselytism, and Common Witness."[34]

What are the defining issues of the dialogue? Catholic Kilian McDonnell has identified five: the hermeneutical moment, infant and believers' baptism, baptism in the Holy Spirit, the church as *koinonia*, and Mary. He states that in a preliminary way the two sides agree on the basic content of the Christian faith: trinity, the divinity of Christ, virgin birth, centrality of the death and resurrection of Jesus, Pentecost as constitutive of the church, forgiveness of sins, and promise of eternal life. "We may look at these areas differently, but there is a measure of agreement on them," he adds.[35] Beyond these theological areas of basic Christian faith, the five issues above emerged in the first three quinquennia and define the dialogue and give it an unmistakable profile.

The dialogue has a special character. The bilateral conversations which the Roman Catholic Church undertakes with other world communions (e.g., the Lutheran World Federation) are prepared to consider problems concerning Church structures and have structural/visible unity as a goal. The Roman Catholic-Pentecostal Dialogue has not had visible unity as a goal. Before it began it was made clear that its immediate scope was not "to concern itself with the problems of imminent structural union," although of course its object was Christians coming closer together in prayer and common witness. Its purpose has been that "prayer, spirituality and theological reflection be a shared concern at the international level in the form of a dialogue" (*FR* I.4).

Since this dialogue represents discussions between a highly structured church, with international authority, and a loosely connected movement without any international governing body, there have been some major challenges in terms of ecumenical method and procedures. These reflect more widely the challenges which will be encountered in future talks between "churches" and "movements." Roman Catholics, especially during the early years of the dialogue, were better trained theologically and exegetically, while many Pentecostals lacked formal theological training and were suspicious of historical critical methods. Furthermore, the fact that there is very little doctrinal unity among Pentecostals often complicated the process for Roman Catholics. In the first dialogue period it was even more difficult, not only because Pentecostals themselves have a great variety of doctrinal emphases, but also Charismatics from older churches were involved.

There is, also, the question of the usefulness of traditional dialogue-patterns in relation to a movement like Pentecostalism. Catholic Peter Hocken has recently discussed why dialogue and cooperation with the "non-ecumenical sector," like the Pentecostal movement, is not easy for a highly structured church like the Roman Catholic. Hocken has also made a comment on a very obvious development taking place in the ecumenical world. On the one hand, there is decline of the (formal) ecumenical movement with decreasing numbers and vitality among official ecumenical bodies, and on the other hand, there is world-wide growth of the "non-ecumenical sectors" (Pentecostals and Evangelicals). His conclusion is that the more institutional expressions of the ecumenical movement have "lost touch with the most dynamic currents of revival and renewal." Hocken, consequently, criticizes his own church for the tendency to insist on bilateral dialogues in which "Church meets Church," noting that the Catholic concept of ecumenism, reestablished as recently as the 1993 release of the new Directory for the Application of Principles and Norms on Ecumenism, operates on the basis of dialoging with Churches or "ecclesial communities."[36]

Hocken articulates four reasons why dialogue and cooperation with the "non-ecumenical sector" (which includes Pentecostals) are difficult. First, there is the incompatibility of fundamentalism and dialogical patterns. Second, there is the refusal to acknowledge non-Evangelicals as Christians and to recognize their Churches as Christian Churches. Third, the perception of the ecumenical movement as a merely human effort to attain unity persists. Lastly, there is the difficulty of dialogue with Christians for whom the reality and concept of Church is not central.

Future Challenges

The original Pentecostal vision of Christian unity, although severely frustrated by subsequent events, carries a lot of ecumenical potential. Despite the fact that most Pentecostals are ambivalent, to say the least, about the value of "formal ecumenism," I see much hope in the steps taken by some courageous pioneers, like David du Plessis and Cecil M. Robeck. They have had to pay the price of being under suspicion, but their vision has been large enough to be shared with others. Pentecostals, like other Christians, do not have the option of choosing *whether* to be engaged in ecumenism. The question is rather *what kind* of ecumenism they see compatible with their own agenda.

Yet, there are in "formal ecumenism" a lot of developments that do not help Pentecostals to be engaged. Theological liberalism, an inclusive attitude toward other religions, and overemphasis on social concern at the expense of proclamation are some of the most obvious. Whether they accurately reflect the agenda of the WCC and related organizations is another issue; but this is the impression given to most Pentecostals.

In many ways, both "mainline" churches and ecumenical constituencies have in recent years shown more openness to Pentecostals than before. There have been even some occasional invitations from the WCC for Pentecostals to bring their contribution. These developments should be welcomed by all. However, let the ecumenical constituencies, especially the WCC, take another look at what it really might mean if Pentecostals would enter official ecumenism on a larger scale. Well known are the pronouncements from Canberra and elsewhere which seem to point to the willingness of "mainline" churches to reach out to Pentecostals/Charismatics, and indeed, some actions have been already taken to that effect. But what would a more massive entrance of Pentecostals/Charismatic into the WCC and Faith and Order mean? Even in terms of numbers of Pentecostals this would most probably bring confusion as much as excitement.

Or, to look at the issue from another perspective: is "ecumenism" defined only in terms of "official" ecumenism? How should we regard the fruitful exchange of Christian goods at the grass-roots level in mission fields and churches around the world, where Pentecostals and other Christians are working side by side? What are the implications for Christian unity of common social projects or evangelistic campaigns (of Rev. Billy Graham and others where there is really an "ecumenical" backing from Pentecostals with other Protestants and Catholics)?

And, what is perhaps the most uneasy challenge to other churches: Now that there is pneumatological resurgence all over the Christian *oikoumene*, are Pentecostals consulted for their contributions to a subject which, in fact, is *the* issue for them? Are other churches humble enough to invite Pentecostals to teach them about the whole spectrum of gifts of the Spirit (from healings to prophecy to exorcism), or Spirit-baptism, or other favorite Pentecostal topics? These are just few of the questions to be faced and discussed. Without such willingness on the part of others to listen, however, Pentecostals may continue to struggle to become "conscious" ecumenists.

Chapter Four

Free Churches, Ecumenism and Pentecostalism

One of the leading topics in recent ecumenical theology has been the question of (confessional) identity. Partly this may be due to the widespread popular interest in identity as a psychological category evidenced in the fast growing "self-help" literature. In part because of this, ecumenical theologizing and praxis have come to a postmodern crossroads. There is no turning back to older junctures with clearly defined positions and confessional boundaries. The issue of identity touches the future of Christian unity and, more widely, Christian identity in relation to other religions. What unites us and what makes us different? The joint declaration from several ecumenical research institutes expressed this in clear terms: "We are convinced that the most urgent task facing them [Christian churches] is that of *joint self-examination.* Today each church must ask itself afresh how far its inheritance and understanding of the gospel is a contribution to the Ecumenical Movement or must be seen as an obstacle on the path to realization of the ecumenical goal."[1]

Identity in the ecumenical *thesaurus* is defined as characteristics and distinctives which a given church or denominational community regards as indispensable for its self-understanding. A religious body cannot exist as a recognizably distinctive collectivity unless it has some beliefs and/or practices by which it can be identified. "Confessional identity" refers to distinctive identities of any given Christian communion. Dialogue with other confessions raises the question of who we are as Catholics, Pentecostals, Lutherans, etc. Consequently, "...confessional identity is no longer seen as the opposite to ecumenical commitment and Christian unity, but as inseparable from it."[2]

The question of identity is integrally related to how the vision(s) of Christian unity is (are) conceived. The short history of ecumenical theologizing attests to a rapidly changing canon here. The last two decades or so in ecumenical theology have been the golden age of "ecumenical models": "organic unity," "concord unity," "conciliar unity," "unity in reconciled diversity," "*koinonia*," etc. Recently, we have heard of expressions like "ecumenism in oppositions" (*Ökumene in Gegensätzen*), and, most paradoxical of all, "ecumenism without unity."[3] Without going into intricacies of these models of unity, suffice it to note that whatever approach is taken, one must have some kind of basic idea of who one is and what is the overall goal of unity. Related questions include: are perceived differences obstacles to unity or can they be seen as complementary? What is the distinctive "confessional profile"? On the one hand, what is stable, and on the other hand, what can be changed?

The purpose of this chapter is to offer reflections on ecumenical identity from a distinctive perspective, namely that of Free Churches. The expression "Free Churches" involves two primary meanings. It designates first those churches with a congregationalist church constitution, and, second, churches affirming a consistent separation of church and state. In this chapter I use the term primarily in the first sense, in order to show how the emergence of Free Churches brings new challenges to the task of defining identity. After a brief look at what global changes in the composition of Christendom mean to ecumenism in general and to identity in particular, I will delve into a Free Church case study, namely Pentecostalism. I will offer a brief consideration of its origins as it relates to identity and critically evaluate some of the most recent attempts for defining identity. I close the chapter putting Free Churches again into the larger ecumenical context, and suggesting some challenges both to them and to older churches.

Identity and Changing Scenes of the Christian *Oikoumene*

The identity-question is both enriched and confused by the emergence of a new kind of Christian mosaic as we approach the third millennium—and this is something that ecumenical theology and work have to take into account in a much more profound way than has been done thus far. What I mean is that "mainline" ecumenism is losing its grip while the fastest growing segment of Christendom, namely Pentecostals and other Free churches, are coming into the forefront. It has been said that after the enthusiasm of the 1970s (cf. the influence of Vatican II), the 1980s were a time of regression in ecumenical perspective, while the 1990s could be labeled an "ice age" of ecumenism. This prompted one of the leading Roman Catholic ecumenists to say: "Word is out among ecumenists that the future of ecumenism is to be found with the Evangelical wing, the new frontier, the unexplored terrain."[4] Another leading ecclesiologist of our days asks if Free Churches are "The Churches of the Future"?[5]

Clearly, a global transformation has been under way during the second half of the twentieth century. From the religion of the so-called First World, Christianity has become a religion of the so-called Two-Thirds World. In the process, it is slowly "shedding its European forms of enculturation and is becoming a genuine global religion with its own varied forms of enculturation."[6] New congregational models are emerging, and many specialists are of the opinion that the Free Church congregational model will be the major paradigm in the third millennium. Even the current Prefect of the Congregation for the Doctrine of the Faith in Rome, who has expressed severe criticism against congregational ecclesiologies, has admitted that this is the direction into which Christian *oikoumene* is heading.[7]

The implications of growth numbers seem to be unavoidable, especially in relation to Pentecostalism and Charismatic movements. From the beginning of the century to the present, Pentecostalism has become the largest single category in Protestantism, the "third force" in Christianity, outstripping the traditional groups that date back to the Reformation such as the Lutheran, Reformed, and Anglican communions. "A growth of from zero to 400 million in ninety years is unprecedented in the whole of church history."[8]

If, currently, Roman Catholics are the largest Christian group, then classical Pentecostals are now the second largest, and gaining fast. In the 1980s the Pentecostals (193 million) exceeded the Orthodox Christians (179 million). Catholics now number about 950,000,000. As of 1990 Roman Catholics constituted 58% of all affiliated Christian church members, while Pentecostals make up 21%. What Harvey Cox said of the silencing of Leonardo Boff might as well apply to older Christian churches in general: "How will the church leaders deal with a restless spiritual energy splashing up from the underside of society and threatening to erode traditional modes of ecclesiastical governance?"[9]

As one might expect, the "newcomers" have not spent as much energy in theologically defining their identity as the older churches have. What the "mainline" churches have failed to do, with their longer history of thinking about identity, is to pay attention to the changing prospects of Christianity. It seems to me that the thinking about identity still goes on as if nothing significant had happened. However, when theological and ecumenical reflection on identity crosses into the third millennium, many new aspects have to be taken into account: What is the defining role of spirituality in identity? Most Free Churches and all Third World churches define themselves in terms of peculiar spirituality rather than discursive doctrinal formulations. What is the role of context on, say, Lutheran, Catholic or Pentecostal identity? How do new concerns, like the role of women or the fate of creation, inform our thinking about identity? Or, how do spiritual gifts (healings, exorcisms, speaking in tongues, and prophecy) bear on it?

As a case study, I will offer some reflections on Pentecostal identity. I have selected Pentecostals as an example of Free Churches for two reasons. First, they represent by far the largest segment and are in that sense representative. Second, a current of self-examination and struggle for identity has been the hallmark of the Pentecostal movement in the last few years.

The Pluriform Origins, Roots, and Theologies of Pentecostalism

As there is not yet a consensus among researchers of Pentecostalism as to the exact origins of the movement (see chapter three), we need to acknowledge the *fact* of the multicultural, heterogeneous origins of the movement. This certainly has bearing upon how its identity is conceived. It accounts for the differentiated, if not contradictory, nature of the spirituality and theology of Pentecostalism worldwide.

This pluralism within Pentecostalism can be seen in the main "theologies" that are now being espoused. First, there are the Wesleyan Pentecostals who emphasize the doctrine of "second blessing" and entire sanctification. They simply add the baptism in the Holy Spirit evidenced by speaking in tongues as a "third blessing." Second, there are Baptistic Pentecostals who came into being with the organization of the Assemblies of God in 1914, currently the largest Pentecostal denomination. They stress gradual sanctification and more presbyterian and congregational forms of church government. Most Pentecostal bodies in the world formed after 1914 reflect this strand. Third are the Oneness Pentecostals, nowadays comprising about one fourth of all Pentecostals and known also as "Jesus Name" Pentecostals, who represent the most radical theological departure of any Pentecostal group. Essentially, these churches teach a "unitarianism" of the Son which denies the traditional doctrine of the Trinity and claims that Jesus is Father, Son, and Holy Spirit. They (re)baptize in Jesus' name. They are the only major group of Pentecostals who teach (or at least imply) that speaking in tongues is necessary to salvation.[10] Fourth, there are Charismatic Pentecostals (also known as "Charismatics") who have decided to stay in their churches after experiencing the new work of the Holy Spirit. Finally, there are also independent Pentecostal Charismatic theologies and spiritualities with diverse agendas. Two of the most recent and most famous are the "Toronto blessing" starting in 1994 and the "Pensacola revival" a few years later.[11]

A related question, that of the roots of the movement—theological, historical, spiritual roots—is also disputed among scholars, as is that of origins. The basic consensus is that the nineteenth century Wesleyan-Holiness heritage lies behind the movement. A Reformed heritage of the nineteenth century has also been posited, but it has not met with wide acceptance. Besides the formative influence of Wesleyan-Holiness movements, there is also, according to Professor Walter Hollenweger, a strong influence of Catholic spirituality that was mediated through Wesley and his writings. From Wesley the Pentecostals received the stress on holiness and sanctification, sometimes called "second blessing" or "baptism of the Spirit," from Catholics the mystical-charismatic spiritual tradition, and from Blacks the enthusiastic, corporeal worship style.[12]

Defining Pentecostal Identity from Its Spirituality?

The complicated origins and present manifestations of Pentecostalism, by far the largest of Free Churches, are evident. Consequently, attempts to define its identity are met with a plethora of challenges. Whoever determines identity for Pentecostals is "placed in a unique and privileged role," since in this definitional act, "there is power."[13] Ironically, Pentecostal identity has sometimes been established as a reaction against other churches, e.g., the Catholic Church with whom Pentecostals have had an international dialogue since 1972. On the one hand, ecumenical contacts have helped Pentecostals to clarify their identity, and on the other hand, as Roman Catholic observer Peter Hocken has recently pointed out, there is the danger of the loss of Pentecostal distinctiveness as Pentecostals become immersed in ecumenical discussions.[14]

In the beginning of the first dialogue phase with Roman Catholics, a statement called "Essence of Pentecostalism" was issued that sought to define the basic identity of Pentecostalism:

> It is the personal and direct awareness and experiencing of the indwelling of the Holy Spirit by which the risen and glorified Christ is revealed and the believer is empowered to witness and worship with the abundance of life as described in Acts and the Epistles. The Pentecostal experience is not a goal to be reached, not a place to stand, but a door through which to go into a greater fullness of life in the Spirit. It is an event which becomes a way of life in which often charismatic manifestations have a place. Characteristic of this way of life is a love of the Word of God, fervency in prayer and witness in the world and to the world, and a concern to live by the power of the Holy Spirit.[15]

This is a good starting point, since it shows that Pentecostals understand themselves first and foremost on the basis of their particular brand of spirituality. According to Margaret Poloma, a historian of Pentecostalism, Pentecostals have offered an "anthropological protest against modernity" by "providing a medium for encountering [the] supernatural...[and] fus[ing] the natural and supernatural, the emotional and rational, the charismatic and institutional in a decidedly postmodern way." She has characterized this "Pentecostal worldview [by] its belief in and experience of the paranormal as an alternate *Weltanschauung* for our instrumental rational modern society."[16]

Donald Dayton (Wesleyan Holiness), in his groundbreaking *Theological Roots of Pentecostalism*, has urged Pentecostals to understand themselves through a paradigm involving several theological factors. There are four he identifies as present in a slightly different form in the American Wesleyan-Holiness movement of the nineteenth century, albeit reconfigured in Pentecostal thinking and popularized in a powerful way by Aimee Semple McPherson (founder of the Foursquare Gospel, one of the oldest and biggest Pentecostal bodies): Jesus was understood to be Savior, Baptizer in the Holy Spirit, Divine Healer, and Coming King.[17] To these were added still one aspect, rooted in the Holiness movements where Pentecostalism came from, and consequently Pentecostals were known as "Full Gospel" Christians. This full gospel was thus comprised of five theological motifs: (1) justification by faith in Christ; (2) sanctification by faith as a second definite work of grace; (3) healing of the body as provided for all in the atonement; (4) the pre-millennial return of Christ; and (5) the baptism in the Holy Spirit evidenced by speaking in tongues.[18] This last motif came to be the most distinctive feature of classical Pentecostalism. Perhaps the "prophethood" of all believers could be added to the priesthood of all believers as a sixth motif.

Walter Hollenweger of Birmingham University has argued that the paradigm for defining Pentecostal identity must be understood even more broadly. His classic description includes the following aspects of Pentecostalism as forming its identity: (1) orality of liturgy; (2) narrativity of theology and witness; (3) maximum participation at the level of reflection, prayer, and decision-making and therefore a form of community that is reconciliatory; (4) inclusion of dreams and visions into personal and public forms of worship where they function as a kind of icon for the individual and the community; and (5) an understanding of the body/mind relationship that is informed by experiences of correspondence between body and mind, the most striking application of this insight being the ministry of healing by prayer.[19] On the basis of this description Hollenweger has argued that Pentecostalism represents a religious movement *sui generis*, "eine neue Konfession" ("a new confession") which cannot be reduced to Fundamentalism, Evangelicalism, or even to Protestantism as such.[20] It was brought into existence not by rational theological analysis but by a sudden outpouring of the Spirit. Experience first, then doctrine. The early years gave the movement its *prodigium*. Several Pentecostal scholars have followed Hollenweger and emphasized that the first ten years of the Pentecostal movement—reflected in the theological-spiritual definitions above—form the heart, not the infancy of Pentecostal spirituality.[21] Of course, Pentecostals have also written doctrinal statements, but these have been secondary to testimonies and enthusiastic worship encounters. Hollenweger, in his *magnum opus*, *Pentecostals* has offered the most comprehensive and cross-culturally representative analysis of the basic systematic theology of early Pentecostalism.[22]

In Search of a "Legitimate Sectarian Identity"

The most important research arena of Pentecostalism, as of other traditions, is provided by the scholarly societies, the most influential of which has been, and continues to be, the Society for Pentecostal Studies (SPS). In recent years, SPS annual meetings have been active in discussing identity.[23] In the 1992 SPS Presidential Address, Episcopalian-charismatic D. William Faupel asked, "Whither Pentecostalism?" Taking his point of departure from the religious developments of the previous century which gave birth to Pentecostalism, he contends that the "Movement has been shaped by the very forces the early adherents set out to critique." Pentecostalism started as an ecumenical, revival movement that sought to revitalize the existing churches. In many respects its vision was not realized. The movement's message to the Church was either ignored or rejected outright. For liberals, Pentecostals were too "conservative" and to Fundamentalists, they were too enthusiastic! This led Pentecostals to create organizations of their own, the idea of which the very first pioneers opposed. To define their identity, it was only natural for them to use the language of their opponents. "They did so by stating they were fundamentalist, but fundamentalists plus" (belief in the current manifestations of the Spirit).[24]

Even today many observers, if not many Pentecostals themselves, regard the movement as a branch of Fundamentalism because of the early developments. According to Faupel, the alignment with Fundamentalism in the early years perhaps helped the movement to overcome the stigma of cultism but it has also paralyzed its ecumenical and theological vision. One example of this is the emergence of the Charismatic movement in the 1960s. One could have expected Pentecostals to welcome it, since the "spread of the fire" was the initial purpose of Pentecostals. But instead, Pentecostals were shocked when its message was suddenly accepted by many within mainline churches. Faupel thus argues that the future of Pentecostal identity has two options. Pentecostalism can see itself as a subgroup of Evangelicalism, sharing its assumptions, its agenda, and its mission; or the initial impulses which gave rise to the Pentecostal movement must be recovered, making it possible for Pentecostals—and other Christians, too—to "perceive Pentecostalism to be an authentic expression of Christian Faith in its own right and not as a subgroup of Evangelicalism."[25]

Two years later, in another SPS Presidential Address, Roger Stronstadt attempted to affirm legitimate diversity among Pentecostals and in relation to others. His point of departure was the Old Testament view of God's people as prophets which was carried on by Luke in his vision of the early church as the eschatological community of prophets upon whom the Spirit of prophecy was resting as it was resting upon her Messiah. Stronstadt contends that very soon after the first generation Christians ceased to function as Spirit-filled prophets, either individually or corporately, when the reception of the Spirit was identified with water baptism, the gifts were institutionalized, and enthusiastic prophetic movements (e.g., Montanists) were expelled. Among both individuals and renewal/pietistic groups, prophets and prophesying sporadically reappeared. "Now, in the twentieth century, Luke's vision of all believers has been permanently, though only partially, restored." The restoration is, of course, the pouring forth of the Spirit and of the complementary gift of prophecy at the beginning of the twentieth century.[26]

Stronstadt, however, laments that the Pentecostal-Charismatic movement does not fully measure up when its adherents are caught up in secondary issues and are not challenged to function in the church and in the society as Spirit-baptized, Spirit-led, Spirit-empowered prophets. As a result, the Pentecostals experience

> tends to be both individualistic, self-centered, and, even, narcissistic. In other words, the experience is sought as a private blessing, rather than as an empowering for ministry. Far too many Pentecostals have been led to receive the blessing of the Holy Spirit in the prayer room and have never been taught to take the empowering of that gift into the streets and marketplaces of society.[27]

In addition, the restoration of prophecy is often trivialized and commercialized.

Ecumenically perhaps the most astute recent treatment of Pentecostal identity is offered by Cheryl Bridges Johns in her 1995 SPS Presidential Address: "The Adolescence of Pentecostalism: In Search of a Legitimate Sectarian Identity." Her focus was on the maturing of Pentecostalism: "Perhaps we should even consider whether or not Pentecostalism is actually maturing as a movement or if, particularly in North America, the movement is experiencing pre-mature aging and early death?"[28] Pentecostalism started as a radical counterculture with ordination of women, racial inclusion, and identification with the poor and wayward. Outside rejection contributed to an intensification of internal bonding. Soon this was replaced by symptoms of "Pentecostal adolescence," with exaggerated self-consciousness and creation of "pseudo-enemies." The enemies of Evangelicals/Fundamentalists became their enemies. This led to a sense of shame that can take forms of exhibition and grandiosity. There was a deep inferiority complex in Pentecostal hearts and minds. As a consequence, Pentecostals wanted to be "as good as others" by building expensive cathedrals, launching ambitious social and educational programs, etc.

What are prospects for future identity? Johns suggests growth by integration rather than substitution or "patch-work." Referring to Old Testament theologian Walter Brueggeman's idea of "The Legitimacy of a Sectarian Hermeneutic," she recommends that Pentecostals read their narrative from the perspective "of an oppressed people yearning and receiving emancipation," not unlike Israelites under the tyranny of the Assyrians (cf. 2 Kings 18–19).[29] Dead orthodoxy and creedal rigidity had hid the face of God from the humble, and now with the new Pentecost it was made available to all people. Rather than hide their shame and vulnerability, Johns advises Pentecostals to learn how to lament. "As such, grief work liberates from the tyranny of self-groundedness." Let them also be willing to offer an imaginative proposal for ordering society in an alternative way. And, according to Johns, let Pentecostals work out the implications of a legitimate sectarian identity in relation to other Christians. They need to go beyond the wall and learn to listen to voices of other Christians too. Johns quotes a moving passage from an anonymous participant of the Azusa Street revival:

> We must give God all the glory in this work. We must keep very humble at His feet. He recognizes no flesh, no color, no names. We must not glory in Azusa Mission, not in anything but the Lord Jesus Christ by whom the world is crucified unto us and we unto the world. We stand as assemblies and missions all in perfect harmony. Azusa Mission stands for the unity of God's people everywhere. God is uniting His people, baptizing them by one Spirit into one body.[30]

Johns sees this kind of maturing as a key to ecumenism: with shame transformed into humility, Pentecostals "would allow the Holy Spirit to bear witness of a shared *oikumene*, and they would be able to see the glory of God reflected in others."[31]

That Pentecostalism was birthed as an ecumenical movement is an established fact. How the movement is going to realize its original vision is one of the major challenges of the future. The answer, whatever it might be, is inseparably linked with the way its identity is formed. As one Pentecostal theologian and ecumenist puts it:

> In tension with the ecumenical potential of Pentecostalism is its designation as a "sectarian" movement....In a positive vein, such sectarianism implies the existence historically of Pentecostalism as a marginalized movement containing elements of prophetic insight and criticism valuable for the whole People of God. However, this sectarianism also stands in considerable tension with the ecumenical meaning of a Pentecostal identity that is true to Pentecost.[32]

Impending Ecumenical Challenges

Confessional identities can no longer be defined in isolation from the rest of the Christian *oikumene*. Identity denotes, on the one hand, in what way we are different from, and, on the other hand, similar to other Christians. This principle has been taken for granted at least since formal ecumenism in terms of the WCC was born. But what is not as clear at all to most of organized ecumenism is that confessional identities (of older churches) can no longer be described without taking into account the fast growing segment of the Free Churches. In fact, soon we are in a situation where Pentecostals and other Free Churches, with their congregational and other church models, are the "mainline" forms of Christianity. The other pole will continue to be the Roman Catholic Church, but Protestant and Orthodox Churches appear to change into "minority" expressions of Christianity. And it is good to keep in mind that neither Catholics nor most Free Churches are members of the WCC.

Free Churches have to be challenged toward a more active ecumenical involvement, without downplaying their distinctives. The entrance of the Orthodox Churches into the WCC in the 1960s made a significant contribution to *oikumene*. In the same way, a more active participation of the Free Churches, not necessarily (only) in the WCC but (also) in other forms of searching for unity, would challenge in a healthy way older participants and their agendas.

The dialogue of Free Churches and movements like Pentecostalism with Roman Catholicism raises a number of issues. The question of the usefulness of traditional dialogue patterns between Free and established churches has already been noted in the previous chapter. Other factors should be noted, like a more active recruiting of "lay theologians" and, consequently, adopting of oral, non-discursive approaches since most theologizing, especially in the Two-Thirds world, is done in that mode. The contribution of spiritualities has also to be taken much more seriously. As we saw with reference to Pentecostalism, Free Churches often define themselves intuitively more in terms of spirituality than doctrines. It is not to say that doctrine is unimportant for them, but doctrine is not the primary way of identification.

Despite some serious historical, theological, and ecclesiological differences between the older churches and the Free Churches, it seems to me there is enough common ground for mutual search for both distinctive confessional identities and common Christian identity. The search for a common "basis of faith," a spiritual and doctrinal core, presupposes that unity as such exists as a gift, and confessional formulations are expressions beyond which we must seek to go. Consequently, different expressions, at a deeper level, could point to the very same "core." The notion of "basic consensus" (*Grundkonsensus*) is used often. Although the "basic consensus" model has come under criticism in more recent ecumenical theology, there is still some justification for it, at least as a helpful analogy.

Karl Rahner captured something significant when he spoke about an "inner groaning" of the Spirit that we all share in the struggle to be true to the unified witness of the peoples of God: "All of us 'know' in the Spirit of God something more simple, more true, and more real than that which we are capable of knowing and expressing in the dimension of our theological concepts."[33] This something is the common basis of faith uniting Christians coming from various traditions with their respective theological formulations and time-bound concepts.

Chapter Five

The Ecumenical Potential of Pneumatology

The last two decades or so in ecumenical theology have been the golden age of "ecumenical models." Overall, there has been a radical scaling down of what unity implies. After the proposal of Oscar Cullman of unity through diversity, in which the New Testament metaphor of the members of the body is taken out of the context of the local congregation and applied to present denominations, we have heard of expressions like "ecumenism in oppositions" (*Ökumene in Gegensätzen*), and, most paradoxical of all, "ecumenism without unity."[1] The last decade has witnessed the rise to prominence of *koinonia*-theology, and it is yet to be seen what are its long-term ecumenical implications.

This chapter reflects on yet another perspective on Christian unity, that of pneumatology. A pneumatological renaissance over the doctrine and spirituality of the Holy Spirit has in these days stirred much interest and even enthusiasm from all theological corners. While I hesitate to call the pneumatological perspective another "model," because that term limits too severely the doctrine and spirituality of the Spirit of God, yet it is also true to say that ecumenical theology in the past has not paid much attention to the role of the Spirit. Konrad Raiser of the WCC has noted that what is most characteristic of ecumenical thought is its *dialogical* nature; it has taken shape in response to challenges both from within and outside the ecumenical movement. Genuine dialogue does not aim at comprehensiveness; it can leave things open or unsaid, to be taken up at a later stage. Dialogue is moved forward by what the respective partners perceive to be the most pressing issues at a given time, allowing for later reformulation of earlier insights once a new challenge arises.[2]

The doctrine of the Holy Spirit is a case in point. Earlier in the twentieth century, Nikolay Berdayev called the theology of the Spirit "the last unexplored theological frontier."[3] For a long time, the need did not seem to be felt in the ecumenical movement to enter more fully into a discussion of pneumatology. It used to be commonplace to say that the Holy Spirit is the Cinderella of the Trinity; when the other two sisters went to the theological ball, the Holy Spirit was left behind every time.[4]

But more recently there is a resurgence of pneumatology across the theological world. The reverberations of this pneumatological renaissance can be seen everywhere, from the WCC Assembly at Canberra, under the title, "Come Holy Spirit—Renew the Whole Creation," to monographs of various sorts, to specialized conferences on the theme, and to worldwide ecclesial programs such as the Roman Catholic Church's emphasis on the Holy Spirit in 1998. Kilian McDonnell, one of the foremost developers of pneumatology in our time, issued already in 1985 a programmatic statement, in which he quoted Karl Barth: "Everything that one believes, reflects and says about God the Father and God the Son...would be demonstrated and clarified basically through God the Holy Spirit, the *vinculum pacis* between Father and Son. The work of God in behalf of creatures for, in, and with humanity would be made clear in a teleology which excludes all happenstance."[5] Nowadays, then, it will not do to speak about the Holy Spirit as the *theos agraptos*—God about whom no one writes (Gregory of Nazianzus in the fourth century)—or as "the forgotten God" (Catholic theologians of the nineteenth century). "The rise of the charismatic movement within virtually every mainstream church has ensured that the Holy Spirit figures prominently on the theological agenda. A new experience of the reality and power of the Spirit has had a major impact upon the theological discussion of the person and work of the Holy Spirit."[6]

The Pentecostal movement, and later Charismatic movements, has challenged the mainline churches and theologies to rethink their attitude toward New Testament type of enthusiastic, charismatic spirituality and theologizing. In this chapter, I want to explore not only the Pentecostal-Charismatic movements, but also the entrance of the Eastern Orthodox Churches into the WCC constituency in the 1960s, and the development of pneumatological reflection in the WCC and the Catholic Church since. Together, these combine as the major developments in the Christian *oikumene* that have contributed to the renaissance of pneumatology. I begin with Eastern Orthodoxy first.

Eastern Orthodox Pneumatology in the Forefront

The doctrine of the Spirit has always played a more prominent role in Eastern Orthodox theology than in the West, with roots in the classical works of Athanasius, Cyril of Alexandria, and Basil the Great. According to many Orthodox theologians, priority is given to pneumatology in the East, and to christology in the West, although both profess the same trinitarian faith. The Eastern tradition pays more attention to the Holy Spirit, both in the doctrine of salvation and in ecclesiology. Greek orthodox theologian and WCC-official Nikos A. Nissiotis, following Vladimir Lossky, has most dramatically articulated the charge of "Christomonism" against Western theology. According to Nissiotis, Christianity in the West is seen as unilaterally referring to Christ, the Spirit being an addition to the church, its ministries and sacraments. Although Nissiotis' and Lossky's critique is one-sided, and may be too harsh, there is no denying that a pneumatological deficiency has existed—and still does, in some quarters—in the Latin Church.[7]

Eastern pneumatologists have remarked that not even Vatican II with its many remarkable achievements was "pneumatological enough."[8] *Lumen Gentium* was first written on christological foundations and pneumatological "tinsel" was added afterward. Catholic Walter Kasper, having listened to the critique of Eastern theologians, adds a keen criticism of Roman Catholic theology in this respect: "In modern theology one often gets the impression that pneumatology has become a function of ecclesiology; the Spirit has become the guarantor of the Church as an institution and pneumatology has become the ideological superstructure on top of ecclesiology."[9]

The Eastern critique of "Christomonism" in the West does not, of course, mean neglecting either Christ or the Trinity in Orthodox theologizing. On the contrary, a good case can be made for the claim that Eastern pneumatology is always anchored in christology rather than operating as an independent theological *locus*.[10]

The ecclesiology of Eastern Orthodoxy, unlike most classical Western theologies, is permeated with pneumatology. Eastern theology never thinks of the Church apart from Christ and from the Holy Spirit. Vladimir Lossky expresses this by speaking of the "two aspects of the Church," the church as the body of Christ and fullness of the Spirit. John Zizioulas speaks of the church as being "instituted" by Christ, and "constituted" by the Spirit.[11] The Spirit belongs to the *esse* (essence), not just to the *bona esse* (well being) of the Church, since she lives in continual Pentecost:

> But the Church is not only hierarchical, it is charismatic and Pentecostal. "Quench not the Spirit. Despise not prophesying" (1 Thessalonians 5, 19–20). The Holy Spirit is poured out upon all God's people....In the Apostolic Church, besides the institutional ministry conferred by the laying on of hands, there were other charismata or gifts conferred directly by the Spirit: Paul mentions "gifts of healing," the working of miracles, "speaking with tongues, and the like (1 Corinthians 12, 28–30). In the Church of later days, these charismatic ministries have been less in evidence, but they have never been wholly extinguished.[12]

Besides ecclesiology, the doctrine of salvation in the Eastern Church is more pneumatologically oriented, with its goal of theosis of men and women in the Spirit. It is interesting that along with resurgence of pneumatology there has also been a new ecumenical enthusiasm about the doctrine of deification, even in Protestant circles. This implies the ecumenical potential of pneumatology for soteriology, too.

The entrance of the Eastern Orthodox Churches to the WCC has contributed to the strengthening and proliferation of pneumatological perspectives in WCC theologies. However, as some leading Eastern theologians have freely admitted, there is still need for further nuancing of Eastern pneumatology, especially in relation to ecclesiology and the Trinity. Zizioulas writes:

> Orthodox theology has no ready-made answers to offer to the problems at hand. It is often assumed that Orthodoxy can be helpful in the ecumenical discussions by contributing its Pneumatology to them. This may be true to some extent, especially if the Orthodox contribution is taken as a corrective to Western excesses in ecclesiology. But when it comes to the point of doing justice to the basic components of the Orthodox tradition itself or—and this is more important—to the point of facing our ecumenical problems with positive propositions, it becomes clear that Orthodox theology needs to work closely together with Western theology.[13]

The Emergence of a Pneumatological Perspective in WCC-Theologies[14]

The Seventh General Assembly of the WCC in Canberra 1991 focused on the Holy Spirit. Rather than analyzing the outcomes of that particular meeting—the results of which are well documented and easily accessible—I will trace briefly the development of a pneumatological perspective in the WCC culminating in Canberra.[15]

Emergence of a pneumatological perspective among WCC churches and elsewhere was partly prepared by the influential theologizing of Jürgen Moltmann of Tübingen, whose *The Church in the Power of the Spirit* awakened expectations that were not disappointed by his magisterial *Spirit of Life.*[16] Certainly now the "forgetfulness" of the Spirit has given way to "a whole flood of writings about the Holy Spirit and its efficacies." His treatment has been labeled as a "systematic, theological elaboration of the World Council of Churches' reflections on pneumatology," but Moltmann himself has not been willing to accept this honor.[17]

Another major pneumatology of this decade, *God the Spirit,* also by a Tübingen systematician, Michael Welker, takes a much more reserved standpoint toward "natural pneumatologies" proposed by Moltmann and others. Welker's work is permeated with explicit biblical argumentation.[18] The appearance of these two pneumatologies reflects the polarity in theologizing about the Spirit, especially in Protestant ecumenical circles.

In the reports of the major ecumenical conferences prior to the formation of the WCC in 1948, reference to the Holy Spirit remains fairly traditional, following the lines of conventional Protestant thinking. The trinitarian confession of faith is acknowledged formally, but the affirmation of the Spirit as person in communion with the Father and the Son remains largely undeveloped. According to Raiser, this relative subordination of the Holy Spirit to the person of Jesus was fairly representative of the general setting of Protestant theology and evangelical piety of those years. The Faith and Order conferences at Lausanne (1927) and Edinburgh (1937) refer to the Holy Spirit mainly in relation to the church, as the one who gives life to the Church. The Spirit sanctifies and renews the Church through word and sacrament and draws it into unity.[19]

The reports of the First Assembly of the WCC at Amsterdam (1948) concentrated on Christ who brings forth the Church. It was affirmed that the Church persists in continuity throughout history through the presence and power of the Holy Spirit. Interestingly enough, the expression "recover[ing] the spirit of prophecy to discern the signs of the times," which became one of the catchwords of Vatican II, was employed here.[20]

The International Missionary Conference at Willingen, and the Faith and Order Conference at Lund, both in 1952, reached a new understanding of the missionary task as participation in the *missio Dei.* Through the Spirit, the church can proclaim God's saving work in Christ and wait for his final victory. The Lund conference affirmed many earlier pronouncements on the Spirit. The continuity of the church in history is assured "by the constant action of the risen Lord through the Holy Spirit," and it is through the "unifying power of His indwelling Spirit" that the organic unity of the body of Christ is sustained.[21]

At the Third Assembly of the WCC at New Delhi (1961), the new orientation became apparent. The basis of the WCC was enlarged to include an explicitly trinitarian, doxological formulation: "to the glory of the one God, Father, Son and Holy Spirit."[22] The preamble to the statement places the understanding of unity in a trinitarian, pneumatological setting:

> The love of the Father and the Son in the unity of the Holy Spirit is the source and goal of the unity which the triune God wills for all men and creation. We believe that we share in this unity in the Church of Jesus Christ....The reality of this unity was made manifest at Pentecost in the gift of the Holy Spirit, through whom we know in this present age the first fruits of that perfect union of the Son with his Father, which will be known in its fullness only when all things are consummated by Christ in his glory.[23]

The Montreal Faith and Order Conference (1963) built on New Delhi and developed the pneumatological perspective, especially in relation to Scripture and tradition as well as to the delicate issue of ministry. The statement on ministry already anticipated the rise of Charismatic movements and the renaissance of *charismata* in the church: "The Holy Spirit dwells in the Church....He also bestows differing gifts (*charismata*) on groups and individuals....All members of the Church are thus gifted for the common good."[24] After the Montreal meeting there came new studies on pneumatology, especially to clarify the pneumatological understanding between East and West from the standpoint of patristic scholarship, and to further explore "Christ, the Holy Spirit, and the Ministry." Another influential study was on the relation of sacraments and the Spirit (Bristol, 1967). But it was not until the Uppsala Assembly (1968) that the first explicit address to the Holy Spirit was issued. Paragraph 8 of section I "proves the fullest summary of ecumenical thinking on the Holy Spirit up to that moment."[25]

Faith and Order at Louvain (1971) gathered together studies initiated at Montreal and paved the way for the most important document of Faith and Order, *Baptism, Eucharist and Ministry*, issued about ten years later.[26] Raiser synthesizes the development of pneumatological perspective after Louvain in four statements. First, there is the role of the Holy Spirit in the confession of the faith. The influential study on *filioque* suggested that there needs to be "a new sensitivity to the person and work of the Holy Spirit as the one who in his fullness both rests upon Jesus Christ and is the gift of Christ to the Church, the Lord and Giver of life to humankind and all creation."[27] The project *Confessing One Faith* has been far-reaching in the study of the Spirit in confessions.[28] It explicates the classical affirmation about the Holy Spirit in the Nicene-Constantinopolitan Creed. Second is the relation of the Spirit and church. Here, of course, *Baptism, Eucharist and Ministry* stands in the forefront. The pneumatological perspective, though, not the focus of the study, is present in relation to sacraments and ministry, based on the pneumatological understanding of the church. Third, the more churches from the Third World have joined the WCC, the more the issues of the Spirit and religious pluralism have come to focus. Moltmann's and others' recent works have nuanced theologically the developments which have come out of the theology of religions and the role of the Spirit in all of it. The fourth aspect of development is the emergence of charismatic renewal among WCC churches as well as in the Roman Catholic Church. Beginning in the 1960s many member churches have experienced manifestations of a charismatic renewal focusing on the baptism of the Holy Spirit, charismatic ministry, and various *charismata*. I will briefly look at the contribution of Pentecostal and Charismatic theologies after I have first surveyed pneumatological perspectives in recent Catholic theologies. The most recent development in the WCC to bear on the pneumatological perspective is the influence of the Faith and Order Conference at Santiago de Compostela (1993). Its emphasis on *koinonia*-theology carries potential for pneumatological developments, since there is a growing consensus on the church as "communion in the Spirit."

The Potential of Catholic Pneumatology after Vatican II

In preparation for crossing into the third millennium, the year 1998 was assigned by Pope John Paul II to special devotion to the Holy Spirit (as the previous year was to the Son and the following to the Father) in the Roman Catholic Church worldwide. Publications were issued, special services were celebrated, lectures were organized and research programs took place as the largest church of Christendom sought to deepen her understanding of pneumatology and develop the cult of the Spirit. The 1996 Catholic Theological Society of America meeting was devoted to pneumatology: "Toward a Spirited Theology: Challenges of the Holy Spirit to Theological Disciplines."[29]

Vatican II, of course, was instrumental in the new Catholic pneumatological renaissance. Pope John XXIII, when formally announcing the Council, wrote: "This getting together of all the bishops of the Church should be like a new Pentecost."[30] This council could be called the "Council of the Holy Spirit," for as Pope Paul VI pointed out, there are two hundred and fifty-eight references to the Holy Spirit in the pages of the Council documents.[31] And since the Council the popes have urged theologians and lay people alike to revive their interest on the Spirit.

In terms of ecclesiology, the most important development of Vatican II was the replacement of the old institutional-hierarchical ecclesiology with a dynamic "People of God" notion, where the church is first of all seen as a pilgrimage people on the way to the Heavenly City. This understanding was very much prepared by the highly influential theological work of Yves Congar, who also had distinguished himself as a pneumatologist. Very soon, several leading Catholic ecclesiologists adopted the theology of *koinonia*, although there are still some major differences between them and the curia about what it means in the Catholic context. Both of these ecclesiological breakthroughs are pneumatologically suggestive. Along with ecclesiological rethinking, reassessment of sacramental theology has taken a pneumatological course, as in Protestant theologies, too, with the idea of the church as the sacrament of the Spirit, and the sacraments consequently integrated with *epiklesis* (the invocation of the Spirit).[32]

The explicit emphasis upon the pneumatic nature of the Church, including the gifts and graces of the Holy Spirit, was secured in the Council by Leon Joseph Cardinal Suenens, who played a critical role in assuring the college of bishops of the importance of the Holy Spirit and of spiritual gifts to the future of the Roman church. Catholic systematician Michael A. Fahey states that "another way that the church is described in the perspective of the Second Vatican Council is as a community of charisms."[33] In this understanding the church is seen as the Body of Christ, "created, ordered, and sustained by the charismatic inspirations of the Breath [Spirit] of the risen Jesus."[34] Paderborn's systematician Heribert Mühlen has developed some of the key ideas of *Lumen Gentium* by arguing that the church is seen "as the continuation of the Anointing with the Spirit of Jesus at his baptism."[35] *Lumen Gentium* and *Apostolicam Actuositatem* as well as *Presbyterorum Ordinis* establish the existence and contribution of charisms under the supervision of shepherds of the church. Vatican II emphasized repeatedly the Spirit's sovereign freedom in dispensing the charisms (*AA* 3; *LG* 7). The council insisted on the universal availability of the charisms.

The Spirit calls all Christians, ordained and lay alike, to some form of charismatic ministry (*AA* 3, 28, 30; *LG* 4).

Jesuit theologian Donald Gelpi, though, criticizes his own church for not taking seriously the charismatic and pneumatological teaching of the Second Vatican Council. He thinks it is not the so called "Catholic Charismatic Movement" that has responsibility to renew the church, but it is precisely the burden of the whole church with her theologians and teachers to implement what was rediscovered in the Council. He argues that the charisms play an indispensable role in the life of the Church and they therefore cannot be confined to the first generation of Christians, as most Catholics before Vatican II were taught to believe.[36] According to Kilian McDonnell, "the charisms of the Spirit play an indispensable role in the life of the Church because they create the shared faith consciousness of the Christian community."[37]

McDonnell, in the course of his extensive writings during the last two decades on various aspects of pneumatology and ecclesiology, has appealed tirelessly for a truly pneumatological ecclesiology.[38] Now it has become more and more obvious to the emerging ecumenical ecclesiology that as the Spirit is constitutive of the identity of Israel as God's people, so does the Spirit belong to the constitutive moment of the existence of the church. It is not enough to add the Spirit later, after the Church has been instituted, as a sort of "decorative tinsel," as it was still with the pneumatology of *Lumen Gentium*, with all its otherwise positive contributions. It builds up the Church in christological terms, and then when the christological moment is all over, the Spirit is added in a second moment, McDonnell laments. This approach he names "consequent pneumatology....[But] [t]his is too late. The Spirit belongs to the first constitutive moment. This has profound implications for the life of the Church, evangelization, preaching, liturgy, the Christian life."[39] This has also been the focus of persistent Greek Orthodox critique of the ecclesiology of Vatican II, as we saw above.

Several Catholic theologians have remarked recently that the pneumatological aspect must be seen together with the fact that the Church, in its confession of faith, is connected with the Holy Spirit. The Church is named in the creeds in the clause after the Holy Spirit. Miguel M. Garijo-Guembe of Spain notes that according to the *Traditio apostolica* of Hippolytus, the third baptismal question runs: "Do you believe in the Holy Spirit in the Church?" Further, as the apostles were baptized in the Holy Spirit at Pentecost, in the same way the communion of the faithful is made fruitful today through the gifts of the Spirit. The close connection between Holy Spirit and Church in the early centuries reveals the three basic convictions which are normative for us, too. First, it was the Spirit who was active in ancient prophets and who had prophesied the coming and experiences of the Savior. Second, the Spirit enlightens the Church and leads her into the truth; it fills her with its charisms, and is effective in sacraments. Finally, the Spirit guarantees the faithful a share in eternal life, that is, victory over death.[40] This ecclesial conviction about the integral relationship between the Spirit and the Church was expressed clearly by Irenaeus: "For where the Church is, there is also the Spirit of God. And where the Spirit of God is, there is also the Church and all grace; for the Spirit is the Truth."[41]

The resurgence of pneumatology and pneumatological ecclesiology and sacramentology has opened up new prospects in the search for Christian unity, too, in Catholic theologies. Several Catholic ecumenists have recently pointed to the indispensable role of pneumatology in ecumenical theology. Avery Dulles, noted for his "models," thinks that the rules of ecumenical theology must be "biblically rooted, ecclesially responsible, open to criticism, and sensitive to the present leading of the Holy Spirit." Philip J. Rosato declares confidently that pneumatology offers the divided Christian communities a new meeting place for dialogue. Dietrich Ritschl has elaborated a "therapeutic task of theology," where the plurality and diversity promoted by the Holy Spirit is acknowledged as a condition for unity. Paul D. Lee, taking up the Johannine image of the Spirit as the *Paraclete*, speaks about a true ecumenical theology as a healer, a consoler, and an advocate. Here the role of the Spirit is seen as "the go-between God," the bond of love, uniting humans beings to God and to each other.[42]

It is noteworthy that the Roman Catholic Church has been the first and, until 1996 when the International Dialogue between the World Alliance of Reformed Churches and World Pentecostal Churches was initiated, the only church to begin official dialogues with Pentecostals and Charismatics. Catholic ecumenist Paul D. Lee has argued that the dialogue has helped Catholic theologians to "test" a truly pneumatological approach to Christian unity.

> This science [i.e. pneumatology] provides a fresh ecumenical meeting-ground, especially as regards a theologically more agreeable understanding of the Church. The Spirit continuously brings to the Church hope, vigor, and new insights. Today's renewed interest in pneumatology among Christians

> has positive implications for a more comprehensive and theo-centric ecclesiology. A growing convergence in the theology of the Holy Spirit promises new breakthroughs, for instance, in the traditional ecclesiological tensions between "the charismatic" and the "institutional," between the laity and the clergy, between the historical and the eschatological, and between understandings of the Church as "an event" and as "an organization."[43]

Pneumatology offers "an eschatological hope to be experienced and realized now," "a new meeting place for dialogue" in the midst of divided Christendom, Lee further contends.[44] It brings with it hope and new challenges for ecumenical work.

The Contribution of Pentecostalism and Charismatic Movements

Two major shapers of Christian *oikumene* after the Reformation/Counter Reformation have been the emergence of ecumenical consciousness—both in terms of the formation of the WCC and the opening up of the Catholic Church to ecumenism as a result of Vatican II—and the birth of the Pentecostal, and later Charismatic, movements. The dramatic spread of the Pentecostal movement throughout the world has made other Christians wake up to its significance. From humble beginnings at the Azusa Street revival in Los Angeles, California, at the beginning of the twentieth century, it has become the largest single category in Protestantism, the "third force" in Christianity, outstripping the traditional groups that date back to the Reformation such as the Lutheran, Reformed, and Anglican communions. The Pentecostal movement is the most rapidly growing missionary movement in the world and in the history of Christendom. There are specialists who expect that in the next century it will overshadow the Catholic Church numerically.[45]

Such a dramatic growth has brought new questions to theology, and the existence of Pentecostal-Charismatic Christianity cannot be overlooked any more, certainly not in ecumenical theology, although—especially in Europe—ecumenical theologizing still goes on like nothing has happened to the tapestry of the Christian Church. The author of *The Secular City* in the 1960s, Harvard theologian Harvey Cox, has, in the 1990s, awakened mainline theologians to stop pretending that the world's largest growing segment is of no interest.[46]

To be sure, Pentecostalism has not developed much theology, being a lay-led charismatic renewal of spirituality. Its mode of doing theology has been oral/experiential rather than the discursive/analytic way familiar to the Western academy. It reflects the way theology is mainly done in Third World cultures where testimonies, songs, visions, and dreams are preferred over lectures, studies, and analytical discussions. "The salient characteristic of Pentecostalism is its belief in the present-day manifestation of spiritual gifts, such as miraculous healing, prophecy and, most distinctively, glossolalia. Pentecostals affirm that these spiritual gifts (charismata) are granted by the Holy Spirit and are normative in contemporary church life and ministry."[47] Many observers of the movement hold that this challenge, in spirituality and enthusiasm—in the "revalorization of the Charismata"—rather than in theological analysis, entails the most important contribution of Pentecostalism and later Charismatic movements. Pentecostalism has also reintroduced a dynamic, enthusiastic type of spirituality to the modern church. The focus of Pentecostal spirituality is experiencing God mystically as supernatural. The category of experience is essential to understanding the spirituality of Pentecostals, and thus its worship.[48]

In other words, the major contribution of Pentecostalism and Charismatic movements to the *oikumene* has been the introduction of charismatic, enthusiastic spirituality with a view of reviving the New Testament type of Christianity.[49] The irony of our day is that most ecumenical theologians are still completely unaware of this. What other contribution to pneumatology would be more valuable than this, especially, when the prospects of the Christian church in the future lie in the expansion of non-western oral cultures rather than the Western academy?

But notwithstanding the Pentecostal emphasis on living out spirituality rather than writing theological treatises, the younger generation of Pentecostals now—and Charismatic Christians, especially Catholics, since the beginning of the Renewal—have also started to develop distinctively Pentecostal pneumatology and theology. One of the most studied topics has been the Pentecostal-Charismatic distinctive, the baptism in the Holy Spirit, with accent on speaking in tongues.[50] The topic has produced a manifold ecumenical exchange between Pentecostal theologians and exegetes and systematicians of other persuasions. James D. G. Dunn's classic *Baptism in the Holy Spirit* has invited numerous responses from Pentecostal and Charismatic theologians.[51] Ecumenically the most far reaching study has been one initiated by the Catholic-Pentecostal dialogue. Kilian McDonnell collaborated with the New Testament exegete George Montague on the monograph *Spirit-Baptism and Christian Initiation in the First Eight Centuries.* The book argues that during the first centuries of Christendom, baptism in the Holy Spirit was expected to be a normative part of Christian initiation (baptism, Eucharist, confirmation) with accompanying spiritual manifestations, like speaking in tongues, prophecy, etc.[52]

Interestingly enough the appearance of Jürgen Moltmann's *Spirit of Life* has drawn considerable ecumenical exchange between Moltmann and Pentecostal-Charismatic theologians. In fact, Moltmann has been one of the first pneumatologists of international caliber to engage in a rather extensive dialogue with Pentecostals-Charismatics. His appearance in the largest Charismatic theological conference at Brighton in 1991 (Theological Forum of the International Charismatic Consultation on World Evangelization) opened some limited exchange between continental theologians and their Pentecostal partners.[53] This was followed by the devotion of the 1996 (vol. 3) *Concilium* issue, edited by Moltmann and Karl-Josef Kuschel, to the topic, "Pentecostal Movements as Ecumenical Challenge," with articles by Pentecostal, Charismatic, Catholic, Orthodox, and Protestant theologians. Another recent author of major pneumatology, Michael Welker, has also engaged in dialogue with Pentecostals, as has his compatriot, the New Testament exegete Eduard Schweizer.[54]

These few examples mainly from Western ways of doing Pentecostal theology do not do full justice to the Pentecostal movement worldwide. Distinctively intercultural Pentecostal-Charismatic theologies are emerging in Africa, Asia, Latin America, and elsewhere.

The WCC has shown some limited interest to dialogue with Pentecostals in developing a more conciliar, contextual pneumatology. A major monograph was produced in 1981 as a result of a consultation, entitled *The Church is Charismatic*.[55] Theologically and ecumenically, perhaps the most significant contribution is that of Hollenweger, who outlines three perspectives to the Spirit: ecclesiological, where the Church is seen as "social experience of God"; cosmological, where the Spirit creates renewal of creation, healing of social relations, and bodily healing; and sacramental, where the Spirit is given to believers to effect conversion and power for holy living.[56]

The Canberra WCC-Assembly (1991) was the first to pay specific attention to the contribution of Pentecostals both in liturgy and theologizing about the Spirit. It recommended to its member churches an open attitude toward the Pentecostals and Charismatics and urged them to dialogue with this enthusiastic type of Christianity: "Insofar as they

[Pentecostals and Charismatics] emphasize the charisms of the Spirit described in the New Testament and represent a discovery of the ministry of healing, they are valid expressions of Christian living. They also represent a commitment to strong faith and fellowship, increased spontaneity, openness and freedom among worshippers, all of them leading to greater participation in the life of the churches."[57]

Prospects for a Truly Pneumatological Ecumenical Approach?

Our descriptive survey of a pneumatological perspective in major theological traditions, with a view to ecumenical potential, has revealed some key principles for further analysis and development. First of all, the resurgence of pneumatology in every theological corner is a fact of enormous ecumenical significance. Seldom, if ever, has there been in the history of theology, in such a short period of time and to such a broad extent, a more distinctive *conciliar* development than the new enthusiasm concerning the Spirit of God. One suspects that behind this enthusiasm is something more than just a passing fascination with the "latest fashion." The emergence of pneumatology has implications, not just for the subject matter of theology, but also for its method, boundaries, expressions, and so on.

Second, it seems that two factors have been the primary catalysts in contributing to this development. On the one hand, the voice of Eastern Orthodox theology, especially after its inclusion in the WCC; on the other hand, the dramatic growth and spread of Pentecostalism and Charismatic movements. To these must be added the reformulation of the theological agenda in Catholic theology as a result of Vatican II. Academic theology, operating up until our days mainly from a Western/European perspective, must now reflect on this truly catholic agenda.

Third, the resurgence of pneumatology operates on two levels: in spirituality, which is the main focus of Pentecostal-Charismatic Christianity, but also to a large measure that of Eastern Orthodoxy, and in theology, with an increasing literature on the topic. Hardly any other theological topic has such a potential for integrating spirituality and discursive theologizing; and there is much in the Western academic enterprise to be learned from both Pentecostals and Third World Christians. The hegemony of one-sided Western theologizing, notwithstanding its massive accomplishments, must give way to a more comprehensive, intercultural theologizing where the whole life, not just intellectualism, comes to bear on our living and thinking. A true *ecumenical* theologizing can never be a possession of one segment of world Christianity, especially of that segment which is diminishing while non-western regions are growing quickly.

Fourth, the existing ecumenical "models," especially the *koinonia*-theology with its leaning toward the role of the Spirit in the search for Christian unity, have to be reworked in order to include the critical role of pneumatology. A truly trinitarian approach to ecumenism always emphasizes the role of the Spirit since—as Eastern theologians have taught us—we can never know the "essence" of God, only his "energies," or the "economy" of the Spirit.

Fifth, it has always been the belief of the church catholic that the Spirit is the uniting factor, not only *ad intra* Trinity but also between Christians, who have been born and empowered with the same Spirit of God. The renaissance of pneumatology bears testimony to what the church has always believed since the time of the first apostles. In the New Delhi WCC Assembly (1961) an ecumenically fruitful statement pointed to the importance of a pneumatological perspective in the search for Christian unity: "We believe that the unity which is both God's will and his gift to his church is being made visible as all in each place...are brought by the Holy Spirit into one fully committed fellowship."[58]

Sixth, and consequently, pneumatology cannot be seen as a separate article in theology in general, or in ecumenical theology, but as an overarching principle of unity, anchored in a trinitarian vision of the unity of all God's people. The *lacuna* of much theologizing about the Holy Spirit, especially in the West, has been either practical subordination of the Spirit, or, even more often, the treatment of the "doctrine of the Spirit" in a separate theological *locus* rather than as an integrating theme permeating and governing all we say about God and his works. In this new kind of holistic view prospects emerge for a new "ecumenical model." In the words of Orthodox ecumenist Boris Bobrinskoy,

> The theology of the Holy Spirit, or pneumatology, is not so much one specific chapter of Christian theology as an essential dimension of every theological view of the church and of its spirituality and liturgical and sacramental life. The Holy Spirit...is first and foremost the Spirit we invoke, the Spirit who presides over the upbuilding and renewal of the church, the Spirit who infuses everyone that comes into the world with the light of Christ.[59]

Part Two

Ecclesiology

Chapter Six

Toward a Pneumatological Ecclesiology

What is the role of the pneumatological dimension in the theology of the church? And, consequently, what is the relationship between christology and pneumatology in ecclesiology? These are the two cardinal, interrelated questions that have occupied ecclesiological thinking from the beginning.

Every theological tradition today confesses that there is some important role assigned to the Spirit, and that christology and pneumatology must not be seen as opposite to each other but rather interrelated and mutual entities. The New Testament shows convincingly that Easter (the work of Christ) and Pentecost (the outpouring of the Spirit) belong together. From ancient times on, the pneumatological aspect is highlighted by the fact that the Church in its confessions of faith is said to be connected with the Holy Spirit. But what exactly is the role of the Spirit in ecclesiological ramifications? What is the role of pneumatology in our view of the church?

Ecclesiologies have been traditionally built on either of the two classical rules, that of Ignatius of Antioch or of Irenaeus. Ignatius suggested the ecclesiality of the church could be secured by reference to Christ's presence: "Wherever Jesus Christ is, there is the universal church." According to Irenaeus what is decisive is the presence of the Spirit of God: "Wherever the Spirit of God is, there is the church, and all grace."[1]

In the New Testament the church is called the body of Christ. Never is the church labeled as the "body of the Spirit," and never are the Christians said to be "members of the Spirit." Therefore, the traditional christological grounding of the church seems plausible. Very soon, however, especially in the East, the question arose as to the role of the Spirit in the building of the church. The answer was obvious: christology and pneumatology must be seen as simultaneous rather than exclusive. And it is noteworthy that this finding was not so much due to sophisticated theological analysis—in fact, as is well known, the Fathers did not have ecclesiology as a separate theological *locus*—but rather it came through a lived experience in the church. Irenaeus, Athanasius, and others were pastors and bishops in the church. Very soon they realized that God works in the world using "both of his hands" as Irenaeus put it.[2] Notwithstanding this early insight, the later history of ecclesiology testifies to a continual struggle in finding a theologically satisfying balance between these two rules.

The purpose of this chapter is to survey major ecumenical approaches to the question of pneumatological grounding of the church. I will conduct my inquiry in critical dialogue with Eastern Orthodox, Protestant, and Roman Catholic ecclesiologies. Rather than trying to be comprehensive in any way, I have chosen three dialogue partners who are ecumenically representative and theologically significant: John Zizioulas, the Metropolitan of Pergamon and the most important living Eastern Orthodox ecclesiologist; Wolfhart Pannenberg, arguably the greatest living Protestant ecumenical theologian, and the late Karl Rahner, the most influential post-conciliar theologian of the Roman Church. I have selected my dialogue partners intentionally not to include "Charismatic" theologians but rather "normal" theologians of each tradition. The reason is obvious: this writing is not an essay in distinctive Charismatic ecclesiology but rather an ecumenical inquiry into the role of the Spirit in classical traditions. I agree with Donald J. Gelpi, S.J., when he argues that it is not the burden of the so-called Charismatic Renewal to renew the church (in his case, the Roman Catholic Church), but it belongs to the whole church and theology to reflect upon the critical role of the Spirit in the Church.[3]

The Church as "Continual Pentecost": Zizioulas

Traditionally, it has been the legacy of Eastern Orthodox theology to highlight the mutuality of christology and pneumatology in the doctrine of the church. The church is founded on a two-fold divine economy: the work of Christ and the work of the Holy Spirit. On the basis of biblical language, Eastern theologians speak about the church as the body of Christ and fullness of the Holy Spirit.[4] Significantly enough, St. Basil contended that "Christ comes, the Spirit goes before. He is present in the flesh, and the Spirit is inseparable from him."[5] This is a noteworthy theological statement since it anchors the work of Christ in the Church in the economy of the Spirit.

The mutual relation between the Son and Spirit is manifested in that just as the Son comes down to earth and accomplishes His work through the Spirit, so the Spirit comes into the world, being sent by the Son (John 15:26). The work of the Spirit is not subordinate to the work of the Son, nor is the Pentecost a "continuation" of the Incarnation, but rather its sequel, its result. As a result of the mutual work of the Son and Spirit, catholicity of the church means two things: unity of the church (as a result of its being the body of Christ) and diversity of the church (as a result of its being the fullness of the Spirit).[6] The Holy Spirit who rests upon Christ, the "Anointed One," communicates himself to each member of this body, creating, so to speak, many christs, the anointed ones.[7] The christological aspect creates the objective and unchangeable features of the church, while as a result of the pneumatological aspect there is the subjective side of the Church. In other words, the christological aspect guarantees stability while in its pneumatological aspect the church has a dynamic character.

John Zizioulas builds critically upon the long tradition of Orthodox ecclesiology. While sympathetic to the works of Lossky and others, he sees the idea of a distinct "economy of the Spirit" as problematic, as well as the idea of the distinction between "objective" (in Lossky's case, sacramental structure of the Church) and "subjective." Zizioulas makes a reference to the critique expressed by Eastern theologians about the lack of pneumatological dimension in Vatican II's explication of the church in *Lumen Gentium* (several Eastern theologians have charged that the Holy Spirit was brought into ecclesiology after the Church was already construed in christological terms), but he admits that even Eastern ecclesiology falls short of a proper balance between christology and pneumatology.[8]

According to Zizioulas, there are two kinds of christologies. Firstly, we may understand Christ as an individual, and secondly, as a whole personal being—Zizioulas uses the term "corporate" personality[9]—in his relationship with his body, the Church. In his terminology, in the former case we speak of Christ as "individual," in the latter as "person." The role of the Spirit comes into focus right here:

> Here the Holy Spirit is not one who *aids* us in bridging the distance between Christ and ourselves, but he is the person of the Trinity who actually

> realizes in history that which we call Christ.... In this case, our Christology is *essentially* conditioned by pneumatology, not just secondarily as in the first case; in fact it is *constituted* pneumatologically.[10]

Consequently, Zizioulas speaks of the Church as "instituted" by Christ and "constituted" by the Spirit. He contends that it is not enough to speak of pneumatology in relation to the Church but rather to make pneumatology, along with eschatology, constitutive, i.e., pneumatology must qualify the very ontology of the Church. The Spirit is not something that "animates" a Church which already exists. "Pneumatology does not refer to the well-being but to the very being of the Church." In other words, pneumatology is an ontological category in ecclesiology.[11]

Zizioulas explicitly attempts to work for a proper synthesis between christology and pneumatology as the basis for ecclesiology. He rightly notes that in the New Testament there is mutuality rather than priority of either one. On the one hand, the Spirit is given by Christ (John 7:39), on the other hand, there is no Christ until the Spirit is at work either at his baptism (Mark) or at his birth (Matthew and Luke). Both of these views could co-exist in the same canon. Confusion came early on the liturgical level due to the separation of baptism and confirmation. As long as these two rites were united, it could be argued that pneumatology (confirmation) and baptism (christology) form one entity.[12]

As already mentioned, the "corporate" personality of Christ is conceived pneumatologically. It is significant that since the time of Paul the Spirit has been associated with the notion of *koinonia*. Pneumatology contributes to christology (and consequently, to ecclesiology) the dimension of communion.

What then are main consequences to the life of the Church given a proper pneumatological orientation? First, it guards from over-institutionalization. Where there is pneumatological deficit, one result is a hierarchical, centralized concept of the Church. Second, it rehabilitates the local church as the primary entity. If pneumatology is not ontologically constitutive of christology, this can mean that there is first one Church and then many churches. However, if pneumatology is made constitutive of ecclesiology, the body of Christ is ontologically constituted by the Spirit. In other words, the Pentecostal event is an ecclesiologically constituting event. Third, all pyramidal notions disappear in pneumatological ecclesiology where the "one" and the "many" co-exist as two aspects of the same being. Fourth, according to Zizioulas, pneumatology helps ecclesiology open up to the eschatological perspective, i.e., to avoid both "meta-historicism" (sometimes attributed to Eastern tradition) and "historization" of ecclesial institutions (a danger within Western churches). Fifth, the pneumatological orientation has consequences to our view of ministry. The ministry of the Church is the ministry of Christ. But when christology is pneumatologically constituted, the Spirit is constitutive of the relation between Christ and the ministry. This is in fact in line with what Paul argues in 1 Corinthians 12. The life and ministry of the body of Christ is conceived pneumatologically, in terms of the gifts of the Spirit. Be it the question of ordination or that of the role of the laity, the proper context is the *koinonia* of the Spirit among the members of the body of Christ. The charismatic life is constitutive of and not derivative from the Church's being.

Interestingly enough, Zizioulas remarks that the fact that Orthodoxy has not experienced situations similar to those of the Western Churches, such as the problem of clericalism, anti-institutionalism, the Charismatic movement, etc. may be taken as an indication that for the most part pneumatology has saved the life of Orthodoxy up to now. Whatever one thinks of the accuracy of this statement in real life of Orthodox Churches, I believe it contains a theological insight worth pondering.

The Church and "The Outpouring of the Spirit": Pannenberg

The most significant program of systematic theology of the latter part of the twentieth century comes from the hand of Wolfhart Pannenberg. It is reflective of our times, that in Pannenberg's ambitious system pneumatology plays a crucial role, e.g., in the doctrine of God and salvation, to name just a couple of the most obvious *loci*.[13] His approach to the doctrine of the church is thoroughly permeated by a pneumatological outlook. It is indicative that he starts his third volume, the theme of which is ecclesiology and pneumatology, with the chapter title, "The Outpouring of the Spirit, the Kingdom of God, and the Church."

Pannenberg, who is always attentive to integral connections between various theological themes, emphasizes that the Spirit he is speaking about in his discussion on the foundations of the church is none else than the Spirit of God active already in creation as God's mighty *ruach*. The same Holy Spirit who is given to believers in a wholly specific way, namely, so as to dwell in them (Rom. 5:9; 1 Cor. 3:16), is none other than the creator of all life in its various forms (*ST* 3.1–2 and 17). If it is true that theology has often neglected the relation between soteriology and pneumatology (*ST* 3.2–3), the same can be said regarding the relation of pneumatology to ecclesiology.

In Pannenberg's ecclesiological vision there is an integral, dialogical relationship between the Spirit and Son based on his strict trinitarian approach.[14] "The christological constitution and the pneumatological constitution do not exclude one another but belong together because the Spirit and the Son mutually indwell one another as trinitarian persons" (*ST* 3.16–17). According to Pannenberg, everywhere the work of the Spirit is closely related to that of the Son from creation through salvation, to the consummation of creation in the eschaton. The reciprocity, rather than asymmetry (usually in the form of christology taking precedence), is accentuated by the fact that in the New Testament Jesus Christ himself is seen as a recipient of the Spirit and his work in conception (Luke), baptism (Mark), and resurrection (Rom. 1:4; 8:11) (*ST* 1.316, 2.84, and 3.4–5). According to John, the Spirit is given to Jesus Christ "without measure" (John 3:34), whereas for believers the Spirit is a gift related to their becoming sons and daughters by fellowship with Jesus Christ (Rom. 5:15; 6:3ff.) (*ST* 3.9). Since the divine Spirit of life wholly permeates the risen Lord, the Lord can impart the Spirit to others insofar as they have fellowship with him (*ST* 1.269).

The gift of the Spirit is not just for individual believers but aims at the building up of the fellowship of believers, "at the founding and the constant giving of new life to the church" (*ST* 3.12). The Spirit thus unites the believers into Christ and into fellowship with others. The story of Pentecost (Acts 2) gives expression to the fact that the Spirit does not simply assure each individual believer alone of fellowship with Jesus Christ, but that thereby he founds at the same time the fellowship of believers (*ST* 3.13).

Pannenberg rightly notes that in Paul, Jesus Christ is the foundation of the church (1 Cor. 3:11), whereas in Luke the church seems to be founded by the "power" of the Holy Spirit. In constructing a systematic appraisal of the New Testament teaching it is important not to see alternatives in these various ideas nor suppress awareness of the differences by harmonizing. Each theological concept of the church must integrate into itself the material aspects articulated in these different orientations in the same canon. To this effect the Johannine statements are helpful because they share with Luke an interest in the Spirit as an independent entity and yet at the same time they deal with the theme of the link between his work and Jesus Christ. The Spirit's work is to glorify Jesus (John 16:

13–14) but as that takes place, Jesus himself, by the Spirit's work, is with his own (John 14:20) (*ST* 3.15–16).

In short, the church is thus the creation of both the Spirit and the Son. Therefore, a one-sided christological grounding for the church must be judged as one that misses and distorts its full reality. It leads, as the history of the Western Church shows—and Eastern theologians are prone to point this out—to an overemphasis on official church structures derived directly from Jesus Christ (*ST* 3.17–19). Christology on the one hand, and an integral relation of pneumatology to creation and to eschatology on the other hand, helps avoid a defective constricting of pneumatology from a christological angle that finds the Spirit's work only in the fellowship of believers and hence exaggerates the Spirit's work which manifests itself in a harmful enthusiasm evident throughout church history (*ST* 3.19–20).

Pannenberg joins in the classical twofold description of the church as the body of Christ which highlights the christological orientation and the fellowship of believers which highlights the pneumatological (*ST* 3.99–102). For Pannenberg the body of Christ is no mere metaphor nor it is just one of the biblical ways of depicting the nature of the church. Instead, it reveals the realism of the inseparable union of believers with Christ. Yet it is the Spirit who by his work builds the body of Christ as he testifies to Jesus Christ in the hearts of believers (*ST* 3.551). The Holy Spirit is the agent who makes possible for believers the immediacy of individuals to Jesus Christ in the church that is his body (*ST* 3.122ff.). The same Spirit is not merely the basis of their immediacy but also the basis of the fellowship of believers in the unity of the body of Christ.

From all this Pannenberg draws an all-important ecclesiological principle, namely that the work of the Spirit releases and reconciles the tension between the fellowship and the individual in the concept of the church, and hence, the underlying anthropological tension between society and individual freedom. The work of the Spirit lifts individuals ecstatically above their own particularity not only to participation in the sonship of Christ but at the same time also to experience the fellowship in the body of Christ that unites individual Christians to all other Christians. Furthermore, the Spirit's work is ecstatic not merely in individual Christians but also in the life of the church (*ST* 3.130–34).

Here then is an outline of the pneumatological ecclesiology of Pannenberg as presented in his *magnum opus*. The twofold constitution of the church by pneumatological and christological categories is clearly outlined as well as the role of the Spirit in uniting believers with

God and into their mutual fellowship. What is lacking in this program are the implications to the rest of ecclesiological topics such as ministry, structure(s) of the church, spiritual gifts and endowments in the service of the church, and Christian unity. Pannenberg, of course, discusses these issues but in my reading he does not unleash the pneumatological potential his ecclesiology allows. The only major exception is the brilliant discussion on the Lord's Supper in which he considers the role of the Spirit in mediating Christ's presence among his people gathered at the table.

"The Dynamic Element in the Church": Rahner

Modern Roman Catholic ecclesiology has experienced significant turns. Although Johann Adam Möhler is rightly considered to be the originator of the highly influential "the Church as continued incarnation" ecclesiology, it is often forgotten that in 1825 he advanced a Spirit-centered ecclesiology with the publication of *Unity in the Church or the Principle of Catholicism* (1825). In that work Möhler clearly opted for the priority of pneumatology in Catholic ecclesiology.[15]

In his later writings, through which Möhler is presently better known, he sought to redress the christological deficit by, obviously, going to the other extreme. Möhler came to emphasize an Incarnation-oriented ecclesiology in definite juxtaposition to classical Protestant theology (Luther, Calvin, Anabaptists) and modern theology (Schleiermacher especially) with its overemphasis on the Spirit. He did not, of course, deny the meaning of Pentecost but made it subordinate to christology and constructed ecclesiology primarily in terms of Incarnation. Incarnational and mystical body theologies, which dominated until Vatican Council II, were built on that foundation. The Spirit's role was marginal.

The twentieth-century renewal of pneumatology in Catholic ecclesiology, revitalized during Vatican II and continuing with vigor since, could be constructed in part as an attempt to reaffirm Möhler's early Spirit-centered approach and to reintegrate it with his later incarnational ecclesiology within a fully developed trinitarian framework. Three theologians played a crucial role for initiating the fuller recovery of the doctrine of the Holy Spirit on the eve of Vatican II and afterward: Yves Congar, Heribert Mühlen, and Karl Rahner.[16] Interestingly enough, history tends to repeat itself. After the resurgence of pneumatological outlook, in line with Möhler's earlier position, a response to reaffirm the christological/incarnational aspects arose through the influential writings of Henri de Lubac, Hans Urs von Balthasar, and, especially, Joseph H. Ratzinger. To oversimplify the issue: these scholars have done to pneumatology of the twentieth century what the later Möhler did to his earlier period, by issuing warnings about an excessive "pneumaticism."

Karl Rahner carefully steers a middle course in his ecclesiology.[17] Already in 1964, during the Council, he wrote a significant pneumatological treatise entitled *The Dynamic Element in the Church.* Rahner issued a powerful call for the charismatic structure of the church by reminding us that the Holy Spirit is promised and given first and foremost to ecclesiastical ministry, not to suppress the free flow of the Spirit but to make room for it. The Church should always be the "Church of the abiding Spirit." Rahner argued that there should be sensitive discerning of and openness to the charismatic element in the church. Since it is usually new and always surprising, it might even have "something shocking about it."[18]

Rahner does not discuss much the relation of christology and pneumatology, but rather his focus is between the Spirit and structures/office of the church—an issue that, of course, must do with pneumatology and christology, as the Eastern tradition has reminded us. Where there is a one-sided emphasis on christology, church structures tend to become dominating (this has also been the result of the older Catholic view of church as continued incarnation).

According to Rahner, the Spirit is constitutive of the Church in a way more basic than its institutional structure. The charismatic element "does not merely stand in a dialectical relationship to the institutional factor as its opposite pole, existing on the same plane. Rather it is the first and the most ultimate among the formal characteristics inherent in the very nature of the Church as such."[19] Rahner also says—but does not specify in detail—that the church is primarily the "historical concretization of the charismatic as brought about by the Spirit of Christ." And it is clear that in Rahner's view the term "charismatic" does not refer to any specific group in the church but to the life and ministry of all believers. If the Church is founded in the sovereign action of the Spirit, then the church must be understood as an "open system."[20] It means that the church cannot be understood or defined from a point within the Church itself but rather from outside, from the Spirit of God.

The practical results from Rahner's view of the charismatic structure of the church are obvious. First, an openness to the promptings of the Spirit: "Do not Stifle the Spirit" was one of his influential speeches on the eve of the Council.[21] Second, the primacy of the Spirit over the structures and offices of the church, even if the structures in themselves are expressive of the Spirit (Rahner never champions individualism). Third, legitimate plurality results from the sovereign action of the Spirit.[22] Fourth, Rahner's pneumatological ecclesiology is open to ecumenism. There is an ultimate unity that already exists among all Christians, a unity brought about by the Spirit of God. In the Spirit "all of us 'know' something more simple, more true and more real than we can know or express at the level of our theological concepts."[23] Rahner's ecclesiology must be assessed against the background of developing Catholic doctrine of the Church and the Spirit both before and after the Council. Rahner attempts to steer a mid-course between incarnational and pneumatic ecclesiologies. His ecclesiology is contextual in that it warns about overemphasis on structures.

The basic problem with Rahner's thinking is that, surprisingly, he does not seem to offer a plausible theological undergirding to his insistence on the priority of charismatic element over against the hierarchic. Rather—and this has been the core of Eastern Orthodox but also to some degree Catholic critique of Vatican II's teaching on the Church, the result of which owes much to Rahner himself—it seems that the pneumatic/charismatic element is added to an already existing institutional/christological foundation to revive something which is in danger of becoming too stable. Even Rahner's *Foundations of Christian Faith*, where he had the opportunity to respond to criticism of his earlier occasional writings, gives the impression that the church is first christologically constructed and then pneumatologically "decorated."[24] If my impression is wrong, it might be because Rahner does not offer enough material to deal with this basic issue of ecclesiology.

After all this is said, one need not underestimate the contribution of Rahner, not only to his own church and Catholic theology, but also to a wider *oikumene*. And perhaps his lasting influence is not so much in what he said explicitly about the church but what could yet be said in light of his over-arching idea of God's self-communication to humanity through his Spirit. Rahner's Christ-centered, anthropologically anchored pneumatological view of grace and revelation will have much more to say about the relation of Spirit and church than he himself expressed.

Toward a Pneumatological Ecclesiology

Pneumatological ramifications of ecclesiology cannot be construed apart from christological and trinitarian orientations. The foundational triad is the relationship between Christ and Spirit, Christ and Church and Spirit and Church. Here it suffices to outline the basic schema and then reflect on the potential and *lacunae* of those three ecclesiologies discussed above.

In the New Testament, christology is never depicted apart from the Spirit. In their own distinctive ways, the Gospels present Christ as the Spirit Bearer before he is to be the Spirit Giver. He is given the Spirit without measure (John 3:34). Christ is conceived and fulfills his ministry in the Spirit.

The only way to construe a viable pneumatological ecclesiology is to reflect very carefully on the relationship between Christ and Spirit on the one hand, and on the relation of the Spirit to the church on the other hand, and then try to see these three as mutual entities that inform each other. Otherwise we end up with either a "Christomonism" (West) with subsequent effects such as a hierarchical church, or a "Spiritomonism" (some Eastern theologies) where Christ as the foundation of the church (however this disputed concept is defined) and head of his body is pushed to the margins.

A pneumatological orientation is needed to overcome the age-old dilemma between "charism and institution." The work of the Spirit lays foundation for both structure and charism. Instead of seeing these two as opposites, we must seek a "charismatic structure." The Church, as the Body of Christ, is a charismatically structured fellowship, a charismatic fellowship. It is not enough to argue for the necessity of charismatic structure if the pneumatological orientation to the foundations of ecclesiology is missing. As we saw above, Pannenberg's and Zizioulas' orientation has the potential since they are built on a proper view of the necessary Spirit-christological foundation of the church whereas Rahner did not pay enough attention to the question (although he, of course, called for a proper acknowledgment of charismatic dimension in the church). In a word, the role of the Spirit in ecclesiology is much more than just a "dimension." Pneumatology is as constitutive to ecclesiology as christology (and the doctrine of the Trinity). The Holy Spirit is to the church more than just the "soul" as the older Catholic ecclesiology held. The Spirit is constitutive moment.

Eastern tradition has been in the vanguard to appeal to the necessary interconnection between christology and pneumatology in its theology and spirituality. Even where its own theologians admit that further reflection is needed to secure balance, the vision has never been lacking in the East. The western wing of the Church has had to come a much longer—and sometimes painful—road to come into the realization of the needed balance between the work of Christ and Spirit. In the Roman Church, a new awakening to the all-important role of the Spirit in the construing of ecclesiology was dramatically strengthened during Vatican II. On the Protestant side, there is a paradoxical situation. On the one hand, older Catholic writers often accused Protestants of a one-sided pneumatological approach to the church (e.g., Möhler's criticism of Schleiermacher). On the other hand, the Protestant ecclesiology betrays a dramatic lack of focus on the Spirit. There were references to the Spirit, but nothing like a pneumatological program.

Zizioulas has critically handled his own Eastern tradition to orient focus on the all-important communion-dimension of ecclesiology. He has been pointing the way toward much of the ecumenical theologizing. Although his trinitarian vision and program of retrieving the concept of "person" in theology has not found universal acceptance, his contribution to the emerging sensitivity to these issues has been unsurpassed.

Rahner's ecclesiology has much more pneumatological potential than his own writings express. Largely due to the contextual factors (especially his critical role in the preparation for Vatican II), his focus on the relation of the Spirit to the church depended mainly on the (older) distinction between the Spirit and institution/structures. What he said about the issue is something every tradition embraces today. Yet what he said was not as theologically grounded as one has the right to expect from such a prominent theologian. One reason may be that his theology in general is so heavily christologically anchored that he did not have a chance to do enough thinking on the pneumatological issues, and his pneumatology in particular is so anthropologically focused that its communal (i.e., ecclesiological) aspects did not receive due attention. Be that as it may, Rahner did not produce a satisfying analysis of the triad of Christ, Spirit and church.

Pannenberg's monumental theological vision combines much of what has been reflected on the relation of Christ, Spirit and church both during history and especially in recent decades. He comes closest to a careful definition of this critical grounding of ecclesiology.

What are some hopes for the future of an emerging ecumenical pneumatological ecclesiology?[25] By definition, life in the Spirit is *experience*.[26] If pneumatology, the doctrine and spirituality of the Holy Spirit, is only discursive theology—as it has been to a large extent, especially in the West—something essential is missing. Theology of the Spirit is a lived experience. The emergence of charismatic gifts, the release of the whole people of God into the ministry by the power of the Spirit, a manifold charismatic testimony by word and deed, a new enthusiasm for evangelization, etc., are but examples of the new vigor of life given by the Spirit to the whole church. Here the enthusiastic, dynamic contribution of Pentecostalism, the Charismatic movements and a host of more recent Free Churches have to be taken into consideration. Their vivid experience of the Spirit points to a crucial dimension of life in the Spirit.

Pneumatological ecclesiology will also enrich ecumenical efforts as the same Spirit who has given birth to Christians and Christian communities strives for unity in the same Spirit—the unity of which is not only "spiritual" being wrought by the Spirit, but will also manifest itself in united witness and service to the world. Michael Welker, in his recent monograph *God the Spirit,* highlights the ecumenical importance of pneumatology in ecclesiology: "The true and real church, the ecumenical and transcontinental church, the church that extends beyond particular epochs, and thus also the visible body of Christ, concretely present here and now, was and is built up by the Holy Spirit (cf. Acts 9:31; 11:24; and passim)."[27]

Pneumatological ecclesiology will also open windows into the world; the Church does not exist for the sake of itself but for the world. Rahner's pneumatology is replete with this orientation. But it would already bring us into another essay.[28]

Chapter Seven

Trinity as Communion in the Spirit

According to Ralph Del Colle, a Catholic charismatic theologian, "the Pentecostal-charismatic experience is intrinsically trinitarian in structure." He contends that through "the pneumatic effusion of Spirit-baptism the Christian is empowered with the Holy Spirit in the mission of Jesus Christ to the glory of God the Father."[1] That all Pentecostals are trinitarian in their spirituality and faith—the order is intended since it is spirituality rather than theology which distinguishes Pentecostalism from other traditions—is not disputed. This statement is true even when we take into account a fairly large number of Pentecostals, in a conservative estimation about one-fourth of all Pentecostals, who are known as "Oneness Pentecostals." Oneness Pentecostals, sometimes also known as "Jesus Only" Pentecostals—since they baptize in the name of Jesus only—do adhere to a trinitarian understanding albeit only on the economic level. They argue that to go beyond the economic level means giving up the economic language of the New Testament and succumbing to philosophical speculations.[2]

However, it must be admitted that until recently Pentecostals have not bothered themselves with formulating their doctrine of the Trinity in cohesive theological terms. On the one hand, this is understandable since Pentecostalism represents a grass roots level movement of charismatic spirituality—a "pneumatic enthusiasm" rather than discursive theology.[3] On the other hand, one might have expected a more concentrated effort to define their trinitarian understanding because the issue of the Trinity arose in the early years of the movement. The "New Issue" raised by Oneness Pentecostals in the formative years of the movement questioned the traditional trinitarian view of the Godhead and resulted in both groups being diametrically opposed to and historically suspicious of each other.[4]

Ironically, Pentecostals have affirmed the classical trinitarian understanding as expressed in creeds, but their attitude toward creeds and creedal formulations has been either pejorative or superficial. "When we 'came out' for Pentecost," wrote the well-known British Pentecostal spokesperson Donald Gee, "we came out not merely for a theory, or a doctrine: we came out for a burning, living, mighty *experience* that revolutionized our lives." This emphasis on experience rather than on creeds is expressed even more clearly in a statement from the first years of the Azusa Street Mission: "We are not fighting men or churches, but seeking to replace the dead forms and creeds...with living, practical Christianity."[5]

For most Pentecostals, creeds indicated a departure from apostolic faith for two reasons: a) because of their lack of concern with practical Christianity, and b) because of their origin in and support for an episcopacy alien to the priesthood of believers and the idea of church as a voluntary community of "believers." This criticism did not mean that Pentecostals were in principle opposed to statements of doctrine; they would occasionally admit that there is some value in creeds. The result has been a mixture of formulae and phrases which "trickle down" from standard Christian creeds and a variety of *ad hoc* statements, especially in relation to questions raised by Oneness Pentecostals.

Like most Western traditions, trinitarian Pentecostals have approached the doctrine of God by discussing the unity of the Godhead and then emphasizing the three eternal and personal distinctions within the divine essence.[6] Proof-texting rather than philosophical or dogmatic argumentation has been characteristic of Pentecostal treatments. Both Pentecostal groups' (trinitarian and Oneness) emphasis on the economic rather than on the imminent Trinity accords well with the dominant theological orientation of our time. The *pro nobis* ("for us") aspect of the Trinity is at the forefront.[7] Yet in recent years, the dialogue with the Catholic Church has helped Pentecostals formulate in theological terms what they have believed. This applies, however, only to trinitarian Pentecostals since Oneness Pentecostals have not been part of the dialogue.

The purpose of this chapter is to inquire into the main perspectives on the Trinity that have emerged from that dialogue. A couple of qualifications are in order to orient the reader. First, the dialogue between Catholics and Pentecostals did not devote much space to the topic of Trinity, as this was not a major issue of contention (especially since the Oneness Pentecostals did not participate in the dialogues). In that sense the agenda of the dialogue differs from most other discussions the Roman Catholic Church has with other communities. Second, and this is ecumenically significant, the context where the discussion on the Trinity came into surface was ecclesiology, the meaning of *koinonia*. The Third Quinquennium (1985–1989) was devoted to the topic of *koinonia*, and it was here that the issues of the Trinity and *filioque* were treated. This is in fact the proper context for the discussion, since it anchors the doctrine of the trinity not in philosophical speculation, but in the concrete life of communion between God and his people. This orientation is also helpful since it guards against the development of pneumatology and pneumatological ecclesiology "independent" from christological and theo-logical ramifications.

The first major part of the chapter will discuss the issue of the Trinity in the context of *koinonia*. The second part will inquire into the meaning of *filioque* from an ecclesiological point of view.

Spirit and Trinity

Koinonia between Christians is Rooted in the Trinitarian Communion

FR III section entitled "The Holy Spirit and the New Testament Vision of *Koinonia*," with the subtitle "Koinonia *with the Triune God*," opens with an important mutual affirmation:

> Both Pentecostals and Roman Catholics believe that the *koinonia* between Christians is rooted in the life of Father, Son and Holy Spirit. Furthermore, they believe that this trinitarian life is the highest expression of the unity to which we together aspire: "that which we have seen and heard we proclaim also to you, so that you may have fellowship with us; and our fellowship is with the Father and with his Son Jesus Christ' (1 John 1:3)." (*FR* III.29)

With this affirmation, *koinonia* is inseparably linked with the doctrine of the Trinity. It is an ecumenical consensus that the communion between Christians in the churches is based on the *koinonia* among divine persons.

At the same time, the unity/communion of the persons of the Trinity is the highest expression of unity for Christians. This is the "deepest meaning of *koinonia*," *FR* III.70 states, echoing the foundational sayings of *Unitatis Redintegratio* and *Lumen Gentium*. It also accords with the Pentecostal Statements of Faith.[8]

The above quoted paragraph emphasizes also the fact that *koinonia* is a two-dimensional concept, comprising both vertical and horizontal aspects: communion with God and among God's people. Since *koinonia* is rooted in the Triune God, believers have "a share in the eternal life which is *koinonia* with the Father and with his Son Jesus Christ (cf. 1 John 1: 2–3), and a communion in the Holy Spirit whom God's Son, Jesus Christ, has given to them (cf. 1 John 3.24; 2 Cor. 13:14)" (*FR* III.70).

Holy Spirit, Trinity, and Communion

Catholics and Pentecostals agree unanimously that "the Holy Spirit is the source of *koinonia* or communion. The Church has been gathered in the Holy Spirit (cf. 2 Cor. 13:13)" (*FR* III.30). There is also a christological concentration since no one can confess the Lordship of Jesus except in the Holy Spirit (1 Cor. 12:3; *FR* III.36).

In his theological position paper, Hervé Legrand, O.P., who gave a short outline of a Catholic trinitarian reading of basic New Testament texts, argued that there is a "comparatively large agreement" between Catholics and Pentecostals as to the reading of the New Testament data referring to the communion with the Triune God.[9] Ecumenically this is an extremely important result in that it points toward a common ground for developing a more consensual view of *koinonia* as both parties take their point of departure from the written Word of God.

According to Legrand, the Father is the one who brings us into communion with his Son and with himself (1 John 3:1, 2:24). The Christians, united among themselves, dwell in the love of the Father and of the Son, like the Father and the Son are dwelling within each other, making them one (John 14:20; 15:4; 17:20–23; 1 John 4:12). Communion with the Son is accomplished especially through the Eucharist (1 Cor. 10:16; 1:9; John 6: 56). The relationship with Christ introduced by baptism is more complex. There the role of the Holy Spirit in the communion with God is much more explicit, since the baptism in the name of Jesus (Acts 2:38; 8:16; 10:48; 19:5; 1 Cor. 6:11) is received through the Spirit of God (1 Cor. 6:11). The baptized become the temple of the Holy Spirit (1 Cor. 8:19). Consequently, the Holy Spirit animates the life of every Christian as well as the whole Church.

Legrand argues that in the New Testament Christ achieves his task by pouring forth the Holy Spirit upon the apostolic community (Acts 2:33). Thus at Pentecost begins the gathering of the messianic community open to all nations (Acts 2:5–11). "The gifts of the Spirit to all Christians do not only set up a deep communion between them (2 Cor. 13:14; Phil. 2:1) but they equally contribute to the construction of the Church (1 Cor. 12:7; 14:

4) and to the building up of the Temple of God (1 Cor. 3:16; Eph. 2:22). The Spirit is always at work for the unity of the body of Christ (1 Cor. 12: 13)." Furthermore, Legrand reminds us that in the New Testament the communion initiated in the Church is an eschatological reality, oscillating between "already" and "not yet." This eschatological dimension, of course, does not negate the visible and historical dimension of the community: "The communion with God, the Father, the Son and the Holy Spirit, is not only eschatological: it gives birth to a Church which is visible and has a mission and a responsibility within history."[10]

Another Catholic team member, Heribert Mühlen, developed his idea of "The Trinity as Communion in the Spirit" from an explicitly pneumatological viewpoint. His idea of a pneumatological ecclesiology built on his *Una Mystica Persona* (1968).[11] Mühlen notes that *Lumen Gentium* §8 speaks of an analogy between incarnation and the Church: "For this reason, by an excellent *analogy*, this reality is compared to the mystery of the incarnate Word....Just as the assumed nature inseparably united to the divine Word serves him as a living instrument of salvation, so, in a similar way, does the *communal structure* of the Church serve *Christ's Spirit*, who vivifies it by way of building up the body (cf. Eph. 4:16)." The Church is thus defined as the mystery of the Holy Spirit or "communion in the Spirit."[12]

Lumen Gentium §7 stresses also the fact that the Spirit is one and the same in Christ and Christians. By this the Council means to say that the Church is the continuation of the anointing of Jesus with the Holy Spirit. Pentecostals are delighted to hear from Catholics that "the central statements of Vatican II about the Church clearly highlight its basically *pneumatological* structure, the Council closely following St Paul in this matter." And, therefore 1 Cor. 12:1–13, one of the cardinal texts for Pentecostals, "assumes an importance for ecclesiology that is similar to that of, say, John 1:14 and Phil 2.5–11 for Christology," Mühlen argues.[13] It is therefore the Holy Spirit,

> dwelling in those who believe and pervading and ruling over the entire Church, who brings about that wonderful communion of the faithful and joins them together so intimately in Christ that he is the principle of the Church's unity.... This is the sacred mystery of the unity of the Church, in Christ and through Christ, with the Holy Spirit energizing its various functions.[14]

Using his somewhat idiosyncratic language, Mühlen notes that since the Holy Spirit is one person out of and in two persons, the divine "we," he brings about the Church as a "relational structure." In the "we" of the witnesses of the life of Jesus, the Holy Spirit makes his appearance in the history of salvation, so that "the effectiveness of the Spirit is and can be experienced when one gains access to the communion of these witnesses." On the basis of this Mühlen can say something which is very crucial to his view of the church: "The Church is the visible and sensorially perceivable form of the Holy Spirit." When we see and hear how other human beings abandon themselves to God, Mühlen states, then we perceive the Holy Spirit himself, or better, his acts.[15]

While both Legrand and Mühlen accentuate the critical role of the Spirit in the creation of church *koinonia* (both vertical and horizontal), there are also differences of emphases. Legrand underlines the sacramental perspective whereas Mühlen's language, in fact, comes extremely close to the Pentecostal understanding of the church. In Mühlen the language of sacramentality seems to go so far toward the pneumatological that the distinction between "sacramental" and "charismatic/pneumatological" is hard to detect.

Trinity, Fellowship, and Experience

The Pentecostal co-chair, Cecil M. Robeck, Jr., accentuated the trinitarian perspective in his position paper. Actually, his whole paper is imbued with trinitarian perspectives as he exegetes some crucial New Testament passages relating to *koinonia*, like 2 Cor. 13:13: "The grace of the Lord Jesus Christ and the love of God and the fellowship of the Holy Spirit be with you all." From this and similar passages (1 Cor. 1:9; Phil. 2:1 etc.), "we can conclude that *koinonia* is a work of God which comes from God. It is descriptive of a unique relationship to God mediated through the Son and made effective by the Holy Spirit."[16]

In the beginning of his paper, he cites an extremely meaningful passage from Emil Brunner, which relates directly to the concerns of Pentecostal thinking about church:

> The Body of Christ is nothing other than a fellowship of persons. It is "the fellowship of Jesus Christ" or "fellowship of the Holy Ghost" where fellowship or koinonia signifies a common participation, a togetherness, a community life. The faithful are bound to each other through their common sharing in Christ and in the Holy Ghost, but that which they have in common is precisely no "thing," no "it," but a "he," Christ and His Holy Spirit.[17]

Interestingly enough, this passage could have been written by a Pentecostal! It betrays several emphases of Pentecostal teaching on the church: first, the "body" language, second, insistence on the fellowship-nature of the church, and third, the primacy given to the Holy Spirit.

These are the emphases that Robeck also finds in the ecclesiology of the New Testament. Two basic texts, which explicitly connect the Spirit and *koinonia*, are Philippians 2:1 and 2 Corinthians 13:13, but there is a *plethora* of others which imply the same: 1 Corinthians 1:9; Romans 11: 17; 1 John 1:3, 6–7 among others. From these passages Robeck draws the conclusion that *koinonia* is a work of God which comes from God: "It is descriptive of a unique relationship to God mediated through the Son and made effective by the Holy Spirit. It has both vertical and horizontal dimensions which may be distinguished but not separated.... *Koinonia* is not something which the church undertakes to do, it is something which God call sinners to experience."[18]

In fact, the most important thing for Pentecostals is not the doctrine *per se*, but the experience of the Trinity. Howard Ervin, in his position paper, contends that the "Pentecostal insistence upon the new birth and the baptism in the Holy Spirit takes seriously a personal *koinonia* with the Son and with the Holy Spirit." Ervin also contends that it is not without significance that the twentieth century Pentecostal renewals of the western churches have led to a renewed emphasis upon the Trinity, not simply on a speculative level, but existentially in a renewed experience of the immediacy of the vertical as well as the horizontal dimension of *koinonia*. "It may hardly be gainsaid, that the Pentecostal revivals of the present century have taken the *koinonia* of/with the Holy Spirit out of the cloistered mystical tradition of the Church, and made it the common experience of the whole people of God."[19] In sum, it can be said that there is no contention between Catholics and Pentecostals concerning the trinitarian foundation of *koinonia* in the Spirit.

Toward a Trinitarian Pneumatology and Ecclesiology

To deepen our analysis of the trinitarian basis of ecclesiology, a brief reference to an important, widely acclaimed essay by Kilian McDonnell entitled "A Trinitarian Theology of the Holy Spirit," will be made before moving to the question of *filioque*.[20] McDonnell contends that the Spirit sets the rules for speaking of God and the Trinity, and that the Trinity sets the control for a healthy pneumatology, and thus for a pneumatological ecclesiology. He is not downplaying the christological concentration of pneumatology, but what he insists is that the first location of both christology and pneumatology is the Trinity. A trinitarian orientation safeguards pneumatology from the danger of either ignoring christological orientation or becoming overly "Pentecost"-centered, although Pentecost is to ecclesiology what Easter is to christology. The Spirit as experienced in history is the point of entry into the christological and trinitarian mystery. Pneumatology, according to McDonnell, is therefore the universal horizon determining the interpretation of Christ and the Trinity. In a diagram, this hermeneutic would look like this:

Ecclesiology ← Pneumatology → Christology → Trinity[21]

The Spirit exercises mutuality through a contact function. The Father touches history and the Church through Christ in the Spirit. The Spirit is also the point of entry into a movement back to the Father. In all of this the Trinity is the control.

Filioque and the Question of Deficient Pneumatology and Ecclesiology

If Pentecostals have paid little attention to the doctrine of the Trinity, the issue of *filioque* ("and the Son") has received even less attention. Nevertheless, many of the underlying issues at stake in the historic controversy over the *filioque* question have been of great interest to Pentecostals, even though most Pentecostals have yet to realize that fact. Most Pentecostals, of course, found themselves confessing, along the Nicene Creed and other Western formulations, *filioque*, but one needs to ask seriously if it is anything other than repeating what others have said earlier.

A definitive interpretation of the doctrine of the Trinity from a Pentecostal viewpoint is subjoined to Article 2 of the Assemblies of God "Statement of Fundamental Truths." It is entitled "The Adorable Godhead," and the relevant section is (d) "Identity and Co-Operation in the Godhead."[22] It defines the Trinity in the traditional Latin way with an explicit *filioque*-clause:

> The Father, the Son and the Holy Ghost are never identical as to Person; nor confused as to relation; nor divided in respect to the Godhead; nor opposed as to cooperation. The Son is in the Father and the Father is in the Son as to relationship. The Son is with the Father and the Father is with the Son, as to fellowship. The Father is not from the Son, but the Son is from the Father, as to authority. The Holy Ghost is from the Father and the Son proceeding, as to nature, relationship, cooperation and authority. Hence neither Person in the Godhead either exists or works separately or independently of the others. John 5:17–30, 32, 37; John 8:17, 18.

With regard to the Catholic-Pentecostal dialogue, it is interesting to note that the *FR* III itself does not address the issue of *filioque* (and no other *Final Report* for that matter). However, there is an extensive discussion in both the Catholic and Pentecostal position papers. Ironically, the Pentecostal team member Howard M. Ervin devoted the most space to the discussion of this problem. He noted that most Pentecostals, not familiar with the nuances of creedal formulations, are often found to be rather inconsistent regarding the issue of *filioque*. Most Pentecostal manuals would likely endorse the Western addition that "the Holy Spirit, then, proceeds (as the creeds declare) from the Father and the Son."[23] While some Pentecostal textbooks are ambiguous about whether the proceeding of the Spirit (John 15:26) is an eternal relationship (as stated in the creeds) or a proceeding into the Church on the Day of Pentecost, others affirm that the Holy Spirit "proceeds eternally from the Father and from the Son."[24] Ervin's own stand is clear in this issue: "Whether the procession is eternal or in time, in John 15:26 the Spirit 'proceeds from the Father' alone. Biblically, and within the presuppositions of a Pentecostal theology this is decisive; the procession of the Spirit is attributed *only* to the Father, never to the Father and the Son."[25]

Ervin makes reference to Pentecostal Raymond M. Pruitt who has addressed the question of the subordination of both the Son and of the Holy Spirit. According to Ervin, Pruitt makes an unwarranted comment that "it is a subordination of functional activity, not of essence." Pruitt, though, "for convenience's sake"[26] sees it advisable to use the traditional (creedal) terms, like "eternal." While Ervin rightly sees the implications of such thinking as "disturbing" to christology and the Trinity, one must note of that Pentecostal theology operates here at a popular, non-analytic level.[27] To confuse eternal relations and temporal mission does not mean that Pentecostal theology is departing from the classical canons.

No more can we cast doubt upon the orthodoxy of Pentecostals Duffield and Van Cleave, when they state that "*koinonia* was applied to the Church as those having a common salvation through a common faith in God and in His Son Jesus Christ."[28] To see here (in the absence of a mention of the Holy Spirit) "lingering echoes of the subordinationism of the *filioque* in the Pentecostal witness to *koinonia*" is to require too much of a theology which until our decades has been mostly in oral form.[29] What it shows is that we are still lacking a coherent Pentecostal systematic theology.

But Ervin is correct when he claims that the question of subordination is not answered by characterizing it as functional rather than ontological.

According to *filioque*, the Spirit proceeds from the Father and the Son, but the Son is not begotten by the Father and the Holy Spirit. Thus the Father and the Son constitute twin principles or sources of the Godhead from which the Holy Spirit is excluded by definition. Since generation and procession are of necessity ontological, this exclusion of the Holy Spirit from the source of the Godhead argues for subordination of the Holy Spirit. Thus *filioque* is open to the charge of ditheism, Ervin concludes.

Implications of Filioque

Even if the charge of ditheism could be avoided, the insertion of *filioque*, according to Ervin, has serious effects on the notion of *koinonia* and church: "The general neglect of the Holy Spirit in the life of the churches is all too obvious. Even when their theologies are formally trinitarian, all too often, life and praxis are crypto-unitarian. It is to the credit of Pentecostals, that despite the opprobrium to which they have been subjected, they continue to bear uncompromising witness to the *koinonia* of the Holy Spirit."[30] Ervin contends that many Pentecostals would find common ground with the Orthodox theologians who argue that there are two negative consequences of the *filioque*, namely, "subordination of the Holy Spirit, [and an] overemphasis on the unity of God."[31] Surprisingly, Ervin is echoing very much the popular sentiment of the Greek Orthodox critique of *filioque*. He sums up: "The objections raised...have this in common, that the *filioque* introduces a distortion in the *koinonia* of the Trinity, and a consequent distortion in the *koinonia* of the Church."[32]

Catholic Hervé Legrand is much more moderate in his assessment of the implications of *filioque*. To him such a causal link between *filioque* and the ecclesial effects attributed to it seems doubtful. If it were the direct cause, we would be forced to claim that Protestant churches make "charism subject to the institution, interior liberty subject to imposed authority, the prophetic subject to the juridical, the mystique subject to the scholastic, the laity subject to the clergy, the universal priesthood subject to the ministerial hierarchy."[33] This Legrand is not ready to admit, although he contends that we must recognize a certain pneumatological deficiency in the Latin Church, which is seen in the weak attention to the epiclesis, the absence of a developed synodality, and the giving of a certain autonomy to the clergy. These are some of the deficiencies that Pentecostal spirituality and theology—perhaps using a less sacramental and less liturgical language—could help correct in the future.

Spirit and Filioque

Mühlen's and McDonnell's insights might help us sharpen our view of the relationship of the Spirit to the Son and the Father. Mühlen points out that it forms part of the stock of the Church's traditional understanding that the Holy Spirit emerges from the Father and the Son, or through the Son, in a single, joint act. Father and Son, then, are not two principles but rather one principle of the Holy Spirit. From all eternity the Holy Spirit emerges out of the Father and the Son, "not as the result of two breaths, but by means of a single breath."[34] The emergence of the Holy Spirit can therefore be described as the joint "we" act of Father and Son. In Mühlen's scenario the mutual relationship between the Father and the Son has a completely different structure from the mutual relationship that exists between the Father and the Son on the one hand and the Holy Spirit on the other.

> The Father is constituted as a person only by means of his relationship to the Son, while the Son is constituted as a person only by virtue of his reverse relationship to the Father. The "breathing" of the Holy Spirit, on the other hand, has its origin in the two persons who *merge into a single act*. The Holy Spirit is *one person out of and in two persons*, the divine "we" in person.[35]

McDonnell notes that, alongside the distinction of two "missions," there is in the New Testament a radical relating of the one to the other. The Father sends the Spirit in the name of the Son (John 14:26), and the Son sends the Spirit from the Father (John 15:26). The source of both is the Father. Luke also has this mutuality of the Spirit and Son (Luke 24: 49; Acts 2:22). In a different perspective Paul reaches the point where the mutuality expressed in "Lord" and "Spirit" becomes almost interchangeable (Rom. 12:5, 11; 1 Cor. 6:11; 2 Cor. 3:17, 18). If then, both missions go out from the Father, McDonnell concludes, both lead to the Father. He reminds us that building on the biblical witness (e.g., Rom. 8:15; Gal. 4:6; Eph. 2:18; 1 Cor. 15:24.), the patristic tradition developed the theology of the movement from the Father through Christ in the Spirit, and back by the same movement to the Father.[36]

Since the *filioque*-clause has not been graced with universal approval and it devalues the unity of the Church, an increasing number of Western Churches are considering suppression of the insertion.[37] The joint study conducted by the Faith and Order has suggested several alternative formulations worthy of consideration:

- the Spirit proceeds from the Father of the Son;
- the Spirit proceeds from the Father through the Son;
- the Spirit proceeds from the Father and receives from the Son;
- the Spirit proceeds from the Father and rests on the Son;
- the Spirit proceeds from the Father and shines out through the Son.[38]

It must be noted, though, that exclusion of the *filioque* from the creeds does not by itself, of course, mean taking it out of the doctrine!

Trinitarian Theology on the Way...

The discussion on the Trinity in the context of ecclesiology helps Catholics and Pentecostals to operate on the *pro nobis* level which has always been characteristic of Pentecostalism and more and more of recent Catholic theology, too. Catholics and Pentecostals agree on the necessary trinitarian basis of *koinonia*. Together they say that *koinonia* between Christians/Churches is a reflection of the divine communion. In this trinitarian context, there is a communion of the Spirit.

Pentecostal theology is still in the making. Pentecostalism represents charismatic spirituality rather than discursive theologizing about the Spirit. The dialogue over the years has helped Pentecostals to think more clearly about their theology of the Trinity and *filioque*. It is yet to be seen, *if* there is any distinctive Pentecostal contribution to these issues, and what directions it might take. *The* distinctive Pentecostal contribution could be the accent on baptism of the Holy Spirit with accompanying charismatic manifestations (speaking in tongues, prophecy, word of knowledge, etc.) which, as was stated in the beginning of the chapter, brings the doctrine of the Trinity into the *experiential* level.[39] This is more in tune with the New Testament emphasis. Yet it is safe to say that one should not necessarily posit a need for a distinctive Pentecostal trinitarian doctrine.

What one could say, however, is that Pentecostalism might be able to sharpen other traditions' perception of the role of the Spirit in the Trinity. Even if it is wise not to blame too hastily the *filioque* for alleged pneumatological deficit in Western theology, it must be admitted that it has bearing upon how the role of the Spirit is conceived. Together with Eastern Orthodox theologians, Pentecostals might be able to correct pneumatological "forgetfulness."

Chapter Eight

The Church as Charismatic Fellowship

When the Pentecostal movement began at the turn of the twentieth century, it reintroduced a dynamic, charismatic spirituality and church life. While regarding the worship services and ministry patterns of older churches as dead—rituals without life—the very mission of the new movement was to revive church life in accordance with the New Testament charismatic power and dynamic. Although at first the older churches strongly opposed the newcomer, later on they began to adopt some Pentecostal and Charismatic emphases, such as dynamic praise and emphasis on the active ministry of all believers, to name just a few of the more evident features.

Eastern Orthodox (then Anglican) priest, Michael Harper of England has suggested that the contribution of Pentecostal church life includes the important role of the Holy Spirit in giving life and power to the individual and through the individual to the Church and world; the active participation of the whole assembly of God's people in acts of worship and administrations of the sacraments; the release of the laity in ministry in the Church and world, and their active role in all parts of church life; the importance of the local church as the gathering of the people of God, and as a corporate expression of Christ's life to the world; the experience of charismatic actions of God as a kind of quasisacramentalism, actively at work in people's lives; and the restoration of experiential apostolicity to the whole Church (while the Roman Catholic Church has stressed its apostolic nature largely in historical terms of apostolic succession, etc., and Protestant Churches have attempted to retrieve the apostles' teaching to the Church, the Pentecostal contribution has been in the restoration of the apostolic signs: healing, miracles, prophecy, speaking in tongues, and so on). But Harper notes that the Pentecostals' greatest contribution may yet be assessed in terms of their ability to instill indigenous principles from the start in the Third World, which in part accounts for their remarkable growth in these areas. Whereas historic church missionary endeavors in the nineteenth century were carried out in the atmosphere of empire building and the westernizing of other cultures, Pentecostal outreach has very largely been free from such taints.[1]

In spite of these contributions to the Church, however, Pentecostals have not attempted to develop a distinctive ecclesiology, a theology of the church. They were "doers" rather than "thinkers," and instead of writing theological treatises they went on living and experimenting with the New Testament type of enthusiastic church life. This led, of course, to a variety of ecclesiological options. For this reason, Catholic Paul D. Lee, an informed analyst of Pentecostalism, raises the question whether it is reasonable to speak about a distinctive Pentecostal ecclesiology at all:

> if Pentecostalism is a movement, is it useful or valid to talk about ecclesiology at all? What does ecclesiology mean to a Pentecostal? At first, Pentecostals were so busy spreading the "good news" of the fresh outpouring of the Spirit "in the last days" that they became unconcerned about forming a denomination. The premillennial urgency of the imminent Kingdom made Pentecostals focus on their readiness, through personal conversion and regeneration, thereby rendering any ecclesiological deliberation rather irrelevant or at least secondary.[2]

This is a legitimate observation, since Pentecostals have written surprisingly little on ecclesiology, the only substantial contribution being the classic *A Theology of the Church and Its Mission: A Pentecostal Perspective*, by Melvin L. Hodges.[3] Peter Hocken, in his article "Theology of Church" in *DPCM*—interestingly enough, written by a Catholic theologian—notes that "the process of denominationalization did not...produce any distinctively Pentecostal view of the Church, except for those bodies seeking to restore the fivefold ministry of Ephesians 4: 11."[4] Understandably, Pentecostal ecclesiology is of an *ad hoc*-nature that leaves much room for improvisation. Since most Pentecostals emphasize the spiritual, thus invisible, nature of the church, much of their writing has been on ecclesiastical polity that is characterized by the restorationist desire to go back to apostolic times. Lee is correct when he says that Pentecostal ecclesiology "is not so much a thematized theology as a lived reality," therefore the answer to the question above, "will almost certainly not be met with a theologically satisfactory answer."[5] But this does not mean in any way that ecclesiology is of little importance or that it is a luxury added to personal spirituality.

The extended dialogue with the Roman Catholic Church has forced Pentecostals to reflect on the church and its life and ministry. While ecclesiological topics were occasionally discussed during the earlier phases of the talks, the Third Quinquennium (1985–1989) was devoted to the theme of the church under the general title of *Koinonia*. The lack of systematized thinking on church among Pentecostals, of course, had bearing on the dialogue with another tradition, the hallmark of which has been rigorous theological and ecclesiological reflection.

The purpose of this chapter is to offer reflections on one aspect of ecclesiology, namely the relationship between charism and institution, on the basis of the discussions in the Catholic-Pentecostal dialogue. Nothing like a comprehensive Pentecostal ecclesiology is attempted in the confines of this chapter. Rather I wish to focus on this particular issue, highlighting two crucial perspectives that guided the talks on ecclesiology during the Third Quinquennium. The first one is the emphasis on the charismatic structure of the church, and the second is emphasis on fellowship, i.e., on *koinonia*.

The Charismatic Structure of the Church

One of the perennial problems of ecclesiology has been the relationship between the Spirit/charisma and institution. Italian Catholic Luigi Sartori reminds us of the obvious fact that theological thinking on ecclesiology must take into account three separate though interrelated factors: authority, the charismatic, and the sacraments.[6] And he argues that now (the year was 1978!) the time has come to "confirm not only that charismatics have their place in the structure of a community but that there are genuine principles for building a 'charismatic structure.'"[7]

Understandably, the Catholic Church has emphasized more the role of hierarchy, ordained ministry, church authority, and sacramental apparatus, whereas Pentecostalism, as a recent revival movement, has sought for the experience of a free flow of charisms in the church. However, it would be oversimplified to leave the issue here, as a closer look at our sources reveals. Without denying this basic difference of emphasis, there is much that both parties can—and *have* to—learn from each other. In fact, both Catholics and Pentecostals are ready to go beyond the all too simplified dichotomy of "charisma *versus* institution" to a more fruitful notion of church which is *both* charismatic *and* structured.

The dialogue reveals to us that Pentecostal ecclesiology is not naive enough to downplay the role of authority/structures, nor is Catholic ecclesiology content with an overemphasis on hierarchy. Pentecostals are seeking for balance between charisma and structure whereas Catholics look for balance between structure and charisma. Both, in their respective ways, seek "charismatic structure," although with divergences that have, of course, much to do with other theological *loci*, such as sacraments and the view of the relationship between local *versus* universal church.

That there has not always been the balance in Catholicism is evident to any observer of the history of the Catholic Church, as many Catholic theologians have argued at least since the appearance of Pope Pius XII's *Mystici Corporis* (1943). Hans Küng sees two basic reasons for neglect and overlooking the importance of the charismatic structure of the church: first, a certain clericalism and legalism, and second, the fact that the ecclesiology of Catholic textbooks tended to be construed on the Pastoral epistles, ignoring for the most part the contribution of (genuine) Pauline letters, especially of 1 Corinthians. He argues that the rediscovery of the charisms is a rediscovery of specifically Pauline ecclesiology, "the importance of which for the problems of Catholicism and ecumenism cannot be overestimated."[8] Yet neither is the Pentecostal side beyond criticism. As a young revival movement, it has had hard times in seeking to find a balance between its passion for the free moving of the Spirit and the inevitable need for order and institution. Perhaps the time is ripe for an attempt to move beyond "the inevitable conflict and difficulty of reconciling ministry [institution] and charism."[9]

Michael Harper, in his position paper for the Pentecostal side entitled "The Holy Spirit acts in the Church, its structure, its sacramentality, its worship and sacraments," argued that the history of God's people in relationship to the Holy Spirit can be viewed in terms of the extent to which the Holy Spirit has been "free to operate *incarnationally* amongst them on the one hand, and the extent to which humans have attempted to *incarcerate* the Holy Spirit in some of the outward aspects of the givenness of the Church—e.g. the scriptures, sacraments, ministry, etc."[10] He mentions three major approaches. First, the Catholic emphasis on sacraments, apostolic succession, and priesthood can degenerate into imprisoning the free Spirit of God and denying his freedom to move beyond church structures. Second, the Protestant Reformation can be viewed as a reaction to this. Here the Spirit can easily be imprisoned in the doctrinal formulae. At the same time, the Reformation opened the way for sectarianism, with its accent on individualism and the freedom of individuals to decide. Finally, Pentecostalism was in part a reactionary movement against both of these, in its desire to break free from the past and to start again without institutions. But—and this is acknowledged by most observers of Pentecostalism—the movement found itself very soon to be caught up with its own institutions and regulations. Its "trap"—according to Harper—is its extreme experience orientation: "In striving to release the Spirit from institutionalism and excessive theological formulae and fundamentalistic pedagogy, Pentecostals tend to trap the Spirit in experiential criteria." And then he adds: "If to Catholics an important question is 'Whose hands were laid on whom?,' and to Protestants, 'What do you believe?,' to Pentecostals the right questions to ask are 'Are you baptized in the Spirit?' and 'Do you speak in tongues?'"[11]

Without hiding differing emphases, a broad agreement was reached as to the inevitability and necessity of church structures: "Roman Catholics are more inclined to see the Spirit operating through certain ecclesial structures, although Pentecostals, too, recognize that the Spirit may work through ecclesial structures and processes" (*FR* III.88). Along the same lines it was also "agreed by both sides of the dialogue that order and structure are necessary to the exercise of ministry" (*FR* II.80). It is ecumenically noteworthy that in other places, too, the Pentecostal side affirmed the necessity of order and institution as something not necessarily opposed to the sovereign work of the Spirit but rather as a channel for the Spirit's flow (*FR* III.105). Pentecostals admit also that sometimes there has been a tendency, among ordinary members as well as charismatic leaders, to overlook the importance of authority in the church (*FR* III.75). Pentecostals tend to downplay the importance of office and authority because they desire to have direct access to the Spirit and his workings (*FR* III.76). Catholics and Pentecostals together affirm, too, the necessity of renewal of church structures and offices, so that "the Spirit can breathe new life into the Church's offices and structures when these become 'dry bones' (Ezek 37)" (*FR* III.106). Both parties are also troubled by the discrepancy between the theology and the practice of their own parishes or congregations (*FR* III.89).

Pentecostals do not agree among themselves concerning how Church structures and institutions should be made up. The views range from congregational to episcopal, but what is important is that they accept the full ecclesial status of the churches ordered in various ways. For Pentecostals there is no single criterion to indicate the "true nature" of a given church. Their view is based on the observation that in the New Testament there appears not to be *the* structure but several structures (*FR* III.84). Consequently, Pentecostals are inclined to criticize the Catholic Church for structures too rigid and authoritative, without legitimate biblical basis, and sometimes seen by Pentecostals as an obstacle to the free work of the Spirit (*FR* III.87). On the whole, Pentecostals propose that "presbyterial and/or congregational ecclesial models express better the mutuality or reciprocity demanded by *koinonia*" (*FR* III.87). Yet there is a definite, historical reason—although probably not seen as such by contemporaries—why early Pentecostals were slow to invest a lot of energy in the structuring of the church. It has to do with eschatology. Eschatology, waiting for the Second Coming of Christ, undergirds the whole of their life and spirituality. If Jesus was coming soon for a Church that was "as a bride adorned for her husband," there was no hope for the institutionalized historic Churches. The main impetus for setting up churches and organizations was to help evangelize the world in the power of the Spirit, before the end would come.

Thus there is different agenda here. While the Catholics (and Protestants in general) tend to look back to their ecclesial foundations, Pentecostals want to forget the past, and look *forward* to their ecclesial fulfillment in the *Parousia*. This explains why Pentecostal ecclesiology, if there is any, is mostly of an ad hoc nature. However, the church structures of Pentecostalism have nevertheless grown. Sure, at the beginning there was little thought for permanence because of the enthusiastic eschatological expectation. However, as time went on there came inevitably the need to form some kind of structures to carry the work on. This was done mainly *ex tempore*. Finally—and this is noted by insiders as well as outsiders—there came the time of "establishment" with bureaucracy, organization, and authority structures like in any other religious movement.[12]

Pentecostalist Harold Hunter recognizes well the tension the Pentecostal movement itself must tackle when trying to find a balance between the principle of *spiritus ubi vult spirat* (the Spirit blows where it wills) and human-made structures: "Tensions between the institutional and the charismatic have appeared throughout canonical and ecclesiastical history. Although the Pentecostal movement is an obvious testimony to the belief in releasing charisms in the community of the faithful, in reality many gifts have been suppressed by dominating authority figures and structures."[13]

Catholics are more inclined to see the Spirit operating through certain ecclesial structures (*FR* III.88), and consider some existing ecclesiastical structures as "God given." Therefore these structures and offices belong to the very essence of church order rather than serving only its well being (*FR* III.83).

But what are the theological resources for understanding the relationship between the charisms and structures? The question must be put into wider theological-ecclesiological ramifications, to the relationship between the Spirit and Church. This line of questioning, however, cannot be properly done without an integral link to christology, since the Spirit we are talking about is the *Spirit of Christ.*

Heribert Mühlen of Paderborn, Catholic team member and one of the most prominent post-conciliar pneumatologists/ecclesiologists of the Roman Church, in his first quinquennium paper, based his view of the integral relationship between charisma and institution on the doctrine of incarnation: "the Spirit of Christ ever since the death of Jesus has become something that it was not before, that is to say, the *uncreated principle of unity in the social structure of the Church.*"[14] Consequently, the Spirit of God does not only descend suddenly and unforeseeably in a vertical line upon an individual person (as Pentecostals affirm), nor is the sovereign Spirit tied to human-made "rites" (of imposition of hands as the sign of succession, as Catholics say) without the history of the experience of the Spirit within the history of the ministry. For Paul, Mühlen notes, an opposition of charisma and ministry would be wholly impossible, for Paul considers the service of the apostle as a charisma (1 Cor. 12:28). In his Third Quinquennium paper, Mühlen noted that *Lumen Gentium* emphasizes that the gifts of the Spirit are among the basic elements of ecclesiastical life, and that, consequently, charisms are "constitutive, fundamental Spirit actions in the church" with the word and sacraments. All these fundamental elements have their origin in one and the same Spirit, and therefore stand in an organic relationship with each other and constitute an "inseparable whole."[15]

Another Catholic team member, John Mahoney, S.J., echoes Mühlen's thoughts. For him, too, discrepancy between office and charisma is untenable in that it "presumes and ignores the intimate connection between pneumatology and ecclesiology." On the one hand, the Spirit is not "an anarchic, wild, interior power," but rather the Spirit of order, and on the other hand, the church structures in themselves are meaningless without the work of the Spirit that makes the Church. Just as every manifestation of the Spirit is for the benefit and upbuilding of the Church, so also the Church itself exists primarily as the instrument of the Holy Spirit.[16]

Koinonia: The Church as Charismatic Fellowship

Pentecostals Peter Kuzmic and Miroslav Volf of former Yugoslavia developed the idea of the charismatic structure of the church along the lines of fellowship-language. Fellowship, a synonym for *koinonia*, is the key to right structuring of the church. Before explicating Volf and Kuzmic's ideas, a short note about the importance of *koinonia*-theology is in order.

Pentecostals have always favored "fellowship-language" for the church. Decades before the ecumenical theology began to hark back to biblical and patristic roots to revive the ancient theological understanding of Christian community as *koinonia*, Pentecostals emphasized fellowship among Spirit-filled sisters and brothers. Pentecostal spirituality and theology has almost from the start appreciated fellowship-language over "institutionalized church" (as hierarchical structure). This is evidenced also in the fact that even nowadays several Pentecostal and Charismatic communities prefer to call themselves by the name "fellowship" rather than "church." In some European languages, e.g. German, the term *Gemeinschaft* catches the meaning. In my home country of Finland, Pentecostal "churches" seldom, if ever, call themselves by the name "church" (*kirkko*), because it carries for them institutionalized connotations; instead they prefer the term *seurakunta*, which can be translated as "church" in English, but which has nothing of the meaning of institution. In (former) Yugoslavia, Pentecostals most frequently use the expression "going in fellowship" referring to church attendance.[17] Clearly, "Pentecostal soteriology and pneumatology point...unmistakably in the direction of an *ecclesiology of the fellowship of persons*."[18]

One reason why *koinonia*/fellowship-language is such a viable option for Pentecostals is its strong biblical attestation. The communion language can be traced to the early church in Acts 2. Kilian McDonnell, the Catholic co-chair of the dialogue, writes: "So, if one is true to the dynamics of Acts, one would add immediately after the imparting of the Spirit, *koinonia*/communion, i.e., community formation together with its Eucharistic expression. The language of Luke is communion language."[19] In its basic meaning, the term "*koinonia*/communion" denotes "a sharing in one reality held in common."[20] Synonyms for *koinonia* are sharing, participation, community, communion.

The Church is a communion in the Spirit, with also a specific christological expression (2 Cor. 1:5; Phil 3:10), even trinitarian. The basic communion themes, especially the Eucharistic one, constituted the ecclesiological supposition "for most, if not all, of the earliest councils," and remained a force as an ecclesiological model for about the first thousand years.[21] The patristic theology of *communio* arises from the biblical witness. Communion language, far from being just an ancient perspective of the past, has shown its relevance in modern church life, and in the modern world. Today we use other terms, "fellowship" and the like, but they convey the same basic meaning. In fact, it can be claimed that communion is not just another notion of ecclesiology but belongs to the *ontology* of human being, and thus we should rather speak of an actual "ontology of communion." This is the basic thrust of the highly influential work, *Being as Communion*, by Greek Orthodox Metropolitan John Zizioulas. He has argued that ecclesial being is bound to the very being of God as communion: "From the fact that a human being is a member of the Church, he becomes an 'image of God,' he exists as God Himself exists, he takes on God's 'way of being.' This way of being...is a way of *relationship* with the world, with other people and with God, an event of *communion*, and that is why it cannot be realized as the achievement of an *individual*, but only as an *ecclesial* fact."[22]

Against this background, Kuzmic and Volf's attempt to develop a Pentecostal view of the church as charismatic fellowship, a pneumatologically constituted reality, can be better appreciated. This is what they see emphasized in the New Testament picture of the church: "[f]ellowship was *a common experience of baptism into the body of Christ through the Spirit* (cf. 1 Cor. 12.13)." This fellowship is something to be experienced, a shared experience, in the everyday life of the community. In this sense the question "Where is the Church?" cannot be answered without reference to the living presence of the Spirit.[23] They have a citation from Lesslie Newbigin which compares Protestant, Roman Catholic and Pentecostal understandings of the church:

> The apostles asked the converts of Apollos one question: "Did you receive the Holy Spirit when you believed?" and got a plain answer. His modern successors are more inclined to ask either "Did you believe exactly what we teach?" or "Were the hands that were laid on you our hands?" and, if the answer is satisfactory, to assure the converts that they had received the Holy Spirit even if they didn't know it. There is a world of difference between the two attitudes.[24]

According to Kuzmic and Volf, then, there are three basic models: first, the traditional Protestant "lecture room" setting where the focus is pulpit and preaching; second, the Catholic church as a "theater setting" where the emphasis falls on the dramatic elements in the worship; third, the Pentecostal "fellowship," where the emphasis is on the community gathered together for mutual edification. Without wanting to exclude the elements of preaching and sacraments, they suggest that in the New Testament the fundamental characteristic of worship is mutual sharing in fellowship. God communicates himself to Christians through more than just written or proclaimed word or ritual cultic activity, "He does so more by the Spirit *through one another*."[25] Quoting Lesslie Newbigin again, they say "that a real congregational life, wherein each member has his opportunity to contribute to the life of the whole body through gifts which the Spirit endows him, is as much part of the *esse* of the church as are ministry and sacraments."[26] The dynamic of the fellowship is concretely lived out through the charismata. "As fellowship should be the unalienable modus of the Church's existence, so the charismata should be a permanent feature of its life."[27]

If every member of the community is provided with the charisms and they depend on each other in their exercise of them, then the hierarchical structures and the question of obedience to the authority should be re-evaluated. Kuzmic and Volf argue that "In the context of the Pauline understanding of fellowship, the term 'hierarchical communio' is a contradiction in adjecto, since this term, communio, can mean nothing else but one-sided 'dependence and obedience,' whereas in the Pauline usage the mutuality belongs to its very heart." But the emphasis on the charismatically structured church does not mean stressing charismata at the expense of structure and institutions. "This would be," the authors note, "both sociologically and historically naive."[28] They say that history teaches us the lesson that the movements which broke through the calcified church structures soon developed their own structures and institutions. The conclusion of Kuzmic and Volf is worth quoting in full:

> It is clear: no social body can permanently exist without structures. The Church is no exception. In the case of the Church, however, it is of fundamental importance that the structures it develops be compatible with the freedom and sovereignty of the Spirit in her own ranks. The NT ecclesiology suggest that *pneumatocracy* cannot be realized through the juridically structured *hierarchy*. Though it may seem paradoxical, if the Church is truly to be ruled *from above*, its structures must arise *from below*. The reason is simple: since

> all members have the Spirit no one of them can monopolize his leading. Since the Spirit's leading is a privilege of all members, the structures of a charismatic fellowship have to arise through the interaction of all its members. Sociologically speaking, they have to be formed according to the laws of group formation. This means that special care has to be given to see that the structures arising *from below* continually remain an outgrowth of the concrete life of the community. Otherwise they develop a tendency to become independent and hinder the life instead of helping it.[29]

This notion of "charismatic structure," which explicitly echoes the earlier call of the Catholic Hans Küng for "the continuing charismatic structure," attempts to move beyond the dilemma of equating the "structured" with "calcified" and the "charismatic" with the "liquefied."[30] In this scenario of Kuzmic and Volf, three characteristics of the church are always present: fellowship, charismatic fellowship, charismatically structured fellowship. And they add one more, which is eschatological. As such the church has four basic tasks: first, the fellowship of mutual edification, second, fellowship of service to each other and to the world, third, fellowship of witness, and fourth, fellowship of worship.

Towards a Participatory Ecclesiology: Promise and Challenge

There are, therefore, three main principles in the Pauline teaching on charisms and charismatic fellowship which Kuzmic and Volf want to underline. First, in the New Testament gifts are universally distributed among the members of the fellowship: "To each is given the manifestation of the Spirit for the common good" (1 Cor. 12:7; cf. Rom. 12:3; Eph. 4:7; 1 Pet. 4:10). There are no functionless members of the body of Christ. "To be a member means to exercise a particular ministry for which one is called and equipped by the Spirit."[31] Consequently, one of the "marks" of the true church is that the life of the community is participatory: each member taking part in it. A characteristic of charismata closely related to universal distribution is their polyformity: there is, in principle, a limitless variety of gifts (1 Pet. 4:10). Pentecostals would certainly welcome the *Baptism, Eucharist and Ministry* (*BEM*) document's principle according to which the church lives "in the power of the Spirit...characterized by a variety of charisms."[32]

Second, there is the Pauline principle of "one-anotherness": the various charismata do not belong to just one individual. Though some have more gifts than others do, the New Testament knows nothing of a universally talented personality in no need of others. "The Church is not a club of self-sufficient charismatics; it is a fellowship of charismatics. The members of the fellowship have different gifts: 'Having gifts that *differ* according to the grace given to us...' (Rom. 12:6)."[33] The complementarity of gifts establishes interdependence among those who exercise them. The Church is thus a fellowship of mutual "giving and receiving" (Phil. 4:15).

This is also what Catholic Hervé Legrand underlines in his paper: "The diversity of gifts of the Holy Spirit in the local Church implies the inter-relationship among charisms, services and ministries."[34] This principle implies the unity-in-diversity-perspective, also expressed in other ways, namely "diversity in unity." Each Christian receives from the Spirit his or her peculiar gifts to contribute to the rich unity of the community. This is the "law of the true humane society," to paraphrase Moltmann.[35] It is made possible through love that is the leading principle of the charisms. The context of charisms in the New Testament is always that of community, *koinonia*: "...one should rather speak of the 'community of the Holy Spirit' in which the gifted ones who are so diverse come together: there are many gifts—but there is only one Spirit. And this unity of the Spirit is the community between the believers who have been called and gifted in diverse ways."[36] To follow this principle is not always easy; it sometimes involves what Rahner called "the burden of a charisma": to be faithful to one's own calling, while at the same time to endure opposition from the rest of the body and appreciate persons with other kinds of gifts.[37]

Third, the gifts are distributed "just as the Spirit wills" (1 Cor. 12:17), as already noted above. In the same way in which the Spirit is sovereign in imparting saving faith to a non-believer, he is also free and sovereign in distributing *charismata* in the fellowship. There is, however, a difference in the way in which the Spirit imparts saving faith and gives *charismata*: in the first case we do not know where the Spirit will move, in the second we do know he is moving in all the people of God for he gives his gifts to every member. But "how and when" we do not know, all we can do is to pray and seek the "best gifts."

Miroslav Volf has in his more recent writings developed the idea of a "participatory ecclesiology."[38] Volf is of the opinion that the real ecclesiological challenge of the Pentecostal movement for other churches lies in motivating them to take seriously the implications of the priesthood of all. Other churches, Volf claims, must discover anew theologically and learn to live out anew today what they have already known and in part lived out from the beginning: the active priesthood of all believers, a priesthood which they originally understood not only soteriologically but also ecclesiologically. The Churches have to acknowledge the fact that in accordance with their being called and endowed by the Spirit of God, all members of a church depict and offer the manifold grace of God through their actions and words (1 Pet. 4:10–11). The church comes into being and comes to life through the communication of salvation by mutual service with the pluriform gifts of the Spirit. This leads, not to underestimating the outstanding importance of those who are "in office," he reminds us, but to the conviction that the whole life of the church is not ordered around official ministers.

All members of the church create the "plausibility structures" in which the communication of faith and life in faith first become possible. "Thus the Spirit does not constitute the church exclusively through those who bear office, but through all members, who serve the others with their gifts."[39] Many churches have criticized the overemphasis of the *BEM* document on the representation of Christ by the ordained ministry (alone). Not until a proper theology of the laity is developed is there any hope for overcoming the perennial problem of bipolarity of person in office *versus* community. When laity are seen as the medium through which the church is constituted by the Spirit of God, then spiritual activity and receptiveness are no longer divided into two groups of persons, but represent two basic activities of each individual: each individual acts in the person of Christ and each is a recipient of this action. Obviously, Volf's participatory ecclesiology is hard to reconcile fully with the teaching of *Lumen Gentium* §10 which, as we saw above, with all its emphasis on the role of the laity, still holds that the "common priesthood" and "hierarchical priesthood" do differ not only in degree but also "essentially."

To transcend this apparent weakness of most churches, which often leads to a paralysis of ministry of all believers, older churches need to have another look at Pentecostals and develop out of their respective traditions a viable view of the church as charismatic *koinonia*. But Pentecostals are too left with challenges. Along with the (necessary) institutionalization and (not always so necessary?) bureaucratization of the movement, one must ask: how well is the idea of church as charismatic fellowship, where all the Spirit-empowered members are functioning to the well-being of the community and to the mission to the world, realized in typical Pentecostal communities? If not, then what are possible reasons for this? Are the reasons theological or pastoral, or both?

The Catholic-Pentecostal dialogue has both challenged and enriched Pentecostal reflection on the church. Whatever will be the future of the emerging Pentecostal ecclesiology, one thing must not be forgotten: the category of community/communion has been critical since the beginning of the Pentecostal movement. In the Two-Thirds world it still is. The community provides the adherents a safe haven against cultural, religious, and sometimes even political oppressions and anomalies. For Pentecostals, charismatic and fellowship belong to the essence, not just to the well being and benefit, of the faith and spirituality.

Chapter Nine

Spirit, Laity, Ministry

The widely acclaimed ecumenical document *Baptism, Eucharist and Ministry* begins the third section, that of "Ministry," with the subtitle, "The Calling of the Whole People of God." It states in a programmatic way:

> The Holy Spirit unites in a single body those who follow Jesus Christ and sends them as witnesses into the world.
>
> The Church lives through the liberating and renewing power of the Holy Spirit...The Spirit calls people to faith, sanctifies them through many gifts, gives them strength to witness to the Gospel, and empowers them to serve in hope and love.
>
> The Holy Spirit bestows on the community diverse and complementary gifts. These are for the common good of the whole people and are manifested in acts of service within the community and to the world.[1]

Notwithstanding the wide ecumenical consensus about the crucial role of the whole people of God in fulfilling the church's task in the world, the actual church life reveals another picture. In most churches, whether Catholic or Protestant, the ministerial duties are exercised by the paid clergy, while the role of the laity is saying "Amen" to priestly rites (Orthodox), reading a few passages in the liturgy (Catholic), or performing some diaconal or witnessing activities (Protestant). Every theological tradition nowadays agrees about the importance of the non-ordained but nothing much seems to change either in praxis or even in theology.

What are the theological resources, and, conversely, hindrances, to the rehabilitation of the whole people of God in the church's ministry? Are there major differences between Catholics (both Eastern and

Western branches) and Protestants? What is the contribution of the currently fastest growing segment of the Church, namely the Free Churches (mainly in the Protestant sphere) and Charismatic Churches (also among Catholics)? What is the role of the Holy Spirit in all of this? Can anything constructive be said at this point of ecumenical developments?

In this chapter, I shall proceed in the following way. First, I will summarize and evaluate critically the contribution of the Protestant insistence on the priesthood of all believers and connect it to present concerns. Second, I shall give a critical assessment of the resources of Roman Catholic theology, especially of *Lumen Gentium*, and put forward my view of its theological significance to our topic. Third, I shall look briefly at how the Free Churches understand ministry and especially the role of the laity. Fourth, as a way of establishing my view of the church, I shall argue (in part from a reading of the New Testament) for a charismatic structure of the church as opposed to one depending upon hierarchical notions. Only a charismatic structure seems to offer a theologically legitimate and sociologically satisfying precedence for an egalitarian model of the church where all persons, regardless of their status (ordained and non-ordained) and gender, are given an opportunity to serve through their manifold gifts. I write as a Protestant theologian, but my arguments are not intentionally Protestant as opposed to Catholic, but rather conciliar and ecumenical.

The Significance of the Protestant "Priesthood of All Believers"

The Reformation doctrine of the priesthood of all believers which built on the theology of the early church and the Middle Ages, about the sharing of all the baptized in the priestly and kingly office of Jesus Christ, appealed especially to 1 Pet. 2:9. According to Martin Luther, sharing in Jesus Christ on the basis of baptism includes also sharing in his priesthood (*WA* 7.56–57).[2] Luther maintains that the church as the "communion of saints," in accordance with the Apostles' Creed, is "called together by the Holy Spirit" (*WA* 7.219; 30.190, 294). His entire understanding of the church as the community of saints can be described by the priesthood as the law of the church's life. When Christ bears our burdens and intercedes for us with his righteousness, he does the work of a priest; mutual bearing of burdens and substitution in the church are also priestly activities. The inner life of the church is the priesthood of Christians for each other. The priesthood of Christians flows from the priesthood of Christ (*WA* 6.407, 564; 10.309; 17.6).

Sharing in Christ's priesthood gives the believer the right to come before God in prayer and teaching for others (*WA* 7.25–26). The priesthood of all believers means for Luther primarily the right of preaching the Word and administration of absolution and discipline (*WA* 7.57; 11.412). The right to preach does not contradict the limitation of public preaching to those who have been called through the community (*WA* 6.408; 11.412). The whole church is also authorized to proclaim the forgiveness of sins (*WA* 2.722), the task which is in fact the community's glory (*WA* 2.273).[3]

According to Paul Althaus, Luther follows two lines of argumentation concerning the foundation of the office: one "from below" and one "from above."[4] On the one hand, all Christians are called to minister in word and sacrament. But in order to avoid confusion, the community entrusts the public service to ordained people, who carry out this duty in the name of the Church (*WA* 12.189; 50.633). In this case, the difference between the one who occupies the office and the other members of the community lies purely on the level of service (see 6.657).

On the other hand, the fullness of the authority of the office is grounded in its institution by Christ, i.e., the office derives directly from its institution by Christ without reference to the universal priesthood (*WA* 50.647). It must be noted, though, that not even the latter nullifies the general priesthood of all believers. The contradiction of these two forms of ministry is solved by deriving the special (ordained) office from the universal. Luther distinguished the exercise of the priestly office "between brother and brother," and in case of necessity from the public exercise of the office in the administration of the ministry of the word for the entire congregation (*WA* 12.189).[5] The special office is necessary for the sake of order (1 Cor. 14:40). "Thus the only distinction between the ecclesiastical office of the ministry and the universal priesthood is the public character of the official ministry of the word and sacrament to the entire community."[6] It is easy to see what Luther's main targets are here: the Catholic idea of a special "priesthood" of ordained persons, and the special status of the clergy by virtue of ordination. Luther denies both of these.

The lasting contributions of the Protestant principle of the priesthood of all believers are obvious. First, it rehabilitates the New Testament usage of the term "priest" as referring, not to individual ordained persons (as in the older Catholic understanding), but to the whole people of God as they fulfill the Christ-given mandate.[7] Second, it abolishes the difference between ordained and non-ordained in the sense of these two groups differing from each other ontologically (even if the difference of ministerial status still remains). Third, the Protestant view sought to legitimize the use of ordained ministry in a way that should not—at least in principle—lessen the importance of the rest of the people of God. In other words, the task of the ordained in the church was to help do what the rest of the church members were doing.

There were also weaknesses, some of which were related to the historical and sociological context of the times. First of all, Luther's approach is more polemical than theological. His argumentation fails to see the relationship between the ministry of the church and the theology of the church itself. It has to do, of course, with the lack of a specific ecclesiology of much of the early Reformation theology. Luther, however, was on the right track in viewing the church as a communion of saints. Unfortunately, he did not develop the idea in relation to ministry. Related to this is the lack of the role of the Spirit in the theology of ministry. With regard to pneumatological resources, Luther's view of the church as gathered in the Holy Spirit, has a lot of potential, but he failed to draw implications. Second, perhaps mainly due to historical reasons, Luther's view of the church still manifested hierarchical notions even if his theology did not necessarily lead to a hierarchical view. At least on a practical, pastoral level, the medieval opposition between the ordained and the laity characterized church life whereas in the churches of the Radical Reformation in similar socio-historical circumstances, this was not the case. Anyhow, the Protestant theology of the priesthood of all believers had a dramatic influence on Vatican II's view of the church.

The Potential and Problematic of Vatican II

In recent decades, after Vatican II especially, there has been a renewed concern in the Roman Catholic Church for the development of the ministry of all believers.[8] Arising from an emerging pneumatological emphasis, Vatican II documents, viewing the church as the temple of the Holy Spirit, came to appreciate the role of all people of God in building up the Church and the advancement of the mission (see *LG* 4 and 12 *LG*). *Apostolicam actuositatem* §2 explicitly drew attention to the "unity in mission" between the hierarchy and laity despite the difference in ministry. This call is based on the teaching of *Lumen Gentium* on the priesthood of all believers and the sharing of all members of the Church in the prophetic (*LG* 12, 31, 35), priestly (*LG* 10, 11, 34), and kingly (*LG* 13, 31, 36) office of Christ on the basis of the baptism, confirmation, and faith (*LG*

10, 12, 30–38; *AA* 2). Vatican II also rightly paid attention to the role of charismatic gifts in enabling the laity to participate in various ministries (*LG* 12; *AA* 3; *Presbyterorium Ordinis* 9).[9]

The main features of the Council's teaching on the role of the laity can be summarized along these lines. All the baptized "share a true equality regarding the dignity and to the activity common to all the faithful for the building up of the Body of Christ" (*LG* 32). All share "in the mission of the whole Christian people with respect to the Church and to the world" (*LG* 31) and "have an active part to play in the life and activity of the Church" (*AA* 10). The laypeople are now "brothers" to their pastors (*LG* 32), and all without exception are called upon by the Lord "to expend all their energy for the growth of the Church and its continuous sanctification" (*LG* 33; cf. *AA*, 2). All the people of God are "commissioned to that apostolate by the Lord Himself" (*LG* 33), and "upon all the laity... rests the noble duty of working to extend the divine plan of salvation ever increasingly to all men of each epoch and in every land" (*LG* 33). All the baptized are "made sharers in the priestly, prophetic, and kingly function of Christ" (*LG* 31; *cf. AA*, 2). The Lord "made them His witnesses and gave them understanding of the faith and the grace of speech" (*LG* 35).[10]

However, *Lumen Gentium* is ambiguous in affirming the role of the laity and at the same time insisting on "essential" difference (rather than difference of "degree" only) between the laity and priests. Vatican II held that the person who occupies the office of priesthood through ordination has a particular power which other baptized Christians do not have, even if someone who holds office in the church is not a Christian in some higher degree.[11] Vatican II continued to use "priesthood" for the office, and by calling it "hierarchical" differentiated this priesthood from that of the entire baptized (see *LG* 12). In my judgment, this is the decisive issue in recent Roman Catholic theology of ministry. It is noteworthy that even among Catholic specialists there have been differing, even contradictory, assessments of the role of the laity in the Council documents.[12]

I have to disagree with Pannenberg's recent appraisal of the matter. He argues: "No matter what term we prefer, the decisive point here is that in principle there is no difference any more between the Roman Catholic and the Reformation view of church office or ministry and the priesthood of all believers."[13] According to Pannenberg, Vatican II's distinction between two kinds of church's ministry corresponds to the Reformation emphasis on the public character of the preaching ministry. Pannenberg's evaluation can be questioned. It is true, as he notes several times, that a decisive change has taken place when Vatican II changed the older view according to which there is an ontological difference between the ordained and the rest of the Church. This change is to be commended. But I do not think that is the major issue in relation to ministry of all believers (whereas it has important soteriological implications). The "essential" distinction seems to be the main issue. It supports the view of the church as a hierarchical, non-egalitarian society. It hinders the majority of the church from taking an active, constitutive role in the life of the church.[14]

However, Christian Duquoc, in his creative work *Provisional Churches: An Essay in Ecumenical Ecclesiology*, underscores the hierarchical nature of ecclesial mediation that is entailed in the requirement that the sacred meal be presided over by an ordained priest, within the context of episcopacy. Duquoc thus contrasts the Protestant and Catholic approaches to Eucharist, regarding the former one as brotherly and sisterly reality of a shared meal and thus something mutual. According to him, in Roman Catholic ecclesiology "authority based on the sacrament favors an indisputable hierarchy and this then appropriates to itself the Word of God of which it should be the servant."[15] If this "provisional" and "ecumenical" ecclesiology in any way is characteristic of post-conciliar view, there are still major challenges for the newer Catholic theology of ministry.

After a brief look at the Free Church view of ministry, I will next discuss the main precedent for the fulfillment of the priesthood of all believers, the principle that is nowadays supported by all churches, namely the charismatic structure of the church. I shall argue both on biblical and theological grounds for the necessity of the charismatic structure of the church. After that I shall come back to *Lumen Gentium* (esp. §10) and related issues that need correction as we attempt to develop a theologically sustainable view of the laity.

Ministry in the Free Churches

The Free Churches have in general continued the tradition of Radical Reformation in their critique of overly inelastic church structures and the limitation of ministry to the ordained clergy. They wanted to put in practice the idea of the priesthood of all believers.[16] Most Free Churches have ordained ministries but there are basically two differences from older churches. Few if any Free Churches understand ordination in sacramental terms as both Catholic Churches do. For most of them, ordination is just a public confirmation of divine call already active in one's life.

The emphasis of the Free Church view of ministry lies in the appeal to the priesthood of all believers, "which connotes access to God and a participation in ministry on the part of all believers."[17] The view of the Disciples of Christ is representative here. According to Harry Clyde Munro,

> Through Jesus Christ...every believer has direct and immediate access to God. He needs no human professional mediator. Or if one does lose touch with God and seems unable to re-establish this personal relationship, a brother Christian may help him find the way back....Unlike the professional priest who remains permanently as the necessary mediator between the believer and God, the pastor or lay brother who serves in this priestly way steps aside as soon as the relationship has been established and the person so helped can become his own priest.[18]

James D. G. Dunn notes that Pentecostal and Charismatic churches have been successful in giving expression to the wider experience and expression of charismatic ministry in their churches.[19] According to David E. Edwards, Pentecostals argue that to restrict priesthood to clergy would appear to be an endeavor either to recognize the institutionalization or else to institutionalize the presence of Jesus. Furthermore, from the Pentecostal perspective the dynamic and vitality of the Holy Spirit needs no institutionalization and institutionalization would, and does, in fact, mitigate against such dynamic and vital recognition.[20] All Pentecostals would certainly affirm Edwards's insistence on the necessity of the principle of priesthood of all, but not all would see it necessarily in such anti-institutional terms. Even with this qualification, it must be admitted that Edwards's view represents many crucial sentiments of the Pentecostal and thus more generally the Free Church view of ministry.

It is perhaps true that whereas the older Churches (especially Catholic Churches) have typically, perhaps one-sidedly, based their understanding of the ministry, office, and authority on the Pastoral Epistles, the Free Churches have opted for the Corinthian model where the charismatically empowered priesthood of all believers is more in focus. Free Churches have not hitherto offered any kind of viable theological foundation for ministry, but they have in practice fulfilled much of what the Protestant principle of the priesthood of all believers means. Not only have the members of the church in general had the opportunity to participate in all kinds of service in the church, but so too have women and those with little or no education at all. The dramatic growth of the Free Churches, especially in the Two-Thirds World, but also in the West, will anyhow pose a major challenge to the established Churches. The sheer growth in numbers makes it impossible for older churches to continue to neglect the Free Churches' contribution.

Charismatic Structure and the Priesthood of All Believers

The church lives through the participation of its members, the laity and the ordained, and is constituted through them by the Holy Spirit. This is the ecumenical consensus. What is disputed is *how* this occurs. A good case can be made for the charismatic structure of the church on the basis of the New Testament data (especially the Pauline view).

According to James D. G. Dunn, one of the most striking features of Paul's understanding of the body of Christ is that each passage in the Pauline letters in which the concept is expounded at some length envisages it as a charismatic community. Dunn summarizes Paul's view (especially in 1 Cor. 12 through 14 but also elsewhere, e.g., Rom. 12) of the integral relationship between charisms and community in these terms. First, there is interdependence and mutuality of church members since all are dependent on the charisms given by God. Second, there is diversity of charisms: each has received according to the manifold grace of God. Third, the number of charisms is not fixed. Fourth, Paul emphasizes that every member of the body should conceive of himself/herself as an active member (1 Cor. 12:7,11). Ministry should not and could not by definition of the "body" be limited to a few.[21] Dunn asks the question whether Paul's vision is unrealistic? His answer is: "...Paul was no mere dreamer of dreams or promoter of merely idealistic blueprints. He was well aware of how far the churches to which he was writing were falling short of his vision."[22] If that can be said of the churches of that time, how much more of our churches?

Dunn further argues that in Paul's exposition of the charismatic body of Christ the more established ministries of apostle, prophet, and teacher are "in a surprisingly marginal" role (they are mentioned only at the end of 1 Cor. 12).[23] Even if one might want to take argument with this interpretation—which does not consider appropriately the crucial role of prophecy, for example, in 1 Cor. 14—there is no denying the overall vision of Paul of the church as a functioning body where all the members are equipped by the Spirit of God with their own distinctive gifts to ministry and service.

Miroslav Volf, in a critical interaction between Roman Catholic, Orthodox, and Free Church ecclesiologies, has outlined a trinitarian ecclesiology where implications of the New Testament's emphasis on the charismatic foundation and structure of the church have been brought to bear on the view of ministry.[24] According to Volf, the question "Where is the Church?" cannot be answered without reference to the living presence of the Spirit. The basic idea of the charismatic structure of the church can be summarized in five principles. First, the thesis that the church is constituted by way of the entire called and charismatically endowed people of God presupposes that the exalted Christ himself is acting in the gifts of the Spirit. The second identifying feature of the charismata is their universal distribution (1 Cor. 12:7; Rom. 12:3; Eph. 4:7; 1 Pet. 4:10). In the community as the body of Christ, there are no members without charisma. Thus the division into those who serve and those who are served is ecclesiologically unacceptable. Universal distribution implies common responsibility for the life of the church as well as mutual subordination. The third characteristic feature for the charismata is their fundamental interdependence (Rom. 12:6; cf. 1 Cor. 12:7–11). Consequently, the life of the church members must be characterized by mutuality. Fourthly, the sovereign Spirit of God allots the charismata "as the Spirit chooses" (1 Cor. 12:11): "...the Spirit works *when* the Spirit chooses; the church cannot determine at which time the Spirit is to bestow its gifts."[25] Finally, Volf argues for the synchronic and diachronic plurality of charismata. Charismata can vary from time to time and from person to person.

Volf emphasizes that his interpretation is not something new in theology or church life. "This model involves...only *reinterpretation* of what is already actually happening in churches."[26] He argues that the model according to which the Spirit constitutes the church through officeholders (Catholic and Orthodox) obscures the ecclesiologically highly significant fact that in all churches, faith is mediated and kept alive by ordinary people.[27] He further notes that the ecclesiological obscuring of the role of the laity in constituting the church is one of the most important theological factors contributing to lay passivity, resulting in the model of "church in passivity."[28]

All churches generally affirm what has been said up to this point about the charismatic structure of the church. There is no doubt that one way the church is described in the Vatican II documents (e.g., *LG* 12 and 30; *Presbyterorium Ordinis* 9) is as a community of charisms (even if the charisms are distinguished between charismatic gifts and hierarchical gifts, as noted above). From the reception of these various charisms, "there arises for each of the faithful the right and duty of exercising them in the church and in the world for the good of human beings and the development of the church." And then, a very significant qualifier is added in *Apostolicam Actuositatem* §3: charisms are to be exercised "in the freedom of the Holy Spirit who 'breathes where he wills.'"

It is ecumenically significant that some recent Roman Catholic ecclesiologists have adopted the ancient Orthodox (mainly Russian Orthodox) concept of *sobornicity*. According to the principle of *sobornicity*, the church is supposed to function as a harmonious symphony of believers who have been gathered in Christ and upon whom the Holy Spirit rests. In virtue of this, there is an organic and even ontological connection between the ordained and the people of God.[29]

So, it seems that there is not much dispute about the basic New Testament idea of the pneumatological constitution of the church and its charismatic structure.[30] The insistence on the universal distribution of charismata which makes all the members of the church equal, is the "law of the true humane society," to paraphrase Jürgen Moltmann.[31] Moltmann's insistence on the charismatic structure of the church is the starting point for his theological presentation of ministry as is clearly visible in his *The Church in the Power of the Spirit.* He criticizes heavily the monarchical grounding of ministry that he ascribes to Ignatius of Antioch.[32]

Yet, even if all the churches embrace the overall idea of the charismatic structure of the church, its implications regarding the equality of all members are not accepted by all. What is disputed in this idea of a charismatically structured church is what it means for the theology and practice of ministry, specifically the public ministries of the Church. Pannenberg, quite consistently, argues that the main task of the public ministry is to secure the unity of the church. This is also attested in *Baptism, Eucharist and Ministry* (I.8).

Reevaluating the Theology of the Laity

It is important to listen carefully to Volf's call for the rehabilitation of the laity since all the members together form "plausibility structures."[33] All churches should rediscover theologically and learn to live out anew today what they have already known and in part lived out from the beginning: the active priesthood of all believers. The Churches have to come to acknowledge the fact that in accordance with their being called and endowed by the Spirit of God, all members of the church depict and offer the manifold grace of God through their actions and words (1 Pet. 4:10–11). This leads not to underestimating the outstanding importance of those who are in office, but to the conviction that the whole life of the church is not ordered around official ministers.

If we want to overcome what Bernard Cooke refers to as the "distancing of God" from the laity in the congregational life and Jaroslav Pelikan calls the "aristocracy of the Spirit," we need to reconsider the role of the Word and sacrament vis-à-vis the charismata in ministry.[34] In the history of the ministry, the work of the Spirit has been viewed as largely confined to the functions of the Word and sacrament. The difficulty here is that the Word and sacrament have been understood as functions of the ordained clergy. Free Church theologian Frank Macchia calls "an important part of the struggle for the Spirit" the attempt to construe a theology of the Word and sacrament in a way that includes an active role for the wider laity. Macchia continues:

> Theologies of Word and sacrament in the past have tended to neglect the diversely gifted ministry of the laity or to reduce the laity to a passive role. Part of the struggle for the diversity of *charismata* in the church will involve the effort to understand the Spirit's work beyond the confines of Word and sacrament, especially as mediated exclusively through clergy. The struggle for the Spirit in the Church involves the effort to view all the people of God as participants in God's gracious self-giving within and through the varied gifts and the communion of saints.[35]

Of course, this correction is not meant to downplay the role of the Word and sacrament in Christian worship but rather to create a greater awareness of the charismata as vital contacts in which God's gracious presence is imparted and experienced by and among all the people of God. This will prevent the sacraments from contributing to an institutionalization of the Spirit. The lively tradition of many Free Churches has helped us see the critical significance of the charismatic gifts as means of opening the sacraments up as wellsprings of a communal life that involve all the people of God as active participants. Clark Pinnock expresses this succinctly when he states: "As well as receiving the sacraments for the Spirit, we need to cultivate openness to the gifts of the Spirit. The Spirit is present beyond liturgy in a wider circle. There is a flowing that manifests itself as power to bear witness, heal the sick, prophesy, praise God enthusiastically, perform miracles and more."[36]

Rightly, many churches have criticized the overemphasis in the *Baptism, Eucharist and Ministry* document on the representation of Christ by the ordained ministry more than by the laity. A corrective to this is the view that all members of the Church, including the clergy, are meant to serve one another in the person of Christ. Not until a proper theology of the laity is developed is there any hope for overcoming the perennial problem of bipolarity of person in office *versus* community. When the laity are seen as the medium through which the church is constituted by the Spirit of God, then spiritual activity and receptiveness are no longer divided into two groups of persons, but represent two basic activities of each individual: each individual acts in the person of Christ and each is a recipient of this action.

The Catholic Church's increasing attention to the lay apostolate, while commendable in principle since it attempts to encourage non-ordained members to find viable avenues for service, is theologically too limited. Rather than rehabilitating the non-ordained, it isolates a category of Christians, those specializing in the work in the "world," from another category of those concentrated in inter-ecclesial activities.[37] The corrective is that all people of God should take responsibility in both the world and in the church.

Volf's proposal for a "participatory ecclesiology" is viable in that it takes seriously the role of the Spirit in ecclesiology, the necessity of the ministry of all people of God in concert with those who are full-time workers, and corresponds to the contemporary sociological climate with its call for equality and democracy. For Catholics this means re-evaluation of their theology of ministry, especially of *Lumen Gentium* §10 which is still based on a hierarchical concept of the people of God and an overemphasis on the role of the bishop (the latter item being something we can only mention here; in fact, because of shortage of ordained priests, the Catholic Church has already started to re-evaluate its theology of ministry by allowing more flexible kinds of ministries, thus continuing the blurring of the boundary between the ordained and the rest of God's people). For the Orthodox, this means re-evaluation of their doctrine of Trinity that for its part results in the hierarchical, episcopate-centered view of church and thus of ministry. For the Protestants in general it means boldness in implementing in real church life what they have believed since the time of Reformation. And for Free Churches in particular, it means reflecting theologically on what is already the rule of faith in their churches, the constitutive participation of all people of God in his mission in the world.

Chapter Ten

The Spirit and the Lord's Supper

From the first beginnings of the New Testament church the celebration of the Lord's Supper has stood at the heart of Christian worship and consequently also of church life. The celebration of the Supper is one of the few rites that almost all Christians practice, and have practiced through history, regardless of differing interpretations of its meaning. The gathering around the table took importance in the belief that at the breaking of bread the crucified and risen Lord was present (Luke 24:30–31; Acts 10:41; John 21:13). Therefore, Christians of all ages have been keen to follow the exhortation of their Lord to continue the table fellowship even after the departure of the Lord (1 Cor. 11:24–25). All Christians agree that Christ is present in the table fellowship that commemorates his cross and resurrection, as an anticipation of the eschatological banquet when all Christians will gather together at an eternal meal. This basic belief has never been seriously contested.

Of all the disputes concerning the Supper, the most significant has to do with the understanding of the presence of the Lord at or in the Supper. Throughout history, especially in medieval times, theologians devoted a lot of energy to develop a more precise understanding of the relation of Christ's presence to the "elements" (bread and wine) of the meal and consequent "changes" in the "substance." Out of this reflection came terms such as "transubstantiation" (Catholic) and "consubstantiation" (Lutheran). It is not wise to too quickly denigrate these efforts which, against the background of their times, were noble endeavors, although they were hardly able to settle the issues.

The more recent discussions on the understanding of the meaning of the Supper have shifted from this emphasis on Christ's presence in the elements to a more personalistic view of the Supper where the focus is on the nature of Christ's presence among his people gathered around the table. Even in the Catholic camp, under the leadership of Karl Rahner, Eduard Schillebeeckx and others, it has been established that the real issue in the doctrine is no longer the terminology (substance and accidents) but the real presence of Christ in the sacrament.[1]

In recent years, there has been an increasing interest in the relationship between the Spirit and the Eucharist. The ecumenical movement has stimulated research in the *Epiklesis* as practiced and understood in the East. This has been one important catalyst for theological reflection. In John Zizioulas' words, "Pentecost is the natural atmosphere of the Eucharist," and in Henri de Lubac's words, "Our churches are the 'upper room' where not only is the Last Supper renewed but Pentecost also."[2] This orientation brings theologizing to issues such as "How is Christ present among His people in the Supper?" and "In what way is the presence of Christ mediated in the meal?"

There is also an ecumenical consensus today that there is an integral relation between the Church and the Supper. Even if not all Christians would feel comfortable to say with Eastern Orthodox and Catholic traditions that the Eucharist makes the Church (conversely, that the church makes the Eucharist), many Protestants today have come to appreciate the indispensable mutual relation of these two. This understanding is in some sense a logical result of the shift in the common understanding of the meal from a "substantial" to a "personalistic" view in which the presence of Christ is seen among the people (i.e., the church) rather than in the materials.

One of the long-standing misconceptions of theology and spirituality has been the alleged contradistinction between the sacraments and the Spirit. Not infrequently it has been imagined that the Roman Catholic Church and the Eastern Orthodox Church identify themselves with sacraments to the degree that not much room is given to the Spirit, while the Protestant churches, especially newcomers like the Pentecostals, favor the Spirit over against the sacraments. Consequently, the Eucharist, the primary sacrament, has had an unfortunate history of pneumatological anemia.

To Eastern Orthodox spirituality has fallen recently the task of directing our attention to the necessary relationship between the Spirit and sacraments of Easter and Pentecost, as the quote from Georges Florovsky clearly reveals: "The sacramental life of the Church is the continuation of Pentecost, and yet much more: the life of the Church has its foundation in two mutually complementary mysteries: the mystery of the Last Supper and the mystery of Pentecost. One will always discover this duality within the concrete existence of the Church."[3] Michael O'Carroll, C.S.Sp., makes the obvious but significant note that in the beginning of Acts where the apostles and others are gathered in prayer, Luke does not mention the breaking of bread until after the descent of the Spirit. Not until the Spirit was poured down from above do we find that "they devoted themselves to the apostles' teaching and fellowship, to the breaking of bread and the prayers" (Acts 2:42).[4]

From these questions it is a short step to the focus of this chapter, namely, the role of the Spirit in the mediation of Christ's presence. I will inquire into the pneumatological horizons of the meaning of the Supper. Until recently, this topic has not received due attention, although it has always been believed that the Spirit has something to do with the mediation of Christ's presence in the table fellowship.[5] I will proceed in the following way. First, I will look at the significance of the ancient term *anamnesis* (memory) at the Lord's Table against the sayings of Jesus about the Spirit's role of reminding us of all that pertains to Jesus. Then I move from *anamnesis* to *epiclesis*, the prayer for the Spirit to effect the coming of the Lord into the midst of his people gathered around his memory. Following that, I will take up two special cases that seem to have direct bearing upon our topic, one of which is a task and the other a promise: 1) the need to "discern the body," i.e., to keep the unity of the Spirit among those celebrating the rite of unity, and 2) the Spirit's role in effecting healing, even physical healing, as has been believed from ancient days on. Finally, I turn my attention to eschatological implications of the work of the Spirit in the celebration of the Supper. The limitations of this chapter are obvious: focusing on pneumatological implications of the Supper, I will touch other issues under debate (e.g., the meaning of sacraments in modern discussion; the importance of "sign(s)" to a reformulation of the doctrine) only insofar as they shed light on our topic.

Anamnesis: In Remembrance of Jesus

"Do this in remembrance of me" (1 Cor. 11:24; Luke 22:19) is the saying of the Lord as he instituted the celebration of this memorial meal. In recent sacramental theology the term *anamnesis* has taken a new significance. The biblical view of memory is reflected in the New Testament usage of the Hebrew verb *zkr* in which "memory and action are intrinsically connected." For the Hebrew people, what was to be "remembered" in this way above all was the covenant made between God and the people. To remember this covenant was to allow the covenant to lay claim on their present reality. This is the essence of the what the Spirit is doing as he, according to the promise of the Johannine Jesus, reminds believers of Jesus and his sayings (John 14:26).

Here anamnesis, the memory, is conceived in dynamic terms. It meant in its everyday meaning a mere recalling things from the past, but in its ancient biblical and liturgical usage it meant that the transformative power of past events could be brought to bear on present realities, as in the Eucharist. Memory in the biblical sense of the term is not simply storage of the sediment of the past; it is also the "humus from which life never stops borrowing."[6] The ecumenical document *Baptism, Eucharist and Ministry* (*BEM*) captures this meaning well when it states the following about the Eucharist: "The *anamnesis* in which Christ acts through the joyful celebration of his Church is thus both representation and anticipation. It is not only a calling to mind of what is past and of its significance. It is the Church's effective proclamation of God's mighty acts and promises."[7]

From the fathers onward, the Supper has been conceived in terms of presentation and re-presentation of the paschal mystery of Christ. Pannenberg adds an important qualifier here. It is of decisive significance if we are to understand eucharistic anamnesis that we do not see merely an act of human remembering of which we are still subjects but the self-presenting of Jesus by his Spirit. Were it only for us remembering Jesus, it would not differ much from what happens at a funeral when the memory of a loved one is honored. According to John Zizioulas, tradition is not just passed on from one generation to another; "it is constantly re-enacted and re-received in the Spirit."[8] This is exactly what happens in the Eucharist.

The pneumatological focus of anamnesis of Christ's cross and resurrection comes into focus in the Johannine saying (19:30) Jesus "gave his spirit."[9] The Holy Spirit comes at the cost of Christ's departure: "the price of his coming is the cross, and he comes in the power of the Easter mystery."[10] Gottlieb Söhngen has tried to spell this out by introducing the concept of *memoria passionis* in which the subject—rather than being the celebrants—is the One who is celebrated. Söhngen stresses in his exposition that this mediation is the work of the Spirit. Protestant Peter Brunner emphasizes the same perspective. According to him, in eucharistic anamnesis we do not have merely an act of human remembering but a work of the Spirit of Christ in believers.[11]

Epiklesis: The Prayer for the Spirit

The Eastern Orthodox tradition of the Church has always seen the link between sacraments and the Spirit more clearly than the West. There is actually a difference between the Eastern and Western approach to the mystery of consecration. The Western tradition for centuries has emphasized *in persona Christi*, while the Eastern tradition has appealed to the Spirit. Among other reasons this difference has to do with a pronounced pneumatological undergirding of Eastern spirituality and theology. John Zizioulas makes the important observation that in primitive Pauline Churches charismatic manifestations took place during the eucharistic gatherings (cf. 1 Cor. 11–14), as well as ordination to the ministry, the latter of which was understood as the outpouring of the Spirit of God.[12]

According to Saint John Damascene, through the epiclesis and the descent of the Holy Spirit the bread and wine are changed into the body and blood of Christ. "[A]s the Holy Spirit once had formed Christ's body in the womb of the Virgin, so now, continuously, He forms Him by the changing of the Eucharistic elements."[13]

It was not until the eve of Vatican II that some leading theologians of the Roman Catholic Church began to see the integral connection of sacraments and pneumatology. Some even came to speak of sacraments, especially of the Eucharist, as "sacraments of the Spirit." One of the fruits of this re-orientation in theology was the re-introduction of the ancient epiclesis into eucharistic liturgies of the Western church (the East had retained it through the centuries). The *BEM* document has adopted the epiclesis into a conciliar understanding (Eucharist §§14–18) as well as into the liturgy itself (Eucharist §27). Similarly, the *Catechism of the Catholic Church* (§1112) sums up the role of the Spirit thus: "The mission of the Holy Spirit in the liturgy of the Church is to prepare the assembly to encounter Christ; to recall and manifest Christ to the faith of the assembly; to make the saving work of Christ present and active by his transforming power; and to make the gift of communion bear fruit in the Church."[14]

Now epiclesis is prayer for the descent of the Spirit—not so much upon the elements of the Supper (although this view is often reflected both in theology and especially in prayers of epiclesis) as upon the people of God gathered around the Table. This orientation has been a helpful aspect of the Eastern tradition. The entire Eucharist prayer is considered consecratory without a specific point in time where the "change" takes place. Likewise, the prayer-cry of the primitive church, "Come Lord Jesus" (*maranatha*, 1 Cor. 16:22) not only requests the eschatological coming of the Lord, but also calls for his coming for table fellowship in anticipation of the coming Kingdom. In this way anamnesis becomes epiclesis, both depending so much on the Spirit. "Anamnesis and epiclesis form the heart of the Church's eucharistic celebration and life: Christ and the Spirit together, both truly present."[15] Thus, *BEM* says that at the eucharistic meal the Holy Spirit makes the crucified and risen Christ truly present for us by fulfilling the promise of the words of institution (Eucharist, §14).

Rediscovery of the epiclesis has been helpful also in that it reminds us of the dependence of the celebration on the Spirit since prayer is petition, not a command. It is not for human beings to secure the coming of the Lord into their midst. What they can do is to pray for it. (To be dogmatically correct, the Holy Spirit is, of course, not inactive in the worship event of the Supper until he is prayed for. What we mean here is his "actual" presence, in distinction from his "real presence.") Our dependence on the Spirit is further enhanced by the realization that the Spirit is the power behind all Christian prayer (Rom. 8:15).

Therefore, the celebration of the Supper is much more than just "remembering" a deceased person. It becomes a spirited event where the celebrants rather than the elements are to be transformed into the image of the one who was crucified and rose from death through the power of the Spirit. The same Spirit effects in them the transformation.

> The transforming work of the Spirit related, then, not merely to the eucharistic elements. As the Eucharist is celebrated, this work embraces the participants as well in significatory anticipation of the eschatological world change. The express prayer for the Spirit rings out in various parts of the liturgy because by themselves, without the Spirit, believers do not know how to give thanks or to pray aright or to bless one another, and they certainly cannot transform themselves in order to dedicate their lives as thank offerings to God any more than they can cause Christ to be present in bread and wine. Only God's Spirit can effect the transforming of this life and only by such transforming can we, by and with bread and wine, be drawn into the movement of the life of the Lord's Supper.[16]

Along with the transformation of believers, the Eucharist, a spirited celebration, always points to the coming transformation of the world through the power of the crucified and risen Lord. Also present in the Eucharist is a missionary dimension. Interestingly enough, Nicholas Cabasilas in the fourteenth century, who accused the Latins of misunderstanding and confusion concerning the Eucharist, linked the Savior's

Pentecostal promise, "you shall receive power" (Luke 24:49; Acts 1:8) with his injunction "Do this in remembrance of me (Luke 22:19; 1 Cor. 11:24): "But he would not have ordered them to do it, if he were not about to give them the power, by which they could do so. And what was the power? The Holy Spirit, the power which descending from on high equipped the Apostles in accordance with the word spoken to them by the Lord: 'Remain in the city of Jerusalem—you shall receive power.'"[17] Consequently, epiclesis is not just on occasional prayer at the meal but a continual dependence upon the coming of the Spirit. Yves Congar captured this dependence well when he entitled the very last section of his three-volume work "The Life of the Church as One Long Epiclesis."[18]

An important ecumenical perspective also bears upon this significance of epiclesis. Roman Catholic Regis A. Duffy asks the all-important question of whether there is an access to a valid sacramental celebration for the separated Christian communities who "firmly desire to do what Christ intended and call down the Holy Spirit in their sacramental celebrations."[19] Therefore, perhaps we should speak about an "ecumenical epiclesis."[20]

Fellowship of the Spirit

The Lord's Table is primarily a meal of unity, at several levels, actually. First of all, it unites those who celebrate together along with the churches who participate in the one body and cup. Of course, we know that if anywhere the testimony of actual Christianity is hampered, it surely is around the Table. Notwithstanding this scandal of disunity on this side of God's kingdom, the eschatological reality of the oneness of all God's people, the anticipation of which is the presence of the one undivided body of their Lord in every Supper, cannot be made void. Since the Table is ultimately the sign of unity, it expresses both a promise to and a task for all the followers of Christ. In other words, our task is to keep the unity of the Spirit (Eph. 4:3).

It is good to remember that the first meal in the early church that we could legitimately call the Lord's Supper in the post-apostolic sense was a result of the outpouring of the Spirit. According to the second chapter of Acts, on the day of Pentecost, after a mighty manifestation of the Spirit's power with accompanying signs and wonders, following the scriptural exposition of Peter, the new converts with the apostles celebrated the meal. Rather than limiting themselves to an occasional sharing of the meal, they started church life with the daily breaking of bread (Acts 2:

42). This formed the basis of the "fellowship of the Sprit" to which we come later in this chapter. Unity of all God's people was at first a powerful means of testimony also to those outside the Church.

It is also significant that the only occasions where Paul gives instruction about the Supper are related to the twin themes of the Spirit and of unity. In 1 Cor. 10, by way of introduction to his orders concerning the celebration itself, Paul gives a typological exposition of the Supper of the old people of God. Then he explains the meaning of the cup of the covenant and the bread of unity (1 Cor. 10:16–17). He focuses concern on the preservation of the unity brought by the Spirit of God. Approaching chapters 12 through 14, his exposition of charisms and their role in the preservation of the unity of the body, he gives the detailed orders concerning the celebration of the Supper in the church (1 Cor. 11:14–27). And to make sure that the relation between the Spirit and unity in the celebration of the Supper is observed, he says, "By one and the same Spirit we are all baptized into the one body, both Jews and Greeks, both slaves and free; one and the same drink of one Spirit" (12:13).

Herein lies the basic meaning of the often quoted, and also debated, word from Paul about "discerning the body" (1 Cor. 11:28). Contrary to the interpretation of older exegesis in terms of moral lapses—although this concern from another perspective is, of course, not without significance—the modern exegesis agrees that what Paul has in mind is discerning the unity of the body of Christ, i.e., the Church. What Paul has in mind is not unworthiness of the celebrants because of their failure in their private Christian walk, but breaches in the fellowship. If the people of God gather around the Table to recollect the one undivided body of Christ and have at the same time internal strife, they oppose the work of the Spirit, the Spirit of unity.[21]

Healing through the Presence of Christ in the Spirit

Very early on, Christians who gathered around the Table looked to the Lord also as the healer of the body. The presence of Christ, through his Spirit, has been seen as effecting renewal not only of our inner being but also of our bodies and emotions. The Fathers spoke of the Eucharist as a *pharmakon* or medicine.[22] The Eucharist is the service of healing. The Lord himself invites us to his table to partake of his very being, to become one with him, offering us healing and wholeness through his body and blood. In a good Catholic and Orthodox tradition, grace is God's self-communication of God's self, thus making union with us possible. This is also being acknowledged by Protestants.[23]

True, after the first centuries, the expectation of healing was channeled along two separate avenues that until our days have not had much to do with each other. On the one hand, along with the development of belief in sacraments as signs which effect what they signify (especially in the Middle Ages), at least in popular piety, high expectations were set upon the healing power of the Eucharist. These expectations, one assumes, had to do more with a quasi-magical understanding of the sacraments than with the power of the Spirit. On the other hand, the Charismatic renewal movements especially inside the Catholic Church but later on also in Protestant Churches, kept alive the belief in the wonder-working power of the Spirit. These Christians did not usually connect it with the Lord's Table but rather with the prayer of faith. They might even have been suspicious of healing through the Eucharist, since they opposed the dangers of sacramentalism as they understood it in the older churches.

An interesting case study is the Charismatic movement inside the Lutheran Church. Lutheran Markku Antola of Finland has shown in his recent dissertation entitled *The Experience of Christ's Real Presence in Faith* that Lutheran Charismatics regard the Eucharist as an avenue for physical and emotional healing.[24] They expect healing to flow from the presence of Christ in the Eucharist as the healing also can come through intercessory prayer or the gift of healing (charism): "a person may receive faith for healing in connection with receiving the Lord's Supper, and many testify to this."[25] Lutheran Charismatics refer to Luther who spoke about the Eucharist as a "medicine which aids and quickens us in both soul and body."[26]

Another interesting case study is the Roman Catholic-Pentecostal International dialogue. Ecumenically it is highly significant that in recent years these two streams have coalesced in the form of a historical dialogue between the oldest and largest historical church, the Roman Catholic Church, and the newest, but extremely rapidly-growing Pentecostal movement. In the dialogue between these two Christian constituencies, the topic of healing has been discussed extensively and, significantly enough, the relation to the Eucharist has also been considered. Now it should be noted that Pentecostalism, as an ecclesial newcomer, clung to the ancient belief and practice of the Christian church even though the purpose of the new movement was to free the church from "rites and rituals" which were believed to be not only meaningless but also a hindrance to the understanding of the Gospel. Pentecostals, understandably, have not devoted much energy to formulating their doctrine(s) of the Lord's Supper. This is in line with the movement's accent on spirituality rather than on doctrine, and its preference for oral rather than discursive theologizing.

Yet, both Catholics and Pentecostals agree that the Lord's Supper may indeed be an avenue for healing (see *FR* II.40). This foundational common affirmation is more important when we take into consideration the fact that the same paragraphs also include an honest look at different emphases in the role of sacramental acts in the expectation of healing. The Eucharist is for Catholics a representation of the healing power of the paschal mystery. As sacrament it is a pledge of the ultimate resurrection of the whole person. Pentecostals avoid speaking of "sacraments" in the area of healing. But for them, too, the meaning of the death of Christ is central, to be commemorated each time the Lord's Supper is celebrated. The Eucharist points to the biblical paradigm in which "[t]he ultimate healing transformation comes from suffering and death borne out of love. This is how the kingdom of God advances. This is how Jesus became Risen Lord and how we too personally share in the Easter victory of Christ. This is what the Paschal mystery is about and scripture could not be more explicit on this point."[27]

Spirit, Eschatology, and the Table Fellowship

One advantage of introducing a pneumatological orientation into the discussion on the Lord's Supper is that it helps us to see the eschatological nature of the meal. The roots of the Supper are not only in the cross but also in the resurrection of the Lord. The resurrection of Jesus was facilitated by the Spirit of the Father (Rom. 4:25). As Pannenberg succinctly says: "In fact, then, the church's existence is made possible only by God's own action in the resurrection of the Crucified and the eschatological gift of the Spirit."[28]

The Spirit, who mediates Christ's presence in the Supper, is none else than the eschatological gift. Therefore, he orients the celebrants' attention to the coming eschatological meal when the work started at the cross and the resurrection will find its completion. As Zizioulas brilliantly notices, the anamnesis of Christ and his work in the cross is realized not as a mere re-enactment of a past event but as an "*anamnesis of the future*," as an eschatological event.[29] This eschatological outlook calls attention to the missionary nature of the celebration of the Lord's Supper. Whatever our interpretation of the meaning of the disputed term "proclaim" (1 Cor. 11:26), it is true that "as the fellowship that celebrates the Lord's Supper, the church is the sign and instrument of humanity's eschatological ordination for fellowship in God's kingdom."[30]

Regular celebration of the Supper therefore reminds us of the indispensable eschatological nature of the church such that it can be called an "eschatological community," even though still, on this side of God's *eschaton*, only in a provisional form. According to Zizioulas, the ultimate essence of the catholicity of the whole Church of God is "revealed in the eucharistic community" in which there is "the transcendence of all divisions in Christ."[31] Even if we do not yet see this fulfilled, the Eucharist testifies powerfully to what God is going to effect in the *eschaton*.

Towards a Deepened Experience of the Spirit in the Supper

Along with the resurgence of a pneumatological outlook in theology in general and ecclesiology in particular, a new interest in the role of the Spirit in the Eucharist and the eucharistic celebration has arisen in ecumenical theology. The attention has shifted from a mechanistic to a more personalistic-dynamic view of the Lord's presence in the meal devoted to his memory.

The meaning of the Eucharist can be captured in two ancient terms, anamnesis and epiclesis, both of which are full of pneumatological potential. The Spirit turns the celebrants' eyes and hearts to the saving and healing sacrifice of the Lord. The Spirit makes the remembering a dynamic process that overcomes the distinction between the past, present, and future by anticipating the final consummation of the Kingdom of the Slain Lamb. The Church acknowledges its dependence on the Lord by continuous prayer for the coming of the Spirit. The epiclesis entails the whole celebration, not just the moment of "consecration." Through an earnest prayer-cry the celebrants are empowered by the Spirit of him who raised the crucified Son from the dead. The people of God rise from the Table to spread the good news of reconciliation to the ends of the earth.

In this chapter we have touched on some crucial perspectives concerning the role of the Spirit in the Eucharist, such as the meaning of anamnesis and epiclesis, the meal as the manifestation of the unity of the body of Christ, Christ's healing presence at the meal through the Spirit, and the eschatological orientation of the banquet. We have not discussed the relationship between the Spirit and grace, another important question for further reflection. Other important tasks for further study include the relationship of the Spirit and sacraments in general, the triadic relationship between the Spirit, Church, and sacraments, and the question of the contribution of an emerging Spirit-christology to the question of a pneumatological understanding of the Eucharist.

Part Three

Soteriology

Chapter Eleven

Grace and the Ecumenical Potential of Theosis

No informed observer of the Eastern Orthodox Church would doubt the centrality of the doctrine of deification (*theosis*, *Vergöttlichung*) in Eastern theology. The idea of a human being becoming a god is far more than just *a* theological locus. It is an overarching principle which permeates all of Eastern theology and spirituality.[1] However, any expert on Reformation theology would have a hard time trying to reconcile the idea of theosis with the doctrine of justification. Historically, these two traditions have been considered to be diametrically opposed to each other. A corollary problem is that—at least for Lutherans—the Eastern soteriology entertains problematic notions of the freedom of will, too positive an anthropology, and, worst of all, the idea of human-divine *synergia* in salvation.[2] When it comes to Pentecostal-Holiness theology, nothing much can be said regarding the idea of deification. Generally speaking, Pentecostalism has adopted the doctrine of justification in its Reformation form (this is true especially among White Pentecostals). What justification is there then for lumping together three traditions so widely differing from each other?

Would it help to ask this question within a pneumatological framework? Even here, some serious questions arise. Pneumatological ramifications certainly permeate Eastern Orthodox theology. However, Reformation theology, especially in its Lutheran form,[3] is built on christological concepts rather than pneumatological. In the Pentecostal tradition, on the other hand, a novice might easily take for granted that Pentecostals have a developed pneumatological theology although it appears to be underdeveloped in this regard. Pentecostals have reintroduced a charismatic spirituality with spiritual gifts, but thus far they have been slow to develop a pneumatological doctrine of salvation, of Scripture, or of the Church, to name just a few of the more obvious examples.

The purpose of this chapter is to advance an ecumenical quest for a conciliar doctrine of deification and a pneumatological concept of grace. This is important for both the Pentecostal-Holiness tradition and their dialogue partners, the Orthodox and the Lutherans. For Pentecostals, it is time to start to develop a theology worthy of the name "Pentecostal." The extended dialogue with Roman Catholics has helped Pentecostals clarify some of the most crucial theological issues. The dialogue under planning with the Eastern Orthodox Church, to which I want to make a contribution here, will require a lot of homework from Pentecostals in trying to identify common concerns and possible convergences. I personally see Eastern Orthodox theology as a very fitting dialogue partner since it carries so much pneumatological potential. In fact, as I will try to show, the very distinctive contribution of Eastern theology to the wider *oikumene*, the idea of theosis, is a thoroughly pneumatological concept.

By including Luther's theology as a third dialogue partner, I have consciously taken a risk. If this chapter had been written a couple of decades ago, not much convergence could have been found either with Eastern or Pentecostal-Holiness soteriologies. In our present days, there are a number of positive ecumenical changes on the horizon, and happily so. Recent Lutheran ecumenical theologizing has unexpectedly discovered the motif of deification and a pneumatological concept of grace within Luther's own writings. The so-called Mannermaa School at the University of Helsinki has provided a promising and yet controversial claim about theosis being one of the images Luther used to describe salvation. These findings have rapidly been introduced into ecumenical conversations, first between the Russian Orthodox Church and the Finnish Lutheran Church, and then within the international Orthodox-Lutheran dialogues. Pentecostals and Lutherans have yet to engage in international theological dialogue although some national and local conversations have been held. The promise and the urgency of that dialogue lies in the fact that much of Pentecostal soteriology has been taken from Lutheran sources. I believe Pentecostals could help Lutherans to read in a fresh way their own sources of the doctrine of soteriology and the Holy Spirit, while Pentecostals themselves could also profit from such an exchange.

In this chapter I will proceed in the following way. After briefly tracing the biblical and patristic roots of the doctrine of theosis, I will discuss Eastern Orthodox, Lutheran, and Pentecostal-Holiness views of deification and underlying pneumatological ramifications. In conclusion I will offer some ecumenical suggestions and topics for further study and dialogue.

"He Became Man That We Might Become Gods"

Biblical and Patristic Roots

The Bible offers a sufficient amount of passages about the idea of human participation in God for it to be taken as an important image of salvation. The two cardinal texts are 2 Peter 1:4 and Psalm 82:6 (cited in John 10:34–35). But Orthodox theologians claim that the doctrine has a solid biblical basis that goes beyond the two explicit texts mentioned above. They refer to other biblical passages like Exodus 34:30 where Moses' face shone, or to Exodus 7:1 which reveals that Moses became a god to Pharaoh. The transfiguration of Peter on Mt. Tabor (Matt. 17:4) is also considered a classic text. Orthodox fathers often cite 2 Corinthians 8:9, Hebrews 4:15, and a host of texts from the Johannine corpus.[4]

The two most often referred to patristic texts are from Irenaeus and Athanasius. Irenaeus says: "The Word of God, our Lord Jesus Christ who because of his limitless love became what we are in order to make us what even he himself is"; Athanasius is more succinct: "Christ became human that humans might become divine."[5] Many more patristic texts could be added, for example, from Symeon the New Theologian, whose view is always toward a pneumatological orientation, to Maximos the Confessor, the Cappadocian Fathers, etc. Basil attributes the experience of theosis to the Holy Spirit who "being God by nature…deifies by grace those who still belong to a nature subject to change."[6] St. Macarios likewise accentuates the role of the Spirit in theosis when he says that the persons to be deified, though they retain their own identity (i.e., do not overstep the distinction between God and human), "are all filled with the Holy Spirit."[7] Even though Orthodox Vladimir Lossky's comment that theosis is "echoed by the fathers and the theologians of every age" might intentionally be an overstatement,[8] it does however reflect the general mindset among patristic fathers. The patristic doctrine of theosis can thus be briefly formulated as follows: "Divine life has manifested itself in Christ. In the church as the body of Christ, man has a share in this life.

Man partakes thereby of 'the divine nature' (2 Pet. 1:4). This 'nature,' or divine life, permeates the being of man like a leaven in order to restore it to its original condition as *imago Dei*."[9]

The distinction between God and the human person is not made void. God still remains God and human remains human though participating in the divine. Orthodox theology, as is well known, has tried to solve this problem by making a distinction between divine essence and divine energies. According to Orthodox understanding, deification means participating in the divine energies, not the divine essence as such.

Theosis in Eastern Orthodoxy

As is well known, there is a pronounced difference in orientation in christology and soteriology between east and west. According to Eastern theology, Latin traditions have been dominated by legal, juridical, and forensic categories. Eastern theology, on the contrary, understands the need of salvation in terms of deliverance from mortality and corruption for life everlasting. Union with God is the goal of Christian life, even becoming in-godded. The underlying anthropology is not necessarily more positive but, instead of operating mainly in guilt-concepts, it looks upward, so to speak, to the image of God to be fulfilled in mortal human beings. The idea of divine-human cooperation in salvation is not only accepted but is enthusiastically championed, while at the same time not nullifying the role of grace.

According to the Eastern view, the descent (*katábasis*) of the divine person of Christ makes human persons capable of an ascent (*anábasis*) in the Holy Spirit. It was necessary that the voluntary humiliation, the redemptive *kénosis*, of the Son of God should take place, so that fallen humans might accomplish their vocation of theosis, the deification of created beings by uncreated grace.

Eastern theologians do not speak of deification only as a metaphor; they also stress the reality of the union with God, promised to the faithful. Lossky writes, "The words of St. Peter are explicit: *partakers of the divine nature.* They leave us in no doubt as to the reality of the union with God which is promised us, and set before us as our final end, the blessedness of the age to come. It would be childish, not to say impious, to see in these words only a rhetorical expression or metaphor."[10] Of course, Eastern thinkers do struggle with the compatibility of the two seemingly opposite ideas: the absolute incommunicability of the divine being and a real partaking of humanity in God. Whatever one may think of traditional Eastern solutions (e.g., essence-energy distinction), there is no denying their passion to affirm the idea of the divine-human union.

The deification of the creature, of course, will be realized in its fullness only in the age to come. Nevertheless, this deifying union must be fulfilled ever more and more even in this present life. Consequently, Eastern theologians do not shy away from speaking of divine-human synergy, cooperation of human beings with God. Humans are to be saved by grace, but not without total devotion and willingness to be transformed. Prayer, asceticism, meditation, humble service, and similar exercises are recommended for the attainment of this noble goal. The notion of merit, though, is foreign to the Eastern tradition. In general, their attitude toward grace and free will is less reserved than their Western partners. In the East, the question of free will has never had the urgency that it assumed in the West from the time of Augustine onward. The Eastern tradition never separates grace and human freedom. Therefore, the charge of Pelagianism (i.e., that grace is a reward for the merit of the human will) is not fair. It is not a question of merit(s), but of a cooperation, of a synergy of the two wills, divine and human. Grace is a presence of God within us, which demands constant effort on our part. In the nineteenth century, Bishop Theophanes, a Russian ascetic writer, asserted that "the Holy Ghost, acting within us, accomplishes with us our salvation" and that "being assisted by grace, man accomplished the work of his salvation."[11]

The role of the Holy Spirit in Eastern soteriology is highlighted by the ultimate goal of salvation. Redemption has our salvation from sin as an immediate aim, but in its ultimate realization in the age to come salvation will be our union with God, the deification of the created beings whom Christ ransomed. But this final realization involves the dispensation of the Holy Spirit. The work of the Spirit is, of course, inseparable from that of the Son. In the words of Athanasius, "God bearing flesh," and Christians, "bearing the Spirit."[12]

Interestingly enough, Eastern Fathers attribute to the Spirit all the multiplicity of names which can be attributed to grace, as is evident for example in St. Gregory Nazianzan and St. Basil. They freely speak about the Holy Spirit as effecting deification, perfection, adoption, and sanctification. Eastern Christians sing: "The Holy Spirit giveth life to souls; he exalteth them in purity; He causeth the sole nature of the Trinity to shine in them mysteriously."[13] The Eastern Church teaches that that which is common to the Father and the Son is the divinity which the Holy Spirit communicates (cf. *perichoresis*) to humans within the Church, in making them partakers of the divine nature. Deification is the highest gift and blessing of the Holy Spirit. In this sense, as St. Seraphim of Sarov said, "the true aim of the Christian life is the acquisition of the Holy Spirit of God."[14]

In fact, the idea of deification cannot be expressed on a christological basis alone, but demands a pneumatological development as well. For the mystical tradition of Eastern Christendom, Pentecost, which confers the presence of the Holy Spirit and the first fruits of sanctification, signifies both the end and final goal of the spiritual life. It is important to note that in the Eastern rite confirmation—"anointing" with the Spirit—follows immediately upon baptism. The Holy Spirit is operative in both sacraments. The Spirit recreates human nature by purifying it and uniting it to the body of Christ. The Spirit also bestows deity upon human persons. Eastern theology even speaks about Christians as "christs," anointed ones: the Spirit who rests like a royal unction upon the humanity of the Son, communicates himself to each member of Christ's body.[15]

The mystical theology of the Eastern wing of the Church is often more experience-based and concrete than Latin theology. "As he who grasps one end of a chain pulls along with it the other end to himself, so he who draws the Spirit draws both the Son and the Father along with it," Basil writes.[16] The role of the Spirit in this understanding—although the language is of course not to be taken at face value—is to make the "first contact," to be followed by the revelation of the Son and, through him, the Father. There is a genuine trinitarian outlook in the Eastern view: "The Father does all things by the Word in the Holy Spirit."[17]

The doctrine of salvation, obviously, has implications for other theological *loci*, in particular ecclesiology. If we construct the doctrine of salvation in christological terms only (which in sacramental theologies is anchored primarily in sacraments), it leads to a "quality of absolute objectivity."[18] But if we wish to safeguard another aspect of the Church, which has a quality of subjectivity no less absolute, it must be based on the dispensation of the Spirit. In the words of Vladimir Lossky:

> The point is that the Incarnation and the redeeming work of Christ, considered apart from the dispensation of the Holy Spirit, cannot justify the Church's personal multiplicity.... The mystery of Pentecost is as important as the mystery of the Redemption. The redeeming work of Christ is an indispensable pre-condition of the deifying work of the Holy Spirit.... But, on the other hand, one may say that the work of the Spirit serves that of the

> Son, for it is by receiving the Spirit that human persons can bear witness in full consciousness to the divinity of Christ.[19]

Theosis in Luther's Theology

Lutheran-Orthodox Conversations on Deification

Two developments in recent years have opened new horizons for a more positive appraisal of the Eastern doctrine of deification by Lutherans: ecumenical conversations between Lutherans and Orthodox and a "new quest for Luther's theology" initiated by the Mannermaa school at the University of Helsinki.

Already in the 1970s, the Finnish Lutheran Church, in its conversations with the Russian Orthodox Church, adopted a number of soteriological statements that compared the Lutheran doctrine of justification with the Orthodox view of deification/theosis.[20] This Finnish-Lutheran dialogue produced a highly influential soteriological document in Kiev 1977 entitled "Salvation as Justification and Deification." The preamble to the theses claims that

> Until recently, there has been a predominant opinion that the Lutheran and Orthodox doctrines of salvation greatly differ from each other. In the conversations, however, it has become evident that both these important aspects of salvation discussed in the conversations have a strong New Testament basis and there is great unanimity with regard to them both.[21]

It was found that the doctrine of deification covers the idea of a Christian's life as righteous and sinful at the same time, as the Lutheran theology has always emphasized. The idea of deification makes more explicit what is sometimes in danger of being underemphasized in Lutheranism, namely the purifying role of grace: "When the Christian has been justified, he takes a new road leading to deification."[22]

Perhaps the greatest obstacle to Lutherans in how they perceive Eastern soteriology is the question of the freedom of human will. The Orthodox speak freely of the freedom of the human person in a strongly ontological sense whereas for Lutherans there is not much left to human initiative.

Deification in Recent Luther Research

The theological grounding of the suggested convergence between Orthodox and Lutheran soteriologies—which has since its publication created debate—was done by Tuomo Mannermaa and his students at

Helsinki. For Mannermaa, the contact point is Luther's idea of "Christ present in faith." According to Mannermaa, the idea of Christ's presence is "real-ontic" for Luther, not just a subjective experience or God's effect on the believer as the neo-Protestant school has exclusively held.[23]

The core of the doctrine of deification from this viewpoint is the idea of real participation in the divine life in Christ. We receive the salvific gifts through participation in Christ. The Lutheran tradition holds to the idea of God living in the believer. This for Mannermaa is analogous with the doctrine of theosis. According to Luther, Christ and thus his person and work is present in the faith itself. For him, the Christ present in faith is the *forma fidei*, i.e., the realization or concrete manifestation of faith. Whereas Catholic theology considers love as a *forma*, Luther regards Christ himself as a link between faith and good works.

Mannermaa's student Simo Peura has written a full-scale monograph on the idea of deification in Luther.[24] Peura shows that even though Luther does not often use the term deification itself—even though it is one image of salvation in him—the idea of deification is an integral motif of his theology. The most explicit passage comes from Luther's *Sermon on the day of St. Peter and St. Paul* (1519): "For it is true that a man helped by grace is more than a man; indeed, the grace of God gives him the form of God and deifies him, so that even the Scriptures call him 'God' and 'God's son'" (*WA* 2.247–48).[25] To cite another obvious example from Luther's Christmas sermon of 1514: "Just as the word of God became flesh, so it is certainly also necessary that the flesh become word. For the word becomes flesh precisely so that the flesh may become word. In other words, God became man so that man may become God. Thus power becomes powerless so that weakness may become powerful. The logos puts on our form and manner..." (*WA* 1.28). It is easy to see that Luther presents here the idea of deification with the help of Athanasius and Irenaeus, as a union of logos and flesh, or word and humanity. Although God does not stop being God and human beings do not stop being human beings, the *unio*, though, is real. It is "a community of being of God and man."[26]

Although the term deification is not frequent in Luther—the terms *deifico/vergotten/durchgotten* appear thirty times in Luther's corpus—the core idea is integral to him. He usually prefers terms like presence of Christ in faith, the participation in God, union with God, *perichoresis*, the famous Eastern term, and others. As already noted, Christ's real presence in the believer is the leading motif in Luther's soteriology. A classic formulation can be found for example in his *Lectures on Galatians* (1535). Speaking about "true faith," Luther says: "It takes hold of Christ in such a way that Christ is the object of faith, or rather not the object, but so to speak, the One who is present in the faith itself....Therefore faith justifies because it takes hold of and possesses this treasure, the present Christ" (*WA* 40.228–29).

The idea of participation in God is related to this. Luther does not hesitate to say that "we are born again into eternal life by faith, that we may live in God and with God and be one with him, as Christ says (John 17:21)" (*WA* 42.48). Participation in Christ, following Paul (Phil. 3) is also participation in his cross. For Luther, the idea of deification is closely linked with his theology of the cross. This is a helpful reminder especially to Pentecostals and Charismatics who easily get carried away by the idea of divinization which borders on the *theologia gloriae*, the arch-enemy of Luther's thinking.

Pneumatological implications of this new approach of Luther scholarship are obvious. The leading idea, Christ present through faith, can also be expressed pneumatically: it is through the Spirit of Christ—it must be remembered that Luther always thinks christologically—that the mediation of salvific gifts is accomplished. Participation in God is possible only through the Spirit of Christ, the Spirit of adoption. In fact, several major research projects at the University of Helsinki are currently underway focusing on pneumatological orientations in Luther. The title of Miikka Ruokanen's dissertation clearly expresses its purpose: *Spiritus vel gratia est ipsa fide* (Spirit or grace is the faith itself), with the subtitle, "A Pneumatological Concept of Grace in Luther's *De servo arbitrio*."[27] Opposite to what is usually thought of Luther's major work *De servo arbitrio* (in which he attacks Erasmus vehemently), Ruokanen argues that the theology of grace and justification is conceived very much in terms of pneumatology. Ruokanen shows that Augustine's concept of pneumatological *gratia increata* (i.e., the personal presence of the Triune God in humanity through the Holy Spirit) might be an indispensable theological background for understanding Luther's pneumatology of grace.

Christ's Real Presence in Faith through the Spirit in Charismatic Lutheran Theology

A highly interesting study for our present purposes is the inquiry into the pneumatological implications of the doctrine of salvation in Charismatic Lutheran theology. Markku Antola, who teaches in Hong Kong, has recently published his dissertation entitled, *The Experience of Christ's Real Presence in Faith*.[28] The Charismatic theology of Lutheranism describes charismatic experience as the presence of the Triune God through the Spirit. The actual purpose of the Holy Spirit's work is to create faith in Christ and lead the believer into a "living union" with Christ. "But the Holy Spirit alone creates true faith, whereby one is actually united with the living Christ as the present and redeeming Lord."[29] It is noteworthy that Christ's presence is often expressed by the concept of union with Christ:

> If any one is in Christ, he is a new creation" (2. Cor. 5:17). The newness is not simply the fact that human nature has been forgiven and cleansed....The newness goes deeper: a person now lives in union with the risen Christ. That which has been created, the "new creation," is precisely this reality of the indwelling Spirit establishing and maintaining the risen Christ and the believer in a living union.[30]

Explicitly using Luther's language, the Charismatic theology maintains that "in the faith itself Christ is present," and, "Faith describes the whole action by which the Holy Spirit brings the living, redeeming presence of Christ into a living union with a human being. The initiative and the power to accomplish this lies with the Spirit."[31]

Also, in line with Luther's own theology—but not necessarily of subsequent Lutheranism—charismatic theologians teach that the forgiveness of sins and the imputation of Christ's work to the believer is to be followed by union with Christ, where Christ comes to live inside the believer as God's gift. In other words, justification does not only include God's favor but also Christ as the gift living inside the Christian. Charismatic Lutheran theology is also helpful in maintaining that—in line with Luther himself, but against his later interpreters—justification and sanctification, rather than being two distinct matters, occur inside each other and happen simultaneously.

An important bridge to Pentecostal-Holiness traditions is the accent on experience: "No one can correctly understand God or his Word unless he has received such understanding immediately from the Holy Spirit. But no one can receive it from the Holy Spirit without experiencing, proving, and feeling it.[32]

Deification, Grace, and Spirit in Pentecostal-Holiness Traditions

Wesley and Holiness Traditions

One of the pressing issues for the Holiness and Pentecostal movements is to establish their identities regarding the larger Christian world. There have been assertions that these two interconnected religious movements constitute a third way of Christianity parallel with the Orthodox and Roman Catholic traditions. Others have argued that both are thoroughly rooted in Reformation Protestantism. Be that as it may, further probing must be made in order to find some common denominators. Some helpful historical precedents exist to start with in relation to our topic.

The idea of deification was embraced not only by the Reformers but also by their counterparts, the Radical Reformers. This is the conclusion of Thomas Finger, a Mennonite theologian, who has compared Eastern Orthodox theology with Anabaptist theology. He demonstrates that for these persecuted people, the doctrine of theosis brought hope and encouragement. Finger lists a host of Mennonite leaders, such as Hans Denck, Melchior Hofmann, Menno Simons, and others who have championed the idea of divinization.[33]

This is highly significant for Pentecostal-Holiness people who, as is well known, have inherited a lot of their theology, especially theology of sacraments, conversion, and church, from the Radical Reformers. In fact, it can be said that the only major differences between the Pentecostal-Holiness and the Anabaptist traditions are their distinctive emphases on the understanding of the Holy Spirit and spiritual gifts. Anabaptists' unexpectedly wide acceptance of the idea of deification points to the fact that, indeed, it is not so foreign to Pentecostal-Holiness traditions as one might suspect.

In fact, Jürgen Moltmann has shown that John Wesley, the theological architect of Holiness traditions, was himself open to the idea of deification and to a pneumatological understanding of the concept of grace. Wesley was able to discern five stages in the sanctification of life from an awakening of the conscience by a preliminary divine grace to a gradual sanctification of life to the final stage: "Believers are wholly interpenetrated by the Holy Spirit and arrive at the state of Christian perfection, the theosis."[34] Moltmann correctly notes that for Wesley, sin is a sickness that requires healing rather than a breach of law requiring atonement. Therefore, Wesley was less interested than Reformation theology in the permanent justification of the sinner, and more interested in the process of a moral renewal. This orientation does, of course, resemble Eastern Orthodox spirituality.

David Bundy, in a research conference at Prague (Fall 1997) where there was a fruitful encounter between theologians from Orthodox, Catholic, Protestant, and Pentecostal-Holiness traditions, read a paper entitled, "Vision of Sanctification: Themes of Orthodoxy in the Methodist, Holiness and Pentecostal Traditions."[35] In his paper, Bundy attempts to detect some common theological roots in Pentecostal-Holiness and Eastern traditions. He refers to several Methodist researchers who have found evidence of Orthodox themes pervading Wesleyan theology. In the 1960s, Albert Outler years ago made the claim that Wesley's reading of Orthodox theologians had a definite influence on Methodist theology.[36] Bundy summarizes his well-documented piece of research on the formative Eastern Orthodox influences through Holiness movements to Pentecostalism:

> [O]ne particular strand of Eastern Christianity can be traced from Clement of Alexandria to Origen to Pseudo-Macarios to Wesley to Madame Guyon and from both of them to the Holiness theologian Thomas Cogswell Upham, Phoebe Palmer, and from them to formative theologians of Pentecostalism including William Seymour, Minnie Abraham and Thomas Ball Barrett.[37]

Wesley's sermons suggest that the goal of the Christian life is "Christian perfection," a movement toward unity with God. Like Eastern spiritual guides, there is emphasis on prayer as a tool for achieving contemplation of God and ascetic life in which every activity and passion of life is part of that struggle for victory over the ungodly influences in life. This was undoubtedly the mentality of (early) Pentecostal meetings where power from on high was expected to finish what was lacking in sanctification and empowerment for service.

Terminologically, there is one identification in Bundy's text which raises question marks (and is often evident in ecumenical conversations between Lutherans and Orthodox). It seems as if he wants to make "theosis" a synonym with "sanctification."[38] This is, of course, not so much wrong as it is one-sided. Sanctification is not only part of what Eastern theologians call deification, it is the goal. Even the whole process of salvation could be called deification, not just its "end station."

Pentecostal Traditions

Bundy sees clear convergence between the spirituality of William J. Seymour, the Black pioneer at Azusa Street, and the Alexandrian Christian tradition of Origen (*praktike, theorike, gnosis*) and others in the matters of justification, sanctification, and baptism in the Holy Spirit.[39] The same applies to two others Bundy discusses: Minnie Abrahams and Thomas Barrett. In fact, Abrahams describes the goal of life as "union with God" which is not unlike both the Orthodox and Luther's traditions. Furthermore, she understands the Christian life as spiritual warfare "which is best waged in prayer and ascetic lifestyle" where one is able to surrender one's self in complete conformity to the will of God. Only through the grace of God's Holy Spirit living through the individual can the individual be successful in this personal renewal. Resembling patristic/Orthodox language, she says that the individual who experiences the infusion of the Holy Spirit can fall away through lack of conformity to God's will. The journey to "union" is developmental from stage to stage. Significantly enough, echoing Luther's language of participation in Christ's cross, Abrahams speaks about being made perfect through conformity to Christ's death and resurrection. She also speaks about the "abiding presence of the fire of the Holy Ghost" in the hearts of those praying and fighting to be conformed to God's image. According to Barratt, the same principles of spiritual life are in operation in that through prayer and perfect submission to the will of God, the Holy Spirit gives grace for victorious life. The goals of this life are power for service and being "in Him, lost in Him and His love."[40]

The International Dialogue between the Roman Catholic Church and Pentecostal Churches (1972–1989) produced a highly significant agreement on a pneumatological understanding of salvation. Notwithstanding serious disagreements concerning soteriology (e.g. sacraments, personal response of faith), both Catholics and Pentecostals agreed that the essence of faith is "fullness of life in the Spirit" or "indwelling of the Spirit in individuals." The common statement uses "union" language in a pneumatological framework: "The Holy Spirit, being the agent of regeneration, is given in Christian initiation, not as a commodity but as he who unites us with Christ and the Father in a personal relationship. Being a Christian includes the reception of grace through the Holy Spirit for one's own sanctification as well as gifts to be ministered to others" (*FR* I.18). It is the Spirit of Christ who unites the believer to Christ and to his people. The grace to save us from the power of sin and death is given through the Holy Spirit. Following Karl Rahner, it can be said that grace is first and foremost God's self-communication and presence through the Spirit to human existence.[41] Ecumenically, it is noteworthy that the giving of the Spirit to dwell in every Christian is cast in a trinitarian context. The Holy Spirit is given in Christian initiation "as he who unites us with Christ and the Father" (*FR* I.18).

Theses for Further Study and Reflection

To facilitate the continuing search for a more conciliar understanding of salvation through the lens of deification and pneumatology, let me suggest the following theses for further study and reflection.

1) Deification is an ecumenically fruitful and biblically-theologically legitimate image of salvation, which, although rarely used by Pentecostal-Holiness people, has some roots in their tradition. There is an important precedent in Lutheran studies. For a long time, it was believed that Reformation and Orthodox soteriologies were diametrically opposed to each other. A closer scrutiny showed that this is not necessarily the case. A faithful reading of Luther's texts shows that the idea of deification is not just occasional but an integral part of the structure of Luther's view of salvation. Even though Luther does not use the concept of deification extensively, other corresponding concepts leave no doubt about the legitimacy of theosis as an image of salvation. Perhaps a similar kind of finding could happen when Pentecostal-Holiness texts are searched. Bundy's reading of some selected texts is a promising step. (However, when one finds occasional terms like "union," one must be careful not to read too much into them.) There is enough documented material already to show that Pentecostal-Holiness theologies do not stand in contradistinction to the idea of deification—participation in God, union with God, etc. The appearance of the idea even in the Anabaptist tradition supports its compatibility with Pentecostal-Holiness traditions.

But why, then, is there such a need to try to establish the legitimacy of the concept of deification? Deification is a suitable image of salvation since it is both faithful to the ancient church and viable for the need of contextualization in the modern world. The idea of deification, rather than being a novelty, is an ancient concept widely used during the first centuries by the Church catholic. Furthermore, it is also highly relevant to the challenges of our days. Living as we are during the time of transformation of religions and cultural patterns, the Church is challenged by all kinds of yearning for spirituality, from crystals to horoscopes to interest in angels. Without getting adjusted to the mindset of our days (cf. Rom. 12:2), we need to respond to challenges also from other religions, and speak about a legitimate kind of "divinization." This is an exercise in the contextualization of theology. With the emergence of an ecumenical quest for the doctrine of deification, Pentecostal-Holiness Christians can both clarify their own identity and soteriological understanding as well as contribute to a conciliar understanding of salvation.

2) The idea of deification is a pneumatologically rich concept, thus helping Pentecostal-Holiness theologies to highlight the role of the Spirit in soteriology. Deification is a pneumatologically loaded image of salvation, and therefore, an ideal candidate for Pentecostal-Holiness soteriology. The pneumatological orientation was acknowledged even in Lutheran-Orthodox conversations. Defining the "the new road leading to deification" as a "process of growing in holiness," the joint document cites two important Pauline texts: "'But we all, with open face beholding as in a mirror the glory of the Lord, are changed into the same image from glory to glory, even as by the Spirit of the Lord' (2 Cor. 3:18). Deification takes place under the influence of the grace of the Holy Spirit by a deep and sincere faith, together with hope and permeated by love (1 Cor. 13:13)."[42]

Ecumenically in general and regarding Pentecostal-Lutheran relations in particular, it is extremely significant that it seems to be possible to express the classical Reformation doctrine of salvation and justification in pneumatological terms. This is especially significant when we take into account the fact that Reformation theology, especially in its Lutheran form, has traditionally been so slow to adopt a pneumatological orientation in its emphasis on forensic-juridical approaches both in christology and soteriology. Luther's original writings, however—as the most recent research has shown—carries clear pneumatological potential. Pentecostal soteriology which is built on the one hand on the christological categories of Latin theology and, on the other hand, on the forensic-juridical concepts of Reformation, is genuinely enriched by exposure to a pneumatological orientation. A pneumatological concept of grace does justice to Pentecostal-Charismatic traditions better than the one-sided forensic approach.

Jürgen Moltmann has a helpful section on soteriology in his *Spirit of Life* where he criticizes the traditional Reformation/Lutheran view for not paying due attention to the role of the Spirit in salvation. Referring to passages like Titus 3:5–7, which speaks about the "washing of regeneration and renewal in the Holy Spirit, which he poured out upon us richly," Moltmann emphasizes that "'[r]egeneration' as 'renewal' comes about through the Holy Spirit" when the "Spirit is 'poured out.'" By making further reference to John 4:14, the metaphor of the divine "wellspring of life" which begins to flow in a human being, he contends that "through this experience of the Spirit, who comes upon us from the Father through the Son, we become 'justified through grace.'" There is also a christological concentration, according to Moltmann, so dear to Luther:

"The medium of regeneration is the Holy Spirit, which is 'richly' poured out. Because the Spirit is mediated through Christ, it must at this point be called 'the Spirit of Christ.'"[43]

Moltmann's theologizing helps Pentecostal-Holiness traditions to reorient their soteriologies in a helpful way; in fact, in a way which does much better justice to their spirituality. First, it focuses on the crucial role of the Spirit in justification and regeneration in accordance with many New Testament witnesses. Second, it puts more stress on the process of sanctification than traditional Reformation doctrine has done. Again, quoting Moltmann: "The operation of the Spirit as we experience it is therefore a double one: it is the justification of the godless out of grace, and their rebirth to a living hope through their installation in their right to inherit God's future. The justification of the godless is the initial operation of the outpouring of the Spirit...."[44] Laying aside the differing interpretations of sanctification, one must say that neglecting the importance of sanctification in Pentecostal and Holiness spiritualities would mean ripping off something essential. The long-standing dialogue with the Roman Catholic Church has helped Pentecostals to draw pneumatological implications from their doctrine of salvation. Hopefully, the dialogue under planning with Eastern Churches will deepen these insights.

3) Encounter with Eastern traditions helps Pentecostal-Holiness theologies to clarify some basic issues which Reformation traditions have found problematic. Traditionally, Reformation theologians have accused Eastern Orthodoxy of two cardinal errors: free will and *synergia*. Interestingly enough, the same accusations are usually leveled against Pentecostal and Holiness people. Pentecostal sources freely speak about the role of human will. Orthodox theology regards freedom as belonging to the constitution of human beings.

The background to the alleged contradistinction may be found in the debates preceding the Reformation concerning the relationship between nature and grace. Lyle Dabney has identified two different models of doing theology. The oldest model he calls the theology of "the first article."[45] It is the scholastic Thomistic model which finds its point of departure in the goodness—although not of course, in the sinlessness—of God's creation. The basic axiom of this type of theology is that grace fulfills that which is in nature: "Grace does not destroy, but rather presupposes and perfects nature."[46] Over and against this claim stands the theology of the sixteenth-century Reformation that is based on the second article (christology), and assumes discontinuity rather than continuity between nature and grace. From Luther to Barth there are various nuances but the same kind of insistence on the incompatibility of human nature and God's grace.

Pentecostal-Holiness soteriology has traditionally identified itself with the Reformation camp because of its fear of Catholicism and their "work-based" view of salvation. Orthodox tradition, as we saw above, does not easily fit either category. It does not operate at all along the lines of the nature-grace opposition. Ironically, both Orthodox and Pentecostal-Holiness seem to be on the same side, so to speak. For both traditions, there is no denying the relative freedom of will and human responsibility, although Pentecostal-Charismatics often have not acknowledged the tension in relation to the strict Lutheran view of human beings as almost inactive.

As a way out of the old dichotomy, Dabney suggests a theology "of the third article," which finds its orientation in the doctrine of the Holy Spirit. It represents "continuity through discontinuity which begins its witness to Christ with the Holy Spirit, is rooted in the Trinitarian event of the cross, and then defines the Christian community in those categories."[47] A pneumatological concept of grace, anchored in the cross of Christ and a trinitarian vision, might help to reassess the traditional dilemma.

The Eastern Orthodox tradition might be helpful here with its insistence on pneumatological orientations on the one hand, and on the need for divine-human synergy, on the other. This enterprise might, of course, border on Pelagian charges. Orthodox theology does not regard itself as semi-Pelagian but rather insists on a different kind of anthropology and a legitimate divine-human synergy. It seems to me that Pentecostals have been so eager to identify themselves with the Reformation doctrine of justification that they have not seen how their anthropology and view of human responsibility is in tension with the Reformation view.

Chapter Twelve

On a Theology and Spirituality of the Cross

> Now it is not sufficient for anyone, and it does him no good to recognize God in his glory and majesty, unless he recognizes him in the humility and shame of the cross.... That person does not deserve to be called a theologian who looks upon the invisible things of God as if it were clearly perceptible in those things which have actually happened.... He deserves to be called a theologian, however, who comprehends the visible and manifest things of God seen through suffering and the cross. (*LW* 31.52; *HDT* 19 and 20)[1]

Pentecostal-Charismatic Christianity has reintroduced to Christian spirituality an ideal of victorious Christian living, an intensive faith expectation, and an emphasis on spiritual power to overcome problems in one's life. The attitude of "overcoming" is characteristic to Pentecostal and Charismatic preaching. Often there is a heightened expectation of divine intervention, even in situations that seem impossible. Even if such an expectation has sometimes led to absurdities such as denying medication to a dying child, these exceptions should not be given undue attention.

What has been much more problematic to Pentecostals/Charismatics is the negative side of the Christian life: disappointments when the healing did not come, agony when one faces the death of a loved one despite prayers of faith, the tragedy of financial breakdown, and so on. In fact, many Pentecostals and Charismatics have been left with few options: deny experiences that seem to shatter one's faith, blame oneself or other persons involved for the lack of faith, or give up one's faith. Pentecostal preachers do not often tackle the problem of unanswered prayers or disappointed faith. Rarely does one find in Pentecostal-Charismatic periodicals honest consideration of life situations where a prayer of faith was either not answered or was bluntly rejected.

The concept of faith plays a crucial role in all these issues. Much of Pentecostal-Charismatic preaching and testimony-giving is meant to increase and strengthen faith, and consequently, to heighten the expectation of miracles. Faith is often understood in "power" categories: the more faith one has, the more one has the right to expect from God. Pentecostalism and the Charismatic movements would lose something very crucial if they neglected talk of faith, power, healing, and miracles. But what is also needed is to ensure that Pentecostal-Charismatic Christians are equipped to come to grips with inevitable questions of life such as the existence of suffering, the duality of human faith, the mystery of God's hiddenness, and the ultimate fate of everyone, death. What is the role of faith here? What is the meaning of faith? How do faith and suffering relate to each other? Questions like these need to be taken up by Pentecostals and Charismatics.

The purpose of the present chapter is to offer resources for Pentecostal-Charismatic Christians and theologians as they face the dark side of life. I will inquire into the theology of the cross as its initial developer, Martin Luther, presented it. By going to the original sources of Luther, as they are highlighted by the most recent ecumenical Luther research in Europe, especially at the University of Helsinki, I believe we can glean helpful perspectives for modern day Christians.[2]

I will proceed as follows. First, I will offer a general orientation to Luther's theology of the cross and then discuss its main aspects, such as how Luther describes the seemingly paradoxical nature of God's works in that God appears to act against us while God conceals himself in the opposite attributes, and how faith and revelation are to be appropriated in that context. I will also touch on Luther's understanding of the relationship between Christ's sufferings and ours, and how Christ's presence could change Christian life, both individual and communal, into a healing "hospital." I will conclude by offering theses and challenges to Pentecostal-Charismatic theology and spirituality as to how to deal with the issues of suffering, disappointments, and failures.

"*Crux sola est nostra theologia*"[3]: Luther's Theological Program

In April 1518, Martin Luther presided over the opening disputation of the chapter of his Augustinian Order at Heidelberg. The disputation concerned a series of theses that Luther had drawn up for the occasion at the invitation of Johannes von Staupitz. In the Heidelberg Disputation a new phrase was added to the Christian *thesaurus*, namely *theologia crucis*, the theology of the cross.

It is a consensus among recent Lutheran scholars that the *theologia crucis*, far more than being just *a* topic among others, is *the* programmatic theme underlying all of Luther's theology. It attacks a false kind of thinking about God and humanity, "the theology of glory," by pointing to the decisive importance of the cross of Christ, where we meet the suffering God. It also introduces two opposite kinds of loves: God's love that is oriented toward bad, sinful humans who are nothing in themselves, and human love that always seeks its own best. Luther's *theologia crucis* takes seriously God and human beings and their relationship held in tension in a world filled with sin and suffering.

"The Works of God Appear Evil"

The leading idea in the Heidelberg Disputation, and in much of Luther's theology, is the difference between two kinds of love: *amor Dei* and *amor hominis*, or the love of God and the love of human beings. The twenty-eight theses, in fact, culminate in this distinction. Human love is always basically selfish, and it fools human beings into seeking God with good works and human wisdom. This perverted love in the final analysis renders people incapable of receiving God's grace (*LW* 31.57; *HDT* 28). Human love is oriented toward objects that are inherently good, where self-love defines the content and the object of the love. Humans love something that they believe they can enjoy. For Luther, love as defined by medieval scholastic theology provided an example of this kind of love.

God loves in a way opposite to human love: "The love of God does not find, but creates, that which is pleasing to it.... Rather than seeking its own good, the love of God flows forth and bestows good" (*LW* 31.57; *HDT* 28). Luther sometimes calls God's love *amor crucis*: "This is the love of the cross, born of the cross, which turns in the direction where it does not find good which it may enjoy, but where it may confer good upon the bad and needy person" (*LW* 31.57; *HDT* 28). It is born out of the cross of Christ and is manifested through God's gracious works in the world.

Luther goes a step further by arguing that the works born out of human love are in fact sin leading to death. Although good works seem to be good in other peoples' eyes, Luther calls them "deadly sins" (*LW* 31.43; *HDT* 3, 5). On the contrary, God's works "are always unattractive and appear evil, (but) they are nevertheless really eternal merits," insofar as they are in accordance with the true love (*LW* 31.44; *HDT* 17). As a fitting conclusion to the section dealing with human works, Luther states that the only way to prepare for receiving grace is to preach about sin and the need for repentance (*HDT* 3).

In order to do works acceptable in God's eyes, a radical change must take place, namely faith. Faith is not something that humans choose for themselves. Rather, it is a gift from God. Faith changes human will in a way that through their works they are not seeking good for themselves but for others as well. The root of evil, and the bedrock of all sin, for Luther is pride and perverted self-confidence. These characteristics will be manifested in relation to God as well as fellow Christians. The lack of fear (of God) is a symptom of this perverted love (*LW* 31.47; *HDT* 8). Whereas good human works appear to be beautiful to human eyes, God's works in this world often appear ugly. Whereas human beings do their best to become good and beautiful by seeking the good and beautiful, according to Luther God works in an opposite way. God conceals himself in lowliness and darkness to reveal the greatness of his love. Consequently, God will not reward human works according to their (alleged) merits, but instead reveals their weakness and sinfulness through the cross and suffering.

The natural mind imagines the works of God beautiful, fine, and attractive. But according to Luther, the opposite is the case. He describes the works of God with biblical pictures: "He had no form of comeliness (*decor*)" (Isa. 53:2), and "The Lord kills and brings to life; he brings down to Sheol and raises up" (2 Sam 2:6). In other words, God makes us "nothing" (*nihil*) and "stupid" to reveal his real love to us (*LW* 31.33; *HDT* 4).[4]

God's Alien Works and God's Proper Works

Here Luther introduces one major aspect of his "theology of paradoxes": God's alien work (*opus alienum Dei*) and God's proper work (*opus proprium Dei*). God's alien work includes putting down, killing, taking away hope, leading to desperation, etc. God's proper work includes the opposite: forgiving, giving mercy, taking up, saving, encouraging, etc. (*LW* 14.95). The following quote gives a clear picture of the meaning of these two terms: "You [God] exalt us when you humble us. You make us righteous when you make us sinners. You lead us to heaven when you cast us into hell. You grant us the victory when you cause us to be defended. You give us life when you permit us to be killed" (*LW* 14.95).

The alien works Luther sometimes calls "the works of the left hand" and the proper works "the works of the right hand." It is important to understand that, while these two kinds of works seem to be opposite to each other, they result from the same love of God. Luther in fact says that God's proper work is veiled in his alien work and takes place simultaneously with it (*LW* 31.50; *HDT* 16). In doing so God turns out to be the devil. To show the paradoxical nature of his theology of the cross, Luther even goes so far as to say that God's works are not just veiled in their opposite, but they also sometimes create bad results (*LW* 31.45; *HDT* 5, 6). To illustrate his point, Luther compares the working of God in this world with a worker with a bad ax: although the worker himself is skillful, because of the tool the results are bad. And furthermore, Luther argues that sometimes God uses even Satan for his *opus alienum* in order to work out his *opus proprium* (*LW* 45; *HDT* 6).[5]

The Paradoxical Nature of God's Revelations: Revelation by Hiding

There is no way for a sinful person to know God directly, apart from God's "covering himself" in the word, incarnate in human flesh.[6] The only meeting point between the majestic God and sinful humanity is the word. Luther's theology is first and foremost a theology of the word. God enters into a saving encounter with humankind only by "clothing" himself and causing himself to be found at a place God has designated. This particular place is Christ, the word incarnate.

Philosophical and scholastic theological speculation about God belong to the category of humanity's autonomous search for God. Such speculation seeks to know God in himself, in his majesty—as he is in heaven. The corrupted nature of sinful human beings cannot, however, achieve this. For if humans able to reach to God that way, to achieve it, what they meet is absolute majesty, naked and unveiled. Sinful humans, however, are not capable of dealing with divinity. Luther goes so far as to say, "Man and God in his majesty are enemies."[7] God adjusts himself to our human ability to comprehend him. Therefore, he does not present himself to us directly, but covers and clothes himself with a mask. God thus comes to us hidden by "fog and shadows."[8]

Luther describes the essence of true theology as *theologia crucis*, the opposite of *theologia gloriae*. He bases his argument on Exodus 33:18–23, where Moses asks, "Show me thy glory." God answers that Moses cannot see his face, "for man shall not see me and live." God lets Moses see only his "back side." This is the theology of the cross: to see God hidden, veiled, covered, because seeing God in his majesty and glory is destructive to humanity. The theology of glory, on the contrary, according to Romans 1:20, seeks "God in heaven." That was, in fact, possible before the Fall but not anymore.

God's invisible nature is described in terms of his majestic attributes, whereas his visible backside is described in terms of his humanity, weakness, and foolishness. Luther wrote, "He who does not know Christ does not know God hidden in suffering" (*LW* 31.53). Here we come to the distinction, crucial to Luther: knowledge of God from his works and knowledge of God from his sufferings: "Because men misused the knowledge of God through works, God wished again to be recognized in suffering, and to condemn wisdom concerning invisible things by means of wisdom concerning visible things, so that those who did not honor God as manifested in his works should honor him as he is hidden in his suffering" (*LW* 31.53).

Our Suffering and the Suffering Christ

Theologia crucis explains the paradox of the hiddenness of God. The cross of Christ is opposed to glory and power, the basic elements of *theologia gloriae.* The theology of glory seeks to know God directly in his majesty and power, whereas the theology of the cross paradoxically recognizes him precisely where he has hidden himself: in his sufferings and in all that which humans consider to be weakness and foolishness. In this way, the theology of the cross destroys humanity's self-confidence and at the same time elevates God. God is free and sovereign to do whatever he wishes. For Pentecostals, used to "name it and claim it" faith-formulas, it is healthy to ponder these kinds of words:

> He, however, who has emptied himself through suffering no longer does works but knows that God works and does all things in him. For this reason, whether God does works or not, it is all the same to him. He neither boasts if he does good works, nor is he disturbed if God does not do good works through him. He knows that it is sufficient if he suffers and is brought low by the cross in order to be annihilated all the more. (*LW* 31.55)

The theology of the cross permeates all of Luther's theology, the "wisdom of the cross" (*LW* 14.305, 309). It has implications for his christology, soteriology, ecclesiology, and overall view of the Christian life. The theology of the cross means that all these realities of theology and the Christian life are hidden because God himself, the source of all theology and life, is hidden! God is not presented to us in power and glory, but paradoxically under helplessness and lowliness. It means also that the means of salvation are hidden. God's grace is hidden under his wrath, or to put it in another way, his gifts and benefits are "so hidden under the cross that the godless can neither see nor recognize them but rather consider them to be only trouble and disaster"; and "Thus the favor bestowed by God on this little group is completely hidden from the world and appears to be nothing but eternal wrath, punishment, and torment from God himself" (*LW*, 14, 58).

Here we come directly to the problem of suffering: the world—and also Christians as part of the world—judges God on the basis of what he does with his own and concludes that he is a devil. And consequently, the devil appears to be God, the Lord of the world. That is the terrible impression the reality of the world gives—the world where God's own are left in despair and suffering, while godless people prosper!

According to Luther, amidst this anxiety human beings sense the presence of death (*LW* 31.55; *HDT* 24) akin to hell and consider God as their opponent. Moreover, Luther even says that afflicted people in fact regard the opposition between God and humans as real. For Luther, this is nothing less than the union between the sufferings of Christ and ours. In his exposition on justification, Luther emphasizes that a justified person does not require anything more of God but is satisfied with becoming more *nihil* (*LW* 31.51; *HDT* 24). To do justice to Luther, a modern psychological interpretation of the loss of self-confidence must be set aside.

In this way, the "way of the Christian is hidden" in the world. Only God knows it. God's children are hidden from the world and even from themselves. Neither they nor the world recognize them for what they are before God. Referring to Psalm 1, which calls the righteous blessed, Luther states: "the blessedness of this name is hidden in the Spirit, i.e., in God, so that it cannot be known except through faith or experience....The man whom the prophet here calls blessed is unanimously declared by the world to be the most wretched of all, as Isaiah looked upon Christ, the Head and Model of the blessed, whom he calls the lowest of all (Isa. 53:3)" (*LW* 14.298).

The theology of the cross also determines Luther's understanding of justification, the cornerstone of his thinking. Those with whom God deals are sinners who deserve the wrath of God alone. These wretched, sinful people are supposed to dare to believe the word of promise and think of themselves as righteous before God. "God's 'yes' to them is hidden in a severe 'no.'"[9]

The Paradoxical Nature of Faith

There is no way to understand the nature of faith in Luther apart from the theology of the cross: "The man who believes must repeatedly pass from this experience to that faith which recognizes the reality of the grace, truth, and faithfulness of God hidden under its opposite."[10] Faith, in Luther's view, means believing against your senses, even against your better judgment! Faith counts on God's promises and his faithfulness even when reason says God has betrayed or forsaken you completely. As Luther puts it, "It is most difficult of all to recognize as king, one who died such a desperate and shameful death. The senses are strongly repelled by such a notion, reason abhors it, experience denies it, and a precedent is lacking. Plainly this will be folly to the Gentiles and a stumbling block to the Jews (1 Cor. 1:23) unless you raise your thoughts above this" (*LW* 14.342).

But through faith, against human senses and against what others may think, the Christian takes hold of the word and believes in this "no" that finally appears to be "no" only to human pride and glory, but "yes" to God's mercy. Luther puts is neatly: faith is "holding fast to the deep and hidden 'yes' under and above the 'no' by firmly trusting in God's word" (*WA* 17.203). Faith is directed toward the word of promise and at first has nothing except this word. The word offers a reality that is hidden and cannot be seen. Faith constantly stands in opposition to, and in conflict with experience. Here "faith is not seeing" as some faith-teachers teach us!

According to *theologia crucis*, as we have already seen, even God, the object of faith, is hidden under his opposite. Glory is concealed in shame, power in helplessness. Therefore, to the natural eye, God seems to be doing the opposite of that which he ultimately will. God hides himself under the disguise of his antagonist, Satan. In this sense, faith must not only live without experience. It even has experience against it and must persevere and assert itself in opposition to experience.

Faith also means to Luther total dependence on God, for human beings are not able to sustain themselves. To understand this we must note that for Luther, creation means creation "out of nothing," *ex nihilo*. For Luther this concept is more than an assertion about the genesis of all things. It is an all-inclusive characteristic of God's creating and working. This is also the definition of God's love. It is directed—in opposition to human love—to "nothingness" and creates out of nothing. Since God works all things everywhere, we are always in his hand. This brings confidence and safety to the Christian. In the final analysis, no matter where one goes, one can fall only into God's hands. Everything is subject to God's power, even Satan and his evil work. This means that the devil must still serve God's will for humanity and for the world. God keeps him in his service and uses him for his own work (*opus alienum*). In this sense, the devil is "God's Satan."

Luther is never an academic theologian alone. He is as much a preacher and a pastor who comforts rootless souls. He speaks thus about the "loneliness of faith" by referring to death. In death, each person is completely alone and must die their own death. In the final analysis, "I am lost if in dying I am not personally as certain of God's word as I am of my own existence."[11]

Christian Life as a Life of "Anfechtung"

True faith for Luther always conflicts with the reality that the world and our experience see. Therefore the Christian life is a constant struggle with *Anfechtung*, a word difficult to translate in English: trial, temptation, assault, perplexity, even doubt. To believe means to live in constant contradiction to empirical reality. As Althaus puts it: "The Christian's existence is in danger because he stands in the midst of reality under that impression of it which reason and rational experience have given him.... Faith must endure being contradicted by reason and experience; and it must break through the reality of this world by fixing its sights on the word of promise."[12] This means that faith is not so much a position on which one takes a stand but a constantly new movement. The only way to overcome the impressions that reality gives us is by holding fast to the promises of the word in faith. Christians are always tempted to allow their impression of reality to cast doubt on the truth of God and view it as alien. Faith stands in constant conflict.

However—and this is important for our understanding of the nature of true faith—for Luther, faith and experience are in dialectical relationship with each other. They are certainly in absolute opposition to and conflict with each other, but there is also such a thing as experience wrought by faith itself. In the course of the Christian life, every now and then, I come to experience that God's word is worth trusting. Although Luther is the first to warn of "self-made faith" that leads to false self-confidence (cf. *LW* 40.241), he admits that there is something like "certainty of faith," although not constant. It comes through the Holy Spirit in the midst of the struggle of faith: "No one can correctly understand God or his word, unless he has received such understanding immediately from the Holy Spirit. But no one can receive it from the Holy Spirit without experiencing, proving, and feeling it" (*LW* 21.299).

The Church as a Hospital for the Incurably Sick

The theology of glory seeks God in heaven and in glory. Consequently, faith based on this kind of theology errs in its object. The object of faith, for Luther, is not God's deity in heaven but in the humanity of Christ. The same is true of our love. Since God has become a man, our love for God should show itself as love for others. Thus, Luther's understanding of love is completely dominated by his faith in the incarnation.

We can certainly do nothing for our salvation, but our neighbors need our work, that is, our love: "Every man is created and born for the sake of others" (*WA* 21.346). For if I do not use everything that I have to serve my neighbors, I rob them of what I owe them according to God's will.[13] Each Christian, then, becomes a "work of Christ," and even more a "christ" to the neighbor. Christians do what Christ does. They identify with the suffering of their neighbor (*LW* 31.55–56; *HDT* 25). The presence of Christ in us through faith makes us act the same way Christ loved those in need of help. According to Luther, "since Christ lives in us through faith...he arouses us to do good works through that living faith in his work, for the works which he does are the fulfillment of the commands of God given us through faith" (*LW* 31.56; *HDT* 27).[14]

Challenges and Tasks for Pentecostal-Charismatic Spirituality

To help Pentecostals and Charismatics cope with the dark side of reality without giving up their distinctive Christian—and may we dare to say, biblical—emphasis on the power of the Spirit to effect healing, mental and physical recovery, and deliverance, I will offer the following suggestions based on my reading of Luther's theology of the cross as guidelines for further reflection.

The problem of evil must be faced in all its seriousness and ugliness. Much of Pentecostal-Charismatic spirituality and theology, especially in its popular, devotional form, is a misguided effort to whitewash the walls of our world with sentimental talk about God's love. The radical nature of evil and sin in human life and creation must also be taken seriously. This brings human life into absolute dependence on God and God's mercy. In Luther, anthropology and theology inform each other, and while evil can never be equated with sin in private life (as Evangelicalism too often has implied), neither can it be downplayed, as "natural" theologies of our day often imply.

The cross of Christ has not only salvific but also revelational importance. The way theology speaks about suffering and evil is determined by the understanding of revelation. For Luther, revelation is the word of the cross. Everything one can say about God and God's world is "mediated" by the cross, and therefore, by the Christ of the cross.

Talk about God's love in a real world is dangerous. Much of the love-talk of Christian piety seems so vague because it has no theological basis. For Luther, God's love means the essence of loving something that is not existent, or that exists in weakness and shame, in order to make it something new. This is what it means to be God: to create something out of nothing. Evangelical theology in general and Pentecostal-Charismatic in particular has not paid much attention to the category of love, but rather has focused on the grace of God. Luther's theology of love, combined with the biblical—especially the Old Testament's—view of God's passionate love, could help Evangelicals to say something worthwhile about *agape.*

God must assume the final responsibility for the evil and suffering in the world—and human beings must leave it with God. For Luther, God is the all-determining power in the world. God not only allows evil but also causes it to some extent and makes use of it in God's alien work. God is not to be excused, but is to be trusted, for out of death new life springs forth. Even though Luther's theology reflects crucial Augustinian and western influences—keep in mind that Luther was not only a member of the Augustinian Order, but also a keen student of Augustine's theology, even after he broke with the Catholic Church—his theology of evil and love does not follow the "Augustinian theodicy"—to utilize the well known typology of John Hick's *Evil and the God of Love.*[15] In the approach of Augustine and many of his followers, the main motive is to absolve the Creator from the responsibility for evil and suffering. This is a seriously mistaken course.

The line between the Christian belief in an all-determining God and other gods is sharp: either God takes responsibility and in the final analysis *is* the solution to the problem of evil or we are left to the power of other forces. The cross shows the final evidence of the fact that God assumed the responsibility over evil by sending God's Son to the cross. This is the way the New Testament—which does not know any kind of philosophical theodicy—talks about evil and suffering. Christian theology about evil should be a theology of hope. Luther's theology of the cross takes suffering and death seriously, so seriously that it also takes the hope seriously: it is constitutive of God to make new life out of death, out of *nihil.*

The concept of "faith" must also be critically scrutinized by Pentecostals/Charismatics. There is too much stress on the human side and too little on what God does. There is reservation in talking about faith as an "empty hand" (George Muller) that reaches to God and his mercy. Faith is not so much needed when one sees God's miracles. Faith is needed when we are facing the dark side of life and the immanence of death.

And finally, even though we suffer as individuals, we recover in community—or we become worse if the community is not what it should be. Pentecostal ecclesiology has another lesson to learn from Luther: the church is not a showplace for the successful but a hospital for the suffering and needy!

Chapter Thirteen

Are Pentecostals Oblivious to Social Justice?

One of the most common criticisms against Pentecostal missions is its alleged lack of social concern. Latin American, African, and Asian observers, among others, have often spoken to this effect. Both Marxist and Catholic writers have often attributed the growth of the movement to foreign resources and leadership, and further assumed that Pentecostals are indifferent to and even obstructionist in their attitudes toward the fundamental issues of social injustice, repression, discrimination, corruption, and poverty. One of the reasons for this distrust is the perception that charismatic Christianity represents a completely "other-world" religion—a religion obsessed by its future destination only. Many take it for granted that Nathan Gerrard's description of Pentecostal Holiness Churches in the United States apply to charismatics across the board: "... despite their strong feelings about the evils of the world, they are completely indifferent to the social gospel and take no interest in politics."[1]

Jürgen Moltmann asks where are the "charismata of the 'charismatics' in the everyday world, in the peace movement, in the movements of liberation, in the ecology movement." He continues: "If charismata are not given to us so that we can flee from this world into a world of religious dreams, but if they are intended to witness to the liberating lordship of Christ in this world's conflicts, then the charismatic movement must not become a non-political religion, let alone a de-politicized one."[2]

One persistent misunderstanding among observers of Pentecostalism has tended to contribute to this one-sided understanding. The earlier generation of sociologically-oriented observers of Pentecostalism tended to regard the birth and appeal of the movement in terms of social deprivation theory. Basically, this view suggests that all religious movements, including Pentecostalism, develop as a result of individuals or groups feeling disadvantaged. This model, however, has been unable to explain why Pentecostalism has also appealed to social classes other than the lower. Contrary to deprivation theories, Luther P. Gerlach and Virginia H. Hine have argued that Pentecostalism and other such movements were both "cause and effect of social change...[and they focus] on movements as mechanisms of change rather than on the conditions of disorganization or deprivation which give rise to them."[3]

Pentecostals have taken up the challenge and begun to engage the perennial question concerning the relationship between proclamation and social justice. In fact, one of the most exciting developments among Pentecostals in recent years has been the emergence of a theologically sophisticated response to this alleged lack of social concern. As a result, an exciting corpus of distinctively Pentecostal social ethics, theology of social concern, and related studies has seen daylight. Pentecostal professor of social ethics Douglas Petersen, referring distinctively to the Latin American context, notes that Pentecostalism, rather than being just a movement "for the people," is actually "a social program" in itself. Even though Pentecostals have not written statements about the "preferential option for the poor," most Pentecostal churches are "churches of the poor."[4]

Although Pentecostal mission is focused on evangelization, it is not to the exclusion of social concern, and never has been so. The "broader mission" (holistic) has been part and parcel of the Pentecostal branch of the family "as an automatic outgrowth of its prioritization" of the Great Commission.[5] And as Juan Sepúlveda, a Latin American Pentecostal, succinctly notes, even though Pentecostals have been cautious to engage in politics, "the Pentecostal communities meant a powerful offering of life-meaning for wide sectors excluded from our communities."[6] In fact, Pentecostals have worked with the poor for social renewal in unobtrusive ways and have initiated major social reform programs and institutions.

This chapter has two main parts. The first part will offer some selected Pentecostal responses to the challenge presented by the title and introduction. In this section, I will first take a look at the theological ramifications of Pentecostal social concern, especially what is the potential and problematic of urgent eschatological expectation to how social justice is perceived. The second part will scrutinize the major results of the recent Roman Catholic-Pentecostal dialogue on mission and social justice. This international dialogue was the first ecumenical occasion for Pentecostals to engage the question of social concern, a topic of vital interest to the Roman Catholic Church which has devoted much time to formulating a theologically and missiologically satisfying view of social justice in recent decades.

Theological Resources for Pentecostal Social Concern

"Kingdom Works Remain": The Potential and Problematic of Eschatology and Kingdom

There is no denying the fact that in the formative years of the movement many Pentecostals' eschatological fervor blurred the meaning of social improvement. Why invest in a world that was believed would fade away? Althoguh much of this mindset still prevails in popular Pentecostalism, some Pentecostal theologians have attempted to develop a more constructive theological view. These theologians have not seen it necessary to surrender to such a pessimistic outlook. Although tension between those with a view which emphasizes the "other-worldliness" of the hope and those with a view toward improvement of the present still continues, for many Pentecostals eschatological hope has brought with it optimism about the work they are doing:

> Pentecostals are exceptionally optimistic about both their present and future existence. Their theological conviction that the God who performed mighty works in the New Testament continues to act in miraculous ways through the empowerment of the Holy Spirit provides the great majority of Pentecostal believers with a sense of hope for the present...[I]t is quite clear that the eschatological certainty of eternal life gives freedom to risk one's present life. The Pentecostals' personal relationship with a caring and compassionate God encourages them also to celebrate their experience of transformation in the present within a community of mutual love and respect.[7]

Pentecostal theologian Peter Kuzmic of the former Yugoslavia argues that to interpret the impending premillennial return of Christ as a doctrine that paralyzes efforts for social improvement is more of a Western cultural-theological creation based upon conservative (American) political positions rather than on a clear reading of Scripture. His colleague, Miroslav Volf, has argued that when Christians create history that is compatible with the Kingdom of God, such projects have eschatological significance: what is valid will remain. Volf contends that eschatological continuity between God's present reign and the reign to come "guarantees that noble human efforts will not be wasted."[8]

It is precisely this view of the Kingdom of God that has informed Pentecostal social thinking during the last decade. Pentecostal exegete Gordon Fee has been at the vanguard of introducing Pentecostals to the concept of the Kingdom of God. God brings his future reign to the present with the proclamation of "Good News to the poor" everywhere. According to Fee, the "final consummation, our glorious future, has been guaranteed...by the resurrection of our Lord. But meanwhile, until that future has come in its fullness, we are to be the people of the future in the present age, who continue the proclamation of the kingdom as good news to the poor."[9] The eschatological Kingdom has a normative moral structure reflective of God's own ethical character. Pentecostals believe that when Christians are empowered with the Spirit of God they are equipped to do "kingdom works" in the midst of human suffering and plight.[10]

Asian and other Pentecostals would be helped by the emerging theological work done by Latin American Pentecostals, especially regarding social concern. Peruvian theologian Dario L. Rodriguez, working in the slums of Lima, argues that there are two central theological themes in Luke's perspective on church's responsibility toward the world: first, God's love as a permanent missionary paradigm, and second, the poor and outcasts as subjects and agents of God's mission.[11]

Race, War, Politics

One of the key issues of social justice in the modern world, racism, has definite roots in the birth of the Pentecostal movement.[12] In the formative years of the movement, the Azusa Street mission was essentially a black church (despite the number of whites who initially attended), and, thus, attained a more universal character than was typical of other churches of that time. The short history of Pentecostalism, however, reflects similar kinds of prejudices, racial segregation, and negative attitudes that have existed in the rest of the churches. Very soon white Pentecostals separated themselves from the Blacks, and separate constituencies were formed. Recently, several Pentecostals in the United States and South Africa, especially, have expressed their concerns over this racial division as working against the paradigm of Pentecost where people of various nationalities were united. In the American context it was not until 1994 that white and black Pentecostal organizations coalesced to celebrate the "Memphis Miracle."[13]

Miroslav Volf addresses racial and ethnic issues from a distinctively theological perspective, and suggests the approach of a "theology of embrace" instead of an attitude of exclusion. The theological basis is the "divine embrace" between the Father, Son, and Spirit, which is a divine model of human community. "Embrace, I propose, is what should happen between different ethnic or cultural groups. Instead of seeking to isolate ourselves from other groups by insisting on our pure identity, we should open ourselves to one another to be enriched by our differences."[14]

Along with racial unity, the first Pentecostals were born with the idea of pacifism. A literalistic reading of the Bible and an enthusiasm caused by the wonder of God's Spirit uniting people of different origins, worshipping in the same community, caused Pentecostals to regard war as belonging to the "old age." Most Pentecostals soon, however, came to embrace the ideology of the majority of their societies, with a view of legitimate warfare. During the last decade there have been calls to revive the early pacifism on the basis of early spiritual and theological ethos of the movement.[15]

It is not right to say that Pentecostals have been totally inactive regarding social concern. It is more accurate to say that they have had a distinctive approach to solving social problems as part of their missionary enthusiasm. One area in which this has been clearly seen is the question of political engagement. Generally, although not exclusively, Pentecostals have been reluctant to take part in political action to further their social concerns. This is not necessarily because of a lack of political dimension but rather because of an alternative way of seeing their mission. Pentecostal theologians of social concern would argue that Pentecostals have created their own alternative institutions that function as instruments of human justice. They will also question the definition of social concern that includes only political, state, and civil categories as the exclusive means of being involved in the improvement of society:

> The definition of social concern that includes only political, state and civil categories cannot capture other equally important areas of social concern. Political involvement is only one alternative among several options of social action to institute social change. Pentecostals have a clear expression of serious and committed Pentecostal views, articulating a beginning agenda for a further discussion of social concern.[16]

A Dialogue on Social Justice between Catholics and Pentecostals

Distinctive Pentecostal Perspectives on Social Justice

The fourth phase of the Roman Catholic Church-Pentecostal dialogue (1990–1997), our focus in the remainder of this chapter, lasted for seven years. The overall topic was mission and proselytism. Before exploring common affirmations and divergences, both parties attempted to define their own positions on social justice as clearly as possible. The dialogue outcomes are significant in view of the fact that this has been the very first time when Pentecostals on a larger scale have attempted to define what they believe about this missiologically crucial issue. The following will summarize the Pentecostal position and then analyze the common positions.

There are various reasons why it took time before Pentecostals started to wrestle with the issue of social concern on a larger scale. During the formative years, most Pentecostals came from the lower levels of society. The lower socio-economic status of early Pentecostals may explain the seemingly passive stand toward the issues of social justice. Pentecostals did not see it necessary to attempt to change society but, rather, to invite people into personal faith. The otherworldliness of Pentecostal belief tended to distance them from the present world. This was partly the heritage of the Holiness tradition, out of which Pentecostals came. The idea of the church as pilgrim traveling through a sinful world, a sense of foreignness, and a premillennial vision of the future served to discourage the social and political involvement of Pentecostals. The evangelistic and revivalist heritage consolidated this kind of orientation. With priority on personal conversion, Pentecostals—with most Fundamentalists and many Evangelicals—were careful not to be associated with the stigmatizing "social gospel." Consequently, the focus of Pentecostals has been on individual change, often to the exclusion of social change. This is not to deny the personal and social consequences of being "saved," "sanctified," and "filled with the Holy Ghost," but to note the obvious one-sidedness of their approach to the larger scale problems.

It would, however, be an oversimplification to claim that the Pentecostal approach to evangelism and personalistic orientation leads necessarily to the exclusion of social concern. As was noted above, it is more accurate to say that Pentecostals do strongly prioritize the need for personal conversion and commitment to the communities of faith, according to their interpretation of the New Testament, and through that process wish to effect social change (*FR* IV.42). The structural change is not the point of departure, but rather the change of individuals and Christian communities to facilitate the changes in a larger scale (*FR* IV.64). For Pentecostals, social justice is not a cause but a consequence of successful evangelistic efforts. Therefore, the perceived lack of stress on structural change does not imply a lack of interest in social issues *per se*, but a distinctive approach to social problems. For Pentecostals, conversion, while being personal, is not simply an individual experience, but also a communal one. In the life of the community, Pentecostals have found a new sense of dignity and purpose in life (*FR* IV.43).

Pentecostals have never been totally inactive regarding social issues. Pentecostals believe that they have been called by God in the "last days" (Acts 2:17) to be Christ-like witnesses in the power of the Spirit (*FR* IV.38). The hope in the imminent coming of the Lord has sustained Pentecostals during persecution, harassment, imprisonment, and martyrdom during the twentieth century. They have consistently taught that the Church must be ready for the coming of the Lord by means of faithful witness and holy living. They have taught that all will have to give account to the righteous Judge for those things that have been done or left undone (*FR* IV.39). Pentecostals today still continue to believe that intense hope has been and will continue to be necessary for endurance, healing, and engagement of the forces—both social and spiritual—which oppress and violate people (*FR* IV.41). On the other hand, the theologically more sophisticated sector of Pentecostalism has come to emphasize that the rebirth of a person by the Spirit is the anticipation of the transformation of the cosmos (cf. 2 Cor. 5:17; Rom. 8:21). "This is why conversion and incorporation into the community of faith cannot be seen apart from the transformation of society. The person filled by the Spirit of God is impelled by that same Spirit to cooperate with God in the work of evangelism and social action in the anticipation of the new creation" (*FR* IV.40).

There is one more factor, aptly noted by the Catholic team in the dialogue, namely perception. It seems that Pentecostals have been more active in terms of social activities than is usually thought. But because of a lack of perception much of the work has gone unnoticed. Pentecostals have continued to speak and act on behalf of those victimized by abortion, pornography, violence, oppression, etc. And even more concretely, they have fed the hungry, clothed the naked, and provided emergency disaster relief. They have expanded their educational efforts in many parts of the world (*FR* IV.44). From their earliest existence, Pentecostals have been active in missionary endeavors in the Two-Thirds world. The churches established there have opposed social evils from the pulpit and interpersonally. This concerns evils such as the Caste-system in India, polygamy in Africa and the Pacific, and genital mutilation in some African countries (*FR* IV.45).

But Pentecostals have not written theological treatises like some liberation theologians. Neither have they formed intellectual academic societies to address the relation of evangelization and social concern. The way most Pentecostals have addressed social problems has been in the oral fashion typical of their non-literary culture. For older, more literary publics, only what is written and documented is perceived as having real existence. Pentecostals have only recently begun to document these kinds of social issues in which they have participated for many years (*FR* IV.44–45).

Now, after the presentation of a Pentecostal self-understanding of social concern, it is time to analyze the main results of the mutual dialogue. The mutual discussions can be summarized under the following rubrics: 1) A trinitarian basis of social justice; 2) *Koinonia* and social justice; 3) the Kingdom of God as the ultimate norm; and 4) spirituality as a source of power for social action.

A Trinitarian Basis for Social Justice

It is ecumenically significant that in principle Catholics and Pentecostals are in agreement that theologically evangelization and social justice belong together and cannot be separated. Both agree that the Word of God is the foundation of both evangelization and social justice (*FR* IV.35). In the Old Testament there is a strong insistence that the people whom God has freed should live justly (e.g., Jer. 21:12; 22:3; Amos 5:7–12; 8:4–6; Mic. 6:12). The fact that we find in the Gospels both the Great Commission to evangelize the nations (Mt 28:16–20; Mark 16:15–18) and the Great Commandment to love God and one's neighbor (Matt. 22:34–40; Mark 12:28–34; Luke 10: 27–28) suggests that there is a continuity between the two (*FR* IV.56).

Models for the practice of evangelization and social justice are also found in the life of the early Church (Acts 2:42–47, 4:32–37). Evangelization and social justice are intrinsically linked so that the Church cannot have one apart from the other. The common agreement shows without the slightest doubt that Pentecostals too, have committed themselves to the integral relation of evangelization and social justice. This does not mean, however, giving up the prioritization of personal evangelism and individual conversion.

Significantly enough, there is a trinitarian approach to the theology of social concern: "Clearly, any striving for social justice in which our faith communities engage needs to be rooted in the life of God/Father, Son, and Holy Spirit" (*FR* IV.59). Life in the Holy Spirit energizes Christians to engage in evangelization and to work for justice in society. "Transformed people are compelled by the Spirit, the Creator and Sanctifier, to transform the world in the light of the in-breaking Kingdom of God" (*FR* IV.59). This is a brilliant theological statement, emphasizing as it does, the radical change of Christians transformed by the Spirit of God.

Koinonia and Social Justice

As previously mentioned, *koinonia* has been one of the major topics in recent dialogue years between Catholics and Pentecostals. In fact, the Third Quinquennium (1985–89) was totally devoted to various ecclesiological topics related to communion. It is significant that in dealing with social concern, some of the implications of the emerging *koinonia*-theology were brought to bear upon the discussion. Pentecostals and Catholics agreed that *koinonia* as lived by the early Christians (Acts 2.42–47; 4:32–37), had social implications. Their communities did not act from a concept of social justice. The concern they showed for the poor, widows, and strangers, was not seen as an entirely separate activity, but rather an extension of their worship (*FR* IV.57).

One of the most influential factors contributing to the Pentecostal social action was the strong sense of community, patterned after the model of the early church. In the life of the community, Pentecostals have found a new sense of dignity and purpose in life. Their solidarity creates affective ties, giving them a sense of equality. These communities have functioned as social alternatives that protest against the oppressive structures of the society at large. Along with some social critics, Pentecostals have discovered that effective social change often takes place at the communal and micro-structural level, not at the macro-structural level (*FR* IV.43).

In living out their Spirit-inspired *koinonia* at the local level, the early Pentecostals challenged current norms of inequality regarding the treatment of minorities, women, and the poor. "Thus, mainline denominations petitioned their societies for social justice, while Pentecostals found justice in their daily relationships with the dispossessed of society."[17] Pentecostalism, with its appeal to marginal groups in society, shattered the norms of middle-class society. During a time when racial and gender inequality was endemic, Pentecostals welcomed black and white, male and female, rich and poor. Ecumenically and theologically it is essential to note that the topic of *koinonia* has played a crucial role in the dialogue regarding both ecclesiology and missiology during the Third Quinquennium (1985–1989) of dialogue.

The Kingdom of God as the Ultimate Norm

Even though Catholics and Pentecostals have slightly differing interpretations concerning the crucial New Testament concept, the Kingdom of God, ecumenically it is significant that both Pentecostals and Catholics can agree upon the Kingdom of God as the Ultimate Norm of social justice:

> Pentecostals and Catholics believe Jesus Christ to be the Lord of the Kingdom He came to proclaim, and in our preaching and understanding, the Kingdom of God and social justice should not be separated. Churches should strive to be faithful to the demands of the Kingdom of God, for in their social and historical existence, churches can sometimes grow slack in pursuing this divine purpose of the Kingdom of God. (*FR* IV.66)

Catholics and Pentecostals thus affirm together that the absolute norm for social justice is nothing less than the Kingdom of God. The Lordship of the King of the Kingdom is the guarantee of its ultimate victory over the forces of evil. The Church received its criteria "from above," by the will of God, as manifested in the Kingdom way of life. The "Kingdom" and "New Creation" are used synonymously. Both are biblical terms that describe the ultimate will of God for the whole creation. They imply peace, justice, and reconciliation between individuals, social classes, and ethnic groups and are, therefore, essential for developing criteria for promoting social well-being on personal, communal, and structural levels.[18]

Spirituality as a Source of Power for Social Action

Social concern is not only a matter of theological and biblical considerations. It has also much to do with our spirituality. And here the Catholic dialogue team was able to deepen Pentecostals' appreciation of prayer and spiritual gifts as a means of promoting social justice. Spirituality, living the life of the Holy Spirit, energizes the Church to do evangelization and social justice. Transformed people cooperate with the Spirit, the Creator, and Sanctifier, in transforming the world. The daily prayer of the people of God for the coming of the Kingdom (cf. Matt. 6:10) is one of the main ways Christians can cooperate with their Lord to better the world (*FR*

IV.52). God's kingdom by its very nature is God's gift and work. We do not construct the Kingdom but rather "ask for it, welcome it and make it grow within us"; "it comes by grace in the power of the Spirit."[19] It is noteworthy that for Pentecostals, who otherwise emphasize "prayer of faith" and spiritual gifts, prayer does not seem to play such a great role in social action, or, at least, they did not emphasize it explicitly. The Catholic team further emphasized that prayer not only empowers God's people; in fact, it demands of them a correct relationship to each other in the community and in the society, for all are redeemed by Christ.

The *Final Report* aptly summarizes the common biblical and theological affirmation in two definitive statements. First, evangelization and love for one's neighbor are intrinsically connected, and basic to this love is active work toward social justice. Second, in the work of evangelization, due attention must be given to the social welfare of other people (*FR* IV.58). Significantly, at the end of the Agreed Account there is a mutual confession that reflects the broad common basis of the 1993 session.

Social Justice and the Future of Pentecostal Theology

Whatever the future course of Pentecostal mission work and missiology will be, Pentecostals can no longer avoid the question of social concern. They have available theological resources as was noted above. But they have also in their tradition some features that seem to work against social involvement.

Two issues seem to be determinative to the future of Pentecostal social concern: eschatology and the view of evangelism. There would not be Pentecostalism without a strong eschatological fervency. Pentecostalism arose out of a sustained eschatological expectation nurtured by the previous generation of revival movements. Eschatological fervency may either paralyze all efforts for the betterment of the world or ignite Pentecostals to work for the coming of Kingdom. Both kinds of attitudes have lived and continue to live among Pentecostals.

The other critical factor is how evangelism is appropriated among Pentecostals. Pentecostals should not give up their priority of evangelism or the importance of targeting individuals with the hope of a radical turning away from the world to God's light. But neither should they see the Catholic view of addressing also societies, cultures, and structures as anti-evangelistic. Ugly tragedies and misconduct among Pentecostals, among some top leaders, should make Pentecostals alert to the importance of structural change, too.

In his *Charismatics and the Next Millennium*, Nigel Scotland expresses the hope that Charismatics will overcome their lack of social activism by rethinking their theology.[20] Another Charismatic, Nigel Wright expresses the hope that the Charismatic Renewal will not simply be absorbed in an individualistic religion of the soul, but will also focus on the whole of God's creation: "In so far as charismatic renewal fails to gain this perspective it will prove to be a capitulation to our culture's desire to privatize religious experience and so domesticate it. This tendency is already clear in some parts of the world where charismatic experience and reactionary politics have become close allies."[21] This is a timely challenge to all Pentecostals, too!

Part Four

Theology of Mission

Chapter Fourteen

Proselytism: A Theological Inquiry

Ironically, there are two opposing trends in modern missiology. On the one hand, there is a widespread resurgence of evangelism, not only in younger churches where active evangelism has always been, but also in older churches, for example in the Roman Catholic Church. On the other hand, the issue of proselytism has emerged as one of the most hotly debated topics of evangelization and mission. Charges that religious groups or individuals are actively engaged in proselytism currently abound. Younger churches and Christian groups, especially those churches and groups with enthusiastic evangelistic and outreach programs, are among the groups most frequently charged with proselytizing activities.

Proselytism, understandably, is a concern of older more established historic churches. Usually proselytizing charges come from the older churches that believe they have the right to define what "proselytism" means. Often younger churches, those regarded by others as "proselytizers," have not been invited to participate in discussions on the subject, nor are they particularly concerned to address the subject themselves. The evangelizing activities of, for example, many Free Churches and their numerous outreach organizations have been effective to the point that a concern has arisen among older churches as to the danger of losing a substantial amount of their members as a result of such activities.

Already in 1954, the WCC originated a study, "Proselytism and Religious Freedom." Two years later, an influential document "Christian Witness, Proselytism and Religious Freedom," was drafted and recommended to member churches in the 1961 meeting. Earlier, the Toronto declaration "The Church, the Churches and the World Council of Churches" (1950), was one of the first ecumenical attempts to define proselytism among the WCC member churches and in relations to the Roman Catholic Church. In the 1960s, the Roman Catholic Church drafted the Vatican II document *Dignitatis Humanae* that addresses among other topics religious freedom and proselytism. In 1970, the WCC produced another joint document, "Common Witness and Proselytism" (1970).

Of the older churches, the Roman Catholic Church has been the most active to enter into mutual dialogues with other churches—the Orthodox Church and younger Christian families, such as Evangelicals, Baptists, and Pentecostals—to discuss this delicate topic. At the multilateral level, the Joint Working Group between the Roman Catholic Church and the WCC has recently published a study entitled "The Challenge of Proselytism and the Calling to Common Witness."[1]

According to the joint document "Common Witness and Proselytism" (1970), the concept of "proselytism" covers all inappropriate attempts at conversion which violate the individual's right to religious freedom and prevent a person from making a religious decision in freedom.[2] The document encourages the avoidance of actions and attitudes which might be rightly considered as proselytism: every kind of violence, moral constraint, pressure, use of material benefits, and so on. It is noteworthy that rather than speaking extensively about the negative sides of proselytism, the document begins by explaining the positive qualities of witness: witness must proceed from the Spirit of love, it must be concerned for the good of God and human beings, not for that of a single community, and it must leave the addressee with full freedom to make a personal decision. The document entitled "Common Witness," produced by the Joint Working Group (1982), develops these basic guidelines. In the Orthodox-Catholic Balamand Report, the division of the churches is presented as a "situation which is contrary to the nature of the Church."[3] The importance of *koinonia* is emphasized as well as the principle of religious freedom. The joint document urges the churches to forgive the past misgivings and move toward unity and common witness.

The purpose of this chapter is to take another look at this most delicate issue and inquire whether there are any positive signs on the horizon. The focus will be on relationships between traditional and younger churches, the arena in which the issue of proselytism most often emerges. As a case study, I will look at a recent dialogue-process that focused on the topics of evangelization, proselytism, and common witness—namely the Roman

Catholic-Pentecostal Dialogue. The importance of this dialogue between the two largest Christian families, is underscored by the fact that these two churches are so different. The older one is an ancient church with established structure and worldwide episcopal leadership, while the younger one is a loose movement of heterogeneous groups without any global leadership. They stand at the extreme ends of the ecclesial spectrum. Consequently, the relationship between these two churches has been poisoned by charges of proselytism; for example, in Latin America about 8,000 Catholics join Pentecostal and other Charismatic churches every day.

I will proceed in the following way. After briefly introducing the emergence and development of the Catholic-Pentecostal dialogue, I will analyze the leading ideas of the document *Evangelization, Proselytism, and Common Witness* on proselytism. Then I will explore the theological and ecclesiological ramifications of the problem of proselytism and its connection to our understanding of apostolicity of the church. My main thesis is that the question of proselytism is integrally tied with the acknowledgment (or the lack of acknowledgment) of the ecclesiality of other churches, and that the question of proselytism cannot be regarded only as a "practical" issue of mission. Finally, I will attempt to offer some guidelines as to the future developments of this discussion especially regarding the relationship between traditional and Free Churches.

An Unlikely Dialogue on the Issue of Proselytism

Since the beginning of the Roman Catholic-Pentecostal dialogue in 1972, the members of this dialogue have committed themselves to addressing the issue of proselytism. Yet it was only after almost twenty years of mutual exchange of ideas and spirituality that the dialogue teams finally dared to take up this issue. The fourth phase of the dialogue (1990–1997) concentrated on mission, proselytism, and common witness. Specific themes for the sessions included The Meaning of Mission and Evangelization (1990); The Biblical and Systematic Foundation of Evangelization (1991); Evangelization and Culture (1992); Evangelization and Social Justice (1993); Evangelization/Evangelism, Common Witness, and Proselytism (1994), and Common Witness (1995). The *Final Report* notes that the fact that "this discussion has at last begun is a sign of the growing trust and maturation of Pentecostal-Roman Catholic relations" (*FR* IV.68). Both teams entered into a conversation on this topic with a number of misgivings, largely because of a long history of mutual suspicion, even hostility, and with a long record of charges of proselytizing and persecution. Some members of both churches do not agree that it is appropriate to discuss this issue. Both the Catholic and the Pentecostal teams have debated with themselves, and then together, the wisdom of undertaking such a discussion in light of possible repercussions on their growing relationship.

The main reason for the existence of the issue of proselytism between Pentecostals and Catholics is the lack of a common understanding of the relationship between the Church, on the one hand, and baptism as an expression of living faith, on the other hand. The rationale and courage for mutual discussion on the issue of proselytism arises out of the acknowledgment that the lack of dialogue has usually led to tension, mutual suspicion, further proselytizing, and countercharges of persecution. The unity of the Church is a concern for Pentecostals and Catholics alike. The goal of this dialogue, however, is not structural unity, but rather to foster respect and mutual understanding.

Toward Convergence in Catholic-Pentecostal Views on Proselytism

For Catholics, proselytism, following *Common Witness and Proselytism*, involves improper attitudes and behavior in the practice of evangelism.[4] Proselytism embraces whatever violates the right of the human person to be free from external coercion in the proclamation of the Gospel and in religion in general. There must be, however, a clear distinction between (positive) evangelization and (negative) proselytizing. The true witness is based on the Great Commandment (Matt. 22:37–39; cf. Lev. 19:18; Deut. 6.5), and its end is the glory of God through the salvation of human beings. Witness, nourished by the conviction that the Holy Spirit brings about the response of faith, respects the free will and dignity of those to whom it is given.

The Catholic dialogue team offered several examples of what is the opposite to this, namely proselytism. They also underlined the fact that if Pentecostals ask Catholics to define the phenomenon of proselytism in concert with rather than apart from them, Pentecostals would do well to define salvation together with Catholics. For Catholics, salvation means *koinonia* with the Father and the Son and the Christian community. Although there are signs that indicate whether *koinonia* is present, ultimately only God can judge whether it is actual in a given believer. The purpose of this note is obvious: it seems to Catholics that Pentecostals are too quick to decide whether given faithful are true believers or not, sometimes using their own criteria rather than criteria worked out together.

Catholics maintain, further, that every Christian and every Church has the right to evangelize even those who belong to other Churches, but the thrust of the evangelizing should be on bringing converts back to the pastoral care of their own churches. Interestingly enough, Billy Graham's evangelistic campaigns as well as those of Youth With a Mission are singled out as positive examples.

Pentecostals have rarely addressed the issue of proselytism,[5] and to date they have not participated directly in the development of any ecumenical documents that address the problem of proselytism. They have been, however, accused of proselytizing. Charges that Pentecostals proselytize merely in order to increase their members at any cost, or that they do so to further some (North American) political agenda, have been largely discredited in recent years by respectable non-Pentecostal scholars who have researched the growth of Pentecostalism. Santiago Faith and Order issued probably the most adequate explanation, regarding newer groups and charges against their proselytizing, when it stated that, "We believe that most groups and persons who are engaged in such activities do so out of a genuine concern for the salvation to whom they address."[6] The same statement, however, continues with a plea for dialogue in order for some methods and intentions to be challenged by other churches.

The Pentecostals in dialogue were very frank about the issue of proselytism: "They [Pentecostals] are, at times, guilty of the charges. They share what they believe to be the Gospel, even attempting to convert people who say that they are part of another tradition." But they also underlined the fact that there must be a reason or a series of reasons for Pentecostals' behavior. Some of these reasons come "as a result of Pentecostal understandings of ecclesiology, of spiritual discipline, of Christian discipleship, of fruit in the Christian life which points to the transformation which has taken place or is taking place in the one who claims to be Christian."[7]

Whatever distorted motives there have been in Pentecostal evangelization—as these are also found in any other Christian proclamation—for the purposes of ecumenical dialogue the records have to be set clear: "In a very real sense evangelization is *the* self-understood *raison d'être* of the Pentecostal Movement."[8] In other words, to speak about Pentecostals is to speak about evangelization. What some other churches consider to be proselytism is for most Pentecostals urgent passion for the fulfillment of their mandate. The early Pentecostals regarded missionaries without passion for the salvation of souls as "abnormal" and themselves, with the power of the Spirit to carry the message to the ends of the earth, as "normal" Christians.

The Pentecostal team defines proselytism as follows:

> Proselytism is a disrespectful and uncharitable recruitment of committed members of Christian communities by persons from other Christian communities. We reject all activities which violate the dignity of human persons, their freedom from external coercion, and manipulation in religious matters, or whatever, in the proclamation of the Gospel, which does not conform to the ways God in Jesus Christ wishes to draw people to Himself in Spirit and truth.[9]

Here the similarity to the Catholic team's view is obvious: both understand as proselytism, an "evangelization" that betrays unworthy, unrespectable attitudes toward the "objects" of evangelization and does not honor human freedom. Both emphasize that the criterion for true evangelization is the God-like love of drawing all people to salvation in Christ. In fact—and this is ecumenically significant—even the Pentecostal definition seems to closely follow the document *Common Witness and Proselytism* (§6). If Pentecostals, as is evident in this dialogue, are ready to agree with the conciliar rejection of proselytism, there is much hope for eliminating conflicts and furthering mutual understanding in the common task.

The Pentecostal definition, however, seems to have subtle nuances, that reflect their distinctive approach. They understand as proselytism, primarily, unworthy recruitment of "*committed members* of Christian communities." What this means, apparently, is that "recruitment" of noncommitted members of other churches, i.e., those baptized but not living out their faith, are seen as legitimate "objects" of evangelization. In fact, this is explicitly said: "All those who have not repented, believed, and are not following Christ are to be evangelized" (even though baptized?).[10] One hopes that the Catholic team would have addressed this formulation, since the overall ethos of the Catholic approach is that those who are baptized are either to be "awakened" by a more effective pastoral care or, if invited back to conscious Christian life with evangelists of other churches, led back to their own church. The Pentecostal view logically follows their soteriology: unlike Catholics, Pentecostals do not see the Christian life as constituted by initiatory sacraments (baptism, Eucharist, confirmation) but by conscious faith responses. It also has to do with Pentecostal ecclesiology: the Church is constituted by people who have made a conscious faith response and want to form a community, based on the New Testament portrait of voluntary decision.

The Pentecostal team wanted to underline the difference between proselytism and persuasion on the one hand and changing church affiliation on the other hand. These must not be equated. All Christians and Christian communities have the God-given mandate to persuade all people (cf. 2 Cor. 5:11), including Christians, though always in love and with respect for other communities. Changing church affiliation is also legitimate if based on a free, conscious decision of any person. The Catholic team, too, emphasized the urgent need for persuasive proclamation for each Christian. It must respect individual freedom. The Catholics did not explicitly mention the issue of changing religious affiliation, although their accent on the necessity of preaching and individual freedom seems to leave the door open to it.

Catholics and Pentecostals reject all claims that the Gospel should not be proclaimed by a Christian community simply because another Christian community has preceded it in a particular geographic area. This is allegedly against claims of some Orthodox and Catholic Churches to have "territorial occupation." Similarly, the idea that Christian communities or their members should not evangelize people simply because they have lived all of their lives in a "Christian" culture is rejected.

A Theological Understanding of Proselytism

Unfortunately, the problem of proselytism has not received much attention from theologians. Usually it has been relegated to the practical questions of missions to be dealt with at the discussion table as part of other "housekeeping" issues. My thesis is, however, that the topic of proselytism concerns the very ecclesiality of the church, i.e., on what conditions a church can be called a church and what right, if any, it must proclaim the Gospel to others.

Of course, there could be a useful division of labor. Accordingly, the question of proselytism, as well as common witness, can—and should—be dealt with on two levels. The first one I will call "attitudinal" and the second one "theological." The first level is usually properly done. This is also the case regarding the Catholic-Pentecostal dialogue. The fruitful discussions in the *Final Report* reveal that very helpful steps have been taken to accomplish this goal. There is an atmosphere of mutual understanding, humility, and willingness to learn from each other, instead of operating with second-hand information and prejudices. The attitudinal level is a critical one. If two churches are not willing to start with a humble and willing attitude, then not much hope is left for improving their relationship. The famous Catholic missiologist Robert J. Schreiter speaks to this level when he, in a recent survey of the developments in the Roman Catholic Church toward proselytism, gives some advice for the future. He suggests among other things that when "competing groups give priority to acknowledging their similarities over their differences...proselytism loses much of its energy."[11] That has happened in this dialogue: "...members of the Dialogue think that Pentecostals and Catholics already agree on critical points of faith" (*FR* IV.69).

The second level, which I call theological, begins at this point. It is crucial to take another look at the problem of proselytism and ask the critical question: What, if any, are the theological resources for avoiding proselytism? Or, how does our understanding of proselytism connect with what we think of the church in general? In fact, the *Final Report* acknowledges the need for a theological orientation to the question of proselytism at the very beginning of its treatment of the subject. It mentions that proselytism exists "in large part because Pentecostals and Catholics do not have a common understanding of the Church." Then it adds this very significant illustration: "...they do not agree on the relationship between the church, on the one hand, and baptism as an expression of living faith, on the other" (*FR* IV.69).

Here is the point, as I see it! Unfortunately, the *Final Report* does not develop this question further. In fact, during the Third Quinquennium (1985–89), there was a fruitful discussion about *koinonia* and related ecclesiological and soteriological topics between Catholics and Pentecostals, but the outcomes of that dialogue are not sufficiently brought to bear upon the dialogue on mission and proselytism. Having very carefully read the *Koinonia*-Report, I have an uneasy feeling that there was not enough courage to deal with the most substantial issue, i.e., what exactly Catholics and Pentecostals understand about *koinonia*, and/or, how does one's view of *koinonia* relate to the question of Christian unity. All that was said was a reiteration of viewpoints that one knows without talking about *koinonia* for several years: Pentecostals opt for a "spiritual" unity whereas Catholics opt for a "visible/structural" unity. This is unfortunate and it reflects the general ecumenical procedure: proselytism is usually discussed apart from theological ramifications, as a sort of "practical" question of mission.

Clearly, everything that can be said about proselytism between traditional churches and younger churches in general and Catholics and Pentecostals in particular finally culminates in theological ramifications—especially two interrelated questions, that of the church and salvation/faith. A related theological question, that of saving faith and its relation to sacraments, must be discussed once more in relation to evangelization, proselytism, and common witness. The Fifth Phase (began in 1998) that focuses on salvation, among other things, raises hopes regarding the issues under consideration here.

Proselytism, Ecclesiality, and Openness to Other Churches

For a step forward in this critical question, I would like to refer to an approach suggested by Miroslav Volf, in his notable work on ecclesiology entitled, *After Our Likeness.* Volf himself was a participant of the Dialogue in several sessions of the third and fourth phases. According to Volf, the all-embracing framework for an appropriate understanding of the church is God's eschatological new creation. From this Volf draws an all-important principle for relationships between churches—"interecclesial minimum" as he calls it—namely "the openness of every church toward all other churches as an indispensable condition of ecclesiality."[12] No church, to be a true church, can alone, in isolation from all other churches, claim to be a church without acknowledging all other churches. Through this openness to other churches, a church necessarily sets out on the path to its future, a path in which it is able to express and deepen its communion, that is "differentiated unity" with all other churches.[13]

What makes this idea so appealing to Pentecostals and other Free Churches is that it allows them to speak only of a plurality of churches rather than of the one church. Even if this idea might sound scandalous to Roman Catholics and other sacramental churches, this is indeed the case. On this side of the eschatological gathering of the whole people of God, there can be no church in the singular.

The implications for proselytism and common witness are evident. No church has the right to set rules for witnessing or evangelization. What can be done is the "proselytism minimum," if you will, which must be worked out: rules, such as those presented in the *Final Report*, designed to stop actions that violate human freedom and the credibility of the Christian message. Every church must be given the right to give its distinctive witness, both to nonbelievers and members of other churches, even if that message disagrees with the doctrines of other churches, without it being labeled as proselytism. In fact, the *Final Report* section on common witness suggests the principle of a "limited measure of common witness" (IV.122) which clearly follows this approach. On this side of the eschatological gathering of God's people, every testimony is partial and fragmentary (cf. 1 Cor. 13:10–13). Furthermore, no church has the right to "occupy territories" and prevent other Christians from sharing their distinctive testimonies.

From this perspective, what Pentecostals accomplished in the dialogue was ecumenically groundbreaking. They showed their willingness to open up to other churches. Or how else could the following affirmations "in relation to Christian communities" be understood: The one church of Jesus Christ, the fellowship of the Spirit, which is comprised of many communities of those who call upon the name of the Lord Jesus Christ; the presence and the power of the Gospel in Christian communities outside the Pentecostal tradition; the need to speak truth in love about all Christian communities (Eph. 4:15); the obligation to portray the beliefs and practices of other Christian communities accurately, honestly, and charitably; cooperative efforts with other Christian communities, wherever possible. Furthermore, Pentecostals affirm that all ought to pray for "the building up the body of Christ until all of us come to the unity of the faith and of the knowledge of the Son of God, to maturity, to the measure of the full stature of Christ" (cf. Eph. 4:12–13).[14] Especially significant are the acknowledgments of the oneness of the Church, the presence of the Gospel in other Christian communities, and the need to speak in love and truth about others. Also, a competitive attitude in regard to other Christian communities is rejected.

These advances, however, do not mean that the issue of proselytism has been resolved. Connected as it is to ecclesiological issues, the question remains regarding how the Church is to be understood. As far as the conditions of ecclesiality are concerned, the episcopal and Free Church traditions differ especially in (at least) three respects. First, according to Catholic and Orthodox traditions, Free Church ecclesiology lacks a bishop to ensure the presence of Christ, while according to the Free Church tradition, such a bishop is not permitted. Second, in the episcopal model, Christ's presence is mediated sacramentally. By contrast Free Churches speak of Christ's unmediated, "direct" presence in the entire local communion. Finally, according to the episcopal tradition, the church is constituted through the performance of objective activities and Christ's constitutive presence is not bound to the subjective disposition (even if the latter is not unimportant). Free Churches, on the other hand, have come to emphasize subjective conditions, namely faith and obedience, to the point that where these are missing, even if the objective side is present, serious doubt arises regarding ecclesiality. During the early Church, the conditions of ecclesiality were debated as the marks of the Church. In what follows, then, I would like to approach this question from the viewpoint of the Church's apostolicity.[15]

Proselytism, Apostolicity, and Mission

One of the classical "notes" of the church is apostolicity. Every Christian church affirms apostolicity even though there are differing and to some extent contradictory understandings of what is the essence of apostolicity. In this chapter, it is, of course, neither feasible nor necessary to delve into this complex question.[16] Yet from the New Testament perspective, the church is "apostolic because it remains in continuity in essentials with the original witnessing of the first-century apostles."[17] What is originally apostolic is being sent to bear witness to the universal and definitive truth of the revelation of God in Jesus Christ. "The apostolicity of the Church is ultimately grounded in God's mission to the world."[18] Primarily, then, apostolicity entails the sending out of apostles to all humanity by the church. The task of mission did not end with the age of the apostles. Part of continuing the apostolic mission is fidelity to the apostolic beginnings, especially to the apostolic gospel.

Consequently, mission and evangelism is therefore an essential aspect of the ecclesiality of the church along the formulation of *Ad Gentes* (§2) of Vatican II that came to speak of the "missionary nature of the church." It is also the most recent emphasis of WCC documents, like Faith and Order of Santiago de Compostela, with its underscoring of the intimate relationship between *koinonia*, common confession of the apostolic faith, and common witness in mission and evangelism.

Primarily, however, the assertion of the church as apostolic should be understood eschatologically. Understanding the church's apostolicity in terms of the apostolic mission points beyond every historical present to the eschatological consummation of the world. The apostolic mission of the church aims at the renewal of all humanity in the kingdom of God, a renewal that has begun already with the advent and cross of Jesus of Nazareth.

Consequently, being a church requires engaging in mission and evangelization and letting other churches to do the same. Clearly understanding that Christian witness is always "broken" and in constant need of being measured by the criterion of the received Word of God, every church in hand with other churches should give its own distinctive testimony. There is no way, as I see it, to eliminate problematic encounters with other churches and their members, since the testimony of each church is unique, though based on the one apostolic Gospel. Thus, no church has the right to claim apostolicity for itself, not even the oldest churches. Apostolicity is much more than formally stipulated rules for a right "succession." It is dynamic reality, integrally connected with living church life and mission. That is the essence of the New Testament apostolic foundations.

Since apostolicity is as much an object of hope as it is a (always only partly) fulfilled reality on this side of God's eschatological gathering of his people, humility and consideration toward brothers and sisters—one sign of which is willingness to enter the table of proselytism talks—should characterize Christian communities rather than blind judgments. In fact, refusal to let other churches give their distinctive testimony to the apostolic Gospel means nothing less than denying their ecclesiality. A church cannot exist if it must ask for its right to exist from other churches. Rather, all churches receive their ecclesiality from the presence of Christ and his Spirit among his people.

In sum, only a healthy ecclesiology can inform discussion about proselytism and evangelization. A sound doctrine of the church sets parameters for the imperative of evangelization, the right and responsibility of all churches as well as rules for ecumenically damaging ways of "evangelization."

Suggestions for the Future

Proselytism is a serious problem both in terms of ecumenical relationships and relationships with the world. Nothing less than the credibility of the Christian Gospel is at stake. How can the Church convince the world of reconciliation in Christ if Christian families cannot be reconciled in their joint efforts of winning the world to Christ? How can they proclaim the message of peace if ecumenical relationships are frustrated by competing, coercive attitudes accompanied with bitterness and hatred?

Using the Roman Catholic-Pentecostal dialogue process as a paradigm, I want to conclude by offering several observations and recommendations as to the future of the treatment of the topic of proselytism.

First, contrary to what evangelistically-minded younger churches believe, the discussion on proselytism is meant to help rather than hinder evangelization. This is clearly stated in the Roman Catholic-Pentecostal mutual statement: "What we both desire is the pure preaching of the Gospel. Most of our conflicts diminish if we agreed that this is what evangelization is all about" (*FR* IV.78).

Second, it is possible for churches that are quite different from each other theologically and culturally, to engage in fruitful discussion of proselytism and work out definitions that help identify the issues and concerns. Even where no total unanimity is reached, the dialogue process itself has created mutual trust and eliminated prejudices.

Third, as a next step in ecumenical, international talks on proselytism, a theological orientation deeply rooted in ecclesiological perspectives regarding soteriology, sacramentology, and the conditions of ecclesiality is needed. Even though proselytism appears to be a "practical problem," it is a result of conflicting theological convictions among various churches. I suggest launching an interdenominational research project on the theological foundations of proselytism. The WCC could serve as a natural initiator of such a project.

Fourth, discussions on proselytism should be bold enough to take up real issues, e.g., the change of church allegiance and problems in joint evangelistic campaigns. The Roman Catholic-Pentecostal dialogue, as I have already noted, serves as a precedent here. The dialogue teams were courageous enough to take up examples with real names and addresses.

Last, but not least, discussion of proselytism and the related topic of common witness is critical in that it can help avoid the polarization of Christianity between those with evangelistic zeal and those without. Mission and evangelization is a constitutive element of ecclesiality without which no church worthy of its name is able to live.

Chapter Fifteen

Culture, Contextualization and Conversion

It is one of the established canons of modern missiology that the Gospel should be contextualized in given context. Now for several decades, missiologists have, on the one hand, criticized their predecessors for an alleged lack of attention paid to local cultures and, on the other hand, have devised ingenuous ways to implement "contextualization."

Yet the term contextualization has become so used that sometimes one is left wondering whether there is a universally accepted definition. The intensive debate about contextualization in recent decades has helped us see more clearly the integral relationship between the Christian message and the context in which those who hear and live it out find themselves. For example, conversion happens both in a human heart and a socio-cultural context. Catholic theology, because of a long tradition of Thomistic view according to which grace fulfills what is lacking in (human) nature, has been keener to the influence of the context of the Christian message. For Protestant missiology in general and Evangelical and especially Pentecostal-Charismatic missiology in particular, it has been a much longer process of coming to grips with this foundational insight.[1] Protestants have tended to emphasize the opposition between what grace is and does and everything related to the human person and his/her activities.

The fourth and latest phase of the Roman Catholic-Pentecostal dialogue has finally dared to take up issues that really make a difference between these two giants, namely extreme delicate topics such as mission, proselytism, and common witness. The motive for selecting evangelization and mission as the main theme was explained in the *Final Report*: "Since many Christians have seen the last decade of the second millennium as one in which to emphasize evangelization, and since significant tensions exist between Pentecostals and Catholics on this issue, it appeared appropriate to concentrate on this topic" (*FR* IV.5).

The 1992 session's overall topic was culture and related themes, such as contextualization, inculturation, and conversion. The questions discussed during that year's session were the following: the complex relationship between culture and gospel; the relationship between conversion and inculturation; the complicated question of secularization, and its relation to social change and the need for contextualization. In this chapter I want to offer some reflections on each of these questions from that significant dialogue. Even though the dialogue did not focus particularly on Asian context, as a former missionary to Thailand and regular visitor to some countries of the area, I think the dialogue outcomes offer fruitful seed for thought on the Asian mission context. As is well known, in Asia the relationship between culture and religion is even more integral than in many other mission areas.

The Complex Relationship between Gospel and Culture

The Gospel tries to transform a culture from within. If it is successful, we speak of "inculturation," which is not to be confused with acculturation, a simple transfer of elements of one culture to another. Societies and cultures often attempt to neutralize the Gospel. When they succeed, we speak of "secularization." This occurs when human dynamics (e.g., rationalism) take precedence over the Gospel. One possible cause of secularization might be that a Christian group, through intellectual or moral weakness, finds itself greatly alienated from culture due to cultural (rather than Gospel) reasons. Catholics and Pentecostals see together that in looking at the subject of evangelism and culture, both theological issues and sociological dynamics must be examined. Often theological and social issues are intertwined.[2]

Catholics and Pentecostals agree that both the evangelist and the one who is evangelized need to realize that neither operates in a cultural vacuum. Evangelists act unjustly toward peoples and cultures if they import political, economic, or social ideologies alongside the Gospel. Those who listen and respond to the Gospel, too, must be aware of their own culture and religious history and discern how their response is faithful to the Gospel as embodied in their own religious history and culture (cf. *FR* IV.30).

Discerning this unavoidable link between Gospel and culture is, however, complicated since the relationship between culture and Gospel is extremely complex. Catholics and Pentecostals are aware of this and they acknowledge that their proclamation and their Christian lifestyle are always embodied in a specific culture. Both accept also that there is considerable good in cultures, notwithstanding the fact of humanity's fall from grace (*FR* IV.28). Perhaps the most challenging question in evangelization is the relationship between conversion and inculturation.

Evangelization, Conversion, and Inculturation

Many Pentecostals are not only suspect but also afraid of the dialogue with Catholics. Those Pentecostals entertain fears that dialoguing about mission and evangelization with Catholics might be an exercise in futility because of an alleged lack of personal evangelism in Catholic theology and practice. That this is not true was attested firmly in the Agreed Account about the conversion: "Pentecostals and Catholics agree that there is no genuine evangelism without the direct and explicit call to repentance and reconciliation to God through Jesus Christ. Evangelization involves conversion, that is interior change, and being taken up in a Christian community."[3] Quoting from one of the most significant recent Catholic statements on mission, *Evangelii Nuntiandi*, Catholics emphasize that evangelization has "for a basis, center and summit...a clear proclamation that, in Jesus Christ, the Son of God made man, who died and rose again, salvation is offered to all men, as a gift of grace and forgiveness."[4]

The common view of conversion notwithstanding, there is, however, a distinct difference of emphasis between the Catholic and Pentecostal orientation to evangelization. Pentecostals emphasize the changing of individuals whom, when formed into a body of believers, bring change into the culture from within. Catholics emphasize that the Gospel can also transform culture itself in its human institution and enterprises (*FR* IV.28). Consequently, Pentecostals are strong on personal evangelism, and they emphasize a "crisis-type" of conversion.[5] Catholics not only see the need to evangelize persons, but also see the need to evangelize cultures, for example, through educational institutions. Furthermore, they have often evangelized through aesthetics that embody religious values (cf. *FR* IV.33).

The Catholic emphasis on a broader orientation of evangelism than just personal evangelism, does not, however, mean downplaying the importance and primary role of evangelizing persons: "...the ultimate focus of evangelization is the person" (*FR* IV.33). In a healthy self-critical way, Catholics acknowledge shortcomings in their evangelization, such as insufficient Christian initiation and discipleship formation and failure in bringing parishioners to a personal faith commitment. These shortcomings, though, are not theologically motivated and can sometimes be due to concrete conditions of the area, like poverty, illiteracy, a shortage of ministers, and the structures of oppression.

It is ecumenically significant that the Catholics in the dialogue process were at pains in trying to convince the dialogue partner of the importance of personal evangelization. In Hervé Legrand's view, "to reduce evangelization to the relationship to culture, to the ecumenical and inter-religious dialogue, to the reconciliation of the competitive nationalism" would be a fatal error.[6] One fatal error of defining evangelization, at the expense of meeting persons, would be to identify it with, for example, political aspirations: "...there are still suspicions about the political Catholicism which existed not so long ago and which tried to use political power to enforce faith and Christian morals."[7] Yet it still seems to me that the difference of emphasis between the Catholic and Pentecostal views of relation of conversion and evangelization is a matter of different concerns rather than clear-cut theological differences. Pentecostals are concerned whether inculturation among nominal Christians and in non-Christian countries remains true to the Gospel "without the direct call to repentance and reconciliation to God through Jesus Christ."[8]

For Catholics, the main concern is not to see conversion in too simplistic terms. Such an approach would see evangelization/conversion completed by the call to repentance, without due attention to inculturation, that is, "to assure the rootedness, continuity, and plausibility of the Gospel message" in any given context. For Catholics, inculturation is a long process, important because a Christian is not "just a soul to be converted, but a person incarnated into a concrete culture." Catholics challenge Pentecostals to do long term patient work in any culture to overcome prejudices, stereotypes, and feelings antithetical to the Gospel message. The call to repentance and reconciliation will not have its full effect until the values, consonant with the Kingdom proclaimed, can be affirmed in the culture and distortions corrected.[9]

One perspective that helps explain the difference between Catholic and Pentecostal approaches to evangelization is the more pessimistic view of the world among Pentecostals. Pentecostals tend to emphasize the sinfulness of the world (cf. 1 John 2:15–17). Catholics, on the other hand, stress the goodness of the world. The more positive view of Catholicism toward the world is based, as I have indicated above, on the Thomistic view of nature and grace, which operates on the notion that grace elevates nature to a higher level. Consequently, Pentecostal emphasis on opposition to the world is felt by Catholics to be too limited, while Catholic emphasis on continuity with the world goes too far for some Pentecostals. Both parties, though, can learn from each other's perspectives.[10]

Secularization, Social Change, and Contextualization

It was noted above that with "inculturation" missiologists usually mean a successful contextualization of the Gospel whereas the term "secularization" in everyday usage of the word refers to failure to establish the values of the Gospel in one's life and in the community. The term "secularization," though widely used in this dialogue as well as in missiological writings elsewhere, is ambiguous. The 1985 symposium of European bishops rightly paid more attention to the empirical and historical—instead of metaphysical—notion of secularization according to which there is probably no such a thing as secularization *per se* but only varied situations which are the result of complex social compromises. In that approach, the term secularization, rather than being just an obstacle to evangelization, was seen as a tool to help one think through the connection between religion and surrounding society. This is, of course, more in tune with a sociological definition of the term. Although the Catholic paper urges both Catholics and Pentecostals to be more precise in their usage of the term, the *Final Report (1990–1997)* as well as other documents of the dialogue seem to be accustomed to the ecclesial meaning of the term: the term connotes the decline of religious/spiritual commitment in our time.[11]

There is a shared concern over secularization: "Both Catholics and Pentecostals recognize that great social changes in Western society result in secularization processes and consequently a decline in religious practice" (*FR* IV.34). Obviously, the term "secularization" here is used in the popular sense that refers to weakening of Christian commitment. It is something to be deplored and condemned therefore but also, more positively, to be met with a Christian message. The tragedy of secularization is that many people face new challenges without guidelines in the fields of religion and ethics. But secularization goes on inside the Church, not just outside, as Christians adopt the values of materialistic culture or use the Gospel for political purposes:

> Both Pentecostals and Roman Catholics see disturbing expressions of "secularization" in their churches and feel the need to adopt pastoral strategies to address it effectively. As an example, Pentecostals cite the increasing tendency for church members to adopt the values of materialistic cultures. Catholics cite as an example the use of the Gospel for materialistic or political purposes.[12]

Massive social changes have taken place and challenged the church in the postmodern, "global village." Over the past thirty years, technological and scientific innovations have radically changed the concrete conditions in which human beings are born and die, not only in the Western world but also elsewhere. Progress in medicine far more than ideologies has influenced our way of seeing the beginning and end of human life (*FR* IV.35). The aging process and well as the conditions of elderly people have dramatically changed, too (see *FR* IV.36). Pentecostalist Everett A. Wilson highlighted the change processes in Latin America with widespread social problems, deterioration of the structures of the society, and increasing feeling of helplessness.[13] The same can be said in Asian context.

Catholic Legrand takes up as a further example in Europe the growing secularization of women. He thinks that major factors for causing so many women in France and northern Europe to become estranged from the Church, rather than being Feminist ideas, are mostly non-ideological, including the progress of medicine and women's paid work in the post-industrial societies. The development of medicine has enabled the control of birth and reduced infant mortality. Financial independence in many cases has been one of the outcomes of the progress as well as yearning for more equality. Legrand argues that women tend to affirm their independence from societies dominated by men, such as the Church.[14]

What, then, is the proper reaction of churches to changing social circumstances, pluralism, and growing secularization? The dialogue members, although entertaining somewhat differing emphases believed that intensification of evangelization and informed contextualization are the necessary means to counter these challenges.

First of all, Cardinal Martini, the president of the Conseil des conférences épiscopales d'Europe, reminded that evangelizing people means loving them, for if they do not feel loved then they will not listen to the message. It also means trusting them and strengthening them in their hope for a better future. It will also require an effort to give rise to authentic Christian communities in an urbanized and secularized culture. Legrand notes that one can see how the European bishops, in their concern for evangelization, have evolved from the denunciation of secularization to a more positive and also more active perspective of a new inculturation of Christian life.[15]

The Pentecostal team referred to the context of Latin America where the principal challenge facing the Church may not be how to stimulate religious interest or how to resist religious change but rather how to recognize and appropriately encourage the spiritual propensities of Latin America. As is well known, the spiritual, the transcendental and the surreal are replete in Latin American culture, nourished, apparently, by profound inner resources of patience, hope, and imagination. This is, I think, not far from the Asian context.

Further, there is in Pentecostal evangelization something that the Catholic Church has come to appreciate more and more, namely a strategy of evangelization of ordinary people by ordinary people. Many observers would say that this has been one of the key factors in the growth of Pentecostalism. Pentecostalism in Latin America has experienced "exponential growth," largely due to evangelization encounters which take place in market places, schools, work places, homes, etc.[16] In the social circumstances of Latin America, with uncertain employment and changing social conditions, Pentecostals are able to spread the Gospel at grassroots levels and draw new adherents to their churches, even if some of the converts tend to lapse after a while.

While both Catholics and Pentecostals are committed to the task of contextualization, there is a certain difference of emphasis. Pentecostals tend to be more flexible to change in order to cope with new conditions while Catholics are concerned about changes which occur too swiftly since they might yield to the spirit of the times. Wilson maintains that one of the key characteristics of the Pentecostal mission in Latin America has been versatility: "The genius of Pentecost is to be free to find new methods, to adopt and adapt practices which reflect their cultural heritage."[17]

In Latin America the Pentecostal movement has grown not only rapidly but also differently. Springing from a variety of situations and methods, the fertile soil of contemporary crisis and change has led to a broad range of movements, including those that reflect the different aspirations of ethnic groups, those built largely on diverse regions or social classes, and those that accommodate diverse doctrinal, polity, and denominational emphases. The readiness to adapt folk music styles, instead of insisting on "sacred music" in the church, is but one example of the versatile nature of the movement. Pentecostals have shown much more flexibility in recruiting women, those of other races, and persons without any or little education than most other Christian groups. Wilson is even of the opinion that the often-criticized—especially from the Catholic viewpoint—tendency of Pentecostal groups to fragment, serves as an extremely effective means of applying a variety of different approaches to difficult problems. The fact notwithstanding, Pentecostals would do well, however, to address this perennial problem from a theological and ecclesiological viewpoint. That this has not been done often is an indication of the (too) pragmatic nature of the movement with the idea of "working methods" as the "right methods."[18]

Conversion, Community and *Koinonia*

Living in a particular culture and context does not mean living in a vacuum. Human life by definition is communal. There was a helpful discussion on the role of the community and *koinonia* during various sessions of the fourth phase (1990–1997). Theologically it is important to note that the topic of *koinonia* has played a crucial role in the dialogue regarding both ecclesiology and missiology. *Koinonia* was the overall topic of the Third Quinquennium (1985–1989). It was agreed that *koinonia* as lived by the early Christians (Acts 2.42–47; 4:32–37) had social implications. Their communities did not act from a concept of social justice. The concern they showed for the poor, widows, and strangers was not seen as an entirely separate activity but rather as an extension of their worship (cf. *FR* IV.57). The faith community—as seen in the New Testament and in our time—evangelizes through its proclamation and its communal life. This is but living out the *koinonia* given to the Church by the Holy Spirit.

In living out their Spirit-inspired *koinonia* at the local level, the early Pentecostals challenged current norms of inequality regarding the treatment of minorities, women, and the poor. "Thus, mainline denominations petitioned their societies for social justice, while Pentecostals found justice in their daily relationships with the dispossessed of society."[19] Pentecostalism, with its appeal to marginal groups in society, shattered the norms of middle class society. During a time when racial and gender inequality was endemic, Pentecostals welcomed black and white, male and female, rich and poor.

Both Catholics and Pentecostals agree that evangelization includes calling people to conversion and membership in a local church. The difference has to do with how Catholics and Pentecostals define the relation of one local church to other local churches. Pentecostals tend to speak about "autonomous" local churches, while Catholics believe there is no such thing as a totally autonomous church.[20] Catholics think that a significant dimension is lacking when the fullness of visible communion with the universal church is absent because this leads in the end to an impoverishment in the confession of faith.

Toward the Future

In current mission discussion there are two determinative issues, namely, the relation of Christianity to other religions (and the corollary question, that of the role of the Holy Spirit in relation to communities, religions, and people outside the *ekklesia*) and the needs and challenges of contextualization. While the former question was also touched in the Roman Catholic-Pentecostal dialogue on mission (see the last chapter in this volume), the latter received a lot of attention. And significantly so, especially in view of the fact that Pentecostals have been very slow to acknowledge the meaning of culture to proclamation. In their own distinctive—one could perhaps say: unthematized way—Pentecostals have reacted to culture by devising all kinds of contextual methods of evangelization and church planting. One has only to think of adoption of all sorts of popular songs in Pentecostal worship, dance and other physical manifestations, not-church-looking church buildings, etc. But this has not been a result of a sustained reflection but rather an outcome of a highly practical mission strategy.

The Roman Catholic-Pentecostal dialogue is ecumenically and missiologically highly significant just because it is so unlikely as it is; not only because Catholics and Pentecostals are so different, but also because the topics selected for the dialogue have not been very popular or acute among Pentecostals (such as proselytism, common witness, conversion, inculturation). The willingness of Pentecostals to engage in the dialogue and the readiness of the Catholics to further the dialogue over almost three decades is a powerful testimony to the importance of an open, honest dialogue.

One of the outcomes of the mutual talks has been the insight that many missiological and ecumenical questions are not only questions of theology and doctrine but also those of attitude. For example, to what degree churches are open to change is, of course, also a matter of theology but also of overall attitude and history of a particular church. I believe this insight applies to culture as much as to any other missiological topic.

The issue of culture is extremely complex—a fact fittingly acknowledged by the dialogue partners. Much work must be done to ascertain what are the theological and attitudinal resources of all Christian churches to take into consideration the pervasive role of culture.

Ecumenical dialogue is at its best an exchange of gifts, a mutual learning experience. Certainly, Pentecostals can learn from Catholics appreciation of culture and the need to address, not only individuals, but also structures with the powerful message of Christ's Gospel. Catholics may want to learn from Pentecostals about the urgency of evangelism and importance of eschatological "haste" in fulfilling the commission of the Master.

Chapter Sixteen

Pneumatology, Eschatology, Missiology

Pentecostal mission has been successful, extremely successful when we look at the numbers. Whatever reservations one might have regarding the calculations of David Barrett and of others, there is no denying the fact that the advance of Pentecostal-Charismatic mission work has been astonishing. Pentecostals, however, would do well if, instead of continuing to glory in church growth numbers, they would have another look at the challenges of the third millennium.[1] Even during the short history of the movement, the world around has changed dramatically, not to speak of mission scenes. The contexts where Pentecostal mission work started in the first decades of the twentieth century have been—and are being—replaced by new complex circumstances.

Leading missiologists of our day speak about Christian mission taking place between "danger and opportunity," some would even say, under crisis.[2] The crisis they are referring to is, naturally, not only a crisis in regard to mission. It affects the entire church, indeed the entire world. The developments which affect church and mission in the third millennium are obvious: the advance of science and technology; the worldwide process of secularization; the slow but steady dechristianization of the West; the effects of history of subjugation and exploitation of peoples of color by the people of "Christian" West; the ever growing gap between rich and poor; the growing refusal of "mission fields" to continue adapting into the cultures of their parent-churches with their yearning for freedom and distinctive identity, etc.

The late South-African missiologist David Bosch, in his momentous *Transforming Mission*, surveyed mission "paradigms" throughout the history of Christian church starting from the times of the New Testament, and concluded the tour by a call for a "postmodern, ecumenical paradigm."[3] The search for a new paradigm is determined by several other developments, besides the examples listed above. First we now live in a pluricentric, rather than Western-dominated world. Second, the structures of oppression and exploitation are today being challenged as never. Third, a profound feeling of ambiguity exists about the value of Western technology and development. Fourth, we inhabit a shrinking global village with finite resources, and this calls for growing mutual interdependence. Fifth, humans are for the first time aware of their capacity to destroy the earth given to them for inhabitation and cultivation. Sixth, societies everywhere now seek their own local cultural identities. Seventh, freedom of religion and greater awareness of other faiths force Christians to re-evaluate their own earlier attitudes toward other faiths. Many other complicating factors could be added to this list, some of them arising from inside the churches, like role of women in the Church and in the society, the rapidly growing missionary force of the Two-Thirds world countries, the call for inculturation and contextualization of the Gospel, etc.

Christian mission in Asia and Pacific has specific challenges. In the nations that border the vast Pacific Ocean, remarkable developments are going on in politics, culture, economy, social life, and in international influences from and to this area. In some parts of the area, Christian churches in general and Pentecostal-Charismatic churches in particular are growing in an amazing way while in most Asian/Pacific countries traditional religions are still in control. In other words, as we are moving "from an old to a new missionary era" and to a "new birth" of missions, a host of impending questions await our responses.[4]

In this chapter, I would like to do no more than sketch the basic components of a theology of mission for the twenty-first century that derives from the heart of the Pentecostal experience of the eschatological Spirit of God. To do so, I will treat, in order, the emergence of the idea of what I call "pneumatological missiology," followed by an explication of three of its distinctive features. I conclude with implications for pneumatological missiology, especially for Pentecostal missiology.

The Emergence of a "Pneumatological Missiology"

Given the previously mentioned renaissance of pneumatology (see chapter five), one is also struck by the omission of a distinctive pneumatological outlook in modern missiology. Take for example any standard theology of mission, and most likely you will not find much about the role of the Spirit. Sadly, this applies to the magisterial work of Bosch as well as to the recent *Dictionary of Mission* written by Catholics and other writers.[5] Of course there have been some works written on the relation of Spirit to mission.[6] For example, one can point to the magisterial works of the late Karl Rahner (transcendence, human being as spirit in the world, etc.). What I mean when I make a reference to the omission of a pneumatological outlook is that there is considerable evidence of there being a lack of a comprehensive pneumatological outline of mission. I do agree with the Dutch missiologist Jan A. B. Jongeneel who has spoken about "a-missionary pneumatologies."[7] Indicative of this lack of established canons in the field of pneumatological missiology/missiological pneumatology is the immediate and very aggressive response to Catholic missiologist Stephen B. Bevans, S.V.D., who recently tried to present a missionary theology of the Holy Spirit.[8]

One could expect a distinctive missiology from Pentecostals and Charismatics who are enthusiastic about mission, and are known for emphasis on the Spirit. However, this has not been the case. One reason is obvious, and that is that the first missiological writings followed the paths explored by evangelicals. Although Pentecostals have thus far not focused on pneumatological implications of missiology, some Pentecostal exegetes have done some serious work in the area of New Testament pneumatology, especially in Luke and Acts, which have a lot of missiological potential.[9]

Pentecostal-Charismatic Christians, however, have intuitively grasped something about the essence of mission, which, even if it is not articulated in theological terms, is theologically speaking extremely revealing about the integral relation between mission, Spirit, and eschatology. In fact, these two themes have been evident in the Pentecostal mission work since the early days as an intensive eschatological expectation and reliance upon the Holy Spirit's power. In the first years of the movement, there was even an unwarranted optimism that speaking in tongues (*xenolalia*), a form of glossolalia in which human languages previously unknown to the speaker could be spoken, would be given by the Holy Spirit to help finish the evangelization of the world before the imminent return of Christ. "So intensely did they expect the Second Coming of Christ that envisioning an additional decade—or even another century—for evangelization would have been inconceivable."[10]

In what follows, I wish to take a lead from this spiritual *experience* of early Pentecostals, and cast it in a theological framework in search of greater understanding of the need for a pneumatological missiology. I will focus on the relation of the Spirit to eschatology and the implications for missions. Because I do not attempt to offer a fully developed pneumatological missiology/missiological pneumatology, I will leave out many cardinal themes such as the role of the Spirit in preparation for the Gospel, the theology of religion (the question of the Spirit outside *ekklesia*), the relation of the Spirit and justice, just to name a few of the obvious. My main discussion partners will be Wolfhart Pannenberg, undoubtedly the greatest living theologian of our day, whose three-volume *Systematic Theology* is a pneumatological treasure and, Gerhard Ebeling, another ecumenical theologian from Germany. I will also make references to both Catholic (Hans Urs von Balthasar) and Eastern Orthodox (John Zizioulas) theologians.

Spirit, Creation, and Eschaton

Theology, and consequently, theology of mission, has often neglected the relation between the soteriological operations of the Spirit in believers, and his activity both as the creator of all life and, eschatologically, as the effector of the new creation and consummation. In both Protestant and Catholic theology and spirituality, there is a tendency to view the Holy Spirit solely as the Spirit of redemption and leave out his role in creation and in bodily life. In the Old Testament of course, the Spirit is already at work in creation as God's mighty breath, the origin of all life.[11]

Notwithstanding the basic difference of the work of the Spirit in believers and the Church vis-à-vis his creative activity in the bringing forth of life in general—an eschatological gift given to all believers (see *ST* 3.11)—in some measure the dynamic of the Spirit imparts itself also to what it brings forth, to that which is outside the Spirit's own existence. This means that one of the roles of the Spirit is to glorify God's creation. The same Spirit who brings forth life in God's creation, raises the Son from the dead, dwells in believers, and finally glorifies God's creation. The distinctive nature of the eschatological gift of the Spirit consists of the fact that by the conferring of the Spirit as a lasting possession of believers, participation in the eternal life of God is made possible, and consequently also their resurrection to a new life. The task of the eschatological Spirit is not only that of glorifying God's creation but also serving as an agent of judgment and transfiguration. Of course, these two works are not opposite to each other, but rather complementary. That which is judged will be transformed to be in conformity with God's holy will. Finally God will be glorified in all. It can be said that the coming again of Christ and the establishing of his Kingdom is but the completion of the work of the Spirit that began in the incarnation and with the resurrection of Jesus (ST 3.7–12 and 622–27).

Hans Urs von Balthasar clearly depicts the comprehensive role of the Spirit along a continuum, from "creation to church to consummation" contending that the Spirit of God not only drives the Church toward consummation, but also drives the world which has been redeemed by the Son of God.[12] He refers to the groaning of the Spirit in creation (Rom. 8:20–22) as reminders of this. Peter Abelard dared to say, "*quod Spiritus Sanctus sit anima mundi*" (literally, "as if the Spirit would animate the world").[13] This is not far from what the Vatican II's *Gaudium et Spes* (§26) says: "The Spirit of God, who, with wondrous providence, directs the course of time and renews the faith of the earth, assists at this development." Yet, *Gaudium et Spes* §39, while not downplaying the meaning of §26, rightly reminds us that "we must be careful to distinguish earthly progress clearly from the increase of the kingdom of God."

Convergence of Spirit and Eschaton in the "Experience of Transcendence"

The locus of pneumatology in classical dogmatic treatments, especially in the West, has been either in trinitarian consideration or in the doctrine of salvation. What has been overlooked is the role of the Spirit in creation and in eschatology, although both of these *loci* have a strong biblical attestation in reference to the Spirit of God.

It is a consensus among Old Testament scholars that whenever *ruach* is associated with an outpouring, it is always eschatological in nature.[14] In the New Testament as well, the Spirit is depicted as the eschatological gift, the "pledge of our inheritance" (Eph. 1:14).[15] One of the chief features common to the primitive Christian understanding of the Spirit is that the gift of the *pneuma* is an eschatological gift, and his working in the community is an eschatological event.

Eschatology was never totally lost in the postbiblical period, but the relation of the Spirit to eschaton seems to have faded from the memory of the Church. At the very least, the implications to theology, spirituality, and mission are not as evident as they should be. Kilian McDonnell rightly notes that eschatology is one of the guarantees that pneumatology is not exclusively appropriated by the interior life or by the structure of the institutional Church, "two prisons in which the Spirit historically has been prisoned."[16] The relation of the Spirit to eschatology ties with the creation and the Kingdom of God as the consummation of creation and thus expands the rather narrow approach to pneumatology so characteristic of earlier treatments.

Gerhard Ebeling has described in clear theological terms the integral relation between pneumatology and eschatology. He begins volume three of his *Dogmatik des christlichen Glaubens* with a programmatic section entitled "Introduction to Pneumatology and Eschatology."[17] Ebeling rightly notes that intensive eschatological expectation finds expression in pneumatic manifestations, to which the long history of enthusiastic charismatic movements in the Christian Church gives witness. What is important is Ebeling's contention that there is a convergence of pneumatology and eschatology from the standpoint of the "experience of transcendence" (*Transzendenzerfahrung*). That which comes to us from the eschaton and that which comes from the Spirit meet in the fact that in both ways the world is transcended. In other words, what is common to pneumatology and eschatology according to Ebeling is the transition from the finite to the eternal. In this both pneumatology and eschatology have their distinctive tasks. The present that is filled with the Spirit can experience the eternal as present (pneumatology); eschatologically, the present that is oriented to the eschaton grasps the eternal as future (eschatology).[18]

According to Ebeling, the meeting point of the transcendental experience, i.e., the convergence of pneumatology and eschatology, is christology: Jesus Christ in whom the Kingdom of God is both present and future at the same time.[19] What Ebeling did not emphasize but what is made clear from biblical testimony, is that Jesus Christ, the content of the message of the Kingdom of God, is an expression of the dynamic of the Spirit of God. In that sense it can be said that the relation between the future and the present of God's kingdom in the person of Jesus was itself already mediated pneumatically. The christological bracketing is healthy since it anchors pneumatology in christology, and opens the way to a trinitarian program.[20]

Spirit and Consummation

Significantly enough, Pannenberg entitles his main section on eschatology as "The Consummation of Creation in the Kingdom of God" (*ST*

3.527ff). According to Pannenberg, the integral relation between pneumatology and eschatology is secured by the fact that it is from the Spirit of Jesus Christ that Christians expect the eschatological fulfillment of believers (Rom. 8:11) and creation (Rom. 8:19–22). That the subject of eschatology has a special relation to the work of the Spirit takes on plausibility when we consider that the Spirit is at work in both individuals and society as well as in whole of creation. Thus Pannenberg notes that the consummating work of the Spirit integrates individual and social aspects of eschatological hope, "which on the one side aims at the totality of individual life and on the other side at the consummation of fellowship through peace in righteousness. In this way the redemptive work of the Spirit overcomes the antagonism between individuals and society that holds sway in this present world" (*ST* 3.552).

The work of the Spirit links the future to the present. "By the Spirit the eschatological future is present already in the hearts of believers. His dynamic is the basis of anticipation of eschatological salvation already in the as yet incomplete history of the world" (*ST* 3.552). Pneumatology and eschatology belong together because the eschatological consummation itself is ascribed to the Spirit, who as an end-time gift already governs the historical present of believers. Consequently then, eschatology does not merely have to do with the future of consummation; it is also at work in the present by the Spirit. According to Pannenberg, we are to view the presence of the eschatological future by the Spirit as an inner element of the eschatological consummation itself, namely, "as proleptic manifestation of the Spirit who in the eschatological future will transform believers, and with them all creation, for participation in the glory of God" (*ST* 3.553).

Jürgen Moltmann rightly reminds us that traditionally theology has spoken about "regeneration/new birth" in individualistic, pietistic terms. In the New Testament, however, the term more often denotes the universal transformation of creation. Referring to texts such as Romans 8: 11, Titus 3:5–7, 1 Peter 1:3, he states that: "In these texts the interpretation of regeneration or rebirth as new creation is christologically based, pneumatologically accomplished and eschatologically orientated."[21]

This view of the consummating work of the Spirit has several important consequences that relate to mission via the doctrine of the Trinity and the church. With regard to the Trinity, we must expound the relation between pneumatology and eschatology, not merely christologically, but also in terms of the doctrine of the Trinity. For we have to think of the consummation of the world and humanity as grounded in God himself. In the early church, as is well known, the confessions of the faith ascribed the work of creation to the Father, that of reconciliation to the Son, but that of the appropriation of salvation, and of consummation to the Spirit. These appropriations however, were seen to be right only on the principle of the unity of the Trinity in its outward works.

Relating the third and final phase of the economy of salvation to the Holy Spirit seems to make sense only however from the standpoint that we can also ascribe to the Holy Spirit the eschatological participation of creation in the life of the Trinity by its glorification. This ties in with our view of the church and its future as an agent of God's all-embracing mission to the world. The appropriate framework for understanding the church is God's eschatological new creation. In the message of Jesus, the gathering of the people of God is grounded in the coming of the Kingdom of God in his person through the Spirit. The church in this view is "the anticipation of the eschatological gathering of the entire people of God."[22] In other words, the future of the church in God's new creation is the mutual personal indwelling of the Triune God and of his glorified people. This becomes clear from the description of the New Jerusalem in the Apocalypse of John (Rev. 21:1–22:5).

The story of Pentecost is an icon of the eschatological gathering of all people of God, The gathering of Jews in Acts 2 from four corners of the earth becomes a proleptic sign of the "new people gathered out of all peoples" as the earlier mission theology used to say.[23] In Luke's view, the church's universal missionary proclamation shows it to be the end-time people of God foretold by the prophet Joel, established as such by the outpouring of the prophetic Spirit. In fact, according to Luke's account, it was Pentecost that provided an indispensable impulse to mission. Likewise in the rest of the Acts it is the gift of the Spirit that determines and regulates the expansion of the church's mission (6:10; 8:14ff.; 10:44ff.; 13:1ff.; 15:28; 16:6ff. 19:1–7).

It follows from this, that the work of the Spirit of God in his church and in believers serves the consummating of his work in the world of creation. Even if we have to say with Pannenberg that there is a "special mode of the presence of the divine Spirit in the gospel and by its proclamation" (*ST* 3.2) vis-à-vis the life-giving presence of God's Spirit in all of creation (and I think it is important to hold this distinction in order to be able to distinguish between spirit[s] and the Spirit of God, the distinction which is not self-evident in all modern pneumatologies), it is the very same Spirit who works in both arenas. The tradition of the

Eastern Church has preserved the linkage between eschatology and creation more clearly than most Western theologies. Western theology has often failed to see continuity between the Spirit's work in creation, our creaturely life, salvation, inspiration, and the consummating of God's work in eschaton.

This is, of course, not to underestimate the role of the church in God's mission, but rather an attempt to pay constant heed to the relation to creation on the one side and to eschatology on the other, and not to limit the Spirit's work in any of this. We have to keep in mind constantly also the fact that as a sign and tool of the coming kingdom of God, the church has its end not in itself, but in the future of a humanity that is reconciled to God. Thus von Balthasar rightly notes that nowhere does the Bible speak about salvation of the church, but rather salvation of the world (John 3:6). Further, the universality of the work of the Son to save the world has its correspondence in the universality of the work of the Spirit, von Balthasar further notes.[24] As such, constitutive for the nature of the Church is a reference to humanity as a whole. Only then can we speak, as Pannenberg does, about the church as an essentially "missionary church" (*ST* 3.45).[25]

The Church of Jesus Christ lives in the Holy Spirit and is in itself the beginning and earnest of the future of the new creation. As the historical community of Christ, the church is the eschatological creation of the Spirit. The church is the meeting point of pneumatology and eschatology, in the midst of the "experience of transcendence," as long as it journeys on this side of God's new creation. The tension between "already" and "not yet" is tangible and unavoidable. With regard to the church, one must add that not only eschatology but also history is included within pneumatology. It is the "Community in the process of the Holy Spirit" on the way to eschaton, the powers of which it has already tasted.[26]

Implications for Pneumatological Missiology

Instead of drawing conclusions, I will attempt to reflect on what all that has been said above means to an emerging missiological pneumatology, and in what way it might shape theological thinking about mission and evangelization. I will first direct some proposals to missiology in general, and then offer seed thought for Pentecostal-Charismatic Christians in particular.

It is not enough to say that eschatology and mission, as well as Spirit and mission, have something to do with each other, if there is no established theological grounding for these three. The focus on eschatology helps mission to gain the healthy tension between "already" and "not yet" that is so characteristic of biblical testimony, and to look for an ultimate standard of mission work, nothing short of the final gathering of all people of God before his throne.

The focus on a comprehensive pneumatology helps mission to obtain a clear vision of the work of the Triune God in the world. Creation and creatures are works of God brought forth by the Spirit, the source of life and movement. The history of Jesus Christ, the content of the message of the Kingdom, is pneumatological. He is not only the giver of the Spirit, but also the bearer of the Spirit, the One who was also raised up by the same Spirit. The church of Christ is constituted by the Spirit and called to missionary service to the nations. The Spirit will bring forth the consummation of God's salvific work toward creation and humanity, redeemed by the Son, to the glory of the Father.

Pentecostal-Charismatic mission, as already stated, has grasped by intensive experience something very crucial about mission: the centrality of the Holy Spirit and eschatological urgency. It is perhaps not an overstatement to say that without these two factors, not much of Pentecostal mission would have taken place. The early Pentecostals relied upon the transforming, equipping power of the Holy Spirit, and their sense of eschatological expectation was such as to urge every believer to give testimony and render service before the Lord's return.

There are also drawbacks to this, and the later history of Pentecostal mission has had to wrestle with them. Eschatological fervency often blurred the meaning of creation and the world improvement. Why invest in a world that was believed to pass away? This kind of reasoning however, goes against the biblical worldview where the creation points to the consummation in eschaton and where the goal of creation and creatures is to glorify the one God. Kingdom works, rather than losing their significance in light of the coming end, will remain and will be transformed into a new order. Miroslav Volf of the former Yugoslavia, has argued that when Christians create history that is compatible with the Kingdom of God, such projects have eschatological significance. What is valid will remain. Volf contends that eschatological continuity between God's present reign and the reign to come "guarantees that noble human efforts will not be wasted."[27]

Furthermore, for most Pentecostals, and to a lesser degree for Charismatics, the role of the Spirit in mission in the final analysis seems to be rather meager.[28] Although there is no denying the significance of "power" (cf. Acts 1:8), the biblical attestation to the Spirit is far more comprehensive. By this I mean to not only give credit to other works of the Spirit such as the fruit of the Spirit, but also attempt to foster a greater understanding of the Spirit's work in the community, in the world, and in creation. In other words, let there be a greater appreciation of "God's mighty works" as seen in creation, creatures, communities, character, and charisms.

To avoid the perils of enthusiasm and triumphalism, finally, I recommend that Pentecostal and Charismatic missionaries pay proper attention to christology and Trinity as they develop criteria for speaking about the Spirit. Also, to avoid the danger of over-individualism and independence, I propose that Pentecostal and Charismatics reflect on the significance of the category of communion in the Spirit's work.

Chapter Seventeen

A Pneumatological Theology of Religion?

> One might expect the Pentecostals to develop a Spirit-oriented theology of mission and world religions, because of their openness to religious experience, their sensitivity to the oppressed of the Third World where they have experienced much of their growth, and their awareness of the ways of the Spirit as well as dogma.[1]

Clark Pinnock, the Canadian Evangelical theologian with a vested interest both theologically and experientially in the works of the Spirit, in his recent pneumatological systematic theology, *Flame of Love: A Theology of the Holy Spirit*, has pointedly challenged Pentecostal-Charismatic missiology: What is the role of the Spirit in the world, outside the confines of the Christian Church?

While Pentecostals/Charismatics have excelled in missionary activities with impressive results by any standards, their thinking about the ministry of the Spirit in the world lags behind. Not only that, but—aligning with the more conservative wing of the church—they have also been the first to raise doubts about any kind of saving role of the Spirit apart from the proclamation of the gospel. Most often Pentecostals/Charismatics have either succumbed to the standard Fundamentalist view of limiting the Spirit's saving work to the church (except for the work of the Spirit preparing for receiving the gospel),[2] or have ignored outright any reflection on what their otherwise strong insistence on the principle *spiritus ubi vult spirat* ("The Spirit blows where it wills," John 3:6) might mean in relation to other religions.

Furthermore with other conservative Christians, Pentecostals have been afraid of the dangers of recent liberal approaches to the issue.[3] A case in point is the recent warning from an official of the Assemblies of God, the largest white Pentecostal denomination in the United States. According to this statement, a pluralistic approach poses a three-fold problem: (1) it is contrary to Scripture; (2) it replaces the obligation for world evangelism; and (3) those who fail to fulfill the Great Commission are ultimately not living under the Lordship of Christ.[4]

So, the question of the "theology of religions"—as it is technically known—is simple: is there salvation, or at least salvific elements, outside the Church/Christ? One does not need to be specialist in the area to figure out what have been the possible approaches. *Exclusivists* hold that salvation is available only in Jesus Christ to the extent that those who have never heard the Gospel are eternally lost. In this scheme, non-Christian religions play no role in the history of salvation. For *pluralists*, other religions are legitimate means of salvation. The mediating group, *inclusivists* hold that while salvation is ontologically founded upon the person of Christ, its benefits have been made universally available by the revelation of God. The last orientation is the official standpoint of the post-conciliar Roman Catholic Church, although, understandably, there are many variations in modern Catholic theology.

Anticipating the results of our inquiry, it can be said that traditionally Pentecostals and many Charismatics have been exclusivists, but in the last two decades or so there have been several theologically-noteworthy attempts to develop a Pentecostal-Charismatic theology of religions moving toward a more inclusivist view. In fact, this latter group, mainly academic theologians, has inquired into the missiological implications of their doctrine and experience of the Spirit.

This chapter proceeds as follows: I will begin by summarizing the two recent international ecumenical dialogues with Pentecostals as to what they state about our problem. Ecumenical dialogues, if anything, are supposed to faithfully reflect the current standpoint of any church. Then I will inquire into earlier endeavors by some Charismatics concerning the role of the Spirit in salvation. Next I will introduce and critically assess the most recent theological advances in the field of Pentecostal scholarship. Finally, I will give my own appraisal of the state of the inquiry among Pentecostals/ Charismatics and present theses for further work.

Since the question under scrutiny is so multifaceted and the material to be covered so vast and rapidly growing, I need to be very brief in my comments. Rather than offering a final word on this most perennial question of missions—who could ever do that?—I will instead attempt to introduce and bring to light the most important perspectives among Pentecostals/Charismatics for the wider ecumenical guild to work together toward a more satisfying conciliar view. I will limit my comments about Pentecostal-Charismatic views on a theology of religions to only pneumatological aspects, i.e., what is the role of the Spirit here. Therefore christological, ecclesiological, and other related issues have to be set aside unless they have direct bearing on the discussion.

Pentecostals in Dialogue on Spirit and Mission

Pentecostals have held international dialogues with both the Roman Catholic Church since 1972 and more recently with the World Alliance of Reformed Churches (WARC) beginning from 1996. There was a tentative discussion on the possibility of salvation during the Second Quinquennium (1978–1982) of the Roman Catholic-Pentecostal dialogue and no unanimity was reached. Although both Catholics and Pentecostals believe that "ever since the creation of the world, the visible existence of God and his everlasting power have been clearly seen by the mind's understanding of created things" (*FR* IV.20; cf. Rom. 1:20; Ps 19:1–4), their perspectives diverged over the existence and/or meaning of salvific elements found in non-Christian religions. The Final Report, for example, records:

> According to contemporary Roman Catholic understanding, to which Vatican II gives an authoritative expression, "All must be converted to Jesus Christ as he is made known by the Church's preaching" (*Decree on the Missionary Activity of the Church*, par. 7). "The Church...is necessary for salvation" (*Constitution on the Church*, par. 14). But Vatican II also says that all without exception are called by God to faith in Christ, and to salvation (*Constitution on the Church*, par. 1, 16; *Declaration on the Relationship of the Church to non-Christian Religions*, par. 1, 2). This is brought about "in an unseen way...known only to God" (*Constitution on the Church in the Modern World*, par. 22; *Decree on the Missionary Activity of the Church*, par. 7). This theology is seen as a legitimate development of the total New Testament teaching on God's saving love in Christ. The classical Pentecostal participants do not accept this development but retain their interpretation of the Scripture that non-Christians are excluded from the life of the Spirit: "Truly, truly I say unto you, unless one is born anew, he cannot see the Kingdom of God' (John 3:3)." (*FR* II.14)

So, whereas *Extra Ecclesiam nulla salus*—"no salvation outside the Church"—has been the traditional understanding of the Church since the time of Cyprian, ironically the present situation sees the Pentecostals defending this classical position and some Catholics attempting reinterpretation.

Most Pentecostals limit the saving work of the Spirit to the church and its proclamation of the Gospel, although they acknowledge the work of the Holy Spirit in the world, convincing people of sin (*FR* IV.20). The rationale for this more exclusivist attitude is found in the fallen state of humankind and in a literal reading of the New Testament, which for Pentecostals does not give much hope for non-Christians (*FR* II.14). Furthermore, Pentecostals, like many of the early Christians, tend to point out the demonic elements in other religions rather than common denominators. However, there are some Pentecostals who would see a convergence toward the Catholic position that the Holy Spirit is at work in non-Christian religions, preparing individual hearts for an eventual exposure to the Gospel of Jesus Christ (*FR* IV.21). Unfortunately, neither the *Final Reports* nor the Pentecostal paper elaborate on what this convergence might mean.

In the Reformed-Pentecostal dialogue, the problem concerning the existence of salvific elements in other religions and the role of the Spirit here was left an open question:

> Whether there are salvific elements in other religions, however, is currently being debated by individual theologians within the Reformed family. While Pentecostals and many Reformed find it impossible to accept the idea that salvation might be found outside Jesus Christ, some Reformed agree with the ecumenical observation made at the world conference on mission and evangelism in San Antonio, Texas, USA in 1989, that "We cannot point to any other way of salvation than Jesus Christ, at the same time, we cannot set limits to the saving power of God" (cf. Acts 17:28).[5]

While Pentecostals generally speaking are much more reserved as to the possibility of the Spirit bringing any kind of salvific knowledge apart from the proclamation of the gospel, the Reformed are more divided on that issue. The Pentecostal exclusivism is based on their view of the biblical teaching. Furthermore, they also emphasize the need for spiritual discernment:

> On the whole, Pentecostals do not acknowledge the presence of salvific elements in non-Christian religions because they view this as contrary to the teaching of the Bible. The church is called to discern the spirits through the charism of the Holy Spirit informed by the Word of God (1 Cor. 12:10, 14:29; cf. 1 Thess. 5:19–21; 1 John 4:2–3). Pentecostals, like many of the early Christians, are sensitive to the elements in other religions that oppose biblical teaching. They are, therefore, encouraged to received the guidance of the Holy Spirit.[6]

It is clear that, as a whole Pentecostals are extremely reserved about any kind of salvific ministry of the Spirit outside the church. What are the potential reasons? In addition to close links with fundamentalism and conservativism, reasons include literal Bible reading and suspicion toward the ecumenical movement, which it sees as a champion of non-restrictive views. However, there has also been openness to those in other faiths, evident in an appreciation of the high morality and devotion among followers of other religions and in some cases even a willingness to learn from them.[7]

The Spirit and Universality: Emerging Charismatic Contributions

The South African charismatic theologian Henry I. Lederle strikes a note that challenges his Pentecostal counterparts who have been slower to reflect on the wider ministry of the Spirit in the world:

> For too long the Spirit and his work has been conceived of in too limited a sense. There was a capitulation at the beginning of the modern era in which faith became restricted to the private devotional life and the latter was then described as "spiritual." The Spirit should not be limited to spiritual experiences and charisms—even though it needs to be recognized that this element still awaits acknowledgment in much of Christianity. We need, however, to set our sights much higher. Not only the reality discovered by Pentecostalism needs to be reclaimed but also the cosmic dimensions of the Spirit's work. The Spirit is at work in the world and should not be degraded to an ornament of piety.[8]

A consultation on Charismatic theology sponsored by the WCC at Geneva in 1980 produced a landmark document, *The Church is Charismatic*. While mission was not the focus, some interesting developments from missiological viewpoint were offered. A summary of a theological group suggested that there are three major orientations to the Spirit's role in the world: 1) an ecclesiological approach: the Spirit works for the unity and united witness of all churches; 2) a cosmological approach: the Spirit renews creation and bestows fullness of life; this encompasses physical healing and healing of social relationships as well; 3) a sacramental approach: the Spirit is mediated through personal conversion, baptism, confirmation, and ordination as sacramental theologies renew their focus on the Spirit.[9]

One of the main differences between Pentecostals and Charismatics who wanted to stay in their own churches is that the latter are more open to embrace the sacramental principle as part of their own church tradition. Furthermore, many Charismatics are also more open to the possibility of the Spirit ministering outside the church. The term "cosmological approach" to the Spirit clearly reveals this orientation. The range of the Spirit's ministry is far wider than the church and personal salvation. Human beings as physical and social creatures are the "object" of the Spirit's work as is also the creation. The same Spirit of God who was instrumental in creation will also re-create the world. In line with this more comprehensive orientation to the role of the Spirit, *The Church is Charismatic* opens up the possibility for the Spirit to minister in "unknown" ways in the world.

In the Two-Thirds world pneumatologies, the holistic, cosmic orientation is even more evident, of which African Independent Church pneumatologies are an excellent case study. The African independent churches are all thoroughly charismatic in their worship and Christian life. Therefore, I believe the Church catholic needs to hear their distinctive testimony as they live out their Spirit-filled life in African soil, even though some of their practices raise legitimate concerns for many other Christians. According to Marthinus L. Daneel, there are four basic orientations to the role of the Spirit in this understanding: (1) The Holy Spirit as Savior of Humankind; (2) The Spirit as Healer and Protector; (3) The Spirit of Justice and Liberation; (4) The Earthkeeping Spirit.[10] Even though the question of the theology of religions is not explicitly touched here, it is clear that this "cosmic pneumatology" is far more inclusive than the doctrine of most of their western counterparts. The Spirit's role is affirmed regarding individual salvation, healing of the earth, and justice.

Theologically the most significant appeal for a truly pneumatological theology of religions among evangelical Charismatics comes from Clark H. Pinnock, who has for years written extensively on a responsible inclusivist position. He started his move toward inclusivism mainly on a christological basis but then later shifted to a definite pneumatological view (without, of course, positing any contradistinction between these two orientations).[11]

Pinnock rightly grasps the basic errors to be avoided: one is to say dogmatically that all will be saved, and the other is to say that only a few will be. The former is widespread in more liberally minded mainline churches (universalism), while the latter is to be found among conservatives (restrictivism), such as most Pentecostals, Evangelicals and many Charismatics. The two poles of the Christian message, the universal will of

God to save all and the finality of salvation only in Christ are to be handled in a way that does not discourage evangelism but on the other hand does not make salvation unavailable to most people. In Pinnock's view, counting against restrictivism is not only God's nature as Father and the universality of the atonement of Christ but also the ever-present Spirit, "who can foster transforming friendship with God anywhere and everywhere."[12]

The gateway for Pinnock to an appreciation of a more unlimited ministry of the Spirit is the "cosmic range to the operations of the Spirit."[13] Emphasis on the Spirit's work in salvation should not be read as a denial of his work in creation on which it is based, as too often has been the case. Pinnock argues that by acknowledging the work of the Spirit in creation, we are actually allowing a more universal perspective of the Spirit's ministry in which the work of preparing for hearing the gospel is not set in antithesis to the fulfillment of the gospel in Christ. "What one encounters in Jesus is the fulfillment of previous invitations of the Spirit."[14]

Pinnock rightly argues that access to grace is less of a problem for a pneumatologically based theology of religions than for an exclusively christologically anchored one. Whereas the incarnation of the Son was confined to a specific place in time and history, its universal effects through the ministry of the Spirit can be transmitted to the farthest ends of the earth. A truly revolutionary insight of Pinnock's is that the religions rather than being either futile human attempts to reach God (conservatives) or outright obstacles to a saving knowledge of God (the young Barth), can be Spirit-used pointers to and means of contact with God. He asks,

> If the Spirit gives life to creation and offers grace to every creature, one would expect him to be present and make himself felt (at least occasionally) in the religious dimension of cultural life. Why would the Spirit be working everywhere else but not here? God is reaching out to all nations and does not leave himself without witness (Acts 14:17). Would this witness not crop up sometimes in the religious realm?[15]

Not only that, but everyday human experiences can likewise be means of divine contact since human beings "as spirit" are created to be open to God.[16] In the final analysis, the ministries of the Son and Spirit can, of course, not to be put in any kind of opposition. Rather they are to be seen as "both-and." "Christ, the only mediator, sustains particularity, while the Spirit, the presence of God everywhere, safeguards universality."[17]

Discerning the Spirit(s): A Pentecostal Experiment

It might not be surprising that the first Pentecostal who has worked hard to construe a pneumatological theology of religions comes originally from Asia where the challenge of pluralism is more pervasive than elsewhere. For Amos Yong, a Pentecostal-Charismatic theology of religions can be best defined "as the effort to understand both the immensely differentiated experiences of faith and the multifaceted phenomena of religious traditions and systems that is informed by experiences of the Spirit in the light of Scripture, and vice versa."[18] Moreover this endeavor should be attempted without on the hand giving up the priority of evangelism and on the other hand commitment to the authority of Scripture.

Yong's ambitious program consists of the following tasks. First, he shows the impasse of the christological approach to the question of a Christian theology of religions. Yong is too good a theologian to undermine the finality of Christ in his program; what he attempts is to show the limits of a christological starting point which finally leads to exclusive particularism.

Second, in critical dialogue with Eastern Orthodox contributions as well as Karl Rahner, Paul Tillich, and Michael Lodahl (whose *Shekinah/Spirit: Divine Presence in Jewish and Christian Religion* purports to offer a pneumatological bridge between these two sibling faiths[19]), Yong argues for the necessity of a pneumatological approach, basing it on a foundational concept of the Spirit as divine presence. He suggests that it is possible to conceptualize divine presence and activity in the world without denying the reality of divine absence. Since these categories are potentially universal, they can be considered as central elements of a more universal theology of the Spirit in the world.

Third, Yong discusses several reasons why Pentecostals and Charismatics should engage the urgent task of a theology of religions: (1) their international roots and global presence; (2) the presence of urgent missiological issues such as syncretism, the denunciation of local traditions as a sign of a dualistic approach to questions regarding the gospel and culture, the balance between gospel proclamation and work for social justice, etc.; and (3) the quest for Pentecostal identity and theological truth. According to Yong, Pentecostal identity cannot be determined apart from relation to other churches (ecumenism) and other religions (theology of religions). In addition, the truth question of any religion cannot be answered without the challenge of competing (or complementary) truth claims.

Fourth, Yong enlists the services of various resources among Pentecostals regarding the theology of religions challenge. He takes up and adapts the basic categories suggested by Harvey Cox in his widely acclaimed book *Fire From Heaven*,[20] such as the Spirit-inspired religious experience in the form of glossolalia and other gifts as a token of the presence of the Spirit in believers' lives and "Pentecostal pragmatism" that expects the miraculous from God but at the same time is committed to activism and service in the world. He also discusses the role of spiritual discernment and a responsible relationship to the demonic. Fifth, Yong ventures into a comparative case study of Umbanda, an Afro-Brazilian tradition, and Pentecostalism to test his emerging pneumatological theology.

It is too early to give a definite assessment of Yong's very recent approach. Nevertheless, his attempt to construct a viable pneumatological theology of religions should be understood as an opener, a way to ask the right questions. It understandably raises some questions and concerns, such as the relationship between christology and pneumatology. I think nearly everyone today agrees that building a theology of religions on christology alone is not the most promising way, but neither is a theology based on the Spirit at the expense of Christ. Furthermore, even with the presence of the case study, Yong's attempt is quite abstract, and several perspectives that he eloquently develops (and which are in themselves very interesting) do not so easily relate to the main problem of the inquiry. These few reservations are, of course, not meant to undermine the value of this groundbreaking study, but rather to warn Pentecostals/Charismatics and others not to be uncritically excited about a potential solution to this ancient dilemma by turning to the Spirit.

As a way toward a more concrete approach to the question under discussion, a recent essay by the Hispanic Pentecostal theologian Samuel Solivan should be noted. Solivan has outlined five principles for Pentecostals for participation in the interreligious dialogue: (1) the fact that the Holy Spirit is the one who leads Christians to all truth; (2) the importance of identification with the poor of the world and need to bring their distinctive voice into the dialogue; (3) the conviction of the prevenient workings of the Holy Spirit in every human being; (4) the empowerment of believers for witness by the Spirit; and (5) the diverse and pluralistic character of the Spirit's manifestations across racial, class, gender, language, and religious boundaries. On this foundation, as a Pentecostal pastor and academic theologian, Solivan is led to "examine the diverse ways the Holy Spirit is at work among other people of faith."[21] Yet he does so critically since there are always pitfalls—such as relativization of the truth—in an approach to mission in which dialogue is the *main* vehicle.

Reflections and Tasks for Further Study

Reflecting on a theology of religions is a task incumbent upon all Christians. But it is especially so for Pentecostals-Charismatics for several reasons. We live in a world in which the rapid development of communication has brought the inhabitants of our "global village," and consequently their religions, into a kind of contact that had been unforeseen in the previous history of the church. Even those who do not want to engage the question of one's relation to other religions and their potential salvific value cannot pretend to ignore these questions, since religions have come to us even if we are not going anywhere. Moreover, this reflection is particularly incumbent upon Pentecostals/Charismatics because of their faith in the unlimited, powerful ministry of the Spirit.

It is also clear—and critical for the future of this highly evangelistic, eschatologically loaded Christian family—that Pentecostals/Charismatics should not give up their enthusiasm for evangelism and for meeting the social needs of people. Whatever the shape of their pneumatological theology of religions, Pentecostals/Charismatics cannot afford to accept it by denying their identity.

A careful reading of the Bible and a new appreciation for Christian tradition—the outgrowth of Spirit-led reflection and spirituality of the whole people of God through the centuries—might open up new ways of appreciating the sovereign, unexpected, powerful work of the Spirit in the world. If Christ died for all and was raised from the dead by the Spirit of the Father to be the Lord of all, certainly the Spirit must sigh in words unutterable for the salvation of human beings. And if Christ came to be the fulfillment of all that has been believed about God, then religions, even when they are confused by sin, misunderstandings, and distortions, cannot be immune to the pervasive, unrestricted presence of the Divine Spirit. While I have expressed my reservations about building a theology of religions at the expense of christology, I still believe that a biblical, systematically coherent theology of religions must stand on a pneumatological foundation; otherwise, the Spirit of God is not a constitutive person of the Trinity. A pneumatological orientation to the theology-of-religions dilemma creates as many problems and challenges as it seems to solve. But how else could anything new come out, anything significant?

Finally, life in Spirit is more than doctrine and right understanding. It is in the final analysis *life*. Aesthetic and emotional aspects belong to the sphere of the Spirit's ministry as well as intellectual and "spiritual." As Pinnock reminds us, "Spirit is the ecstasy of divine life, the overabundance of joy, that gives birth to the universe and ever works to bring about a fullness of unity."[22] If so, then the Spirit is the essential contact point between the world and God. Right talk about God, the Triune God, leads to right adoration and acceptance of his bountiful gifts. God's gifts are meant for everyone.

> When we render God in this way, not only atheists might come to love him, but even Christians, for we ourselves often lack a sense of God's beauty and adorableness. God is the ever-expanding circle of loving, and the Spirit is the dynamic at the heart of the circle. Through him we all have access in one Spirit to the Father, on behalf of whom the Spirit and the Bride say, "Come!" Let us all join in the dance.

Endnotes

Preface

1. (Grand Rapids, Mich.: Baker Academic, 2002).

Introduction

1. This template structures the framework of Stanley Horton, ed., *Systematic Theology: A Pentecostal Perspective* (Springfield, Mo.: Logion, 1994).

2. See V.-M. Kärkkäinen, *Spiritus ubi vult spirat: Pneumatology in Roman Catholic-Pentecostal Dialogue (1972–1989)*, Schriften der Luther-Agricola-Gesellschaft 42 (Helsinki: Luther-Agricola Society, 1998), and *Ad ultimum terrae: Evangelization, Proselytism and Common Witness in the Roman Catholic-Pentecostal Dialogue 1990–1997*, Studies in the Intercultural History of Christianity 117 (Frankfurt: Peter Lang, 1999).

3. V.-M. Kärkkäinen, *Pneumatology: The Holy Spirit in Ecumenical, International, and Contextual Perspectives* (Grand Rapids: Baker Academic, 2002); *Ecclesiology: An Ecumenical, Historical, and Contextual Introduction* (Downers Grove: InterVarsity, 2002); *Christian Theology of Religions: An Introduction* (Downers Grove: InterVarsity, forthcoming in 2003); *One With God: Salvation as Deification and Justification*, and *To Know Christ: A Contemporary Introduction to Christology* (the last two manuscripts are under review with major publishers at the time of writing).

4. See, e.g., William Hordern and Frederick Dale Bruner, *The Holy Spirit—Shy Member of the Trinity* (Minneapolis: Fortress, 1984).

5. See Barth's "Evangelical Theology in the 19th Century" in his *The Humanity of God* (Richmond, Va.: John Knox, 1972), 24–25; my thanks to Frank Macchia for this reference. Cf. Philip J. Rosato, *The Spirit as Lord: The Pneumatology of Karl Barth* (Edinburgh: T. & T. Clark, 1981).

6. For argument of this movement in Tillich's theology, see Pan-Chiu Lai, *Towards a Trinitarian Theology of Religions: A Study in Paul Tillich's Thought* (Kampen: Kok, 1994), esp. 115–16.

7. The studies are legion. Representative are Yves M.-J. Congar, *I Believe in the Holy Spirit*, 3 vols., trans. David Smith (New York: Seabury, 1983); Donald L. Gelpi, *The Divine Mother: A Trinitarian Theology of the Holy Spirit* (Lanham: UPA, 1984); Jürgen Moltmann, *The Spirit of Life: A Universal Affirmation*, trans. Margaret Kohl (Minneapolis: Fortress, 1992); Michael Welker, *God the Spirit*, trans. John F. Hoffmeyer (Minneapolis: Fortress, 1994); John McIntyre, *The Shape of Pneumatology: Studies in the Doctrine of the Holy Spirit* (Edinburgh: T. & T. Clark, 1997); Gary D. Badcock, *Light of Truth, Fire of Love: A Theology of the Holy Spirit* (Grand Rapids: Eerdmans, 1997); Lee Snook, *What in the World is God Doing? Re-Imagining Spirit and Power* (Minneapolis: Fortress, 1999); Rebecca B. Prichard, *Sensing the Spirit: The Holy Spirit in Feminist Perspective* (St. Louis: Chalice, 1999); Nancy M. Victorin-Vangerud, *The Raging Hearth: Spirit in the Household of God* (St. Louis: Chalice, 2000); and Donald Bloesch, *The Holy Spirit: Works and Gifts* (Downers Grove: InterVarsity, 2000).

8. See, e.g., Steven G. Smith, *The Concept of the Spiritual: An Essay in First Philosophy* (Philadelphia: Temple Univ. Press, 1988); Miroslav Volf, *Work in the Spirit: Toward a Theology of Work* (Oxford: Oxford Univ. Press, 1992); Patrick Sherry, *Spirit and Beauty: An Introduction to Theological Aesthetics* (Oxford: Clarendon, 1992); and Mark I. Wallace, *Fragments of the Spirit: Nature, Violence, and the Renewal of Creation* (New York: Continuum, 1996), just to name the impact of pneumatology on some of areas of theological knowledge.

9. Formally launching this possibility is Henry Pitt van Dusen, *Spirit, Son, and Father: Christian Faith in the Light of the Holy Spirit* (New York: Charles Scribner's Sons, 1958).

10. See the overview of Gelpi's theological program in Yong, "In Search of Foundations: The *Oeuvre* of Donald L. Gelpi, S.J., and Its Significance for Pentecostal Theology and Philosophy," *Journal of Pentecostal Theology*, forthcoming.

11. See Clark H. Pinnock, *Flame of Love: A Theology of the Holy Spirit* (Downers Grove: InterVarsity, 1996).

12. See D. Lyle Dabney, "Jürgen Moltmann and John Wesley's Third Article Theology," *Wesleyan Theological Journal* 19, nos. 1–2 (1994): 140–48; "Otherwise Engaged in the Spirit: A First Theology for the Twenty-first Century," in Miroslav Volf, Carmen Krieg, and Thomas Kucharz, eds., *The Future of Theology: Essays in Honor of Jürgen Moltmann* (Grand Rapids: Eerdmans, 1996), 154–63; and "Starting with the Spirit: Why the Last Should Now Be First," in Gordon Preece and Stephen Pickard, eds., *Starting with the Spirit*, Task of Theology Today II (Hindmarsh, Australia: Australia Theological Forum; Openbook Publishers, 2001), 3–27. All of this is a prelude to Dabney's work in progress toward four volumes in systematic theology beginning with pneumatology, proceeding through christology and patrology, and ending with Trinity.

13. See Yong, *Spirit-Word-Community: Theological Hermeneutics in Trinitarian Perspective*, New Critical Thinking in Biblical Studies and Theology (Aldershot, UK; Burlington, Vt.: Ashgate, 2002).

Chapter One

1. Murray W. Dempster, "Paradigm Shifts and Hermeneutics: Confronting Issues Old and New," *Pneuma* 15, 2 (1993): 129. The entire issue of *Pneuma* 15 (1993), introduced by Dempster's editorial article, was devoted to the issue of Pentecostal hermeneutics, especially of postmodern developments.

2. Walter J. Hollenweger, *The Pentecostals* (London: SCM, 1972), xvii.

3. Ibid., "The Critical Tradition of Pentecostalism," *JPT* 2 (1992): 7, 9, and 17.

4. "Preface" by Jürgen Moltmann and Karl-Josef Kuschel, eds., in "Pentecostal Movements as an Ecumenical Challenge," *Concilium* 3 (1996): viii.

5. Gordon D. Fee, "Hermeneutics and Historical Precedent: A Major Problem in Pentecostal Hermeneutics," in Russell Spittler, ed., *Perspectives on the New Pentecostalism* (Grand Rapids: Baker Book House, 1976), 119.

6. Kenneth J. Archer, "Pentecostal Hermeneutics: Retrospect and Prospect," *JPT* 8 (1996): 64.

7. Steven J. Land, *Pentecostal Spirituality: A Passion for the Kingdom*, JPTSup 1 (Sheffield, UK: Sheffield Academic, 1993), 360.

8. Cited in Jerry L. Sandidge, *Roman Catholic-Pentecostal Dialogue (1977–1982): A Study in Developing Ecumenism*, vol. 1, SIHC 44 (Frankfurt am Main: Peter Lang, 1987), 141.

9. Archer, "Pentecostal Hermeneutics," 64, citing Grant Wacker, "The Functions of Faith in Primitive Pentecostalism," *Harvard Theological Review* 77 (1984): 361.

10. Archer, "Pentecostal Hermeneutics," 67.

11. Cited in Joseph Byrd, "Paul Ricoeur's Hermeneutical Theory and Pentecostal Proclamation," *Pneuma* 15, 2 (1993): 204.

12. Archer, "Pentecostal Hermeneutics," 65, citing Wacker, "The Functions of Faith," 365.

13. Land, *Pentecostal Spirituality*, 55–56.

14. Jean-Daniel Plüss, "Azusa and Other Myths: The Long and Winding Road from Experience to Stated Belief and Back Again," *Pneuma* 15, 2 (1993): 191.

15. Scott A. Ellington, "Pentecostals and the Authority of Scripture," *JPT* 9 (1996): 26.

16. See Walter J. Ong, *Orality and Literacy: The Technologizing of the Word* (London & New York: Methuen, 1982), and *The Presence of the Word: Some Prolegomena for Cultural and Religious History* (New Haven & London: Yale Univ. Press, 1967).

17. See Vinson Synan, "Fundamentalism," in *DPCM*, 324–27. Basically the term can have two meanings: on the one hand, it refers to a group of Christians from various Christian traditions that fights for biblical inerrancy, (often) right-wing political values, etc. On the other hand, it is used to denote an extremely conservative way of defining biblical inspiration, without reference to any group or movement. Cf. French L. Arrington, "Dispensationalism," in *DPCM*, 247–48.

18. Timothy Cargal, "Beyond the Fundamentalist-Modernist Controversy: Pentecostals and Hermeneutics in a Postmodern Era," *Pneuma* 15, 2 (1993): 167–68.

19. Led by Gerald T. Sheppard, "Pentecostalism and the Hermeneutics of

Dispensationalism: The Anatomy of an Uneasy Relationship," PNEUMA 6, 2 (1984): 5–34.

20. Ellington, "Pentecostals and the Authority of Scripture," 17.

21. Ibid., 21.

22. See Land, *Pentecostal Spirituality*, 100 and 106.

23. Howard M. Ervin, "Hermeneutics: A Pentecostal Option," PNEUMA 2, 2 (1981): 22. Charismatic Evangelical theologian, Clark H. Pinnock, in his article "The Work of the Holy Spirit in Hermeneutics," *JPT* 2 (1993): 4, urges us to give up the artificial, even confusing, distinction between inspiration and illumination; see also Pinnock's *The Scripture Principle* (San Francisco: Harper & Row, 1984), chs. 7–9.

24. Howard M. Ervin, "Hermeneutics: A Pentecostal Option," in Jerry L. Sandidge, ed., *The Roman Catholic/Pentecostal Dialogue: A Study in Developing Ecumenism*, vol. 2, SIHC 44 (Frankfurt am Main: Peter Lang, 1987), 100–121. This slightly modified version of this paper was published in PNEUMA (see preceding note). The references hereafter to Ervin, "Hermeneutics," refer to the Sandidge rather than to the PNEUMA version.

25. Ervin, "Hermeneutics," 101.

26. Ibid., 107, emphasis Ervin's.

27. Ibid., 108–109, emphasis added.

28. Ibid., 113.

29. Ibid., 115 and 118.

30. Ibid., 115–16.

31. [Editor's note: By "New Hermeneutics," Ervin is referring to the post-Bultmannian school of interpretation characteristic of the existential theologies of the 1960s which sought to apply a general hermeneutic to the Bible understood as needing to be read as any other book. Ervin cites specifically Gerhard Ebeling's essay, "Word of God and Hermeneutics," which has been reprinted numerous times, most accessibly in James M. Robinson and John B. Cobb, Jr., eds., *The New Hermeneutic* (New York: Harper & Row, 1964), 78–110.]

32. Ervin, "Hermeneutics," 105, emphasis added.

33. Ibid., 118.

34. Ibid., 103 and 110. From the viewpoint of modern Luther research the phrase "ontological union" is highly interesting. The new paradigm of Luther research among Finnish Lutheran scholars, under the mentorship of Tuomo Mannermaa, has shown evidence of the ontological understanding of the presence of Christ in salvation, etc. More on this in chapter eleven.

35. Ibid., 116–17, citing Orthodox Timothy Ware, *The Orthodox Church* (London: Penguin, 1972), 253–54.

36. French L. Arrington, "Hermeneutics, Historical Perspectives on Pentecostal and Charismatic," in *DPCM*, 376–89.

37. Paul D. Lee, *Pneumatological Ecclesiology in the Roman Catholic-Pentecostal Dialogue: A Catholic Reading of the Third Quinquennium (1985–1989)* (Ph.D. diss., Univ. of Thomas, Rome, 1994), 68–69.

38. Ibid., 69–71.

39. Cargal, "Beyond the Fundamentalist-Modernist Controversy," 173–74.

40. Ibid., 174, citing Arrington, "Hermeneutics," 382.

41. Jackie David Johns, "Pentecostalism and the Postmodern World," *JPT* 7 (1995): 73. Johns, in outlining major characteristic of the Pentecostal worldview in relation to postmodern developments, dialogues with the emerging systems thinking as explained, e.g., by Timothy Lines, *Systemic Religious education* (Birmingham, Ala.: Religious Education, 1987). For a technical introduction, see Ervin Laszlo, *Introduction to Systems Philosophy: Toward a New Paradigm of Contemporary Thought* (New York: Harper & Row, 1972).

42. Johns, "Pentecostalism," 89–91.

43. Ibid., 92.

44. Ibid.

45. Peter Stuhlmacher, *Vom Verstehen des Neuen Testaments: Eine Hermeneutik* (Göttingen: Vandenhoeck & Ruprecht, 1979), 125–32, and *Historical Criticism and Theological Interpretation of Scripture: Toward a Hermeneutics of Consent*, trans. R. A. Harrisville (Philadelphia: Fortress, 1977), 84–85.

46. Cargal, "Beyond the Fundamentalist-Modernist Controversy," 165.

47. Daniel E. Albrecht, Richard D. Israel, and Randy McNally, "Pentecostals and Hermeneutics: Texts, Rituals, and Community," PNEUMA 15, 2 (1993): 139.

48. Ibid., 143. This essay by three young Pentecostal scholars is a textbook example of the approach of a postmodern Pentecostal hermeneutics with an awareness of the requirements of a general hermeneutics: "Pentecostals and Hermeneutics: *Texts, rituals and Community*" (emphasis mine). They discuss biblical texts, Pentecostal worship "rituals" and Pentecostal community as the "text" to be interpreted.

49. See Byrd, "Paul Ricoeur's Hermeneutical Theory," 206–207.

50. Gerald T. Sheppard, "Biblical Interpretation after Gadamer," PNEUMA 16, 1 (1984): 125.

51. Paul Ricoeur, *The Symbolism of Evil* (Boston: Beacon, 1967), 5, qtd. in Byrd, "Paul Ricoeur's Hermeneutical Theory," 208. Walter J. Hollenweger, *Umgang mit Mythen: Interkulturelle Theologie* 2 (Münich: Chr. Kaiser Verlag, 1982), qualifies a true myth on the conditions that it stands a threefold test. First, it must be applicable to the present social, cultural and economic conflicts. Second, it will always relate to the Christ-event on the cross. Third, it yields a promise beyond history.

52. Byrd, "Paul Ricoeur's Hermeneutical Theory," 210.

53. For more on Pentecostalism and narrative theology, see Jean-Daniel Plüss, *Therapeutic and Prophetic Narratives in Worship: A Hermeneutic Study of Testimony and Vision*, SIHC 54 (Bern: Peter Lang, 1988).

54. Paul Ricoeur, *Interpretation Theory: Discourse and the Surplus of Meaning* (Fort Worth, Tex.: Texas Christian Univ., 1976), 71–72.

55. Arrington, "Hermeneutics," 383.

56. Albrecht, Israel and McNally, "Pentecostals and Hermeneutics," 145.

57. See Rickie D. Moore, "Deuteronomy and the Fire of God: A Critical Charismatic Interpretation," *JPT* 7 (1995): 1–33.

58. Robert O. Baker, "Pentecostal Bible Reading: Toward a Model of Reading for the Formation of Christian Affections," *JPT* 7 (1995): 34–48. See also R. Jerome Boone, "Community and Worship: The Key Components of Pentecostal Christian Formation," *JPT* 8 (1996), 129–42, and Cheryl Bridges Johns, *Pentecostal*

Formation: A Pedagogy Among the Oppressed, JPTSup 2 (Sheffield, UK: Sheffield Academic, 1993).

59. See Robert Menzies, "Jumping Off the Postmodern Bandwagon," *Pneuma* 16, 2 (1994): 115–20; Sheppard, "Biblical Interpretation," 121–41; and Hannah K. Harrington and Rebecca K. Patten, "Pentecostal Hermeneutics and Postmodern Literary Theory," *Pneuma* 16, 2 (1994): 109–14.

Chapter Two

1. Richard Gaillardetz, *Teaching with Authority: A Theology of the Magisterium in the Church* (Collegeville, Minn.: Liturgical, 1997), 69.

2. Joseph H. Ratzinger, "Dogmatic Constitution on Divine Revelation: Origin and Background," in Herbert Vorgrimler, ed., *Commentary on the Documents of Vatican II*, vol. III (New York: Herder & Herder, 1969), 190–91.

3. This formulation, interestingly enough, comes directly from *DV* 11 and 19 which sees infallibility as a logical result of the Spirit's inspiration.

4. Gerald O'Collins, "Revelation Past and Present," in René Latourelle, ed., *Vatican II: Assessment and Perspectives—Twenty-Five Years After (1962–1987)*, vol. 1 (New York: Paulist, 1988), 125–37, quote from 125; see also O'Collins, *Fundamental Theology* (New York: Paulist, 1981), 100–102. He calls the past revelation, the definitive revelation in Christ, "foundational," and the present revelation, "dependent." This distinction goes back to Paul Tillich (*Systematic Theology*, vol. 1. [Chicago: Univ. of Chicago Press, 1951], 126–28), who speaks in this connection of "original" and "dependent" revelation, and others, like Anglican John Macquarrie (*Principles of Christian Theology* [New York: Scribner's, 1968], 80–81), who speaks of "original" and "repetitive" revelation. A fine study of the "actualization" of the word of God and its relation to exegesis and Bible reading in the Church is offered by Ugo Vanni, "Exegesis and Actualization in the Light of *Dei Verbum*," in Latourelle, ed., *Vatican II*, 344–63.

5. See Maurice Gilbert, "New Horizons and Present Need: Exegesis since Vatican II," in Latourelle, ed., *Vatican II*, 321–43.

6. Paul D. Lee, *Pneumatological Ecclesiology in the Roman Catholic-Pentecostal Dialogue: A Catholic Reading of the Third Quinquennium (1985–1989)* (Ph.D. diss., Univ. of Thomas, Rome, 1994), 66.

7. This striking image comes from Lee, *Pneumatological Ecclesiology*, 76–78.

8. Kilian McDonnell, "Canon and *Koinonia/communio*: The Formation of the Canon as an Ecclesiological Process" (unpublished manuscript, 1997), 1.

9. See James S. Tinney, "Doctrinal Differences Between Black and White Pentecostals," *Spirit: A Journal of Issues Incident to Black Pentecostalism* 1, 1 (1977): 38. Millard Erickson, the Evangelical systematician, in *Christian Theology*, vol. 1 (Grand Rapids: Baker Book House, 1985), 221, defines the doctrine of inerrancy thus: "This is the doctrine that the Bible is fully truthful in all of its teachings."

10. Lee, *Pneumatological Ecclesiology*, 72.

11. The keen observer of Pentecostalism, Walter J. Hollenweger, "From Azusa Street to Toronto Phenomenon: Historical Roots of Pentecostalism," *Concilium* 3 (1996): 6, writes that, "[o]ccasionally Pentecostalists describe themselves as fun-

damentalists"; but "that is to misunderstand themselves, for fundamentalism, first, is younger than the Pentecostal movement and secondly, was and is its most bitter opponent."

12. Cecil M. Robeck, Jr., "National Association of Evangelicals," in *DPCM*, 634–36.

13. The door, however, was cautiously left open by Pentecostals for the possibility of using critical methods already in the Second Quinquennium: "Also in need of further discussion is whether the various methods of exegesis, for example the form-critical method which most Catholic exegetes use, are compatible with classical Pentecostal principles" (*FR* II.30).

14. Ervin, "Hermeneutics: A Pentecostal Option," in Jerry L. Sandidge, ed., *The Roman Catholic/Pentecostal Dialogue: A Study in Developing Ecumenism*, vol. 2, SIHC 44 (Frankfurt am Main: Peter Lang, 1987), 103 and 118; and French L. Arrington, "Hermeneutics, Historical Perspectives on Pentecostal and Charismatic," *DPCM*, 387.

15. See James B. Shelton, *Mighty in Word and Deed: The Role of the Spirit in Luke-Acts* (Peabody, Mass.: Hendrickson, 1991), and Donald A. Johns, "Some New Directions in Hermeneutics of Classical Pentecostalism's Doctrine of Initial Evidence," in Gary B. McGee, ed., *Initial Evidence: Historical and Biblical Perspectives on the Pentecostal Doctrine of Spirit Baptism* (Peabody, Mass.: Hendrickson, 1991), 145–67.

16. Lee, *Pneumatological Ecclesiology*, 73.

17. Ibid., 56.

18. Pentecostals' use of *claritas Scripturae* goes back, of course, to the Protestant Reformation. For an informed assessment of the *claritas Scripturae's* use in recent Protestant and especially (American) Evangelical theology, see James Patrick Callahan, "*Claritas Scripturae*: The Role of Perspicuity in Protestant Hermeneutics," *Journal of Evangelical Theological Society* 39, 3 (1996): 353–72. [Editor's note: See also Callahan's recent booklength treatment: *The Clarity of Scripture: History, Theology and Contemporary Literary Studies* (Downer's Grove: InterVarsity, 2001).]

19. Walter J. Hollenweger, "The *Koinonia* of the Establishment," PNEUMA 12, 2 (1990): 154–55.

20. The "sensus fidei" is described by scholars in various terms: "a free and intense sensibility, intimate inclination, experiential intuition, sympathy, congeniality, connatural and spontaneous knowledge of the truth of Christ" (Lee, *Pneumatological Ecclesiology*, 87). See also John J. Burkhard, "*Sensus Fidei*: Theological Reflection since Vatican II: 1965–1984," *Heythrop Journal* 34 (1993): 58ff., for a comprehensive assessment of the literature. For the infallibility of the magisterium, see Francis A. Sullivan, *Magisterium: Teaching Authority in the Catholic Church* (New York: Paulist, 1983), esp. chs. 5–6.

21. Howard M. Ervin, "The Ties that Divide," in Sandidge, ed., *The Roman Catholic/Pentecostal Dialogue*, vol. 2, 244.

22. Ibid., 283. For the use of Acts 15 as a Pentecostal paradigm, see also French L. Arrington, "Hermeneutics, Historical Perspectives on Pentecostal and Charismatic," in *DPCM*, 387; and John Christopher Thomas, "Women, Pentecostals and the Bible: An Experiment in Pentecostal Hermeneutics," *JPT* 5 (1994): 41–56.

23. See Edward J. Kilmartin, "Reception in History: An Ecclesiological

Phenomenon and Its Significance," *JES* 21 (1984): 34–54. [Editor's note: The recent definitive study of Catholic reception theory is Ormond Rush, *The Reception of Doctrine: An Appropriation of Hans Robert Jauss' Reception Aesthetics and Literary Hermeneutics* (Roma: Pontificia Universita Gregoriana, 1997).]

24. Jeremy Miller, *John Henry Newman on the Idea of the Church* (Shepherdstown: Patmos, 1987), 151–52.

25. Gaillardetz, *Teaching With Authority*, 233–34.

26. Lee, *Pneumatological Ecclesiology*, 80.

27. See also Yves M.-J. Congar, *Tradition and Traditions: An Historical and a Theological Essay* (New York: Macmillan, 1967).

28. Karl Rahner, *Foundations of Christian Faith: An Introduction to the Idea of Christianity*, trans. William V. Dych (New York: Crossroad, 1982), 363, when speaking of tradition in Catholic understanding as living, Spirit-inspired process, says that "it can make Christ himself present in every age."

29. Gaillardetz, *Teaching With Authority*, 76.

30. O'Collins, "Revelation," 129.

31. Vatican II's view of a single font of divine revelation represents an obvious departure from those post-Tridentine theologies that viewed tradition as a distinct, additional source of revelation apart from Scripture. One of the more technical aspects of the conciliar debate concerned whether it was possible to speak of the material sufficiency of Scripture, the belief that there were no teaching found in tradition that could not at least implicitly be found in Scripture. This question was left open.

32. Ervin, "The Ties that Divide," 255–56.

33. J.-M. R. Tillard, *Church of Churches: The Ecclesiology of Communion*, trans. R.C. De Peaux. (Collegeville: Liturgical, 1992), 141.

34. See the seminal study by Nicholas Lash, *Change in Focus: A Study of Doctrinal Change and Continuity* (London: Sheed & Ward, 1973).

35. See, e.g., John Breck, "Orthodox Principles of Biblical Interpretation," *St. Vladimir's Theological Quarterly* 40 (1996): 77ff.

36. This goes back to Paul Evdokimov, "La Bible dans la piété orthodoxe," *Irenikon* (1950): 177–86, qtd. in Yves M.-J. Congar, *Diversity and Communion* (London: SCM, 1984), 134.

Chapter Three

1. Cecil M. Robeck, Jr., "Taking Stock of Pentecostalism: Reflections of a Retiring Editor," *Pneuma* 15, 1 (1993): 39.

2. Walter J. Hollenweger, *Pentecostalism: Origins and Developments Worldwide* (Peabody, Mass.: Hendrickson, 1997), 355–56.

3. One could, though, dispute Hollenweger's remark about the Charismatic movement since in many ways Charismatics have been far more open to ecumenism than most Pentecostals. It is yet to be seen which direction the Charismatic movement in general is going to take. My guess is that most Charismatic Christians do not start forming their own constituencies but rather stay in their own churches, even integrate more fully into them. This is the impression from the Charismatic Renewal in the Roman Catholic Church.

4. Two recent scholarly treatments of the topic are Cecil M. Robeck, Jr., "Pentecostal Origins from a Global Perspective," in Harold D. Hunter and Peter D. Hocken, eds., *All Together in One Place: Theological Papers from the Brighton Conference on World Evangelization*, JPTSup 4 (Sheffield: Sheffield Academic, 1993), 166–80, and Augustus Cerillo, Jr., "Interpretive Approaches to the History of American Pentecostal Origins," PNEUMA 19, 1 (1997): 29–52.

5. This last view of an "unmediated" emergence of Pentecostalism was popularized by Assemblies of God (USA) historian Carl Brumback, *Suddenly...From Heaven* (Springfield, Mo.: Gospel, 1961), 48–63.

6. Walter J. Hollenweger, "The Pentecostal Movement and the World Council of Churches," *ER* 18, 3 (1966): 313.

7. Robeck, "Taking Stock," 37. He refers to several original sources: Parham, Carothers, and Seymour.

8. Ibid., 39.

9. Charles F. Parham, *A Voice Crying in the Wilderness*, 3rd ed. (Baxter Springs, Kans.: Apostolic Faith College, 1910), 61.

10. W. F. Carothers, *The Baptism with the Holy Ghost and Speaking in Tongues* (Houston: W. F. Carothers, 1906–1907), 25, qtd. in Robeck, "Pentecostals and Ecumenism: An Expanding Frontier," in Jean-Daniel Plüss, ed., "Crossing Borders: Conference Papers on Pentecostal and Charismatic Research in Europe, 3–6 July 1991, Haus der Stille, Kappel, Switzerland" (unpublished), 1.

11. Cornelius van der Laan, *Sectarian Against His Will: Gerritt Roelof Polman and the Birth of Pentecostalism in the Netherlands*, Studies in Evangelicalism 11 (Metuchen, N.J.; London: Scarecrow, 1991), 23, qtd. in *Spade Regen* 12, 3 (June 1919): 37.

12. Ibid., 305.

13. Thomas B. Barratt, *In the Days of the Latter Rain* (London: Simpkin, Marshall, Hamilton, Kent, 1909), 145, emphasis orig.

14. See Jon Ruthven, *On the Cessation of the Charismata: The Protestant Polemic on Postbiblical Miracles*, JPTSup 3 (Sheffield: Sheffield Academic, 1993), 14.

15. Vinson Synan, "Pentecostalism: Varieties and Contributions," PNEUMA 8, 2 (1986): 36–37.

16. Robeck, "Taking Stock," 39.

17. Harvey G. Cox, *Fire From Heaven: The Rise of Pentecostal Spirituality and the Reshaping of Religion in the Twenty-first Century* (Reading, Mass.: Addison-Wesley, 1995), 74.

18. Gee, "Possible Pentecostal Unity," *Pentecost* 13 (Sept. 1950): 19.

19. Robeck, "Taking Stock," 39.

20. The Constitution and Bylaws of the Assemblies of God (USA), the world's largest Pentecostal denomination, contains some very strict guidelines concerning the ecumenical movement and participation of ministers in it; see Article IX.B.2.

21. For references, see Gee, "Possible Pentecostal Unity," 17; WCC constitution, §I: Basis, in Michael Kinnamon, ed., *Signs of the Spirit: Official Report: Seventh Assembly* (Geneva: WCC Publications; Grand Rapids: Eerdmans, 1991), 358; and *National Council of Churches (USA)/Report* 1984, 1.

22. Robeck, "Taking Stock," 40.

23. For the objectives of PFNA, which clearly show the effort to build unity, see W. E. Warner, "Pentecostal Fellowship of North America," in *DPCM*, 704.

24. Robeck, "Taking Stock," 43.

25. The remarkable story of du Plessis, usually called "Mr. Pentecost," is recorded in Martin Robinson, "To the Ends of the Earth: The pilgrimage of an Ecumenical Pentecostal, David J. du Plessis (1905–1987)" (Ph.D. diss., Univ. of Birmingham, UK, 1987).

26. Qtd. in Arnold Bittlinger, *Papst und Pfingstler: Der römische katholische-pfingstliche Dialoge und seine ökumenische Relevanz* (Frankfurt am Main: Peter Lang, 1978), 317.

27. Ibid., 322.

28. For a complete listing of Pentecostal Churches which are members of the WCC as of 1997, see Hollenweger, *Pentecostalism*, 384–87.

29. For the Canberra recommendations to the WCC-member churches to enhance their awareness and participation in Pentecostal spirituality and movements, see Jeffrey Gros, "Toward a Dialogue of Conversion: The Pentecostals, Evangelicals, and Conciliar Movements," *Pneuma* 17, 2 (1995): 192–93.

30. Simon Chan, "Sharing the Trinitarian Life—John 17:20–26, 1 John 1:1–4," in Thomas F. Best and Günther Gassmann, ed., *On the Way to Fuller Koinonia* (Geneva: WCC Publications, 1993), 85–90.

31. Gros, "Toward a Dialogue," 197 and 195.

32. Kilian McDonnell, "Can Classical Pentecostals and Roman Catholics Engage in Common Witness?" *JPT* 7 (1995): 97.

33. Paul D. Lee, *Pneumatological Ecclesiology in the Roman Catholic-Pentecostal Dialogue: A Catholic Reading of the Third Quinquennium (1985–1989)* (Ph.D. diss., Univ. of Thomas, Rome, 1994), 36–46. For other academic treatments of the Dialogue, see the following published dissertations: Bittlinger, *Papst und Pfingstler*; Jerry L. Sandidge, *Roman Catholic-Pentecostal Dialogue (1977–1982): A Study in Developing Ecumenism*, 2 vols. (Frankfurt am Main: Peter Lang, 1987); and V.-M. Kärkkäinen, *Spiritus ubi vult spirat: Pneumatology in Roman Catholic-Pentecostal Dialogue (1972–1989)* (Helsinki: Luther Agricola-Society, 1998), and *Ad ultimum terrae: Evangelization, Proselytism, and Common Witness in the Roman Catholic-Pentecostal Dialogue 1990–1997*, SIHC 117 (Frankfurt am Main: Peter Lang, 1999).

34. See the Final Report in *Pneuma* 21, 1 (1999): 11–51.

35. Kilian McDonnell, "Five Defining Issues: The International Classical Pentecostal/Roman Catholic dialogue," *Pneuma* 17, 2 (1995): 175–88, quote from 175.

36. Peter D. Hocken, "Ecumenical Dialogue: The Importance of Dialogue with Evangelicals and Pentecostals," *One in Christ* 30 (1994): 101–23, quotes from 104 and 112.

Chapter Four

1. *Reformation Churches and the Ecumenical Movement*, A Memorandum of Ecumenical Institutes in Bernsheim, Bern, Copenhagen, Prague and Strasbourg, Nov. 1984, 1985. For discussions of Christian identity beyond (intra-Christian) ecumenism, see, e.g., Stephen Sykes, *The Identity of Christianity: Theologians and the Essence of Christianity from Schleiermacher to Barth* (London: SPCK, 1984),

and *Studies on the Identity of the Church*, Summary Report and Evaluation of the Methodologies of Ecclesiology and Identity Studies, Lutheran World Federation (Geneva: Department of Studies, 1979).

2. *Ecumenical Relations of the Lutheran World Federation*, Report of the Working Group on the interrelations between the various bilateral Dialogues, revised by the Executive Committee (Divonne: Feb. 1977). For a discussion of religious identity as involving both beliefs and practices, see George A. Lindbeck, *The Nature of Doctrine: Religion and Theology in a Postliberal* Age (London: SPCK, 1984).

3. See Erich Geldbach, *Ökumene in Gegensätzen*, Bemsheimer Heft 66 (Göttingen: Vandenhoeck and Ruprecht, 1987); Laurentius Klein, "Theologische Alternative zur Konsensusökumene," *Theologischen Quartalschrift* 166, 4 (1986): 268–78; and E. Le Coutre, "Ökumene ohne Einheit," *Der Überblick* 24, 3 (1988). Charismatic Reformed ecumenist Henry I. Lederle of South Africa, "The Spirit of Unity: A Discomforting Comforter. Some Reflections on the Holy Spirit, Ecumenism and the Pentecostal-Charismatic Movements," *ER* 42, nos. 3–4 (1990): 291, calls this last model the "cheapest," without any meaning. A succinct introduction to ecumenical models and ways of unity is offered by Thomas F. Best, "Models of Unity," and "Ways to Unity," in Nicholas Lossky et al., eds., *Dictionary of the Ecumenical Movement* (Geneva: WCC Publications, 1991), 1041–43, 1043–47 respectively.

4. Kilian McDonnell, "Improbable Conversations: The International Classical Pentecostal/Roman Catholic Dialogue," PNEUMA 17, 2 (1995): 163.

5. Miroslav Volf, *After Our Likeness: The Church as the Image of the Trinity* (Grand Rapids: Eerdmans, 1998), 11.

6. Ibid., 11–12.

7. Cardinal Joseph H. Ratzinger, with Vittorio Messori, *The Ratzinger Report: An Exclusive Interview on the State of the Church* (San Francisco: Ignatius, 1985), 45ff.

8. Walter J. Hollenweger, "From Azusa Street to Toronto Phenomenon: Historical Roots of Pentecostalism," *Concilium* 3 (1996): 3. The phrase "third force" was coined by Henry Pitt van Dusen, "The Third Force in Christendom," *Life* 44 (1958): 13. For statistics see David Barrett, *World Christian Encyclopedia* (London: Oxford Univ. Press, 1982), 838, and "Signs, Wonders, and Statistics in the World of Today," in Jan A. B. Jongeneel et al., ed., *Pentecost, Mission, and Ecumenism: Essays on Intercultural Theology: Festschrift in Honor of Professor Walter J. Hollenweger* (Frankfurt am Main: Peter Lang, 1992), 189–96.

9. Harvey G. Cox, *The Silencing of Leonardo Boff: The Vatican and the Future of World Christianity* (Oak Park: Meyer Stone, 1988), 17.

10. For Oneness Pentecostals see David A. Reed, "Oneness Pentecostals," in *DPCM*, 644–51.

11. The preceding categorization follows that of Vinson Synan, "Pentecostalism: Varieties and Contributions," PNEUMA 8, 2 (1986): 34–36, with the exception of the last item which does not appear in Synan's list.

12. The main work arguing for the Wesleyan-Holiness heritage is Donald W. Dayton, *Theological Roots of Pentecostalism* (Grand Rapids: Zondervan, 1987); cf. Edith Waldvogel, "The 'Overcoming Life': A Study in the Reformed Evangelical Origins of Pentecostalism" (Ph.D. diss., Harvard Univ., 1977), and Walter J. Hollenweger, "After Twenty Years' Research on Pentecostalism," *IRM* 75 (1986): 4.

13. Cecil M. Robeck, Jr., "Pentecostal Origins from a Global Perspective," in Harold D. Hunter and Peter D. Hocken, eds., *All Together in One Place: Theological Papers from the Brighton Conference on World Evangelization*, JPTSup 4 (Sheffield: Sheffield Academic, 1993), 169.

14. Qtd. in David Cole, "Current Pentecostal/Ecumenical Tensions," *Ecumenical Trends* 24, 5 (1995): 11.

15. Qtd. in Jerry L. Sandidge, *Roman Catholic-Pentecostal Dialogue (1977–1982): A Study in Developing Ecumenism*, vol. 1 (Frankfurt am Main: Peter Lang, 1987), 141.

16. Margaret Poloma, *The Assemblies of God at the Crossroads: Charisma and Institutional Dilemmas* (Knoxville: Univ. of Tennessee Press, 1989), ch. 1, qtd. in Timothy Cargal, "Beyond Fundamentalist-Modernist Controversy: Pentecostals and Hermeneutics in a Postmodern Age," *Pneuma* 15, 2 (1993): 163.

17 See Dayton, *Theological Roots of Pentecostalism*; Robeck, "Pentecostal Origins," 168, offers a recent evaluation of this schema.

18. Steven J. Land, *Pentecostal Spirituality: A Passion for the Kingdom*, JPTSup 1(Sheffield, UK: Sheffield Academic, 1993), 18.

19. Hollenweger, "After Twenty Years' Research," 6. He has presented this kind of list in numerous other writings, and most observers of the movement, both insiders and outsiders, have enthusiastically cited it.

20. Hollenweger, "Verheissung und Verhängnis der Pfingstbewegung," *Evangelische Theologie* 53, 3 (1993): 265–88.

21. See, e.g., Land, *Pentecostal Spirituality*, 14 and 47.

22. Walter J. Hollenweger, *Pentecostalism: Origins and Developments Worldwide* (Peabody, Mass.: Hendrickson, 1997), 291–456.

23. The spring 1993 issue of *Pneuma* (15, 1) was devoted to the topic of Pentecostal identity; Murray W. Dempster's editorial article, "The Search for Pentecostal Identity," 1–8, overviews the contributions as well as the wider context.

24. William D. Faupel, "Whither Pentecostalism?" *Pneuma* 15, 1 (1993): 22–23.

25. Ibid., 26.

26. Roger Stronstadt, "Affirming Diversity: God's People as a Community of Prophets," *Pneuma* 17, 2 (1995): 155. [Editor's note: see also Stronstadt's recent booklength argument: *The Prophethood of All Believers: A Study in Luke's Charismatic Theology*, JPTSup 16 (Sheffield: Sheffield Academic, 1999).]

27. Stronstadt," Affirming Diversity," 156.

28. Cheryl Bridges Johns, "The Adolescence of Pentecostalism: In Search of a Legitimate Sectarian Identity," *Pneuma* 17, 1 (1995): 3.

29. Ibid., 13, referring to Walter Brueggemann, "The Legitimacy of a Sectarian Hermeneutic," *Horizons in Biblical Theology* 7 (1985): 1–42.

30. Johns, "The Adolescence of Pentecostalism," 15–16, quoting "Beginning of World Wide Revival," *The Apostolic Faith* 1 (Sept. 1906): 2.

31. Johns, "The Adolescence of Pentecostalism," 16.

32. Frank Macchia, "The Tongues of Pentecost: The Promise and Challenge of Pentecostal/Roman Catholic Dialogue," *JES* 35, 1 (1998): 4.

33. Karl Rahner, "On the Theology of Ecumenical Discussions," *Theological Investigations* XI (New York: Seabury, 1974), 38ff.

Chapter Five

1. Oscar Cullman, *Einheit durch Vielfalt* (Tübingen: Mohr, 1986); for other references, see ch. 4, n. 3.

2. Konrad Raiser, "The Holy Spirit in Modern Ecumenical Thought," *ER* 41, 3 (1989): 375.

3. Nikolay Berdyaev, *Spirit and Reality*, trans. George Reavey (London: Bles, 1964), 22.

4. Both Alistair McGrath (*Christian Theology: An Introduction* [Oxford, UK; Cambridge, USA: Blackwell, 1994], 240), and Jürgen Moltmann (*The Spirit of Life: A Universal Affirmation*, trans. M. Kohl [London: SCM, 1992], 1), use this striking illustration.

5. Kilian McDonnell, "A Trinitarian Theology of the Holy Spirit?" *Theological Studies* 46 (1985): 193, quoting Barth, *Schleiermacher-Auswahl mit einem Nachwort von Karl Barth*, ed. Heinz Bolli (Munich: Siebenstern-Taschenbuch, 1968), 311. Karl Barth also called pneumatology "the future of Christian theology"; see Paul D. Lee, *Pneumatological Ecclesiology in Roman Catholic-Pentecostal Dialogue: A Catholic Reading of the Third Quinquennium (1985–1989)* (Ph.D. diss., Univ. of Thomas, Rome, 1994), 200.

6. McGrath, *Christian Theology*, 240. For an overview of this pneumatological renaissance, see V.-M. Kärkkäinen, "Towards a Theology and Ecclesiology of the Spirit: Marquette University's 1998 Symposium, 'An Advent of the Spirit: Orientations in Pneumatology,'" *JPT* 14 (1999): 65–80; and *Pneumatology: the Holy Spirit in Ecumenical, International, and Contextual Perspective* (Grand Rapids: Baker Academic, 2002).

7. Nikos A. Nissiotis, "The Main Ecclesiological Problem of the Second Vatican Council and Position of the Non-Roman Churches Facing It," *JES* 6 (1965): 31–62; and Vladimir Lossky, *In the Image and Likeness of God*, ed. John H. Erickson and Thomas E. Bird (Crestwood, N.Y.: St. Vladimir's, 1985), esp. ch. 4 entitled, "The Procession of the Holy Spirit in Orthodox Trinitarian Doctrine." See also Yves M.-J. Congar, *I Believe in the Holy Spirit*, vol.1: *The Experience of the Spirit* (New York & London: Seabury/Chapman, 1983), 152–266, who chronicles in detail the ethos of "forgetfulness of the Spirit" in Catholic theology starting from Robert Bellarmine (1542–1621) until the Second Vatican Council (1962–1965). Lee, *Pneumatological Ecclesiology*, 195, names as the most obvious deficiencies of the West: (1) a weak regard for the epiclesis in the past, (2) the absence of a developed synodality, and (3) a certain clerical autonomy *vis-à-vis* the Christian community as a whole.

8. E.g., John Zizioulas, *Being as Communion: Studies in Personhood and the Church* (Crestwood, N.Y.: St. Vladimir's, 1985), 123ff.

9. Walter Kasper, *The God of Jesus Christ* (London: SCM, 1984), 138–39.

10. See Constantine N. Tsirpanlis, *Introduction to Eastern Patristic Thought and Christian Theology*, Theology and Life Series 30 (Collegeville, Minn.: Liturgical, 1991), 85: "Those who speak of an Orthodox 'Pneumatocentrism' opposed to the so-called 'Christocentrism' of the Roman Church, may express their own personal theology, but they speak a language alien to the Fathers and to the saints of the

Eastern Orthodox Church. The three Persons, in the Holy Trinity, share in activity of each of them. The Father and the Son are included in every action of the Spirit."

11. Vladimir Lossky, *The Mystical Theology of the Eastern Church* (Crestwood, N.Y.: St. Vladimir's, 1957), 174ff., and Zizioulas, *Being as Communion*, 140.

12. Timothy Ware, *The Orthodox Church* (London: Penguin, 1993), 249–50; see also 240 and 243.

13. Zizioulas, *Being as Communion*, 126.

14. The reason I use the term WCC-*theologies* (in plural rather than in singular) reflects the conviction that there is no *definite* WCC-theology since that would be a contradiction in terms for a constituency that provides a forum for cooperation but not a defined communion.

15. For documentation of Canberra, see Michael Kinnamon, ed., *Signs of the Spirit: Official Report of the Seventh Assembly* (Geneva: WCC, 1991). In what follows, I am heavily indebted to Raiser, "The Holy Spirit in Modern Ecumenical Thought." Also useful is Albert Outler, "Pneumatology as an Ecumenical Frontier," *ER* 41, 3 (1989): 363–74.

16. Moltmann, *The Church in the Power of the Spirit: A Contribution to Messianic Ecclesiology* (New York: Harper & Row, 1977), and *The Spirit of Life: A Universal Affirmation* (London: SCM, 1992). The subtitle in the German original, *Eine ganzheitliche Pneumatologie* stresses the basic intention of the author of writing a "holistic pneumatology." The quote in the next sentence is from page 1 of later book.

17. See Mark W. G. Stibbe, "A British Appraisal," *JPT* 4 (1994): 6; cf. Jürgen Moltmann, "A Response to my Pentecostal Dialogue Partners," *JPT* 4 (1994): 61.

18. Michael Welker, *God the Spirit* (Minneapolis: Fortress, 1994). Welker identities this volume as a realistic biblical pneumatology.

19. Edinburgh, III.29, in Lukas Vischer, ed., *A Documentary History of the Faith and Order Movement 1927–1963* (St Louis: Bethany, 1963), 45.

20. Amsterdam II, in *The Church's Witness to God's Design* (New York: Harper and Brothers, 1948), 222; cf. Amsterdam I.11, in Vischer, ed., *A Documentary History of the Faith and Order Movement*, 78.

21. Lund I.19, in Vischer, ed., *A Documentary History of the Faith and Order Movement*, 90.

22. W. A. Visser't Hooft, "The Basis: its History and Significance," *ER* 2 (1985): 170ff.

23. New Delhi I, in Vischer, ed., *A Documentary History of the Faith and Order Movement*, 144. Raiser, "The Holy Spirit in Modern Ecumenical Thought," 378, pays special attention to the Orthodox contribution to this unity formula and refers to the important article by Nikos A. Nissiotis, "The Witness and the Service of Eastern Orthodoxy to the One Undivided Church," in Constantin G. Patelos, ed., *The Orthodox Church in the Ecumenical Movement* (Geneva: WCC, 1978), 231ff.

24. Montreal III.92, in Patrick C. Rodger and Lukas Vischer, eds., *The Fourth World Conference on Faith and Order, Montreal 1963* (New York: Association, 1964), 65.

25. Raiser, "The Holy Spirit in Modern Ecumenical Thought," 380; see also Norman Goodall, ed., *The Uppsala Report 1968: Official Report of the Fourth Assembly of the World Council of Churches, Uppsala, July 4–20, 1968* (Geneva: WCC, 1968).

26. *Baptism, Eucharist and Ministry*, Faith and Order Paper 111 (Geneva: WCC, 1982).

27. See Lukas Vischer, ed., *Spirit of God, Spirit of Christ: Ecumenical Reflections on the Filioque Controversy* (London: SPCK, and Geneva: WCC, 1981), 18.

28. *Confessing One Faith: Towards an Ecumenical Explication of the Apostolic Faith*, Faith and Order Paper 140 (Geneva, 1987).

29. Judith A. Dwyer, ed., *PCTSA* 51 (1996).

30. Germain Marc'hadour, "The Holy Spirit over the New World: II," *The Clergy Review* 59, 4 (1974): 247.

31. Ibid., 248; see also E. E. O'Connor, *The Pentecostal Movement in the Catholic Church* (Notre Dame: Ave Maria, 1971), 184.

32. For a good overview of the most recent developments in ecclesiology (especially *koinonia*-theology) and pneumatology, see the seminal study by Michael G. Lawler and Thomas J. Shanahan, *Church: A Spirited Communion* (Collegeville, Minn.: Liturgical, 1995), and Miguel M. Garijo-Guembe, *Communion of the Saints: Foundation, Nature, and Structure of the Church*, trans. Patrick Madigan (Collegeville, Minn.: Liturgical, 1994).

33. Michael A. Fahey, "Church," in Francis Schussler Fiorenza and John Galvin, eds., *Systematic Theology: Roman Catholic Perspectives*, vol. 2 (Minneapolis: Fortress, 1991), 39.

34. Donald L. Gelpi, "The Theological Challenge of Charismatic Spirituality," *Pneuma* 14, 2 (1992): 187. He refers to the following Vatican II documents: *LG* 6, 32, 48, 50; *UR* 3; and *AA* 3.

35. Heribert Mühlen, "Charismatic and Sacramental Understanding of the Church: Dogmatic Aspects of Charismatic Renewal," *One in Christ* 12 (1976): 333ff. This is, of course, totally different from what the earlier textbooks said about the church as the continuation of Christ's incarnation.

36. Gelpi, "The Theological Challenge," 188–89. See also Donald L. Gelpi, *Charism and Sacrament* (New York/London: Paulist/SPCK, 1976), 97–110, and, especially *The Divine Mother: A Trinitarian Theology of the Holy Spirit* (Lanham, Md.: UPA, 1984), 103ff.

37. Kilian McDonnell, "Communion Ecclesiology and Baptism in the Spirit: Tertullian and the Early Church," *Theological Studies* 49 (1988): 671ff.

38. See, e.g., Kilian McDonnell, "A Trinitarian Theology of the Holy Spirit?"; "The Determinative Doctrine of the Holy Spirit," *Theology Today* 39 (1982): 142–61; "Pneumatology Overview: Trinitarian Guidelines for Speaking About the Holy Spirit," *PCTSA* 51 (1996): 188–98; and "Vatican II (1962–1965), Puebla (1979), Synod (1985): *Koinonia/Communio* as an Integrating Ecclesiology," *JES* 25 (1988): 399–427.

39. McDonnell, "Pneumatology Overview," 188–90.

40. Garijo-Guembe, *Communion of Saints*, xi and 1.

41. *Adv. Haer.* 3.24.1.

42. See, in order, Avery Dulles, "Method in Ecumenical Theology," in Dulles, *The Craft of Theology: From Symbol to System* (New York: Crossroad, 1992), 195; Philip J. Rosato, "Called by God, in the Holy Spirit: Pneumatological Insights into Ecumenism," *ER* 30 (1978): 110–26; Dietrich Ritschl, "The Search for Implicit Axioms behind Doctrinal Texts," *Gregorianum* 74, 2 (1993): 219; Lee,

Pneumatological Ecclesiology, 33–34; and John V. Taylor, *The Go-Between God: The Holy Spirit and Christian Mission* (London, 1972), 43–44.

43. Lee, *Pneumatological Ecclesiology*, 2.

44. Ibid., 277.

45. Walter J. Hollenweger, "From Azusa Street to Toronto Phenomenon: Historical Roots of the Pentecostal Movement," *Concilium* 3 (1996): 3.

46. Harvey G. Cox, *Fire from Heaven: The Rise of Pentecostal Spirituality and the Reshaping of Religion in the Twenty-first century* (Reading, Mass.: Addison-Wesley, 1995). See also Cox, "Why God Didn't Die: A Religious Renaissance Flourishing Around the World—Pentecostal Christians Leading the Way," *Nieman Reports* (The Nieman Foundation at Harvard University) 47.2 (Summer 1993): 6–8, 47–49.

47. Jon Ruthven, *On the Cessation of the Charismata: The Protestant Polemic on Postbiblical Miracles*, JPTSup 3 (Sheffield: Sheffield Academic, 1993), 14.

48. For Pentecostal spirituality, see: Daniel E. Albrecht, "Pentecostal Spirituality: Looking through the Lens of Ritual," *Pneuma* 14, 2 (1992): 107–25; Russell Spittler, "Spirituality, Pentecostal and Charismatic," in *DPCM*, 804–9; Walter J. Hollenweger, "After Twenty Years' Research on Pentecostalism," *IRM* 75 (1986): 3–12. The major monograph on theological interpretation of Pentecostal experience and spirituality is Steven J. Land, *Pentecostal Spirituality: A Passion for the Kingdom*, JPTSup 1 (Sheffield: Sheffield Academic, 1993).

49. This was explicitly acknowledged in Canberra 1991: "The development of the Pentecostal movement has profoundly influenced the life and worship of many churches related to the WCC" (*Signs of the Spirit*, 107).

50. The basic text is Henry I. Lederle, *Treasures Old and New: Interpretations of 'Spirit-Baptism' in the Charismatic Renewal Movement* (Peabody: Hendrickson, 1988). Various aspects of the distinctive Pentecostal view (not followed by the majority of Charismatics in other churches) of Spirit-Baptism with the "initial evidence" of speaking in tongues, is discussed *pro* and *con* in the collection of essays by Gary B. McGee, ed., *Initial Evidence. Historical and Biblical Perspectives on the Pentecostal Doctrine of Spirit Baptism* (Peabody, Mass.: Hendrickson, 1991).

51. See James D. G. Dunn, *Baptism in the Holy Spirit: A Re-examination of the New Testament Teaching of the Spirit in Relation to Pentecostalism Today* (London: SCM, 1970), and responses by Harold D. Hunter, *Spirit-Baptism: A Pentecostal Alternative* (Lanham, Md.: UPA, 1983); Roger Stronstadt, *The Charismatic Theology of St. Luke* (Peabody, Mass.: Hendrickson, 1984); and Robert Menzies, *The Development of Early Christian Pneumatology with Special Reference to Luke Acts* (Sheffield: Sheffield Academic, 1991), among others.

52. See Kilian McDonnell and George Montague, *Spirit-Baptism and Christian Initiation in the First Eight Centuries* (Collegeville, Minn.: Liturgical, 1991). An ingenious attempt to try to integrate the Pentecostal (non-sacramental) and sacramental (Catholic and other sacramental traditions) approaches to Spirit-baptism is made by a Pentecostal theologian from Hong Kong, Tak-Ming Cheung, "Understandings of Spirit-Baptism," *JPT* 8 (1996): 115–28.

53. The first half of the *JPT* 4 (1994) issue was devoted to "A Global Pentecostal Dialogue with Jürgen Moltmann's *The Spirit of Life: A Universal Affirmation*."

The proceedings of the Brighton forum are collected (including Moltmann's key-note address with responses) in Harold D. Hunter and Peter D. Hocken, eds., *All Together in One Place: Theological Papers from the Brighton Conference on World Evangelization*, JPTSup 4 (Sheffield: Sheffield Academic, 1993).

54. Frank Macchia, "Discerning the Spirit of Life: A Review of *God the Spirit* by Michael Welker," *JPT* 10 (1997): 3–28; Michael Welker, "Spirit Topics: Trinity, Personhood, Mystery and Tongues," *JPT* 10 (1997): 29–34; and Eduard Schweizer, " A Very Helpful Challenge: Gordon D. Fee's *God's Empowering Presence*," *JPT* 8 (1996): 7–21.

55. Walter J. Hollenweger and Arnold Bittlinger, eds., *The Church is Charismatic: Renewal and Congregational Life* (Geneva: WCC, 1981).

56. Hollenweger, "Towards a Church Renewed and United in the Spirit," in *The Church is Charismatic*, 21ff.

57. *Signs of the Spirit*, 107; for a complete listing of recommendations, see 107–8 and 250–51.

58. Report on section on unity, para. 2, in Harold E. Fey, ed., *The Ecumenical Advance: A History of the Ecumenical Movement*, vol. 2: *1948–1968* (Geneva: WCC, 1986), 4.

59. Boris Bobrinskoy, "Holy Spirit," in Nicholas Lossky, et al., ed., *Dictionary of the Ecumenical Movement* (Geneva: WCC, and Grand Rapids: Eerdmans, 1991), 470–73.

Chapter Six

1. Ignatius, *Smyrn.* 8.2; Irenaeus, *Adv. Haer.* 3.24.1.

2. Irenaeus, *Adv. Haer.* 4.Pref.4.

3. Donald L. Gelpi, "The Theological Challenge of Charismatic Spirituality, " *Pneuma* 14, 2 (1992): 188–89. [Editor's note: As a participant in the Catholic charismatic renewal since 1967, Donald Gelpi's own theological contributions over the years are noteworthy. His book on ecclesiology is in progress even while this volume is going to press.]

4. The two aspects of the church (christology and pneumatology) is illustrated by the chapter title of Vladimir Lossky, *The Mystical Theology of the Eastern Church* (Crestwood, N.Y.: St. Vladimir's Press, 1976), ch. 9: "Two Aspects of the Church."

5. *De Spiritu Sancto*, 19, 49, qtd. in Lossky, *The Mystical Theology*, 157.

6. For the understanding of the catholicity in Eastern tradition, see Lossky, "Concerning the Third Mark of the Church: Catholicity," in Lossky, *The Image and Likeness of God*, ed. John H. Erickson, et al. (Crestwood, N.Y.: St Vladimir's Press, 1985), 169–80.

7. Lossky, *The Mystical Theology*, 174; see also 166. Herein lies the basis for a pneumatological understanding of theosis, the doctrine of deification, the most distinctive aspect of Eastern soteriology.

8. John Zizioulas, *Being as Communion: Studies in Personhood and the Church* (Crestwood, N.Y.: St Vladimir's Seminary Press, 1985), 124–26.

9. Ibid., 130.

10. Ibid., 110–11, emphases in the text. Zizioulas argues that such a pneumatologically constituted christology is biblical since in the Bible Christ becomes a historical person only in the Spirit (Matt. 1:18–20; Luke 1:35). He is even ready to say, "Christ *exists only pneumatologically*" (111, emphasis orig.). In line with the Eastern trinitarian sensitivity, he adds that to speak of Christ means speaking at the same time of the Father and the Holy Spirit. He also says, "Thus the mystery of the Church has its birth in the entire economy of the Trinity and in a pneumatologically constituted Christology" (112).

11. Ibid., 131–32.

12. Ibid., 126–29.

13. See Wolfhart Pannenberg, *Systematic Theology*, 3 vols., trans. Geoffrey W. Bromiley (Grand Rapids: Eerdmans, 1988, 1994, and 1998), 1.370–84 (on God), and 3.135–210 (on salvation). Further references in this chapter to Pannenberg's *Systematic Theology* will be located within the text as *ST* followed by volume and page number. In the following exposition, I rely primarily on *ST* 3.

14 Pannenberg's trinitarian doctrine is grounded on an accent on the mutuality of the persons of the Trinity (cf. Augustine's idea of the Spirit as bond of love between the Father and son, making him "impersonal") where the Father gives the Spirit who proceeds from him so that the Son gives him back and in this way proves his self-distinction from the Father as he Son who in eternity receives from the Father the Spirit who raises him to life. The main trinitarian discussion is found in *ST* 1, ch. 5.

15. For an extended treatment of Möhler's position see Bradford E. Hinze, "The Holy Spirit and the Catholic Tradition: The Legacy of Johann Adam Möller," in Donald J. Dietrich and Michael J. Himes, eds., *The Legacy of the Tübingen School: The Relevance of Nineteenth Century Theology for the Twenty-first Century* (New York: Crossroad Herder, 1997), 75–94; and Michael J. Himes, *Ongoing Incarnation: Johann Adam Möhler and the Beginning of Modern Ecclesiology* (New York: Crossroad Herder, 1997).

16. For an exposition and evaluation of the emergence of a pneumatological perspective in post-conciliar Vatican ecclesiology and ecumenism (with references to Congar, Mühlen, Rahner, and others) see my *Spiritus ubi vult spirat: Pneumatology in Roman Catholic-Pentecostal Dialogue 1972–1989*, Schriften der Luther-Agricola-Gesellschaft 42 (Helsinki: Luther Agricola Society, 1998), 18–26 and 54–63.

17. In what follows, I rely on John R. Sachs, "'Don't Stifle the Spirit': Karl Rahner, the Legacy of Vatican II and Its Urgency for Theology Today," *PCTSA* 51 (1996): 15–38.

18. Rahner, *The Dynamic Element in the Church*, trans. W. J. O'Hara (New York: Herder & Herder, 1964), 47–48 and 82–83.

19. Rahner, "Observations of the Factor of the Charismatic in the Church," in *Theological Investigations, XII* (New York: Seabury, 1974), 97.

20. Ibid., 86–88.

21. Rahner, "Do Not Stifle the Spirit," in *Theological Investigations VII* (New York: Herder, 1971), 72–87.

22. See Rahner, "Heresies in the Church Today?" *Theological Investigations*

XII (New York: Seabury, 1974), 117–41. Note also the suggestion by Avery Dulles, *The Resilient Church* (Garden City: Doubleday, 1977), 27–28, that the developments after the publication of *Dei Verbum* (and, of course, *Lumen Gentium*) have led to a "pluralistic" model of authority even for Roman Catholic theology.

23. Rahner, "Some Problems in Contemporary Ecumenism," in *Theological Investigations XIV* (London: Darton, Longman and Todd, 1976), 245–53, quote from 251; see also "Church, Churches, and Religions," *Theological Investigations X* (New York: Herder, 1973), 42ff.

24. Rahner, *Foundations of Christian Faith: An Introduction to the Idea of Christianity*, trans. William V. Dych (New York: Seabury, 1978).

25. For some important aspects, see Christopher O'Donnell, "Pneumatology and Ecclesiology," in O'Donnell, ed., *Ecclesia: A Theological Encyclopedia of the Church* (Collegeville, Minn.: Liturgical, 1996): 367–71, and "Church, the," in Michael O'Carroll, ed., *Veni Creator Spiritus: A Theological Encyclopedia of the Holy Spirit* (Collegeville, Minn.: Liturgical, 1990), 46–49.

26. I know how problematic the notion of "experience" and the "turn to experience" in theology is; however, in the confines of this chapter I cannot discuss it. [Editor's note: see Donald L. Gelpi, *The Turn to Experience in Contemporary Theology* (New York: Paulist, 1994).]

27. Michael Welker, *God the Spirit*, trans. John F. Hoffmeyer (Minneapolis: Fortress, 1994), 308.

28. See chapter 17.

Chapter Seven

1. Ralph Del Colle, "Oneness and Trinity: A Preliminary Proposal for Dialogue with Oneness Pentecostalism," *JPT* 10 (1997): 86; see also Del Colle, "Trinity and Temporality: A Pentecostal-Charismatic Perspective," *JPT* 8 (1996): 101 and 111–12.

2. The most comprehensive and sophisticated Oneness exposition is David K. Bernard, *The Oneness of God* (Hazelwood, Mo.: Word Aflame, 1983).

3. Gerald T. Sheppard, "Nicean Creed, *Filioque*, and Pentecostal Movements in the United States," *Greek Orthodox Theological Review* 31, 3–4 (1986): 402. See also Donald W. Dayton, "Pneumatological Issues in the Holiness Movement," *Greek Orthodox Theological Review* 31, nos. 3–4 (1986): 361–88.

4. For the history of this issue, consult Edith L. Blumhofer, *The Assemblies of God: A Chapter of American Pentecostalism*, Vol. 1: *To 1941* (Springfield, Mo.: Gospel, 1989), 217–47 (from a trinitarian viewpoint), and Arthur L. Clanton, *United We Stand: A History of Oneness Organizations* (Hazelwood, Mo.: Pentecostal, 1970), 13–26 (from a Oneness viewpoint). In the Assemblies of God Statement of Faith a lengthy statement on "The Adorable Godhead" was added in 1916 in response to the "Jesus Only controversy" (to be quoted later in the present chapter).

5. See Donald Gee, "Tests for 'Fuller Revelations,'" *The Pentecostal Evangel* (14 Feb. 1925); and *The Apostolic Faith* 1, 1 (1906): 2.

6. See, e.g., Ernest Swing Williams, *Systematic Theology*, vol. 1 (Springfield, Mo.: Gospel, 1953), 199ff.; the section is entitled, "The Unity of God—The Trinity."

7. See Amos Yong, "Oneness and Trinity: The Theological and Ecumenical Implications of Creation *Ex Nihilo* for an Intra-Pentecostal Dispute," *Pneuma* 19, 1 (1997): 81–107. For more on the *pro nobis* aspect of the Trinity, see Catherine Mowry LaCugna, *God For Us: The Trinity and Christian Life* (San Francisco: Harper & Row, 1991).

8. For a recent Pentecostal exposition of the meaning of trinitarian life, see Simon Chan, "Sharing the Trinitarian Life, John 17:29–26; 1 John 1:1–4," in Thomas F. Best and Günther Gassmann, eds., *On the Way to Fuller Koinonia* (Geneva: WCC, 1993), 85–90, his presentation at the Canberra 1991 Assembly of the WCC. See also *UR* 2, and the explicit trinitarian structure in the first paragraphs of *LG* 2–4 devoted to Father, Son, and Spirit.

9. Hervé Legrand, "Koinonia, Church and Sacrament," a Catholic position paper at the 13th dialogue session at Venice, Italy, 1–8 Aug. 1987 (unpublished), 5.

10. Legrand, "Koinonia," 3–4.

11. Heribert Mühlen, *Una Mystica Persona: Die Kirche als das Mysterium der Identität des Heiligen Geistes in Christus und den Christen-eine Person in vielen Personen* (Paderborn: Ferdinand Schöningh, 1967). See also Mühlen's *Der Heilige Geist als Person: In der Trinität bei der Inkarnation und Im Gnadenbund-Ich-Du-Wir*, 3rd ed. (Muenster: Verlag Aschendorff, 1969), and "Charismatic and Sacramental Understanding of the Church: Dogmatic Aspects on Charismatic Renewal," *One in Christ* 12 (1976), 334 (the published version of his position paper read at the First Quinquennium meeting in 1974).

12. Mühlen, "Charismatic and Sacramental Understanding," 333–34 (emphasis added), and "The Holy Spirit and the NT View of Communion," a Catholic position paper read at the 12th dialogue session, Pasadena, Calif., 24–30 May 1986 (unpublished), 1–2.

13. Mühlen, "Charismatic and Sacramental Understanding," 335, emphasis added.

14. *UR* 2; cf. Mühlen, "The Holy Spirit," 1.

15. Mühlen, "The Holy Spirit," 14–15.

16. Cecil M. Robeck, Jr., "The Holy Spirit and the NT Vision of *Koinonia*," a Pentecostal position paper read at the 12th dialogue session, Pasadena, Calif., 24–30 May 1986 (unpublished), 7.

17. Emil Brunner, *The Misunderstanding of the Church*, trans. Harold Knight (Philadelphia: Westminster, 1953), 10–11, qtd. in Robeck, "The Holy Spirit," 1.

18. Robeck, "The Holy Spirit," 4, 7.

19. Howard M. Ervin, "Koinonia, Church and Sacraments," a Pentecostal position paper read at the 13th dialogue session, Venice, Italy, 1–8 Aug. 1987 (unpublished), 8–9.

20. Kilian McDonnell, "A Trinitarian Theology of the Holy Spirit," *Theological Studies* 46 (1985): 191–227.

21. See also Kilian McDonnell, "The Determinative Doctrine of the Holy Spirit," *Theology Today* 39 (1982): 148 and 159.

22. Statement of Fundamental Truths Approved by the General Council of the Assemblies of God, 13, in Minutes of the General Council of the Assemblies of

God, St. Louis, Mo., 1–7 Oct. 1916. For a helpful discussion, see Sheppard "Nicean Creed," 409ff.

23. Ervin, "Koinonia," 2, quoting Guy P. Duffield and Nathaniel M. van Cleave, *Foundations of Pentecostal Theology* (Los Angeles: L.I.F.E. Bible College, 1983), 109.

24. The former is a non-committal view implied in Duffield and Van Cleave, *Foundations*, 109. The latter is from Raymond M. Pruitt, *Fundamentals of Faith* (Cleveland, Tenn.: White Wing, 1981), 284, qtd. in Ervin, "Koinonia," 3. In reference to John 15:26, though, it has not been noted that the text obviously is about the economy of the Spirit rather than theo-logy.

25. Ervin, "Koinonia," 3, emphasis orig.

26. Pruitt, *Fundamentals of Faith*, 102.

27. Ervin, "Koinonia," 4.

28. Duffield and Van *Cleave, Foundations*, 447.

29. Ervin, "Koinonia," 12. Ervin, though, concedes that this omission of the Spirit might "represent nothing more than the strictures of theological method, i.e., a verbal accommodation to specific texts of Scripture."

30. Ibid., 6.

31. Ibid., 4, quoting Timothy Ware, *The Orthodox Church* (London: Penguin, 1972), 235.

32. Ervin, "Koinonia," 7.

33. Legrand, "Koinonia," 13–14, quoting phrases from Vladimir Lossky, *The Mystical Theology of the Eastern Church* (London: J. Clarke, 1957), 155–56, 163, 166, 185.

34. Mühlen, "The Holy Spirit," 10, quoting from Henricus Denzinger and Adolfus Schönmetzer, eds., *Enchiridion Symbolorum* (Barcinore: Herder, 1963), 460.

35. Mühlen, "The Holy Spirit," 13, emphases his.

36. McDonnell, "A Trinitarian Theology," 210–11.

37. Gennadios Limouris, *Confessing the One faith: An Ecumenical Explication of the Apostolic Faith as it is Confessed in the Nicene-Constantinople Creed (381)*, Faith and Order 153 (Geneva: WCC, 1991).

38. Faith and Order, "The *Filioque* Clause in Ecumenical Perspective (1979)," in Günther Gassman, ed., *Documentary History of Faith and Order 1963–1993* (Geneva: WCC, 1993), 188.

39. For a theological analysis of the trinitarian nature of Pentecostal spirituality and affections see Steven J. Land, *Pentecostal Spirituality: A Passion for the Kingdom*, JPTSup 1 (Sheffield, UK: Sheffield Academic, 1994), 125ff.

Chapter Eight

1. Michael Harper, "The Holy Spirit Acts in the Church, its Structures, its Sacramentality, its Worship and Sacraments," *One in Christ* 12 (1976): 323.

2. Paul D. Lee, *Pneumatological Ecclesiology in the Roman Catholic-Pentecostal Dialogue: A Catholic Reading of the Third Quinquennium (1985–1989)* (Ph.D. diss., Univ. of Thomas, Rome, 1994), 15.

3. Melvin L. Hodges, *Theology of the Church and Its Mission: A Pentecostal Perspective* (Springfield, Mo.: Gospel, 1977). Peter Kuzmic and Miroslav Volf,

"Communio Sanctorum: Toward a Theology of the Church as a Fellowship of Persons," a Position Paper read at the International Roman Catholic-Pentecostal Dialogue, Riano, Italy, 21–26 May 1985 (unpublished), 2, remark that the lack of writings on ecclesiology is not limited just to Pentecostals but also to Evangelicals at large. For a recent attempt to construe an Evangelical ecclesiology, see George Vandervelde, "Ecclesiology in the Breach: Evangelical Soundings," *Evangelical Review of Theology* 23, 1 (1999): 29–51.

4. Peter D. Hocken, "Theology of Church," *DPCM*, 213.

5. Lee, *Pneumatological Ecclesiology*, 16–17.

6. Luigi Sartori, "The Structure of Juridical and Charismatic Power in the Christian Community," *Concilium* 109 (New York: Seabury, 1978), 58ff. In this discussion we will not touch the issue of sacraments although it was widely discussed as a part of *Koinonia*; for details, see chapter ten.

7. Ibid., 57. See also the important statement of the *Mystici Corporis* (in Henricus Denzinger and Adolfus Schönmetzer, eds., *Enchiridion Symborolum* [Barcinore: Herder, 1963], 3801). According to Sartori, this is the first admission that the charisms belong to the structure of the Church, although it does not place them in opposition to the hierarchy.

8. Hans Küng, *The Church*, trans. Ray and Rolaseen Ockenden (New York: Sheed & Ward, 1967), 180–81.

9. Enrique Dussel, "The Differentiation of Charisms," *Concilium* 109 (New York: Seabury, 1978), 53.

10. Harper, "The Holy Spirit," 319–20. Michael Harper of England read this paper during the First Quinquennium when among the Pentecostals there were also some representatives from the Charismatic movement among the older churches (Anglican, Lutheran, and Catholic). He represented at that time the Anglican Church; nowadays he is a communicant of the Eastern Orthodox Church in England.

11. Ibid., 320.

12. Ibid., 323.

13. Harold D. Hunter, "We are the Church: New Congregationalism—A Pentecostal Perspective," *Concilium* 3 (1996): 18.

14. Heribert Mühlen, "Charismatic and Sacramental Understanding of the Church: dogmatic Aspects of Charismatic Renewal," *One in Christ* 12 (1976): 346, emphases mine.

15. Mühlen, "The Holy Spirit and the NT View of Communion," a position paper read at the International Roman Catholic-Pentecostal Dialogue, Pasadena, Calif., 14–30 May 1986 (unpublished), 32–33, referring to *LG* 12.

16. John Mahoney, "Discernment of Spirit," *One in Christ* 13 (1977): 68–69.

17. See Kuzmic and Volf, "Communio Sanctorum," 16.

18. Ibid., 2, emphasis orig.

19. Kilian McDonnell, "Communion Ecclesiology and Baptism in the Spirit: Tertullian and the Early Church," *Theological Studies* 49 (1988): 674.

20. Johannes Willebrands, "The Future of Ecumenism, " *One in Christ* 11 (1975): 313, qtd. in McDonnell, "Communion Ecclesiology," 674.

21. John Zizioulas, *Being as Communion: Studies in Personhood and the Church* (Crestwood, N.Y.: St. Vladimir's, 1985), 156.

22. Ibid., 15, emphases orig.; see especially ch.1 "Personhood and Being."

23. Kuzmic and Volf, "Communio Sanctorum," 14, emphasis orig.

24. See Lesslie Newbigin, *The Household of God* (London: SCM, 1955), 95.

25. Kuzmic and Volf, "Communio Sanctorum," 15, emphasis theirs.

26. Ibid., 16, quoting Newbigin, *The Household of God*, 106.

27. Ibid., 16.

28. Ibid., 22–23.

29. Ibid., 23.

30. This is the title of one section of Küng's *The Church*, 179–91.

31. Kuzmic and Volf, "Communio Sanctorum," 17. Küng, *The Church*, 227, says the same: "The members of the body of Christ are always seen as the bearers of charisms."

32. As noted by Hunter, "We are the Church,"18.

33. Kuzmic and Volf, "Communio Sanctorum," 19.

34. Hervé Legrand, "Commune Sanctorum: The Triple Meaning of the Expression in the Creed and the Catholic Tradition," a position paper read at the International Roman Catholic-Pentecostal Dialogue, Riano, Italy, 21–26 May 1985 (unpublished), 12.

35. Jürgen Moltmann, "The Spirit Gives Life: Spirituality and Vitality," in Harold D. Hunter and Peter D. Hocken, eds., *All Together in One Place: Theological Papers from the Brighton Conference on World Evangelization*, JPTSup 4 (Sheffield: Sheffield Academic, 1993), 34–35.

36. Moltmann, "The Spirit Gives Life," 35.

37. Rahner, *The Dynamic Element in the Church* (New York: Herder & Herder, 1964), 77.

38. Miroslav Volf, *After Our Likeness: The Church as the Image of the Trinity* (Grand Rapids: Eerdmans, 1998). The basic features of Volf's participatory ecclesiology take their lead from the first Baptist theologian John Smyth, albeit in a critical dialogue with Catholic (represented by Joseph H. Ratzinger) and Orthodox (represented by Metropolitan John Zizioulas) ecclesiology.

39. Miroslav Volf, "A Protestant Response to We are the Church: New Congregationalism," *Concilium* 3 (1996): 38.

Chapter Nine

1. *Baptism, Eucharist and Ministry*, Faith and Order Paper 111 (Geneva: WCC, 1982), I.1, I.3 and I.5.

2. Citations of Luther in this chapter will be made parenthetically in the text, and reference the standard German/Latin original of *Luthers Werke, Weimerer Ausgabe* or Weimer edition (*WA*, by volume and page number).

3. It is noteworthy how close Hans Küng's, *The Church* (New York: Doubleday, 1976), 361–480, comes to Luther's view.

4. Paul Althaus, *The Theology of Martin Luther*, trans Robert C. Schultz (Philadelphia: Fortress, 1966), 323–29.

5. I follow here the interpretation of Althaus, *Theology of Martin Luther*, 324–25. The issue is debated among Luther experts. For discussion, see Wolfhart

Pannenberg, *Systematic Theology*, 3 vols., trans. Geoffrey W. Bromiley (Grand Rapids: Eerdmans, 1988, 1992, 1998), 3.375–77. Kilian McDonnell, *John Calvin, the Church, and the Eucharist* (Princeton, N.J.: Princeton Univ. Press, 1967), 183, has affirmed that the priesthood of all Christians had significance for Calvin's doctrine of the ordained ministry. This too is a disputed question. For a recent appeal by a Presbyterian for returning the ministry to the entire people of God, see Greg Ogden, *The New Reformation: Returning the Ministry to the People of God* (Grand Rapids: Zondervan, 1990).

6. Althaus, *Theology of Martin Luther*, 327.

7. I am well aware of the fact that the term "priest" in the New Testament occupies various nuances and the trajectory is quite complex. A general exegetical and theological consensus nowadays is that, in contradistinction to the Old Testament usage, the New Testament does not coincide with the (patristic and medieval) understanding of "priest" as a sacramentally designated person in the church.

8. Miguel M. Garijo-Guembe, *Communion of the Saints: Nature and Structure of the Church*, tr. Patrick Madigan (Collegeville, Minn.: Liturgical, 1994), 133–34, reminds us that the theology of the laity, after the Reformation, played no role in Catholicism. The term practically disappeared from the vocabulary of Catholic theology, since the Reformers had used it in an anti-hierarchical sense (according to Catholic understanding). In fact, Trent explicitly rejected Luther's opinion that "all Christians are in the same way priests of the new covenant or that all are entrusted without differentiation with the same spiritual powers." At the same time one must remember that the *Catechismus Romanus* speaks expressly of the priesthood of all believers. The encyclical *Mediator Dei* (1947) was one of the first attempts to draw attention to the role of the laity, although with the caution that this must not be understood in an anti-hierarchical sense. For references to Trent and *Mediator Dei*, see Henricus Denzinger and Adolfus Schönmetzer, eds., *Enchiridion Symbolorum* (Barcinore: Herder, 1963), 1767 and 3849–53 respectively.

9. For a survey of Vatican II's teaching on charism and ministry, see Christopher O'Donnell, *Ecclesia: A Theological Encyclopedia of the Church* (Collegeville, Minn.: Liturgical, 1996), 87–91. *LG* 4 does make a theological distinction between "charismatic" and "hierarchical" gifts. This distinction is problematic, not only because it lacks any kind of biblical support, but also since it tends to support a hierarchical ecclesiology.

10. I am indebted here to Bonaventure Kloppenburg, *The Ecclesiology of Vatican II*, tr. Matthew J. O'Connell (Chicago: Franciscan Herald, 1974), 263ff., for an exhaustive analysis of Council texts on the topic.

11. *LG* 10: "Though they differ *essentially* and not only in *degree*, the common priesthood of the faithful and the ministerial or hierarchical priesthood are none the less ordered one to another; each in its own proper way shares in the one priesthood of Christ" (emphases added).

12. Kloppenburg, *The Ecclesiology of Vatican II*, 263–64, goes so far as to claim that the theology of the laity took such a decisive role in the documents that it causes many to ask why there should continue to be ordained ministers at all! On the contrary, Michael G. Lawler and Thomas J. Shanahan, *Church: A Spirited Communion* (Collegeville, Minn.: Liturgical, 1995), 71–87, lament that "thirty

years after Yves M.-J. Congar's plea that laity should not be defined negatively ('not-cleric'), the only definition of laity that could be offered by a council...was precisely a negative one": the term "laity" refers to "all the faithful except those in holy orders and those in a religious state sanctioned by the church" (cf. *LG* 31).

13. Pannenberg, *Systematic Theology*, 3.374.

14. Representative of a hierarchical, non-egalitarian view is, e.g., Hans Urs von Balthasar, *Exploration in Theology*, vol. II: *Spouse of the Word* (San Francisco: Ignatius, 1991), 315–31, esp. 319 and 325.

15. Christian Duquoc, *Provisional Churches* (London: SCM, 1986), 103.

16. For a survey of older and more recent Free Church views of ministry and priesthood of all believers, see James Leo Garrett, *Systematic Theology: Biblical, Historical, and Evangelical*, vol. 2 (Grand Rapids: Eerdmans, 1995), 560–63. For the Baptists, see Robert G. Walton, *The Gathered Community* (London: Carey, 1946), 102, Herschel H. Hobbs, *You are Chosen: The Priesthood of Believers* (San Francisco: Harper & Row, 1990), and Paul Beasley-Murray, "The Ministry of All and the Leadership of Some: A Baptist Perspective," in Paul Beasley-Murray, ed., *Anyone for Ordination?* (Tunbridge Wells, UK: Monarch, 1993), 157–74. For the Congregationalists, see Cyril Eastwood, *The Priesthood of All Believers: An Examination of the Doctrine from the Reformation to the Present Day* (London: Epworth, 1960), 164–71. For the Quakers, see Douglas Gwyn, *Apocalypse of the Word: The Life and Message of George Fox (1624–1691)* (Richmond: Friends United, 1984), 166. Finally, for the Pentecostals, see my *Spiritus ubi vult spirat: Pneumatology in Roman Catholic-Pentecostal Dialogue (1972–1989)*, Schriften der Luther-Agricola-Gesellschaft 42 (Helsinki: Luther-Agricola-Society, 1998), 332–45.

17. Balthasar Fischer, "Catholic Liturgy in the Light of Vatican II and the Post-Conciliar Reform of the Liturgy," *One in Christ* 13 (1977): 28–30.

18. Quoted in Garrett, *Systematic Theology*, vol. 2, 561.

19. James D. G. Dunn, *The Christ and the Spirit*, vol. 2: *Pneumatology* (Grand Rapids: Eerdmans, 1998), 293 especially.

20. David H. Edwards, "A Pentecostal Perspective of the Church," in Jerry L. Sandidge, ed., *The Roman Catholic/Pentecostal Dialogue (1977–1982): A Study of Developing Ecumenism*, vol. 2 (Frankfurt am Main: Peter Lang, 1982), 418.

21. James D. G. Dunn, *The Theology of Paul* (Grand Rapids: Eerdmans, 1998), 555–604. Dunn has argued according to the same lines in several of his earlier writings; for the sake of convenience, I u se here his most recent major work.

22. Ibid., 562.

23. Ibid., 566.

24. Miroslav Volf, *After Our Likeness: The Church as the Image of the Trinity* (Grand Rapids: Eerdmans, 1998). The ecumenical groundwork for the rehabilitation of the charismatic structure of the church was done by several scholars, some of the most important being the following: Hans von Campenhausen, *Ecclesiastical Authority and Spiritual Power in the Church of the first three Centuries* (1953; reprint London: Black, 1969), 68–71, restated the emphasis of Rudolph Sohm by insisting that for Paul the Spirit is the organizing principle of the church and that ministry is the employment of a gift which the Spirit bestows. Ernst Käsemann, "Ministry and Community in the New Testament," in

Essays on the New Testament Themes (London: SCM, and Naperville: Allenson, 1964), 63–94, attempted even more vigorously than Campenhausen to transcend the antithesis of charism and office by viewing them in dialectical relationship. Finally, see also Hans Küng, *The Church*, 187ff., who enthusiastically spoke for the "the continuing charismatic structure" of the church as part of its "fundamental structure," and Dunn, *The Theology of Paul*, 567–68.

25. Volf, *After Our Likeness*, 232, emphasis in the text. Therefore, we have to criticize the opinion of John Zizioulas, *Being as Communion: Studies in Personhood and the Church* (Crestwood, N.Y.: St. Vladimir's, 1985), 142, according to which all the charismata are to be channeled through the hands of the bishop in the Eucharist gatherings. This idea goes back to Zizioulas' insistence that the only occasion for the charismata in the New Testament was the celebration of the Eucharist. Both of these claims are half-truths at their best.

26. Volf, *After Our Likeness*, 227, emphasis in the text.

27. One must emphasize here the mediated character of faith. If faith is ecclesiological in nature—being, of course, also deeply personal—it must be mediated. The older distinction between Catholic and Protestant ecclesiologies (so, e.g., Robert Haight: "On Systematic Ecclesiology," *Toronto Journal of Theology* 8 [1992]: 226), according to which in the former the faith is mediated through sacraments and in the latter through the Word, is not the point here. Whatever the role of the sacraments and the Word (which act in accordance rather than being either/or), the fact is that in any church context the basic mode of mediation of faith is the people of God and the ordinary life. Free Churches' participatory, "democratic" church life reflects this more adequately, although many Free Church theologians often mistakenly maintain that in their churches faith is not mediated but rather "comes directly from heaven."

28. Volf, *After Our Likeness*, 227.

29. Michael A. Fahey, "Church," in Francis Schüssler Fiorenza and John P. Galvin, eds., *Systematic Theology: Roman Catholic Perspectives*, vol. 2 (Minneapolis: Fortress, 1991), 41–42; see also Garijo-Guembe, *Communion of Saints*, 139–40.

30. Ecumenically the comment by John Zizioulas, *Being as Communion. Studies in Personhood and the Church* (Crestwood, N.Y.: St. Vladimir's, 1985), 215, is significant when he says that the historical contradistinction between the Catholic theology of ministry and the Protestant idea of the priesthood of all believers is already being overcome on the basis of the New Testament studies.

31. Jürgen Moltmann, *The Spirit of Life: A Universal Affirmation* (Minneapolis: Fortress, 1992), 34–35.

32. Jürgen Moltmann, *The Church in the Power of the Spirit: A Contribution to Messianic Ecclesiology* (New York: Harper & Row, 1977), 305.

33. Volf, *After Our Likeness*, 226–27.

34. See Bernard J. Cooke, *The Distancing of God: The Ambiguity of Symbol in History and Theology* (Minneapolis: Fortress, 1990), and Jaroslav Pelikan, *The Christian Tradition: A History of the Development of Doctrine*, vol. 1: *The Emergence of the Catholic Tradition (100–600)* (Chicago: Univ. of Chicago Press, 1971), 107. I am indebted to Frank Macchia for both of these references.

35. Frank Macchia, "The Struggle for the Spirit in the Church: The Gifts of the Spirit and the Kingdom of God in Pentecostal Perspective," *Theology and Worship Tidings* 10 (2000): 16–17.

36. Clark H. Pinnock, *Flame of Love: A Theology of the Holy Spirit* (Downers Grove, Ill.: InterVarsity, 1996), 129.

37. Cf. Jacques Servais, "The Lay Vocation in the World according to Hans Urs von Balthasar," *Communio* 23 (Winter 1996): esp. 558–59, and Russell B. Shaw, *To Hunt, to Shoot, to Entertain: Clericalism and the Catholic Laity* (San Francisco: Ignatius, 1993). See also See John Paul II, *Christifideles laici* (Apostolic Exhortation, 1988), in *Acta Apostolica Sedis* 81 (1989): 433–35.

Chapter Ten

1. See, e.g., Karl Rahner, "The Presence of Christ in the Sacrament of the Lord's Supper," in *Theological Investigations IV* (London: Darton, Longman & Todd, 1966), 287–311; Eduard Schillebeeckx, *The Eucharist*, trans. N. D. Smith (New York: Seabury, 1968); and Robert Sokolowski, *Eucharistic Presence: A Study in the Theology of Discourse* (Washington: Catholic Univ. of America, 1993). Vatican II's *Sacrosanctum Concilium* (§7) came to speak about the manifold presence of Christ in liturgy. The four forms are the sacrifice of the Mass, the eucharistic elements, the baptism, and the word. This widening of the notion of Christ's presence has been helpful to Catholic theology although the *Sacrosanctum Concilium* in general and §7 in particular do not pay sufficient attention to the role of the Spirit. See further, Michael G. Witczak, "The Manifold Presence of Christ in the Liturgy," *Theological Studies* 59 (1998): 680–96.

2. Both quotes in Paul McPartlan, *The Eucharist Makes the Church: Henri de Lubac and John Zizioulas in Dialogue* (Edinburgh: T. & T. Clark, 1993), 254. For more on a pneumatological understanding of the Eucharist, see John H. McKenna, *Eucharist and the Holy Spirit: The Eucharistic Epiclesis in the 20th Century Theology* (London: Great Wakering, 1976); Yves M.-J. Congar, *I Believe in the Holy Spirit*, vol. 3: *The River of Life Flows in the East and the West* (New York and London: Seabury/Chapman, 1983), 228–74; P. McGoldrick, "The Holy Spirit and the Eucharist," *Irish Theological Quarterly* 50 (1983): 48–66; and Edward J. Kilmartin, "The Active Role of Christ and the Spirit in the Sanctification of the Eucharistic Elements," *Theological Studies* 45 (1984): 225–53.

3. Georges Florovsky, "Le corps du Christ vivant: Une interprétation de l'Église," in Florovsky, *La sainte Église universelle* (Paris: Delachaux et Niestlé, 1948), 19, qtd. in Miguel M. Garijo-Guembe, *Communion of the Saints: Foundation, Nature, and Structure of the Church*, trans. Patrick Madigan (Collegeville, Minn.: Liturgical, 1994), 4.

4. Michael O'Carroll, "Eucharist, The," in *Veni Creator Spiritus: A Theological Encyclopedia of the Holy Spirit* (Collegeville, Minn.: Liturgical, 1990), 78. O'Carroll suggests that there is actually need for deeper reflection on the twofold aspect of the problem of the Spirit and the Eucharist: the relationship between the Spirit and Christ present in the Eucharist and the relationship between the Spirit and

the grace which comes to the individual through the Eucharist. We will focus in this chapter on the first question.

5. Even James D. G. Dunn, noted for his powerful pneumatological orientation to the New Testament theological *loci*, fails to see the connection between the Lord's Supper and the Spirit (whereas he has a good section on the relation of the Lord's Supper to christology): *The Theology of Paul* (Grand Rapids, Mich.: Eerdmans, 1998), 620ff. One of the most powerful expositions of pneumatological implications of the Supper, on which I rely heavily in this chapter, is to be found in Wolfhart Pannenberg's *Systematic Theology*, vol. 3, trans. Geoffrey W. Bromiley (Grand Rapids: Eerdmans, 1998), 283–336, esp. 320–24. For the relationship between the Spirit and Christ in relation to the Eucharist, see Neville Clark, "Spirit Christology in the Light of Eucharistic Theology," *Heythrop Journal* 23 (1982): 270–84.

6. J.-M. R. Tillard, *Church of Churches: The Ecclesiology of Communion*, trans. R. C. De Peaux (Collegeville, Minn.: Liturgical, 1992), 141. Liturgical scholar Mary Collins, *Contemplative Participation* (Collegeville, Minn.: Liturgical, 1990), 55, writes about the biblical meaning of "memory": "Anamnesis is biblical language which was long ago taken up by the Church and recently recovered as liturgical language.... We can perhaps best understand anamnesis by considering it indirectly. Anamnesis speaks about a distinctive kind of human remembering. In common speech we are more likely to talk about its opposite, amnesia.... 'Anamnesis' and 'amnesia' come from a common Greek root. The biblical and liturgical use of the word 'anamnesis' rises from a perception that there is a disorder analogous to clinical amnesia that plagues the human community."

7. "Eucharist" II.B.7, in *Baptism, Eucharist and Ministry*, Faith and Order Paper 111 (Geneva: WCC, 1982), 11. This kind of understanding of memory has, of course, implications to other theological *loci*, the inspiration and interpretation of Scripture being the most important; for this, see V.-M. Kärkkäinen, "'Reading in the Spirit in Which It Was Written': Pentecostal Bible Reading in Dialogue With Catholic Interpretation," *One in Christ* 4 (1998): 337–59.

8. John Zizioulas, *Being as Communion: Studies in the Church and Personhood* (Crestwood, N.Y.: St. Vladimir's, 1985), 207.

9. See Raymond E. Brown, *The Gospel according to John XIII–XXI: A New Translation with Introduction and Commentary*, Anchor Bible Commentary 29A (Garden City, N.Y.: Doubleday, 1970), 913 and 931.

10. Jürgen Moltmann, *The Spirit of Life: A Universal Affirmation* (Minneapolis: Fortress, 1992), 69.

11. See Gottlieb Söhngen, *Christi Gegenwart in Glaube und Sakrament* (München and Salzburg: A. Pustet, 1967), and Peter Brunner, *Worship in the Name of Jesus* (St. Louis: Concordia, 1968), 145, both referenced in Pannenberg, *Systematic Theology*, 3.306–7. Here, Pannenberg himself explains the Spirit's work in eucharistic anamnesis with the help of one of his favored concepts, the form of "ecstatic" elevation. It simply means that the celebrants are outside (*ekstatic*) themselves with Christ as they recall their Lord's passion. "Only as they are outside themselves with Christ in the act of recollection is Jesus Christ, the one whom they remember, present to them."

12. Zizioulas, *Being as Communion*, 190–93. One may not want to say—as Zizioulas seems to think—that charismatic manifestations appeared *exclusively* in eucharistic gatherings, although it is highly significant that the only two eucharistic texts we have from Paul come to the fore amidst his teaching and warning concerning charismata. For a recent discussion on the Eastern view of epiclesis, see Jack Figel, "The Epiclesis of the Byzantine Liturgy," *Eastern Churches Journal* 5, 1 (1999): 103–26, who speaks about the development of "liturgical pneumatology"; and Alexander Schemann, *The Eucharist: Sacrament of the Kingdom* (Crestwood, N.Y.: St. Vladimir's, 1988), 222, who maintains that the whole liturgy is accomplished through the Holy Spirit: "It is entirely, from beginning to end, an epiclesis, an invocation of the Holy Spirit, who transfigures everything done it, each solemn rite, into that which it manifests and reveals to us."

13. *Adv. Jud.*, 10; *PL* 2, 11, 666AB, qtd. in Constantine N. Tsirpanlis, *Introduction to Eastern Patristic Thought and Orthodox Theology* (Theology and Life Series 30; Collegeville, Minn.: Liturgical, 1991), 134.

14. See also Regis A. Duffy, "Sacraments," in Francis Schüssler Fiorenza and John P. Galvin, ed., *Systematic Theology: Roman Catholic Perspectives*, vol. 2 (Minneapolis: Fortress, 1991), 187–88, and Paul Lebeau, "Vatican II and the Hope of an Ecumenical Eucharist," *One in Christ* 5 (1969): 379–404.

15. Robert P. Imbelli, "The New Adam and Life-Giving Spirit: The Paschal Pattern of Spirit Christology," *Communio* 25 (1998): 251. Imbelli also speaks about the "perichoretic unity" between christology and pneumatology as a necessary precedent for the recovery of a pneumatological outlook on the Eucharist.

16. Pannenberg, *Systematic Theology*, 3.324. Roman Catholic Edward J. Kilmartin, *Christian Liturgy I: Theology* (Kansas City: Sheed & Ward, 1988), 248–49, says the same: "The sacraments combine the community's self-offering to the Father through Christ in the Spirit, with a prayer for the sanctification of the subject in whose favor the celebration takes place...or for the assembled faithful"; see also his "The Active Role of Christ and the Holy Spirit in the Sanctification of the Eucharistic Elements," *Theological Studies* 45 (1984): 225–53. I am indebted to Duffy, "Sacraments," 206, for these references.

17. *The Exposition of the Divine Liturgy*, *PG* 150, 425, qtd. in O'Carroll, "Eucharist," 78.

18. Congar, *I Believe in the Holy Spirit*, 3.267–74.

19. Duffy, "Sacraments," 206–7.

20. Cf. Alois M. Kothgasser, "Die Katholische Pneumatologie im zwanzigsten Jahrhundert," in *Credo in Spiritum Sanctum*, vol. 1 (Rome: Liberia Editrice Vaticana, 1983), 654.

21. For a balanced discussion, see Gordon D. Fee, *The First Epistle to the Corinthians* (Grand Rapids: Eerdmans, 1987), 558ff.; cf. Pannenberg, *Systematic Theology*, 3.326 ff.

22. See further, Stanley Samuel Harakas, *Health and Medicine in the Eastern Orthodox Tradition* (New York: Crossroads, 1990), 91, and Kenneth L. Bakken, "Holy Spirit and Theosis: Toward a Lutheran Theology of Healing," *St Vladimir's Theological Quarterly* 38, 4 (1994): 419ff.

23. Bakke, "Holy Spirit and Theosis," 419–20.

24. Markku Antola, *The Experience of Christ's Real Presence in Faith: An Analysis on the Christ-Presence-Motif in the Lutheran Charismatic Renewal*, Schriften der Luther-Agricola-Gesellschaft 43 (Helsinki: Luther-Agricola Society, 1998). [Editor's note: For a more accessible and summary version of Antola's thesis, see his "The Experience of Christ's Real Presence in Faith as a Goal for Lutheran Charismatic Renewal," *Cyberjournal for Pentecostal-Charismatic Research* 6 (1999) [http://www.pctii.org/cyberj/cyber6.html].]

25. Larry Christenson, ed., *Welcome Holy Spirit: A Study of Charismatic Renewal in the Lutheran Church* (Minneapolis: Fortress, 1987), 286. Antolas' study is a careful analysis of this document, which represents the most comprehensive international statement of faith by Lutheran Charismatics.

26. *Welcome Holy Spirit*, 177: "we must never regard the sacrament as a harmful thing from which we should free, but as a pure, wholesome, soothing medicine which aids and quickens us in both soul and body. From where the soul is healed, the body has benefited also....Here in the sacrament you receive from Christ's lips the forgiveness of sins, which contains and conveys God's grace and Spirit with all his gifts, protection, defense, and power against death and the devil and all evils."

27. Charles Gusmer, "The Ministry of the Healing in the Church," *One in Christ* 21 (1985): 153. Catholic Gusmer discusses in his dialogue-paper the relationship between sacramental (healing through anointing and Eucharist) and charismatic (through prayer of healing) healings and concludes that they are in no way opposed to each other but rather complementary.

28. Pannenberg, *Systematic Theology*, 3.291.

29. Zizioulas, *Being as Communion*, 254, italics orig.

30. Pannenberg, *Systematic Theology*, 3.292.

31. Zizioulas, *Being as Communion*, 162.

Chapter Eleven

1. See, e.g., Vladimir Lossky, *The Mystical Theology of the Eastern Church* (Crestwood, N.Y.: St. Vladimir's, 1976), 9 and 11–12.

2. It might be important that at least some Roman Catholic theologians can hold that "the Roman Catholic Church has always taught the deification of man through God's grace"—even if this sounds a bit overstatement! Miguel M. Garijo-Guembe, "Schwesterkirchen im Dialog," *Catholica* (1994): 279–93, quote from 285, qtd. in Risto Saarinen, "Salvation in the Lutheran-Orthodox Dialogue. A Comparative Perspective," *Pro Ecclesia* 5 (1996): 203. A fine introduction to a Catholic appropriation of the idea of deification is offered by Hans Urs von Balthasar, *Theologik III: Der Geist der Wahrheit* (Basel: Johannes Verlag, 1987), 169ff. (Here, as always, von Balthasar's terminology is a bit idiosyncratic.) The reason for a much more positive view among Roman Catholics probably must do with their anthropology and a view of salvation that gives more weight to human responsibility. These two concepts have, in fact, been the main targets of traditional Reformation critique of Catholic soteriology.

3. The term "Lutheran" has two meanings: it can denote either Martin Luther's theology as it is expressed in his own writings or theology/theologies of Lutheran confessions and subsequent Lutheran formulations. During the course of the discussion I will show that these two have to be distinguished from each other since they do not only have some differing emphases but can also end up in contradictory orientations especially in the cardinal doctrine of justification. This is, of course, not my personal thought but is substantiated by recent Lutheran scholarship.

4. For a comprehensive listing of texts, see Daniel B. Clendenin, "Partakers of Divinity: The Orthodox Doctrine of Theosis;" *Journal of the Evangelical Theological Society* 37, 3 (1994): 369ff.; Clendenin writes: "The Bible speaks extensively about theosis, according to the Orthodox theologians, and thus so must we." See also Timothy Ware, *The Orthodox Church* (London: Penguin, 1964), 236–37.

5. Irenaeus, *Adv. Haer.* 5, Preface; Athanasius, *De incarnatione* 54.

6. Basis, *De Spiritu Sancto* 1.2. For a detailed treatment of some selected patristic texts/authors, see e.g., Panayiotis Nellas, *Deification in Christ: Orthodox Perspectives on the Nature of the Human Person*, trans. Norman Russell (Crestwood, N.Y.: St. Vladimir's, 1987), and Donald Winslow, *The Dynamics of Salvation: A Study in Gregory of Nazianzus*, Patristic Monograph Series 7 (Cambridge, Mass.: Philadelphia Patristic Foundation, 1979). A sample of representative texts, relevant to the purposes of the present theme, is also to be found in Stanley M. Burgess, *The Holy Spirit: Eastern Christian Traditions* (Peabody, Mass.: Hendrickson, 1989).

7. Cited in Clendenin, "Partakers," 374; cf. Timothy Ware, *The Orthodox Way* (Crestwood, N.Y.: St. Vladimir's Seminary, 1990), 168.

8. Vladimir Lossky, *The Mystical Theology*, 134. See also Georgios Mantzaridis, *The Deification of Man: St. Gregory Palamas and the Orthodox Traditions*, trans. Liadain Sherrar (Crestwood, N.Y.: St. Vladimir's, 1984), 105.

9. Tuomo Mannermaa, "Theosis as a Subject of Finnish Luther Research," *Pro Ecclesia* 4, 1 (1995): 42; cf. F. W. Norris, "Deification: Consensual and Cogent," *Scottish Journal of Theology* 43, 4 (1996): 411–28; Vladimir Lossky, *In the Image and Likeness of God* (Crestwood, N.Y.: St. Vladimir's, 1985), ch. 5 entitled, "Redemption and Deification," esp. 97–98; and John Meyendorff, *Byzantine Theology: Historical Trends and Doctrinal Themes* (New York: Fordham Univ. Press, 1974), 159–65.

10. Lossky, *Mystical Theology*, 67. This emphasis is very important in relation to the Luther-interpretation of the Mannermaa-school that thinks in terms of "real-ontic" nature of deification in Luther's theology. The next section of the paper delves into details.

11. Cited in Lossky, *Mystical Theology*, 199. The idea of synergy relates to other theological *loci* in Eastern theology; e.g., the doctrine of the inspiration of Scripture is understood as a cooperative effort between the Spirit and the human instrument who receives divine revelation; see John Breck, "Orthodox Principles of Biblical Interpretation," *St Vladimir's Theological Quarterly* 40, 1–2 (1996): 77ff.

12. Athanasius, *De incarnatione* 8; see also, Lossky, *In the Image*, 103ff.

13. Antiphon in the 4th tone from the Sunday Office.

14. Cited in Ware, *The Orthodox Church*, 230; see also Lossky, *The Mystical Theology*, 196.

15. Lossky, *Mystical Theology*, 170ff. For a fine exposition of confirmation-chrism in the Eastern tradition, see Constantine N. Tsirpanlis, *Introduction to Eastern Patristic Thought and Orthodox Theology* (Collegeville, Minn.: Liturgical, 1991).

16. Basil, *Letter* 38, 4; *PG* 32.332.

17. Athanasius, *A Serap.* 1, 31; *PG* 26.605. For pneumatological implications in general, see Meyendorff, *Byzantine Theology*, ch. 13 entitled, "The Holy Spirit."

18. Lossky, *In the Image*, 108.

19. Ibid., 109; see also Lossky, *The Mystical Theology*, 156ff.

20. Hannu Kamppuri, ed., *Dialogue between Neighbours: The Theological Conversations between the Evangelical-Lutheran Church of Finland and the Russian Orthodox Church 1970–1986* (Helsinki: Luther-Agricola Society, 1986). For appraisals and analyses, see Risto Saarinen, "Salvation in the Lutheran-Orthodox Dialogue. A Comparative Perspective," *Pro Ecclesia* 5 (1996): 202–13, and *Faith and Holiness: Lutheran-Orthodox Dialogue 1959–1994* (Göttingen: Vandenhoeck & Ruprecht, 1997). It is noteworthy that even the Evangelical Church of Germany (EKD), which has been the most ardent critic of Eastern soteriology, in the fifth round of conversations with the Rumanian Orthodox Church (1988), could produce a joint document *Rechtfertigung und Verherrlichung (Theosis) des Menschen durch Jesus Christus* (Justification and Glorification [Theosis] of the Human Person through Jesus Christ).

21. *Dialogue between Neighbors*, 73.

22. Ibid., 75.

23. Mannermaa's basic ideas were first represented in his *Der im Glauben gegenwärtige Christus: Rechtvertigung und Vergottung Zum ökumenischen Dialog* (Hannover: Lutherisches Verlagshaus, 1989), which actually translates from Finnish several of his writings, also those touching the relationship between faith and love, a critical question to Lutheran studies in relation to Eastern Orthodox views. For a helpful synopsis of basic ideas and philosophical-methodological orientations of Mannermaa school, see his "Theosis as a Subject of Finnish Luther Research," *Pro Ecclesia* 4, 1 (1995): 37–48. For a critical philosophical scrutiny and critique of the concept of Christ's "real-ontic" presence in Lutheran studies, see Dennis Bielfedlt, "The Ontology of Deification," in Oswald Bayer, Robert W. Jenson und Simo Knuuttila, eds., *Caritas Dei: Beiträge zum Verständnis Luthers und der gegenwärtigen Ökumene*, Festschrift für Tuomo Mannermaa zum 60. Geburtstag (Helsinki: Luther-Agricola-Gesellschaft, 1997), 90–113, and Risto Saarinen, "The Presence of God in Luther's Theology," *Lutheran Quarterly* 3, 1 (1994): 3ff.

24. Simo Peura, *Mehr als ein Mensch? Die Vergöttlichung as Thema der Theologie Luthers von 1513 bis 1519: Veröffentlichungen des Institus für Europäische Geschichte* (Mainz: Philipp von Zabern, 1994).

25. Citations of Luther in this chapter will be made parenthetically in the text, and reference the standard German/Latin original of *Luthers Werke, Weimerer Ausgabe* or Weimer edition (*WA*, by volume and page number).

26. Mannermaa, "Theosis," 44.

27. Still in an unpublished version (Univ. of Helsinki, 1991). The classic introduction to Luther's pneumatology is Regin Prenter, *Spiritus Creator*, trans. John M. Jensen (Philadelphia: Muhlenberg, 1953).

28. Markku Antola, *The Experience of Christ's Real Presence in Faith: An Analysis on the Christ-Presence-Motif in the Lutheran Charismatic Renewal*, Schriften der Luther-Agricola-Gesellschaft 43 (Helsinki: Luther-Agricola-Society, 1998). The primary source of the study was the International Lutheran Charismatic Renewal Leader's consultation from the years 1981–1985, published as Larry Christenson, ed., *Welcome Holy Spirit: A Study of Charismatic Renewal in the Church* (Minneapolis: Fortress, 1987).

29. *Welcome Holy Spirit*, 141.

30. Ibid., 142; Antola, *The Experience*, 56–57.

31. *Welcome Holy Spirit*, 142–43 and 69.

32. Ibid., 117–18; Antola, *The Experience*, 61.

33. See Thomas Finger, "Post-Chalcedonian Christology: Some Reflections on Oriental Orthodox Christology from a Mennonite Perspective," in Paul Fries and Tiran Nersoyan, eds., *Christ in East and West* (Macon, Ga.: Mercer Univ. Press, 1987), 162; cf. Finger, "Anabaptism and Eastern Orthodoxy: Some Unexpected Similarities," *JES* 31 (1994): 67–91.

34. Moltmann, *The Spirit of Life: A Universal Affirmation*, trans. M. Kohl (London: SCM, 1992), 165, with references to both Wesley's original works and his interpreters' works.

35. David Bundy, "Vision of Sanctification: Themes of Orthodoxy in the Methodist, Holiness and Pentecostal Traditions," paper presented to the European Pentecostal Charismatic Research Association in conjunction with the International Charismatic Consultation on World Evangelization, 1997 (unpublished). [Editor's Note: Bundy taught at Christian Theological Seminary, Indianapolis, Indiana, for many years, and has assumed, as of the summer of 2002, a teaching post at Fuller Theological Seminary.]

36. Albert Outler, *John Wesley* (Oxford: Oxford Univ. Press, 1964), 9n. 26. Cf. Randy Maddox, "John Wesley and Eastern Orthodoxy: Influences, Convergences and Divergences," *Asbury Theological Journal* 45, 2 (1990): 29–53; and Ted A. Campbell, *John Wesley and Christian Antiquity: Religious Vision and Cultural Change* (Nashville: Kingswood, 1991). For ecumenical implications of the doctrine of union with God and pneumatological understanding of grace, see also: Thomas Oden, *Systematic Theology*, vol. 3: *Life in the Spirit* (San Francisco: Harper, 1992), part II, especially the section entitled, "Union with Christ and Sanctification" (205–60).

37. Bundy, "Visions of Sanctification," 2, with references to original sources. Bundy notes that it is not "always a simple straight line transmission or a complete appropriation of the earlier texts. It is argued that through this network, there is, because of contact with Pseudo-Macarius, a continuity of themes and that these were definitive for the development of the concept of sanctification/entire sanctification/theosis within the Methodist, Holiness and Pentecostal traditions."

38. E.g., "It has been demonstrated that the interest in 'sanctification' or 'theosis' resulted in a steady stream of essays and books" (Bundy, "Visions of Sanctification," 9).

39. Bundy, "Visions of Sanctification," 17–18. Cf. St. Isaac the Syrian who distinguished three stages in the way of union: penitence, purification, and perfection. Lossky, *Mystical Theology*, 204.

40. Ibid., 18–20, with references to original sources for both Abrahams and Barrett.

41. For Rahner's basic idea, see, e.g., his *Foundations of Christian Faith: An Introduction to the Idea of Christianity* (New York: Crossroads, 1982), 116–26.

42. *Dialogue Between Neighbours*, 75, qtd. in Risto Saarinen, "Salvation," 203.

43. Moltmann, *Spirit of Life*, 146.

44. Ibid., 146–47.

45. D. Lyle Dabney, "Why Should the Last be First?" unpublished lecture in a research seminar entitled, "An Advent of the Spirit: Orientations in Pneumatology," at Marquette University (Milwaukee, Wisc.), 17–19 April 1998. For details, see Lyle Dabney, *Die Kenosis des Geistes: Kontinuität zwischen Schöpfung und erlösung in Werk des Heiligen Geistes* (Neukirchen-Vlyun: Neukirchener Verlag, 1997). [Editor's note: The published version of Dabney's essay is "Why Should the Last be First? The Priority of Pneumatology in Recent Theological Discussion," in Bradford E. Hinze and D. Lyle Dabney, eds., *Advents of the Spirit: An Introduction to the Current Study of Pneumatology*, Marquette Studies in Theology 30 (Milwaukee, Wisc.: Marquette Univ. Press, 2001), 240–61.]

46. "Gratia non destruit, sed supponit et perficit naturam." The classic locus of this axiom is in Thomas Aquinas, *Summa Theologica* 1a.1.8.

47. Dabney, "Why Should the Last be First?" 19.

Chapter Twelve

1. The standard American edition of *Luther's Works*, 55 vols., Jaroslav Pelikan, ed. (St. Louis: Concordia, 1955–1986), will be referenced in the main text as *LW* followed by volume and page number. Periodically throughout this chapter, I will cite from the standard German/Latin original of *Luthers Werke, Weimerer Ausgabe* or Weimer edition (*WA*, by volume and page number). References to the *Heidelberg Disputation* are noted as *HDT* followed by the number of the thesis. The most reliable original (Latin) version of the *Disputation* is found in Martin Luther, *Studienausgabe*, hrsg. von Helmar Junghans, et al. (Berlin: Evangelische Verlangsanstalt, 1979). Surprisingly, in the last sentence, the English translation is not only inadequate but also misleading as it gives almost the opposite idea from the original. The term *posteriora* (*Dei*), here translated "manifest," means literally "rearward," i.e. (God's) back (referring to Luther's exposition of Exod. 33 where Moses is allowed to see only God's back instead of God's face).

2. In recent years, Luther's theology of the cross has elicited a great deal of new ecumenical research worldwide. After Vatican II several Catholic scholars have developed *theologia crucis* and appreciated its ecumenical potential. For an introduction, see J. E. Vercruysse, "Luther's Theology of the Cross: Its Relevance for Ecumenism," *Centro pro Unione* 35 (Spring 1989): 2–11, 19, and, from an Evangelical perspective, Alistair McGrath, *Luther's Theology of the Cross: Martin Luther's Theological Breakthrough* (Oxford and New York: Oxford Univ. Press, 1985).

3. "The cross is our only theology."

4. The frequency of the use of *nihil* in Luther has two main connotations. On the one hand, it denotes total dependence—ontological dependence—of human being on God. Human beings are *nihil ex se*, they have no existence of their own

but are totally dependent on God both for existence and activity. On the other hand, *nihil* in Luther is also an indication of the sinfulness of the human being. For Luther, sin can be identified in the formal sense with *nihil*.

5. For more details, V.-M. Kärkkäinen, "'Evil, Love, and the Left Hand of God': The Contribution of Lûther's Theology of the Cross to Evangelical View of Evil," *Evangelical Quarterly* (forthcoming).

6. "It is therefore insane to argue about God and the divine nature without the word of any covering.... Whoever desires to be saved and to be safe when he deals with such great matters, let him simply hold to the form, the signs, and the coverings of the Godhead, such as his word and his works" (*LW* 1.13). "But those who want to reach God apart from these coverings exert themselves to ascend to heaven without ladders (that is, without the word)" (*LW* 1.14).

7. See Paul Althaus, *The Theology of Martin Luther* (Philadelphia: Fortress, 1966), 21.

8. Ibid., 21.

9. Ibid., 32 (Althaus's paraphrase).

10. Ibid., 31 (Althaus's paraphrase).

11. Ibid., 54–55; cf. *LW* 51.70.

12. Althaus, *The Theology of Martin Luther*, 33.

13. Luther also describes the essence of sin as "robbery of God," e.g., in *LW* 32.224.

14. Cf. V.-M. Kärkkäinen, "The Christian as Christ to the Neighbor: On Luther's Theology of Love," *International Journal of Systematic Theology* (forthcoming).

15. See John Hick, *Evil and the God of Love* (New York: Harper & Row, 1966).

Chapter Thirteen

1. Nathan L. Gerrard, "The Holiness Movement in Southern Appalachia," in Watson E. Mills, ed., *Speaking in Tongues: A Guide to Research on Glossolalia* (Grand Rapids: Eerdmans, 1986), 213).

2. Jürgen Moltmann, *Spirit of Life: A Universal Affirmation* (Minneapolis: Fortress, 1993), 186.

3. Luther Gerlach and Virginia H. Hine, *People, Power, Change: Movements of Social Transformation* (Indianapolis: Bobbs-Merrill, 1970), xxii-xxiii, responding to the social deprivation model of explanating Pentecostal origins. Advocates of the latter include Robert Anderson, *Vision of the Disinherited: The Making of American Pentecostalism* (New York: Oxford Univ. Press, 1979) and Nils Bloch-Hoell, *The Pentecostal Movement: Its Origin, Development and Distinctive Character* (Oslo: Universitatsforlag, 1964). For an overview of the issues, see Albert Miller, "Pentecostalism as a Social Movement," *JPT* 9 (1996): 97–144.

4. Douglas Petersen, *Not by Might, Nor by Power: A Pentecostal Theology of Social Concern* (Oxford: Regnum, 1996), 9. Other booklength Pentecostal publications in social ethics include: Frank Macchia, *Spirituality and Social Liberation: The Message of the Blumhardts in the Light of Wuertemberg Pietism* (London and Metuchen, N.J.: Scarecrow, 1993), and Eldin Villafañe, *The Liberating Spirit: Toward an Hispanic American Pentecostal Social Ethics* (Grand Rapids: Eerdmans, 1992). See also the special theme issue devoted to "Pentecostals and Social

Ethics," PNEUMA 9, 2 (1987): 103–93, followed by a Pentecostal-Evangelical discussion under the guest editorship of Murray W. Dempster in *Transformation: An International Dialogue on Evangelical Social Ethics* 11 (Jan./March 1994): 1–33.

5. L. Grant McClung, "Pentecostal-Charismatic Perspectives on Missiology for the Twenty-first Century," PNEUMA 16 (1994): 14.

6. I have been unable to trace the source of this quotation.

7. Petersen, *Not by Might*, 107–8.

8. Miroslav Volf, "On Loving With Hope: Eschatology and Social Responsibility," *Transformation* 7 (July/Sept. 1990), 29; cf. Peter Kuzmic, "History and Eschatology: Evangelical Views," in Bruce Nicholls, ed., *Word and Deed: Evangelism and Social Responsibility* (Grand Rapids: Eerdmans, 1985).

9. Gordon D. Fee, "The Kingdom of God and the Church's Global Mission," in Murray W. Dempster, Byron D. Klaus, and Douglas Petersen, eds., *Called and Empowered: Global Mission in Pentecostal Perspective* (Peabody, Mass.: Hendrickson 1991), 16–17.

10. Murray W. Dempster, "Evangelism, Social Concern, and the Kingdom of God," in Dempster, Klaus, and Petersen, eds., *Called and Empowered*, 24. Cf. Dempster, "The Church's Moral Witness: A Study on Glossolalia in Luke's Theology of Acts," *Paraclete* 23 (1989): 1–7.

11. Dario L. Rodriguez, "The Liberating Mission of Jesus: A Reading of the Gospel of Luke in a Missiological Key," *Transformation* 14, 3 (1997): 23–30.

12. See Vinson Synan, *The Holiness-Pentecostal Movement in the United States* (Grand Rapids: Eerdmans, 1971), 165–84, and Ian MacRobert, *The Black Roots and White Racism of Early Pentecostalism in the USA* (New York: St. Martin's, 1988). An excellent historical perspective on racial relations among Pentecostals is Cecil M. Robeck, Jr., "Historical Roots of Racial Unity and Division in American Pentecostalism," paper presented at "Pentecostal Partners: A Reconciliation Strategy for 21st Century Ministry," Memphis, Tenn., 18 Oct. 1994. [Editor's note: Robeck's paper is available as "The Past: Historical Roots of Racial Unity and Division," at the homepage of the Pentecostal-Charismatic Churches of North America: http://www.pccna.org/. Click on the "Papers delivered to PCCNA conferences" tab.]

13. For background and elaboration on the significance of this event, see the "Roundtable: Racial Reconciliation" reflections by six Pentecostal scholars in PNEUMA 18, 1 (1996): 113–40.

14. Miroslav Volf, "When the Unclean Spirit Leaves: Tasks of the Eastern European Churches After the 1989 Revolution," *Cross Currents* 41 (1991): 84–85; see also Volf, *Exclusion and Embrace: A Theological Exploration of Identity, Otherness, and Reconciliation* (Nashville: Abingdon, 1996).

15. For an informed survey and assessment of the idea of pacifism among early Pentecostals, see Joel Shuman, "Pentecost and the End of Patriotism: A Call for the Restoration of Pacifism among Pentecostal Christians," *JPT* 9 (1996): 70–96, and Murray W. Dempster, "Reassessing the Moral Rhetoric of Early American Pentecostal Pacifism," *Crux* 26, 1 (1991): 23–36. [Editor's note: The recent work of Paul Alexander at Southwestern Assemblies of God University should also be considered: "An Analysis of the Emergence and Decline of Pacifism in the History of the Assemblies of God" (Ph.D. diss., Baylor Univ., 2000), and "Spirit

Empowered Peacemaking: Toward a Pentecostal Peace Fellowship," *Journal of the European Pentecostal Theological Association* (forthcoming).]

16. Petersen, *Not By Might*, 231.

17. See Murl O. Dirksen and Karen Carroll Mundy, "Social Justice and Evangelism: A Pentecostal Perspective," a Pentecostal position paper presented at the International Roman Catholic-Pentecostal Dialogue, Paris, France, 1993 (unpublished), 1–2.

18. "Agreed Account," A.7; so also A.9. The "Agreed Account" is unpublished material of the International Dialogue between the Roman Catholic Church and Pentecostals, held in Paris, France, in 1993, currently preserved in the archives of the St. John's Univ. Library, Collegeville, Minn.

19. "Hard Questions: Catholic Answers," §3). The "Hard Questions" is also unpublished material of the International Dialogue between the Roman Catholic Church and Pentecostals, held in Paris, France, in 1993, that is preserved in the archives of the St. John's Univ. Library, Collegeville, Minn.

20. Nigel Scotland, *Charismatics and the Next Millennium: Do They Have a Future?* (London: Hodder & Stoughton, 1995), 264.

21. Quoted in Francois G. Wessels, "Charismatic Christian Congregations and Social Justice: South African Perspective," *Missionalia* 25, 3 (1997): 362.

Chapter Fourteen

1. See "Uniatism, Method of Union of the Past, and the Present Search for Full Communion," Joint International Commission for the Theological Dialogue between the Roman Catholic Church and the Orthodox Church: Seventh Plenary Session, Balamand School of Theology, Lebanon, June 17–24, 1993, published in *Information Service* 83 (1993): 95–99; "Evangelical and Roman Catholic Dialogue on Mission, 1977–1984: A Report," *IBMR* 10, 1 (1986): 2–21; available in book form by John R. Stott and Basil Meeking, ed., *The Evangelical Roman Catholic Dialogue on Mission, 1977–1984* (Grand Rapids: Eerdmans, 1986); "Summons to Witness to Christ in Today's World: A Report of the Baptist-Roman Catholic International Conversations, 1984–1988," in *Information Service* 72 (1990): 5–14; and "The Challenge of Proselytism and the Calling to Common Witness," in *Joint Working Group between the Roman Catholic Church and the World Council of Churches Seventh Report* (Geneva: WCC Publications, 1998).

2. "Common Witness and Proselytism: A Study Document of the Joint Working Group of the Roman Catholic Church and the World Council of Churches," *Information Service* 14 (1971): 18–23, §§4–8.

3. "Uniatism," §6.

4. In what follows, I rely in part on "Catholic Answers to Hard Questions by the Pentecostal Team, 1994," III (unpublished dialogue material preserved in the archives of the St. John's Univ. Library, Collegeville, Minn.).

5. The most comprehensive up-to-date discussion is offered by the Pentecostal co-chair Cecil M. Robeck, Jr., in his position paper for the 1993 session entitled, "Evangelization, Proselytizing and Common Witness: A Pentecostal Perspective," unpublished; cf. his "Mission and the Issue of Proselytism," *IBMR* 20, 1 (1996): 2–

8, and "Evangelization or Proselytism of Hispanics? A Pentecostal Perspective," *Journal of Hispanic/Latino Theology* 4, 4 (1997): 42–64. See also Miroslav Volf, "Fishing in the Neighbor's Pond: Mission and Proselytism in Eastern Europe," *IBMR* 20, 1 (1996): 26–31.

6. See Thomas F. Best and Günther Gassmann, eds., *On the Way to Fuller Koinonia: Official Report of the Fifth World Conference on Faith and Order*, Faith and Order Paper No. 166 (Geneva: WCC Publications, 1994), 257. Cf. David Stoll, *Is Latin America Turning Protestant? The Politics of Evangelical Growth* (Berkeley: Univ. of California Press, 1990), xiv–xv.

7. Robeck, "Evangelization, Proselytism and Common Witness," 11.

8. Ibid., 6. He quotes (n. 11) the Assemblies of God, USA, Constitutional Declaration that says, "the priority reason-for-being of the Assemblies of God is to be an agency of God for evangelizing the world."

9. "Pentecostal Answers to Hard Questions by the Catholic Team, 1994," I.3 (unpublished dialogue material preserved in the archives of the St. John's Univ. Library, Collegeville, Minn.). The following discussion also draws significantly from this material.

10. Ibid., I.1.

11. Robert J. Schreiter, "Changes in Roman Catholic Attitudes toward Proselytism and Mission," in James A. Scherer and Stephen B. Bevans, eds., *New Directions in Mission & Evangelization*, vol. 2: *Theological Foundations* (Maryknoll, N.Y.: Orbis, 1994), 113–25, quote from 124.

12. Miroslav Volf, *After Our Likeness: The Church as the Image of the Trinity* (Grand Rapids: Eerdmans, 1998), 156–57.

13. Ibid., 157.

14. "Pentecostal Answers to Hard Questions by the Catholic Team, 1994" II.2.a.

15. [Editor's note: See, e.g., Amos Yong, "The Marks of the Church: A Pentecostal Re-Reading," *Evangelical Review of Theology* 26, 1 (2002): 45–67.]

16. For major options and literature, see V.-M. Kärkkäinen, "Apostolicity of Free Churches: A Contradiction in Terms or an Ecumenical Breakthrough," *Pro Ecclesia* 10, 4 (2001): 389–400, and "Pentecostalism and the Claim for Apostolicity," *Evangelical Review of Theology* 25, 4 (2001): 323–36. Cf. also Margaret O'Gara, "Apostolicity in Ecumenical Dialogue," *MID-STREAM: Ecumenical Movement Today* 37, 2 (April 1998): 175–212.

17. Michael A. Fahey, "Church," in Francis Fiorenza and Galvin *Systematic Theology: Roman Catholic Perspectives*, vol. II (Minneapolis: Fortress, 1991), 43.

18. Geoffrey Wainwright, *Doxology: The Praise of God in Worship, Doctrine and Life* (New York: Oxford Univ. Press, 1980), 135.

Chapter Fifteen

1. A comprehensive treatment of Pentecostal missiology is yet to appear, although Paul A. Pomerville's *The Third Force in Mission: A Pentecostal Contribution to Contemporary Mission Theology* (Peabody, Mass.: Hendrickson, 1985) is a good beginning. For further aspects, see V.-M. Kärkkäinen, "Mission, Spirit, and Eschatology: An Outline of a Pentecostal-Charismatic Theology of

Mission," *Mission Studies* 16–1, 31 (1999): 73–94; "Pentecostal Missiology in Ecumenical Perspective: Contributions, Challenges, Controversies," *IRM* 88, 350 (1999): 207–25; and "Missiology, Pentecostal and Charismatic," in Stanley M. Burgess and Eduard M. van der Maas, eds., *The New International Dictionary of Pentecostal Charismatic Movements*, rev. and expanded ed. (Grand Rapids: Zondervan, 2002), 877–85.

2. *Agreed Account* 1991, Introduction and I.1 (unpublished dialogue material preserved in the archives of the St. John's Univ. Library, Collegeville, Minn.).

3. Ibid., I.4.

4. John Paul II, *Evangelization in the Modern World: Apostolic Exhortation "Evangelii Nuntiandi,"* (Washington, D.C.: United States Catholic Conference, 1975), §13.

5. See Everett A. Wilson, "A Paradigm of Latin American Pentecostalism," a Pentecostal position paper read in Rocca di Papa, Italy, 1992 (unpublished), 10–14 gives vivid illustrations of the crisis-orientation of Pentecostal preaching and conversions in the Latin American context; cf. *Agreed Account* 1992, II:2.b. [Editor's note: The published version of this paper can be found in Everett A. Wilson, "The Dynamics of Latin American Pentecostalism," in Daniel R. Miller, ed., *Coming of Age: Protestantism in Contemporary Latin America* (Lanham, Md.: UPA, 1994), 89–116. All references and quotations in this chapter, however, will be to the unpublished version of Wilson's paper.]

6. Hervé Legrand, O.P., "A Paradigm: 'Evangelizing in Secularized Pluralistic Europe' according to Some Bishops of the CCEE," a Catholic position paper read in Rocca di Papa, Italy, 1992 (unpublished), 30.

7. Ibid., 6–7.

8. "Catholic answer to Pentecostal hard question" (unpublished dialogue material), 1992, §1. Cf. *Agreed Account* 1992, II:2.c, which states that "...whereas Catholics aim for a true Christianization of a culture, Pentecostals are focused more directly on evangelizing individuals."

9. "Catholic answer to Pentecostal hard question," 1992, §1.

10. *Agreed Account* 1992, II.2.a.

11. Legrand, "A Paradigm," 13–14 notes that in a wealth of Catholic literature there is still the older attitude toward the term secularization which tends to denounce it together with materialism, hedonism, individualism and so on.

12. *Agreed Account* 1992, I.6.

13. Wilson, "A Paradigm of Latin American Pentecostalism," 2: "Human aspiration for betterment, a legitimate concept in the Western cultural legacy that in Europe and North America has played an important role in social cohesion and development, has often been frustrated in Latin America. Most people have been left to fashion for themselves, within the resources of their own experience, satisfactory responses to insecurity, rejection and injustice, often reverting atavistically to traditional beliefs and organizational structures."

14. Legrand, "A Paradigm," 14ff.

15. See Hervé Legrand, ed., *Les éveques d'Europe et la nouvelle évangélisation*, Conseil des conférences épiscopales d'Europe. Coll. "Documents des Églises" (Paris: Cerf, 1991), §31.6 and 34.

16. Wilson, "A Paradigm of Latin American Pentecostalism," 7–13.

17. Ibid., 30; the quotation is attributed to William R. Read, without citation.

18. Ibid., 31–33.

19. Murl O. Dirksen and Karen Carroll Mundy, "Social Justice and Evangelism: A Pentecostal Perspective," a Pentecostal position paper presented at the International Roman Catholic-Pentecostal Dialogue, Paris, France, 1993 (unpublished), 1–2.

20. See *Agreed Account* 1992, II.3.

Chapter Sixteen

1. See the healthy, self-critical look at Pentecostal missiology by one of the most noted writers in the field, Gary B. McGee, "Pentecostal Missiology: Moving Beyond Triumphalism to Face the Issues," *Pneuma* 16, 2 (1994): 275–81.

2. David Bosch, *Transforming Mission. Paradigm Shifts in Theology of Mission* (Maryknoll, N.Y.: Orbis, 1991), 1. See also James A. Scherer and Stephen B. Bevans, eds., *New Directions in Mission & Evangelization*, vol. I: *Basic Statements 1974–1991* (Maryknoll, N.Y.: Orbis, 1994), xi. James A. Scherer, *Gospel, Church and Kingdom: Comparative Studies in World Mission Theology* (Minneapolis: Fortress, 1987), 21.

3. Part 3 of Bosch, *Transforming Mission*, 349 ff., outlines the major characteristic of this new emerging paradigm. See also F. J. Verstraelen, et al., eds., *Missiology: An Ecumenical Introduction: Texts and Contexts of Global Christianity* (Grand Rapids: Eerdmans, 1995).

4. Scherer, *Gospel, Church and Kingdom*, 9ff., and Robert J. Schreiter, "Changes in Roman Catholic Attitudes toward Proselytism and Mission," in James A. Scherer and Stephen B. Bevans, eds., *New Directions in Mission & Evangelization*, vol. 2: *Theological Foundations* (Maryknoll, N.Y.: Orbis, 1994), 122ff.

5. See Karl Müller, et al., eds., *Dictionary of Mission: Theology, History, Perspectives* (Maryknoll, N.Y.: Orbis, 1996).

6. E.g., John V. Taylor, *The Go-Between God: The Holy Spirit and the Christian Mission* (London: SCM, 1972). Unfortunately, this work has not been further developed.

7. Jan A. B. Jongeneel, "Ecumenical, Evangelical and Pentecostal-Charismatic Views on Mission as a Movement of the Holy Spirit," in Jongeneel, et al., eds., *Pentecost, Mission and Ecumenism: Essays on Intercultural Theology* (Frankfurt am Main: Peter Lang, 1992), 233.

8. See Stephen B. Bevans, "God Inside Out: Toward a Missionary Theology of the Holy Spirit," *IBMR* 22, 3 (1998): 102–5, and Frederick Dale Bruner, "The Son is God Inside Out: Response to Stephen B. Bevans, S.V.D.," in *IBMR* 22, 3 (1998): 106–8. Bevans argued that there must be reciprocity between the Spirit and the Son, and that the role of the Spirit must be emphasized much more than it has been done thus far. Bruner's response was that Bevans had substituted christology for pneumatology in ecclesiology and mission. Bruner's critique is indicative of views that are unable to see the reciprocal relation of pneumatology and chris-

tology, but rather posit them as opposites to each other. His answer thus reveals more of his own problematic in connecting Christ and Spirit than of Bevans' argumentation that follows recent ecumenical guidelines.

9. See, e.g., Roger Stronstadt, *A Charismatic Theology of St. Luke* (Peabody, Mass.: Hendrickson, 1984); Robert Menzies (a Pacific Rim missionary), *The Development of Early Christian Pneumatology with Special Reference to Luke-Acts* (Sheffield: Sheffield Academic, 1991), and *Empowered for Witness: The Spirit in Luke-Acts*, JPTSup 6 (Sheffield: Sheffield Academic, 1996); and John Michael Penney (Australian), *The Missionary Emphasis of Lukan Pneumatology*, JPTSup 12 (Sheffield: Sheffield Academic, 1997). Paul A. Pomerville, *The Third Force in Missions: A Pentecostal Contribution to Contemporary Mission Theology* (Peabody, Mass.: Hendrickson, 1985), and Murray W. Dempster, Byron D. Klaus and Douglas Petersen, eds., *Called and Empowered: Global Mission in Pentecostal Perspective* (Peabody, Mass.: Hendrickson, 1991), both offer some theologically serious perspectives, the latter by a younger generation of Pentecostal academics. Yet neither volume develops the distinctive *theological* contribution of pneumatology to missiology.

10. Gary B. McGee, "Pentecostal and Charismatic Missions," in James M. Phillips and Robert T. Coote, eds., *Toward the Twenty-first Century in Christian Mission: Essays in Honor of Gerald H. Anderson* (Grand Rapids: Eerdmans, 1993), 42. For formative influences of eschatology to emerging Pentecostal spirituality, theology, and mission, see William D. Faupel, *The Everlasting Gospel. The Significance of Eschatology in the Development of Pentecostal Thought*, JPTSup 10 (Sheffield: Sheffield Academic, 1996), and Andrew M. Lord, "Mission Eschatology: A Framework for Mission in the Spirit," *JPT* 11 (1997): 111–24.

11. For details, see Wolfhart Pannenberg, *Systematic Theology*, 3 vols., trans. Geoffrey W. Bromiley (Grand Rapids: Eerdmans, 1988, 1994, and 1998), 3.32, 195ff., and 347–48. Further references to the Pannenberg's *Systematic Theology* in this chapter will be cited in the text by *ST*, volume and page number.

12. Hans Urs von Balthasar, *Theologik III: Der Geist der Wahrheit* (Basel: Johannes Verlag, 1987), 385.

13. In Henricus Denzinger and Adolfus Schönmetzer, eds., *Enchiridion Symbolorum* (Barcinore: Herder, 1963), 722.

14. Arthur E. Sekki, *The Meaning of Ruah at Qumran* (Atlanta: Scholars, 1989), 82. In this regard, it seems to me that for many Old Testament students there is a danger to restrict the Spirit entirely to eschatology.

15. James D. G. Dunn has argued for this vigorously in several of his writings; see, e.g., *The Theology of Paul* (Grand Rapids: Eerdmans, 1998), 416–19. So also Gordon D. Fee, *God's Empowering Presence: The Holy Spirit in the Letters of Paul* (Peabody, Mass.: Hendrickson, 1994), 897: "Crucial to the Spirit's role is the thoroughly eschatological framework within which Paul experienced and understood the Spirit.... The outpoured Spirit was the primary cause of Paul's radically altered eschatological perspective."

16. Kilian McDonnell, "Pneumatology Overview: Trinitarian Guidelines for Speaking About the Holy Spirit," *PCTSA* 51 (1996): 193.

17. Gerhard Ebeling, *Dogmatic des christlichen Glaubens*, Band III (Tübingen: Mohr, 1979).

18. Ibid., 21–29. For the tension between the "Present of Pneuma" and "Future of Eschaton," see esp. 24–25. Eastern Orthodox bishop John Zizioulas expresses the same by using his own language: the Spirit is the *beyond* history, and when he acts in history he does so in order to bring into history the eschaton (cf. Acts 2:17); see Zizioulas, *Being as Communion: Studies in Personhood and the Church* (New York: St. Vladimir's, 1985), 130–31.

19. Ebeling, *Dogmatik*, 41–45. So also Zizioulas, *Being as Communion*, 183: "In the same Spirit of God, Christ contains us in Himself, by His very constitution as Christ in the Spirit. He thus in the Spirit contains by definition the eschata, our final destiny..."; and Jürgen Moltmann, *The Spirit of Life: A Universal Affirmation*, trans. Margaret Kohl (Minneapolis: Fortress, 1993), 69, who correctly notes that it is pneumatology that brings christology and eschatology together: "There is not mediation between Christ and the kingdom of God except the present experience of the Spirit, for the Spirit is the Spirit of Christ and the living energy of the new creation of all things."

20. Ebeling does not for some reason or another develop the trinitarian program here although his approach clearly leans toward it. Perhaps the reason is that, oddly enough, he puts the doctrine of the Trinity at the end of his systematic theology (chapter 42), thus following Schleiermacher (and *contra*, e.g., Barth). See also Pannenberg, *ST* 3.553, and von Balthasar, *Theologik III*, 31ff.

21. Moltmann, *The Spirit of Life*, 147.

22. This program has been clearly articulated in Miroslav Volf's trinitarian ecclesiology: *After Our Likeness: The Church as the Image of the Trinity* (Grand Rapids: Eerdmans, 1998), 128ff., quote from 128.

23. Adolf von Harnack, *The Mission and Expansion of Christianity in the First Three Centuries*, vol. I (London: Williams and Norgate, 1904), qtd. in Pannenberg, *Systematic Theology*, 3.13.

24. Hans Urs von Balthasar, *Theologik II:* Wahrheit Gottes (Basel: Johannes Verlag, 1986), 234.

25. For the definition of the church as essentially missionary, see *Ad Gentes*, §9: "The pilgrim Church is missionary by its very nature."

26. Cf. Jürgen Moltmann, *The Church in the Power of the Spirit: A Contribution to Messianic Ecclesiology* (New York: Harper & Row, 1977), passim, esp. 33, 198 and 291.

27. Miroslav Volf, "On Loving With Hope: Eschatology and Social Responsibility," *Transformation* 7 (July/Sept. 1990): 17.

28. Cf. von Balthasar, *Theologik III*, 367, where he poses some critical questions to Charismatic Christians, one of which is whether they understand the receiving of the power of the Spirit to be primarily for the purpose of mission, rather than for hedonistic enjoyment as sometimes happens in Charismatic churches.

Chapter Seventeen

1. Clark Pinnock, *Flame of Love: A Theology of the Holy Spirit* (Downers Grove: InterVarsity, 1996), 274.

2. A quick survey of Pentecostal manuals shows this clearly: Ernest Swing Williams, *Systematic Theology* (Springfield, Mo.: Gospel, 1953), 3; Ned D. Sauls,

Pentecostal Doctrines: A Wesleyan Approach (Dun, N.C.: Heritage, 1979), 54; Guy P. Duffield and Nathaniel M. Van Cleave, *Foundations of Pentecostal Theology* (Los Angeles: L.I.F.E. Bible College, 1983), 268–70; Aaron M. Wilson, *Basic Bible Truth: A Doctrinal Study of the Pentecostal church of God* (Joplin, Mo.: Messenger, 1987), 115; and Mark D. McLean, "The Holy Spirit," in Stanley M. Horton, ed., *Systematic Theology: A Pentecostal Perspective* (Springfield, Mo.: Logion, 1994), 392.

3. For details, see V.-M. Kärkkäinen, "The Universe of Faiths: The Theological Challenges of John Hick's Religious Pluralism," *Dharma Deepika* (forthcoming).

4. Harold Carpenter, "Tolerance or Irresponsibility: The Problem of Pluralism in Missions," *Advance* 31, 2 (1995): 19.

5. "Word and Spirit, Church and World," *Final Report of the International Pentecostal-Reformed Dialogue* (Geneva: WARC, 2000), 12. The quote within this extract comes from "Reports of the Sections: Section I: Turning to the Living God," *IRM* 78, 311–12 (1989): 351.

6. "Word and Spirit, Church and World," 12.

7. For details see Amos Yong, *Discerning the Spirit(s): A Pentecostal-Charismatic Contribution to Christian Theology of Religions*, JPTSup 20 (Sheffield: Sheffield Academic, 2000), 185–97. While I will return below to engage Yong's work, for now it is important to note that he offers a detailed discussion of the work and thinking of other Pentecostals who have begun to rethink this question of the religions. For interesting perspectives into Asian Pentecostalism and its attempts to appreciate cultural and religious elements of other faiths, see Julie Ma, "A Comparison of Two Worldviews: Kankana-Ey and Pentecostals," in Wonsuk Ma and Robert Menzies, eds., *Pentecostalism in Context: Essays in Honor of William M. Menzies*, JPTSup 11 (Sheffield: Sheffield Academic, 1997), 265–90. [Editor's Note: For more on Ma's work, including a summary and analysis of her book-length report, see Yong, "Going Where the Spirit Goes...: Engaging the Spirit(s) in J. C. Ma's Pneumatological Missiology," *JPT* 10, 2 (April 2002): 125–43.]

8. Henry I. Lederle, *Treasures Old and New: Interpretations of Spirit-Baptism in the Charismatic Renewal Movement* (Peabody, Mass.: Hendrickson, 1988), 338.

9. "Towards a Church Renewed and United in the Spirit," in Arnold Bittlinger, ed., *The Church is Charismatic* (Geneva: WCC, 1981), 21–28.

10. Martinus L. Daneel, "African Independent Church Pneumatology and the Salvation of All Creation," in Peter D. Hocken and Harold D. Hunter, eds., *All Together in One Place: Theological Papers from the Brighton Conference on World Evangelization*, JPTSup 4 (Sheffield: Sheffield Academic, 1992), 96–126. See also "A Response to M. L. Daneel" by Derek B. Mutungu in the same volume. Both articles give basic bibliographical guidance for further research. [Editor's note: For Daneel's most recent and comprehensive statement, see his *African Earthkeepers: Wholistic Interfaith Mission* (Maryknoll, N.Y.: Orbis, 2001), esp. ch. 11.]

11. Clark H. Pinnock, "The Finality of Jesus Christ in a World of Religions," in Mark A. Noll and David F. Wells, eds., *Christian Faith and Practice in the Modern World: Theology from an Evangelical Point of View* (Grand Rapids: Eerdmans, 1988), 152–68; "Toward and Evangelical Theology of Religions," *Journal of the Evangelical Theological Society* 33 (1990): 359–68; *A Wideness in God's Mercy: The Finality of Jesus Christ in a World of Religions* (Grand Rapids: Zondervan, 1992);

"Evangelism and Other Living Faiths: An Evangelical Charismatic Perspective," in Hocken and Hunter, eds., *All Together in One Place*, 208–18; "An Inclusivist View," in Dennis L. Ockholm and Timothy R. Phillips, eds., *More Than One Way? Four Views of Salvation in a Pluralistic World* (Grand Rapids: Zondervan, 1995), 93–148; *Flame of Love*, esp. 185–215.

12. Pinnock, *Flame of Love*, 186–87.

13. Ibid., 49. In an ecumenical spirit, Pinnock quotes here with approval from Pope John Paul II who speaks of "the breath of life which causes all creation, all history, to flow together to its ultimate end, in the infinite ocean of God" (citing Pope John Paul II's encyclical, "On the Holy Spirit in the Life of the Church and the World," published as *An Encyclical Letter of the Supreme Pontiff, John Paul II* [Sherbrooke, Quebec: Editions Paulines, 1986], 95).

14. Pinnock, *Flame of Love*, 63. A case in point is evangelical theologian W. H. Griffith Thomas, *The Holy Spirit of God* (Grand Rapids: Eerdmans, 1964), 187, 196, 201, who prefers to bypass the cosmic activities of the Spirit as he sees them threatening the uniqueness of the Gospel.

15. Pinnock, *Flame of Love*, 200–201.

16. Ibid., 73. Here one can see the influence of Karl Rahner on Pinnock's thinking, although he doesn't explicate it in this context. Wolfhart Pannenberg's theological anthropology also operates with this idea.

17. Ibid., 192. For an appreciation of Pinnock's overall scheme but also a critique of his theological methodology here, see Amos Yong, "Whither Theological Inclusivism? The Development and Critique of an Evangelical Theology of Religions," *Evangelical Quarterly* 71, 4 (1999): 327–48.

18. Yong, *Discerning the Spirit(s)*, 24. In addition to this monograph, see also his "Whither Theological Inclusivism"; "The Turn to Pneumatology in Christian Theology of Religions: Conduit or Detour," *JES* 35 (1998): 39–65; "'Not Knowing Where the Spirit Blows...': On Envisioning a Pentecostal-Charismatic Theology of Religions," *JPT* 14 (1999): 81–112; and, most recently, *Beyond the Impasse: Toward a Pneumatological Theology of Religions* (Grand Rapids: Baker Academic, 2002).

19. Michael Lodahl, *Shekinah/Spirit: Divine Presence in Jewish and Christian Religion* (New York: Paulist, 1992).

20. With the subtitle, *The Rise of Pentecostal Spirituality and the Reshaping of Religion in the Twenty-first Century* (Reading, Mass.: Addison-Wesley, 1995).

21. Samuel Solivan, "Interreligious Dialogue: An Hispanic American Pentecostal Perspective," in S. Mark Heim, ed., *Grounds for Understanding: Ecumenical Responses to Religious Pluralism* (Grand Rapids: Eerdmans, 1998), 37–45, quote from 43.

22. Pinnock, *Flame of Love*, 48; also source of the concluding quotation.

Name Index

Subject Index

CPSIA information can be obtained at www.ICGtesting.com
Printed in the USA
LVOW05s2021091214

418015LV00028B/1299/P

9 780761 823896